THE AMERICAN
POLITICAL TRADITION

The American Political Tradition

And the Men Who Made It

BY

RICHARD HOFSTADTER

With a Foreword
by Christopher Lasch

Vintage Books
A Division of Random House, New York

VINTAGE BOOKS EDITION, April 1974
Copyright 1948, © 1973 by Alfred Knopf, Inc.
Foreword Copyright © 1973 by Christopher Lasch

Library of Congress Cataloging in Publication Data

Hofstadter, Richard, 1916–1970.
The American political tradition and the men who made it.

Reprint of the ed. published by Knopf, New York.
Bibliography: p.
1. United States—Politics and government.
2. United States—Biography. I. Title.
E178.H727   1974   320.9'73 [B]   73-20353
ISBN 0-394-70009-0

CONTENTS

FOREWORD

Even though his career was cut short in its prime, leaving us immeasurably impoverished by the loss, Richard Hofstadter left a full and rounded body of work, not merely one or two important books, which is the best that most historians can hope for. Each of Hofstadter's books bore an important relation to its predecessors and to those that were to come; none, accordingly, can be seen in isolation from the others. Hofstadter's imagination never rested for long, and his thought ranged widely, embracing political, social, and cultural history —he was impatient with such distinctions—and extending to all periods of American history. Yet his ideas constantly return to certain central preoccupations stated at the outset of his career. A continuing encounter with the progressive tradition—the tradition on which he and most other intellectuals had been "reared," as he put it in the introduction to *The Age of Reform*, but in which he found much to criticize—informs all Hofstadter's work and provides a direct link, for example, between *The American Political Tradition*, first published in 1948, and *The Progressive Historians*, which came out twenty years later.

The continuity of Hofstadter's altogether remarkable career is all the more apparent if one remembers that his first published essay, appearing in 1938, dealt with Charles A. Beard's interpretation of the Civil War, and that other early writings included essays on Frederick

Jackson Turner, on V. L. Parrington, and once again on Beard—the same writers to which he returned toward the end of his life.[1]

Hofstadter's lifelong engagement with the progressive historians immediately tells us something about *The American Political Tradition*—the witty, caustic, daring book that first brought Hofstadter's writing to general attention. That book took shape in a confrontation not only with liberalism in politics but with liberal historiography and specifically with the three towering figures who had exercised such a powerful influence on the generation of historians immediately preceding Hofstadter's own, and for that matter on Hofstadter himself, as he tells us in *The Progressive Historians*. Having taken up American history in the thirties "under the inspiration that came from Charles and Mary Beard's *The Rise of American Civilization*" (just as another generation was to take up American history under the inspiration that came from *The American Political Tradition*), Hofstadter quickly became dissatisfied with the distortions and simplifications associated with the interpretation of American history as a continuing conflict between antagonistic forms of property—more crudely, as a conflict between the people and "the interests." [2] By the middle thirties, this progressive or populist interpretation of the American past had lost whatever critical content it might once have possessed and had become identified with a resurgence of American cultural chauvinism, a tiresome celebration of the American past—its indige-

---

1. "The Tariff Issue on the Eve of the Civil War," *American Historical Review*, 1938, pp. 50–5; "Parrington and the Jeffersonian Tradition," *Journal of the History of Ideas*, 1941, pp. 391–400; "Turner and the Frontier Myth," *American Scholar*, 1949, pp. 433–43; "Beard and the Constitution," *American Quarterly*, 1950, pp. 195–213.

2. *The Progressive Historians*, p. xiv.

nous traditions of popular radicalism, the crude vitality of its popular culture, and the national regeneration allegedly in progress under the New Deal. The progressive interpretation of American history, in other words, had helped to bring into being a "literature of hero-worship and national self-congratulation," which it was one of the stated purposes of *The American Political Tradition* to deflate.

The most curious aspect of this degeneration of a once critical tradition of thought into a form of cultural nationalism is that it occurred under left-wing auspices. The emergence of the Popular Front in 1935 and the Communist Party's reassuring announcement that communism could be regarded as "twentieth-century Americanism" had given the signal for the repatriation of a generation of alienated intellectuals. Estheticism, anti-Americanism, and the cultivation of the inner life went abruptly out of fashion along with the super-revolutionism of "third-period" communism, which had dismissed the reform tradition in the United States as petty bourgeois reaction and the New Deal as incipient fascism. Progressivism and the progressive interpretation of history underwent a revival, and the search for native traditions of politics and culture became a minor industry. Van Wyck Brooks, formerly an astringent critic of American culture, embarked on his nostalgic evocations of the nineteenth century in *Makers and Finders*. The debunking biographical essays of the twenties and early thirties gave way to filiopietistic commemorations of popular heroes—Sandburg's Lincoln, Van Doren's Franklin, Freeman's Lee—in which the sheer accumulation of empirical detail served to lull readers into an acquiescent, appreciative mood. Archibald MacLeish, always a reliable weather-vane, forsook the avant-gardism of his Poundian phase and threw down what he described as

"loudmouthed, disrespectful, horse-laughing challenges
to those who tell us poetry is 'pure' . . . [and] written
about the feeling of being dreadfully alone." Other poets
responded eagerly to his call for "public speech."
Thomas Hart Benton underwent a similar conversion,
moving from New York to Missouri and from abstract
art to populist neo-regionalism, proclaiming the death
of "the great cities." Frank Lloyd Wright and Lewis
Mumford exalted regionalism over urbanism. "Instead
of clinging to the sardonic funereal towers of metropoli-
tan finance," intoned the latter, "ours to march out to
newly plowed fields, to create fresh patterns of political
action, to alter for human purposes the perverse mecha-
nisms of our economic regime, to conceive and to germi-
nate fresh forms of human culture." [3]

The most effective criticism of the excesses and ab-
surdities associated with this latest and much-acclaimed
"American renaissance" came from the left, like the "renaissance" itself—notably from the group of intellectuals
affiliated with or close to *Partisan Review*. This magazine broke away from the Stalinist literary movement
in 1936 and reemerged a year later as an independent

---

3. "Our age is rich in political and spiritual conversions," wrote
Morton Dauwen Zabel in a fierce polemic against MacLeish,
"The Poet on Capitol Hill," *Partisan Review*, January–February
1941, pp. 7, 9; see also Meyer Shapiro on Benton, "Populist
Realism," ibid., January 1937, pp. 53–7, and on Mumford, "Looking Forward to Looking Backward," ibid., July 1938, pp. 12–24.
An important essay on the thirties by Warren Susman ("The
Thirties," in Lorman Ratner and Stanley Coben, eds., *The Development of an American Culture* [1970], pp. 179–218) points
out that the popularization of the concept of culture—in the
sense of a whole way of life, organically rooted in the everyday
experience of the folk—provides an important clue to one of the
overriding intellectual preoccupations of the decade: the search
for native political traditions and for the roots of an authentic
popular culture.

journal, Marxist in its general intellectual outlook, anti-Stalinist in its politics, and resolutely opposed to the subordination of art and culture to the political needs of the moment. The *Partisan Review* critics charged neo-populist writers with "ransacking" the past, as Richard Chase put it in an attack on Mumford—that is, with "conducting armed raids on history" so as to build up an ersatz cultural tradition, a mythical organic community. Without denying the connection between culture and politics, or the need for historical criticism of both, these intellectuals drew a distinction between history conceived as a "usable past"—the conception promoted by Brooks, Beard, and Carl Becker—and history seen as an accumulation of experience; between "using" the past and assimilating it. Just as children do not "use" their mothers but are formed by them, so, they insisted, each generation is formed by its predecessors, and the problem for historical analysis is not to invent a past relevant to the needs of the present but to become critically conscious of these influences.[4]

The position formulated by the *Partisan Review* critics implied an emphatic rejection of the progressive historiography of Parrington, Beard, and Becker, and also, it should be noted, of Frederick Jackson Turner's frontier theory of American history. American progressivism, these writers correctly perceived, was historically bound up with "the optimistic idea of an expanding American world," a vision of "limitless space" that "idealizes an

---

4. Richard Chase, "The Armed Obscurantist," *Partisan Review,* summer 1944, pp. 346–8; William Phillips and Philip Rahv, "Some Aspects of Literary Criticism," *Science and Society,* winter 1937, p. 217. For the concept of a "usable past" see Van Wyck Brooks, "On Creating a Usable Past," *Dial,* April 11, 1918, pp. 337–41, and Carl Becker's well-known essay, "Everyman His Own Historian" (1931).

earlier stage of popular rule as a norm of democracy constantly threatened and regained." [5] Not only the superficiality of progressivism but the radical discontinuity of American culture, it seemed to these writers, derived from the ceaseless search for new beginnings of which the frontier had provided the most durable set of images—the flight from complexity, the flight from the past, the belief that the past is an encumbrance that can painlessly be discarded in the restless search for a better future.

It is not difficult to recognize in this critique of progressive political culture and its "Marxist" offshoots of the thirties the central themes of Hofstadter's early work. Like the *Partisan Review* critics, Hofstadter had been drawn to Marxism and to the economic interpretation of history, only to witness at close range their degeneration into an official culture (as Meyer Shapiro put it in his polemic against Benton) "local in content, national in scale." Personally as well as temperamentally Hofstadter was close to the *PR* group. Shapiro, Chase, F. W. Dupee, Lionel Trilling, Eric Bentley, and C. Wright Mills were his colleagues at Columbia. His friend Alfred Kazin, a frequent contributor to *Partisan Review*, wrote one of the most compelling indictments of the nationalist revival in the last chapter—"America, America!"—of his brilliant study of American letters, *On Native Grounds*. It is possible to see *The American Political Tradition*, which appeared only six years after Kazin's book, as an attempt to do for the study of American politics something of what Kazin had done for literary history. Both books place the problem of American traditions at the center of attention (thereby revealing

5. Meyer Shapiro, "Populist Realism," *Partisan Review*, January 1937, pp. 55–6.

their origins in the literary wars of the late thirties); but instead of celebrating these traditions, in the manner of progressive and neo-populist historians, they remorselessly reveal their inadequacies.

Highly critical of their predecessors, both writers nevertheless absorbed whatever was valuable in their work. Just as Kazin's method retains the best of Van Wyck Brooks, Hofstadter's analysis still shows the influence of Beard. Like Beard, Hofstadter admires the political realism of the Founding Fathers and associates this quality, throughout *The American Political Tradition*, with an understanding of the "economic basis of politics." But whereas Beard had seen the Jeffersonian tradition as a clear-cut alternative to the Federalist tradition, and the continuing conflict between the two as the major theme of American history, Hofstadter treats Jefferson precisely as the first in a long series of opportunists whose principal role in American politics was to blur ideological conflicts and to promote business interests while rhetorically denouncing them in the name of agrarian democracy. Instead of two clearly defined and opposing traditions *à la* Beard and Parrington, Hofstadter finds in American history a series of opportunistic evasions, compromises, and self-delusions. The ironic juxtapositions so often emphasized in the titles of these essays are intended not merely to debunk the literature of hero-worship—forcing us to see Lincoln, for example, as an important source of the self-help ideology or Theodore Roosevelt as a conservative—but to point up the confusion of roles, the bizarre disguises leading statesmen have been forced to adopt, the conflicts between intentions and consequences that abound in a political system lacking any firm ideological basis (except insofar as the tradition of economic realism survived as an undercurrent).

In stressing the lack of serious ideological conflict in American society—as when he brilliantly revised the conventional interpretation of the Jacksonians as a movement of embattled farmers confronting the money power, showing them instead to have been aspiring capitalists chafing under centralized restraints—Hofstadter undoubtedly helped to prepare the way for the consensus theorists of the 1950's, who saw ideological agreement not only as a principal feature of the American system but as the source of its stability. Hofstadter's intention in *The American Political Tradition*, however, had nothing in common with the celebration of American "pragmatism." On the contrary, he saw this agreement as a form of intellectual bankruptcy and as a reflection, moreover, not of a healthy sense of the practical but of the domination of American political thought by popular mythologies: the frontier, the sturdy yeoman, self-help, God and motherhood. An urbanite to the core, writing at a time when the best writers and critics were in recoil from the updated version of the agrarian myth associated with the neo-populism of the thirties, Hofstadter found in sentimental agrarianism a particularly flagrant example of the unreality of American political rhetoric—a nation of industrialists, clerks, and workers pretending to be sturdy sons of the soil. His attack on the agrarian illusion reaches comic heights in the essay on Bryan—a representative figure, in Hofstadter's view, not only because he clung to the agrarian myth long after it had lost all semblance of reality but because he gave his constituents "not so much leadership as expression," thereby "freezing the popular cause at its lowest level of understanding."

Ostensibly a book about politics, *The American Political Tradition* is really a study of popular political culture, which treats politicians "as leaders of popular

thought"—"not their most impressive function," Hofstadter cannot resist adding. The impulse behind the
book has much in common with the impulse that gave
rise, in the same period—the middle forties—to Dwight
Macdonald's polemics against the lib-lab mentality and
"cultural Bolshevism," and to Irving Howe's attack on
"sentimental fellow-traveling" and the neo-populist mystique of the folk. In the thirties, those who condemned
the culture of the Popular Front did so in the name of an
independent socialist movement, which they imagined
was about to emerge from the depression and the struggle against fascism—a movement that would be equally
critical of capitalism and of the perversion of socialism
in the Soviet Union. "My own assertion of consensus history in 1948," Hofstadter says elsewhere, "had its sources
in the Marxism of the 1930's." [6] By the middle forties,
however, this Marxism had been greatly modified by the
need to defend the autonomy of culture against literary
Stalinism and "the intellectuals' tradition" of independent critical thought against the intellectuals' own "deep-
seated need to accept as its own—if only periodically—
the official voice of society." [7] As cultural issues increasingly predominated over political issues, the Marxist
content of this criticism became progressively diluted.

The Marxism of the thirties had also been transformed
by the fading of hopes for a radical social movement,
in the absence of which Marxism appeared more and
more as a purely intellectual alternative to capitalism.
As the prospects for socialism grew increasingly dim,
many intellectuals shifted their attention to the criticism
of popular culture. "Their earlier economic criticism of
capitalistic society," as Edward Shils perceptively noted

---

6. *The Progressive Historians,* p. 452 n.
7. William Phillips, "The Intellectuals' Tradition," *Partisan
Review,* November–December 1941, p. 490.

in an otherwise undistinguished essay, "has been transformed into a moral and cultural criticism of the large scale industrial society." [8] This "transmogrified Marxism" did not come into being, however, because capitalism had eliminated the economic injustices to which socialists had formerly addressed themselves—Shils's explanation—but because the possibilities of a political attack on capitalism appeared by the middle forties to be so greatly diminished, and because in any case a purely political analysis no longer seemed adequate to an understanding of the international crisis that had produced fascism, Stalinism, and the vast technological destruction of the Second World War. As Dwight Macdonald wrote in 1946, "The difficulties lie much deeper, I now think, than is assumed by the Progressives, and the crisis is much more serious." [9]

The political culture of progressivism now came to be seen as itself part of the modern crisis rather than its solution. In the face of the organized barbarism of modern life, the progressive still clung to a naïve trust in science, progress, and the "march" of history, while the genuine radical, according to Macdonald, made man rather than history the center of his politics. "The Progressive thinks in collective terms (the interests of society or of the working class); the Radical stresses individual conscience." [10] These distinctions also figure in *The American Political Tradition*, which criticizes the intellectual poverty of the progressive tradition while dealing sympathetically with Wendell Phillips, the agitator—the only figure in Hofstadter's selection (it has

---

8. Edward Shils, "Daydreams and Nightmares: Reflections on the Criticism of Mass Culture," *Sewanee Review*, 1957, p. 590.

9. "The Root Is Man," *Memoirs of a Revolutionist* (1958), p. 30.

10. Ibid., p. 29.

frequently been pointed out) who never held a public office or even aspired to one, and who conforms closely to Macdonald's definition of the radical as one who "is pleased if history is also going his way, but . . . is stubborn about following his own road, that of 'ought' rather than 'is.'" [11]

Since a cult of history and historical progress was a central feature of the progressive mentality, it was impossible for Hofstadter to criticize the progressive political tradition without also criticizing the progressive or "Whig" interpretation of history, as he later came to call it. In *The Progressive Historians,* where this historiography is discussed in detail, he attributes to the Whig interpretation the following characteristics: "It is avowedly partisan, it takes the side of dissenters and protestants against establishments . . . it seems to be telling a story of steady progress, pointing toward a certain satisfaction with the enlightened ideas of the present." [12] Because of their partisanship, progressive historians like Parrington simplify conflicts so as to make it possible to create opposing traditions, the antagonism between which is seen as persisting throughout history in a sort of timeless vacuum: liberalism and conservatism, Jeffersonians and Hamiltonians, debtors and creditors, agrarians and their oppressors. Among other things, this procedure, according to *The Progressive Historians,* leads to a "lack of concern with the immediate terms on which intellectual problems present themselves to the makers of history." [13] Thus Parrington's "tendency to see two sets of completely opposed ideas in conflict made it impossible for him to see the shared Calvinism of Roger Williams and John Cotton, the basic similarity of

11. Ibid.
12. *The Progressive Historians*, p. 428.
13. Ibid., p. 400.

the ideas of Thomas Hooker and the Massachusetts theocrats, or the common Whiggery between the friends and opponents of the Constitution." [14]

The introduction to *The American Political Tradition* strikes a very similar note, and the essays that follow are devoted to an exploration of the common ground that was shared by the Federalists and the Jeffersonians, the Jacksonians and their enemies, and by twentieth-century liberals and "conservatives." In the introduction, Hofstadter explains that his principal reason for stressing agreement rather than conflict is a desire to avoid the excessive partisanship characteristic of the progressive tradition, which causes historians endlessly to repeat the controversies of the past.

Later generations, finding certain broad resemblances between their own problems and those of an earlier age, will implicitly take sides with the campaigners of former years; historians, who can hardly be quite free of partisanship, reconstruct the original conflict from the surviving ideas that seem most intelligible in the light of current experience and current conviction. Hence the issues of the twentieth century are still debated in the language of Jefferson's time, and our histories of the Jefferson era are likewise influenced by twentieth-century preconceptions that both Jefferson and his opponents might have found strange. While the conflicts of Jefferson's day are constantly reactivated and thus constantly brought to mind, the commonly shared convictions are neglected.

The "principle" that these common convictions are often more important than the conflicts of the past (in this case, for example, helping to explain "the common end at which, willy-nilly, both Jefferson and the Federalists

---

14. Ibid., p. 419.

arrived") became the basis not only of much of Hofstadter's later work but of some of the best historical writing of the 1950's.

Much of this work sprang from the same impatience with the way in which a narrow partisanship had caused historians to debate issues in the same terms in which they were debated by contemporaries. Stanley Elkins's path-breaking study of slavery, for example, begins with a complaint similar to Hofstadter's: "There is a coerciveness about the debate over slavery: it continues to be the same debate. The same tests for the rightness or wrongness of slavery remain in use year in and year out." [15] The determination to achieve a certain detachment from the moral coercions of former debates—not to be confused with the illusion of scientific "objectivity" that characterizes the work of many social scientists—produced a body of historical writing that is now stigmatized, either wrongly or irrelevantly, as conservative in its political implications. It is true that in the writings of those who tried to convert "consensus" into a general principle of historical interpretation, the idea of consensus, originally rooted in a critique of progressive historiography launched from a position to the left of progressivism, eventually came to be identified with a celebration of American "pragmatism" and with what Daniel Bell referred to as the "end of ideology." [16] Even this

15. *Slavery: A Problem in American Institutional and Intellectual Life* (1959), p. 1.

16. This was especially true of Daniel Boorstin, whose early work, especially *The Lost World of Thomas Jefferson* (1948), criticized the intellectual vacuity of the liberal tradition but whose later writings found in the American aversion to political theories a source of great strength; see his *The Americans: The Colonial Experience* (1958) and *The Americans: The National Experience* (1965). See also Louis Hartz, *The Liberal Tradition in America* (1955). The best criticism of these theorists has been made by Hofstadter himself. In a characteristic passage he writes:

work, however, is full of insights that remain to be absorbed and put to full use—insights, indeed, which in many cases still remain even to be understood. Instead of attempting to distinguish between what is useful in consensus history and what is patently ideological, too many historians have returned to a position in many ways indistinguishable from that of the progressive historians themselves. The worst features of progressive historiography reappear under the auspices of the new left: drastic simplification of issues; synthetic contrivance of political and intellectual "traditions" by reading present concerns back into the past; strident partisanship.[17] Worse still, the new emphasis on conflict has given rise to demands that historians cultivate an "activist outlook" and that history be subordinated to the needs of the "movement." Thus Howard Zinn asks historians to decide "from a particular ethical base what is the action-need of the moment, and to concentrate

---

"One may differ as to whether to call the impassioned arguments of the North and South 'ideological' differences—but if this was not an ideological conflict (and I think it was), we can only conclude that Americans do not *need* ideological conflict to shed blood on a large scale. In the face of this political collapse, what does it matter if Professor Hartz reassures us that, because the Southern states were simply adhering to their own view of the Constitution which they incorporated into the Confederate constitution, the Civil War does not represent a real failure of the American consensus? . . . I can best put my own dissent by suggesting a cartoon: a Reb and a Yank meet in 1865 to survey the physical and moral devastation of the war. 'Well,' says one to the other consolingly, 'at least we escaped the ultimate folly of producing political theorists.'" (*The Progressive Historians,* p. 462.)

17. For the construction of artificial traditions, to which contemporaries had no sense of belonging and the continuity of which appears only to the historian in retrospect, see for example Staughton Lynd's *Intellectual Origins of American Radicalism* (1968).

on that aspect of the truth-complex which fulfills that need." [18] In the face of such critics, the consensus historians need no defense.

This is not the place to discuss Hofstadter's own later work, his relation (always ambiguous) to the consensus theorists and to the political and cultural currents of the 1950's, or the considerations that made him decide, at the end of the sixties, that consensus history "no longer seems as satisfactory to me as it did ten or twenty years ago." [19] The leading themes of this later work, as I have already indicated, are implicit in *The American Political Tradition* and in the cultural battles out of which that book emerged. His highly critical treatment of populism in *The Age of Reform,* and of rightist movements as a form of perverted populism in *The Paranoid Style in American Politics,* extended the critique of neo-populism formulated by Marxist intellectuals in the late thirties. His later preoccupation with anti-intellectualism grew out of the traumas of the McCarthy period but had their ultimate origins in the attempt of left-wing intellectuals to discover a tradition of their own, at a time when they found themselves increasingly isolated from left political movements and perceived intellectual values to be under attack from all political positions. The germ of Hofstadter's *Anti-intellectualism in American Life* is already present in William Phillips's essay of 1941, "The Intellectuals' Tradition," in which Phillips treats the best of modern art and thought as an expression of the "distinct group culture" of the intelligentsia, formed in its

18. Howard Zinn, "Abolitionists, Freedom-Riders, and the Tactics of Agitation," in Martin Duberman, ed., *The Antislavery Vanguard* (1965), p. 430.

19. *The Progressive Historians,* p. 444 n.

"permanent mutiny against the regime of utility and conformity." [20]

On the whole, these later books seem to me more vulnerable to criticism than *The American Political Tradition*. The interpretation of populism as a nostalgic and backward-looking movement glosses too easily over the genuinely radical elements in populism. The defense of the intellectuals' tradition against popular anti-intellectualism ignores the anti-intellectualism of the intellectuals themselves and confuses intellect with the interests of intellectuals as a class.[21] Even as I write these reservations, however, I am struck by their inadequacy in the face of the richness and complexity of Hofstadter's work and of the difficulty of arriving at an assessment of it. There is one other aspect of that work that particularly commands our attention: its sheer bulk. I mention this not because quantity is necessarily equivalent to quality but because it conveys something essential about the man and perhaps also about the times through which we are passing.

In order to have produced such a large body of first-rate work, Hofstadter had to have not only superabundant energy but an undivided devotion to his craft. It sometimes puzzled me that he refused to be diverted from the writing of his books even by the need to defend them against attacks that were outrageously ill-tempered

---

20. *Partisan Review*, November–December 1941, pp. 482–3. The attempt to discover an "intellectuals' tradition" is open to many of the same criticisms that apply to the work of progressive and neo-populist historians. The thirties' desperate search for roots affected even the critics of the nostalgia it so often evoked in the writings of Brooks, Mumford, and others.

21. In two of my own works I have tried to deal with these issues at some length; see *The Agony of the American Left* (1969), ch. I, for a discussion of populism, and *The New Radicalism in America* (1965), ch. IX, for a consideration of the "anti-intellectualism of the intellectuals."

and unfair.[22] It was not simply that he regarded other things as more important. He had supreme confidence in the historical profession itself and its ability to reach reasonable judgments on work in the field, including his own.[23] This confidence, together with his faith in Columbia University as a center of disinterested scholarship, his younger colleagues have not always found it possible to share. We find ourselves uncomfortable in academic life and often at odds with the profession and the university; and it is for this reason, perhaps, that we find it so difficult to match the unswerving devotion to history as a calling that was the mark of the best historians of Hofstadter's generation. For whatever reasons, we have written much less history than they did; nor can we console ourselves that at least we have reformed the university and the political system of which it is a part. More than a decade has passed since the first peremptory challenges to the consensus historians were bravely thrown down; the university and the political system remain essentially unreformed (though the prospects are by no means hopeless), while the new history—the history that was to have represented so striking an advance over the work of the forties and fifties—remains largely unwritten. Our generation has seen too many brave beginnings, too many claims that came to nothing, too many books unfinished and even unbegun, too many broken and truncated careers. As activists, we have achieved far less than we hoped; as scholars, our record

---

22. I have especially in mind Norman Pollack's "Hofstadter on Populism: A Critique of The Age of Reform," *Journal of Southern History,* 1960, pp. 478–500.

23. At the same time he had little use for the ceremonial and self-promotional aspects of professional life. He rarely attended meetings of the historical associations. Nor did he worry much about his own reputation and standing in the profession, trusting these matters to take care of themselves.

is undistinguished on the whole. It is not too late to achieve something better, but it is no longer possible to be complacent about our accomplishments or the superiority of our own understanding of American society to that of the last generation of historians.

CHRISTOPHER LASCH

PREFACE

✿

The following preface was written for the Hebrew edition at the request of its publisher.

I WELCOME the opportunity to write a brief new introduction to the Hebrew edition of *The American Political Tradition,* and to set down for the first time in print certain facts about its inception and publication. One's books are in some ways like one's children. Given time enough and a little good fortune they seem to grow up and have a separate identity of their own. They are always one's own and any radical dissociation is hardly possible but one acquires a certain measure of detachment about them. This book, begun in 1943 when I was twenty-seven, was finished in 1947, and published in 1948. It is, I trust, visibly a young man's book in any case, but what may not be so apparent is that though it appeared on the eve of the 1950's it was to a very large extent an intellectual product of the experience of the 1930's. It represents a kind of distillation of what I had learned about American history as an undergraduate and as a graduate student from 1933 to the early 1940's, and what I had learned and unlearned about politics during the same years. To a very large extent, it was a product of the social criticism of the 1930's, a book in which the American political tradition is being seen from a vantage point well to the left, and from the personal perspective of a young man who has only a limited capacity for identifying with those who exercise power.

This book was not written in order to establish some single overarching theory about American politics or American political leadership, but rather to make a number of interpretive and critical comments on certain political figures on whom I had done some special work or who particularly captured my interest. Circumstances, however, made it seem in the end somewhat more ambitious than it had been meant to be, and these had to do mainly with changes suggested by the publisher as it moved toward publication. My original title, which was less demanding and more faithful to the random and unsystematic character of my intentions, was *Men and Ideas in American Politics.* Somewhere in the editorial offices of Alfred A. Knopf, Inc., the conviction formed that this was an unsaleable title and that one more promising should be found. After a few other improbable titles had been temporarily settled upon and fortunately abandoned, we arrived at the present title and subtitle, *The American Political Tradition: And the Men Who Made It,* which indeed seems to have been consistent with saleability, but which left me unhappy on two counts: the subtitle, when cited in conjunction with the title, made it long and awkward, and it suggested a kind of complete coverage of the basic figures in the American political tradition that I never pretended to. (Even sympathetic reviewers asked, reasonably enough, how one could "cover" the American political tradition without a chapter on Alexander Hamilton, or Daniel Webster, or Henry Clay.) Another, and to my mind happier, suggestion came from my editor to the effect that the book consisted of a series of unrelated parts and needed some kind of brief introduction to condense its meaning and pull it together. I recognized the truth of this, but I suppose that this had been exactly the challenge I had been trying to evade, since I was in a period of intellectual transition and had sense enough to know that I had not arrived at a point in my life at which I was either learned or settled enough to be ready to put together a synthetic statement about the meaning of the American political tradition. Nonetheless, all the sketches had been the conception of a single mind, and it seemed reasonable for my editor to ask if there was not in fact some single and distinctive angle of vision from which my cast of characters had been seen and which might not be generalized in a brief introductory passage.

And so I hazarded my six-page introduction, which has probably made as much trouble for me as any other passage of comparable length. When in writing this introduction I asked myself what it was that I had been saying, it seemed to me that I had been looking at certain characters in American political history not only somewhat from the political left but also from outside the tradition itself, and that from this external angle of vision the differences that seemed very sharp and decisive to those who dwelt altogether within it had begun to lose their distinctness, and that men on different sides of a number of questions appeared as having more in common, in the end, than one originally imagined. As it turned out, this introduction which was only an afterthought proved to be the first statement, at least for my own generation, of a very controversial point of view, which has been the subject of a very large literature in recent years—now generally called consensus history.

Consensus history, conceived in reaction to the very strong and often oversimplified emphasis on conflict that had preoccupied American historians since the time of Frederick Jackson Turner and Charles A. Beard, refers

to the work of a number of historians who have emphasized the common, bourgeois, entrepreneurial assumptions of most of the effective forces in American political
life and the tendency of these forces to group ideologically around a Whiggish center rather than to be polar-
ized in sharp ideological struggles. It is the absence of
deep, persistent, and consistent class conflict that has
preoccupied the consensus historians and the process by
which certain common political and social beliefs usually cut across and link most of the effective segments of
political society. Where the consensus historians take
note of conflict they tend to reduce it to a very *ad hoc*
basis—that is, they postulate it as an affair of shifting
groups and coalitions rather than as a continuing struggle based on enduring sets of fixed classes, such as agrarians and capitalists, or workingmen and industrialists.
It is the hazy multiplicity of American conflict that the
consensus historians have emphasized, as against the
efforts of their predecessors to see sharp and continuous
struggle and profound social dissonance.

This has been very awkward for me, in the sense that
it has linked me with other historians with whom I have
significant differences, and because I have some serious
misgivings of my own about what is known as consensus
history. Consensus history has a certain validity, as I see
it, in that no society can function at all unless there are
certain very broad premises, moral and constitutional,
on which the overwhelming majority of its politically
active citizens can agree at any given time. It is important for the historian to be as aware of these premises
as he is of the sources of conflict. It is also true that the
dynamics of historical change becomes somewhat more
comprehensible if we frequently penetrate beneath the
surface of the formulated issues and look at the elements
of consensus that are at work. Those historians of the

generation of Frederick Jackson Turner and Charles A. Beard who had put the conflict between groups of classes so firmly in the center of the historical frame had carried this point of view so far that between the 1940's and 1950's a corrective was visibly necessary and the pendulum could only have swung rather far in the opposite direction. In this respect, I still think that what I wrote in my introduction about Jefferson and the Federalists is essentially valid and useful. Again this approach proved illuminating when applied to the Progressive era, and has probably held up well against the test of time and further inquiry. However, the consensus point of view is limited in that it is only an assertion about the frame or the configuration of history and not about what goes on in the picture. Once the valid essence in the consensus view has been absorbed, its limitations will also be keenly felt. Americans may not have quarreled over profound ideological matters, as these are formulated in the history of political thought, but they quarreled consistently enough over issues that had real pith and moment. And their unappeasable conflicts finally brought them in 1861 to one of the momentous and tragic political failures in modern history. Even in more tranquil phases of our history, an obsessive fixation on the elements of consensus that do undoubtedly exist strips the story of the drama and the interest it has. William James used to say that there is not much difference between one man and another but that the little difference there is is of great importance. The same is true of the political conflicts that we can find in the history even of states that are permeated by a strong feeling of consensus.

I have never been tempted to revise or to extend this book and such little temptation as I might have felt has

diminished with time. It would be difficult for me to find
my way back into the intellectual frame of reference in
which I was working in the 1940's, and a new frame of
reference would require a new book. I can however give
some general suggestions about the misgivings I have
had and just a few illustrations of how the work might
have been changed. To a certain extent this volume is a
kind of intellectual history of the assumptions behind
American politics, and I think that coming as I did out
of an age of intense ideological dispute and unusual (for
Americans) doctrinal consciousness, I was somewhat
disposed to downgrade the men I was writing about,
even though I was well aware that the general guiding
ideas of American politicians were not their strongest
point. Secondly, I was less interested in the art of the
exercise of power than I was in the art of acquiring it,
and this I suppose to some extent set limits upon the
value of what I had to say about several members of my
cast of characters. For example, if I were writing about
Jefferson again today I could not so easily thrust aside
the great test of Jeffersonianism that came with the
Napoleonic Wars and the endless difficulties called into
being by Jefferson's embargo policies. Today the dilemmas of foreign policy and the inconsistencies and acts
of tyranny that were entailed upon Jefferson by his attempt to execute the embargo would be matters of far
more concern, and they would require a modification,
though I think not a complete abandonment, of my
conception of the undoctrinaire and pragmatic Jefferson.

Again, in writing of Theodore Roosevelt I was, I
think, unduly taken with my "discovery" of the element
of sham in his progressivism and was led to arrive at a
conclusion which I would now take as my starting point
if I were to write about him again. Instead of viewing
T.R. as a bogus progressive, suppose one were to begin

with the assumption that he was indeed distinctly a conservative at heart, but a most flexible and adroit conservative? Some of the problems of his administration would fall into different perspective, and so indeed would much of the significance of our political tradition. But one could go on. There is hardly a portrait in this book whose lines I would not alter in at least one significant dimension, if I were to redo it now.

It is easy for me to suggest how I might at so many points change this book, but it is perhaps not for me to try to say too much about why it has enjoyed such an enormous readership in the United States and stimulated such continuing interest over two decades, especially in the schools and colleges. Perhaps more than anything else it is because young Americans, excessively nourished on the national tendency toward self-celebration, enjoy its iconoclasm and even in many cases learn from it for the first time that American political heroes are not saints in plaster but live and vulnerable figures of controversy.

RICHARD HOFSTADTER

September 29, 1967

INTRODUCTION

❦

IN times of change and danger when there is a quicksand of fear under men's reasoning, a sense of continuity with generations gone before can stretch like a lifeline across the scary present.   JOHN DOS PASSOS

SINCE Americans have recently found it more comfortable to see where they have been than to think of where they are going, their state of mind has become increasingly passive and spectatorial. Historical novels, fictionalized biographies, collections of pictures and cartoons, books on American regions and rivers, have poured forth to satisfy a ravenous appetite for Americana. This quest for the American past is carried on in a spirit of sentimental appreciation rather than of critical analysis. An awareness of history is always a part of any culturally alert national life; but I believe that what underlies this overpowering nostalgia of the last fifteen years is a keen feeling of insecurity. The two world wars, unstable booms, and the abysmal depression of our time have profoundly shaken national confidence in the future. During the boom of the twenties it was commonly taken for granted that the happy days could run on into an indefinite future; today there are few who do not assume just as surely the coming of another severe economic slump. If the future seems dark, the past by contrast looks rosier than ever; but it is used far less to locate and guide the present than to give reassurance.

American history, presenting itself as a rich and reward-
ing spectacle, a succession of well-fulfilled promises, in-
duces a desire to observe and enjoy, not to analyze and
act. The most common vision of national life, in its fond-
ness for the panoramic backward gaze, has been that of
the observation-car platform.

Although the national nostalgia has intensified in the
last decade, it is by no means new. It has a history of its
own, particularly in political traditions. A longing to
recapture the past, in fact, has itself been such a basic
ingredient of the recent American past that no history of
political thinking is complete which does not attempt to
explain it. In American politics the development of a
retrospective and nostalgic cast of mind has gone hand
in hand with the slow decline of a traditional faith.
When competition and enterprise were rising, men
thought of the future; when they were flourishing, of the
present. Now—in an age of concentration, bigness, and
corporate monopoly—when competition and opportunity have gone into decline, men look wistfully back
toward a golden age.

In the early days of the Republic the Founding Fathers, despite their keen sense of history, felt that they
were founding novel institutions and gloried in the newness of what they were doing. As the decades passed,
this feeling faded. Where the Founding Fathers dreamed
of and planned for a long-term future, the generation of
Webster, Clay, and Calhoun was busily absorbed with a
profitable present. The following generation, North and
South, was consciously concerned to preserve and defend what its fathers had built. Lincoln, for example,
believed that he was stabilizing his America and erecting bulwarks against undesirable change. Although he
helped to form a new party, uprooted slavery and the
aristocracy of the South, led a revolutionary change in

the structure of national power, and paved the way for the success of industrial capitalism, he did all these things with the intent of restoring the Union as it had been, saving the common man's control of the government, and protecting the existing rights of free labor.

The post Civil War generation, witnessing a spurt of economic expansion, lived once again in the present and the future. But beginning with the time of Bryan, the dominant American ideal has been steadily fixed on bygone institutions and conditions. In early twentieth-century progressivism this backward-looking vision reached the dimensions of a major paradox. Such heroes of the progressive revival as Bryan, La Follette, and Wilson proclaimed that they were trying to undo the mischief of the past forty years and re-create the old nation of limited and decentralized power, genuine competition, democratic opportunity, and enterprise. As Wilson put it, the machinery of democratic government was to be revivified *"for the purpose of recovering what seems to have been lost . . .* our *old* variety and freedom and individual energy of development." Even Theodore Roosevelt, who realized and at times candidly stated the impossibility of any such undertaking, so far as it concerned the country's economic structure, was careful to do things that caused him to be acclaimed as a "trustbuster."

Among postwar statesmen, Herbert Hoover, who is not usually thought to have much in common with these men of the progressive era—and whose methods and temper, in fact, were quite different—still adhered to much the same premises and accepted the same goals. Like the progressives, he expected to see a brilliant and expansive future, but he expected to reach it along the traditional highway. Franklin D. Roosevelt stands out among the statesmen of modern American liberalism—

and indeed among all statesmen since Hamilton—for his sense of the failure of tradition, his recognition of the need for novelty and daring. His capacity for innovation in practical measures was striking, and the New Deal marked many deviations in the American course; but his capacity for innovation in ideas was far from comparable; he was neither systematic nor consistent, and he provided no clearly articulated break with the inherited faith. Although it has been said repeatedly that we need a new conception of the world to replace the ideology of self-help, free enterprise, competition, and beneficent cupidity upon which Americans have been nourished since the foundation of the Republic, no new conceptions of comparable strength have taken root and no statesman with a great mass following has arisen to propound them. Bereft of a coherent and plausible body of belief—for the New Deal, if it did little more, went far to undermine old ways of thought—Americans have become more receptive than ever to dynamic personal leadership as a substitute. This is part of the secret of Roosevelt's popularity, and, since his death, of the rudderless and demoralized state of American liberalism.

The following studies in the ideology of American statesmanship have convinced me of the need for a reinterpretation of our political traditions which emphasizes the common climate of American opinion. The existence of such a climate of opinion has been much obscured by the tendency to place political conflict in the foreground of history. It is generally recognized that American politics has involved, among other things, a series of conflicts between special interests—between landed capital and financial or industrial capital, between old and new enterprises, large and small property —and that it has not shown, at least until recently, many signs of a struggle between the propertied and unpropertied classes. What has not been sufficiently recognized is the consequence for political thought. The fierceness of the political struggles has often been misleading; for the range of vision embraced by the primary contestants in the major parties has always been bounded by the horizons of property and enterprise. However much at odds on specific issues, the major political traditions have shared a belief in the rights of property, the philosophy of economic individualism, the value of competition; they have accepted the economic virtues of capitalist culture as necessary qualities of man. Even when some property right has been challenged—as it was by followers of Jefferson and Jackson—in the name of the rights of man or the rights of the community, the challenge, when translated into practical policy, has actually been urged on behalf of some other kind of property.

The sanctity of private property, the right of the individual to dispose of and invest it, the value of opportunity, and the natural evolution of self-interest and self-assertion, within broad legal limits, into a beneficent social order have been staple tenets of the central faith in American political ideologies; these conceptions have been shared in large part by men as diverse as Jefferson, Jackson, Lincoln, Cleveland, Bryan, Wilson, and Hoover. The business of politics—so the creed runs—is to protect this competitive world, to foster it on occasion, to patch up its incidental abuses, but not to cripple it with a plan for common collective action. American traditions also show a strong bias in favor of equalitarian democracy, but it has been a democracy in cupidity rather than a democracy of fraternity.

Almost the entire span of American history under the present Constitution has coincided with the rise and spread of modern industrial capitalism. In material power and productivity the United States has been a flourishing success. Societies that are in such good working order have a kind of mute organic consistency. They do not foster ideas that are hostile to their fundamental working arrangements. Such ideas may appear, but they are slowly and persistently insulated, as an oyster deposits nacre around an irritant. They are confined to small groups of dissenters and alienated intellectuals, and except in revolutionary times they do not circulate among practical politicians. The range of ideas, therefore, which practical politicians can conveniently believe in is normally limited by the climate of opinion that sustains their culture. They differ, sometimes bitterly, over current issues, but they also share a general framework of ideas which makes it possible for them to cooperate when the campaigns are over. In these pages I have tried, without neglecting significant conflicts, to keep sight of the central faith and to trace its adaptation to varying times and various interests.

It is in the nature of politics that conflict stands in the foreground, and historians usually abet the politicians in keeping it there. Two special interests, striving to gain control of government policy, will invoke somewhat different ideas to promote their causes. The material interests in good time will be replaced by others as the economic order changes, but their ideas, which already have wide acceptance, will be adapted again and again with slight changes to new conditions. Later generations, finding certain broad resemblances between their own problems and those of an earlier age, will implicitly take sides with the campaigners of former years; historians, who can hardly be quite free of partisanship, reconstruct the original conflict from the surviving ideas that seem most intelligible in the light of current experience and current conviction. Hence the issues of the twentieth century are still debated in the language of Jefferson's time, and our histories of the Jefferson era are likewise influenced by twentieth-century preconceptions that both Jefferson and his opponents might have found strange. While the conflicts of Jefferson's day are constantly reactivated and thus constantly brought to mind, the commonly shared convictions are neglected.

These shared convictions are far from unimportant. Although the Jeffersonians and Federalists raged at each other with every appearance of a bitter and indissoluble opposition, differences in practical policy boiled down to a very modest minimum when Jefferson took power, and before long the two parties were indistinguishable. If their ideas are to be tested in action, we must give due weight to the relatively slight differences in policies that they gave rise to. This seems to me to be one of the keys to historical analysis because it leads us to consider the common end at which, willy-nilly, both Jefferson and the Federalists arrived. The same principle can profitably be extended to the rest of American history. And if it is true of some of the more serious conflicts, how much more true will it be of the innumerable presidential campaigns in which the area of agreement was so large and the area of disagreement so small that significant issues could never be found! Above and beyond temporary and local conflicts there has been a common ground, a unity of cultural and political tradition, upon which American civilization has stood. That culture has been intensely nationalistic and for the most part isolationist; it has been fiercely individualistic and capitalistic. In a corporate and consolidated society demanding international responsibility, cohesion, centralization, and planning, the traditional ground is shifting under our feet. It is imperative in a time of cultural crisis to gain fresh perspectives on the past.

The subjects of these essays were chosen as figures of singular human interest who were excellent representatives of main currents in American political sentiment. With one exception, Wendell Phillips, who introduces a contrast between the agitator and the practical politician, they were prominent major-party figures and holders of high office. Others might well have been added, but these at least seemed indispensable.

These portraits are not painted in roseate colors. I am here analyzing men of action in their capacity as leaders of popular thought, which is not their most impressive function. Further, I am trying to re-emphasize facets of their careers which I feel have not had sufficient attention; this has inevitably led me to pass over perspectives, often more favorable, to which pietistic biographers have frequently done justice. A great deal more than I have chosen to say might be said, for example, about Jefferson's democracy or Jackson's and Lincoln's nationalism; but in all historical and biographical writing, and above all in the brief essay, selection from a mass of material and a large number of themes is necessary. Even in a full-length biography it is all but impossible to arrive at comprehensive understanding of a public personality, and I have taken for myself no such ambitious goal. Finally, I have no desire to add to a literature of hero-worship and national self-congratulation which is already large. It seems to me to be less important to estimate how great our public men have been than to analyze their historical roles. A democratic society, in any case, can more safely be overcritical than over-indulgent in its attitude toward public leadership.

R. H.

January 1948

THE AMERICAN
POLITICAL TRADITION

CHAPTER I

THE FOUNDING FATHERS:
AN AGE OF REALISM

❦

WHEREVER *the real power in a government lies, there is the danger of oppression. In our Government the real power lies in the majority of the community.* . . . JAMES MADISON

POWER *naturally grows* . . . *because human passions are insatiable. But that power alone can grow which already is too great; that which is unchecked; that which has no equal power to control it.* JOHN ADAMS

LONG ago Horace White observed that the Constitution of the United States "is based upon the philosophy of Hobbes and the religion of Calvin. It assumes that the natural state of mankind is a state of war, and that the carnal mind is at enmity with God." Of course the Constitution was founded more upon experience than any such abstract theory; but it was also an event in the intellectual history of Western civilization. The men who drew up the Constitution in Philadelphia during the summer of 1787 had a vivid Calvinistic sense of human evil and damnation and believed with Hobbes that men are selfish and contentious. They were men of affairs, merchants, lawyers, planter-businessmen, speculators, investors. Having seen human nature on display in the marketplace, the courtroom, the legislative chamber,

3

and in every secret path and alleyway where wealth and power are courted, they felt they knew it in all its frailty. To them a human being was an atom of self-interest. They did not believe in man, but they did believe in the power of a good political constitution to control him.

This may be an abstract notion to ascribe to practical men, but it follows the language that the Fathers themselves used. General Knox, for example, wrote in disgust to Washington after the Shays Rebellion that Americans were, after all, "men—actual men possessing all the turbulent passions belonging to that animal." Throughout the secret discussions at the Constitutional Convention it was clear that this distrust of man was first and foremost a distrust of the common man and democratic rule. As the Revolution took away the restraining hand of the British government, old colonial grievances of farmers, debtors, and squatters against merchants, investors, and large landholders had flared up anew; the lower orders took advantage of new democratic constitutions in several states, and the possessing classes were frightened. The members of the Constitutional Convention were concerned to create a government that could not only regulate commerce and pay its debts but also prevent currency inflation and stay laws, and check such uprisings as the Shays Rebellion.

Cribbing and confining the popular spirit that had been at large since 1776 were essential to the purposes of the new Constitution. Edmund Randolph, saying to the Convention that the evils from which the country suffered originated in "the turbulence and follies of democracy," and that the great danger lay in "the democratic parts of our constitutions"; Elbridge Gerry, speaking of democracy as "the worst of all political evils"; Roger Sherman, hoping that "the people . . . have as little to do as may be about the government"; William Livingston, saying that "the people have ever been and ever will be unfit to retain the exercise of power in their own hands"; George Washington, the presiding officer, urging the delegates not to produce a document of which they themselves could not approve simply in order to "please the people"; Hamilton, charging that the "turbulent and changing" masses "seldom judge or determine right" and advising a permanent governmental body to "check the imprudence of democracy"; the wealthy young planter Charles Pinckney, proposing that no one be president who was not worth at least one hundred thousand dollars—all these were quite representative of the spirit in which the problems of government were treated.

Democratic ideas are most likely to take root among discontented and oppressed classes, rising middle classes, or perhaps some sections of an old, alienated, and partially disinherited aristocracy, but they do not appeal to a privileged class that is still amplifying its privileges. With a half-dozen exceptions at the most, the men of the Philadelphia Convention were sons of men who had considerable position and wealth, and as a group they had advanced well beyond their fathers. Only one of them, William Few of Georgia, could be said in any sense to represent the yeoman farmer class which constituted the overwhelming majority of the free population. In the late eighteenth century "the better kind of people" found themselves set off from the mass by a hundred visible, tangible, and audible distinctions of dress, speech, manners, and education. There was a continuous lineage of upper-class contempt, from pre-Revolutionary Tories like Peggy Hutchinson, the Governor's daughter, who wrote one day: "The dirty mob was all about me as I drove into town," to a Federalist like Hamilton, who candidly disdained the people. Mass unrest was often received in the spirit of young Gouverneur Morris: "The mob begin to think and reason. Poor reptiles! . . . They bask in the sun, and ere noon they will bite, depend upon it. The gentry begin to fear this." Nowhere in America or Europe—not even among the great liberated thinkers of the Enlightenment—did democratic ideas appear respectable to the cultivated classes. Whether the Fathers looked to the cynically illuminated intellectuals of contemporary Europe or to their own Christian heritage of the idea of original sin, they found quick confirmation of the notion that man is an unregenerate rebel who has to be controlled.

And yet there was another side to the picture. The Fathers were intellectual heirs of seventeenth-century English republicanism with its opposition to arbitrary rule and faith in popular sovereignty. If they feared the advance of democracy, they also had misgivings about turning to the extreme right. Having recently experienced a bitter revolutionary struggle with an external power beyond their control, they were in no mood to follow Hobbes to his conclusion that any kind of government must be accepted in order to avert the anarchy and terror of a state of nature. They were uneasily aware that both military dictatorship and a return to monarchy were being seriously discussed in some quarters—the former chiefly among unpaid and discontented army officers, the latter in rich and fashionable Northern circles. John Jay, familiar with sentiment among New York's mercantile aristocracy, wrote to Washington, June 27, 1786, that he feared that "the better kind of people (by which I mean the people who are orderly and industrious, who are content with their situations, and not uneasy in their circumstances) will be led, by the insecurity of property, the loss of confidence in their rulers, and the want of public faith and rectitude, to consider the charms of liberty as imaginary and delusive." Such men, he thought, might be prepared for "almost any change that may promise them quiet and security." Washington, who had already repudiated a suggestion that he become a military dictator, agreed, remarking that "we are apt to run from one extreme to the other."

Unwilling to turn their backs on republicanism, the Fathers also wished to avoid violating the prejudices of the people. "Notwithstanding the oppression and injustice experienced among us from democracy," said George Mason, "the genius of the people is in favor of it, and the genius of the people must be consulted." Mason admitted "that we had been too democratic," but feared that "we should incautiously run into the opposite extreme." James Madison, who has quite rightfully been called the philosopher of the Constitution, told the delegates: "It seems indispensable that the mass of citizens should not be without a voice in making the laws which they are to obey, and in choosing the magistrates who are to administer them." James Wilson, the outstanding jurist of the age, later appointed to the Supreme Court by Washington, said again and again that the ultimate power of government must of necessity reside in the people. This the Fathers commonly accepted, for if government did not proceed from the people, from what other source could it legitimately come? To adopt any other premise not only would be inconsistent with everything they had said against British rule in the past but would open the gates to an extreme concentration of power in the future. Hamilton saw the sharp distinction in the Convention when he said that "the members most tenacious of republicanism were as loud as any in declaiming the vices of democracy." There was no better

expression of the dilemma of a man who has no faith
in the people but insists that government be based upon
them than that of Jeremy Belknap, a New England
clergyman, who wrote to a friend: "Let it stand as a
principle that government originates from the people;
but let the people be taught . . . that they are not able
to govern themselves."

II

If the masses were turbulent and unregenerate, and
yet if government must be founded upon their suffrage
and consent, what could a Constitution-maker do? One
thing that the Fathers did not propose to do, because
they thought it impossible, was to change the nature of
man to conform with a more ideal system. They were
inordinately confident that they knew what man always
had been and what he always would be. The eighteenth-
century mind had great faith in universals. Its method,
as Carl Becker has said, was "to go up and down the
field of history looking for man in general, the universal
man, stripped of the accidents of time and place." Madison declared that the causes of political differences and
of the formation of factions were "sown in the nature
of man" and could never be eradicated. "It is universally
acknowledged," David Hume had written, "that there
is a great uniformity among the actions of men, in all
nations and ages, and that human nature remains still
the same, in its principles and operations. The same motives always produce the same actions. The same events
always follow from the same causes."

Since man was an unchangeable creature of self-
interest, it would not do to leave anything to his ca-

pacity for restraint. It was too much to expect that vice could be checked by virtue; the Fathers relied instead upon checking vice with vice. Madison once objected during the Convention that Gouverneur Morris was "forever inculcating the utter political depravity of men and the necessity of opposing one vice and interest to another vice and interest." And yet Madison himself in the *Federalist* number 51 later set forth an excellent statement of the same thesis:[1]

> Ambition must be made to counteract ambition. . . . It may be a reflection on human nature that such devices should be necessary to control the abuses of government. But what is government itself, but the greatest of all reflections on human nature? If men were angels, no government would be necessary. . . . In framing a government which is to be administered by men over men, the great difficulty lies in this: you must first enable the government to control the governed; and in the next place oblige it to control itself.

Political economists of the laissez-faire school were saying that private vices could be public benefits, that an economically beneficent result would be providentially or "naturally" achieved if self-interest were left free from state interference and allowed to pursue its ends. But the Fathers were not so optimistic about politics. If, in a state that lacked constitutional balance, one class or one interest gained control, they believed, it would surely plunder all other interests. The Fathers, of course, were especially fearful that the poor would

---

1. Cf. the words of Hamilton to the New York ratifying convention: "Men will pursue their interests. It is as easy to change human nature as to oppose the strong current of selfish passions. A wise legislator will gently divert the channel, and direct it, if possible, to the public good."

plunder the rich, but most of them would probably have admitted that the rich, unrestrained, would also plunder the poor. Even Gouverneur Morris, who stood as close to the extreme aristocratic position as candor and intelligence would allow, told the Convention: "Wealth tends to corrupt the mind and to nourish its love of power, and to stimulate it to oppression. History proves this to be the spirit of the opulent."

What the Fathers wanted was known as "balanced government," an idea at least as old as Aristotle and Polybius. This ancient conception had won new sanction in the eighteenth century, which was dominated intellectually by the scientific work of Newton, and in which mechanical metaphors sprang as naturally to men's minds as did biological metaphors in the Darwinian atmosphere of the late nineteenth century. Men had found a rational order in the universe and they hoped that it could be transferred to politics, or, as John Adams put it, that governments could be "erected on the simple principles of nature." Madison spoke in the most precise Newtonian language when he said that such a "natural" government must be so constructed "that its several constituent parts may, by their mutual relations, be the means of keeping each other in their proper places." A properly designed state, the Fathers believed, would check interest with interest, class with class, faction with faction, and one branch of government with another in a harmonious system of mutual frustration.

In practical form, therefore, the quest of the Fathers reduced primarily to a search for constitutional devices that would force various interests to check and control one another. Among those who favored the federal Constitution three such devices were distinguished.

The first of these was the advantage of a federated government in maintaining order against popular uprisings or majority rule. In a single state a faction might arise and take complete control by force; but if the states were bound in a federation, the central government could step in and prevent it. Hamilton quoted Montesquieu: "Should a popular insurrection happen in one of the confederate states, the others are able to quell it." Further, as Madison argued in the *Federalist* number 10, a majority would be the most dangerous of all factions that might arise, for the majority would be the most capable of gaining complete ascendancy. If the political society were very extensive, however, and embraced a large number and variety of local interests, the citizens who shared a common majority interest "must be rendered by their number and local situation, unable to concert and carry into effect their schemes of oppression." The chief propertied interests would then be safer from "a rage for paper money, for an abolition of debts, for an equal division of property, or for any other improper or wicked project."

The second advantage of good constitutional government resided in the mechanism of representation itself. In a small direct democracy the unstable passions of the people would dominate lawmaking; but a representative government, as Madison said, would "refine and enlarge the public views by passing them through the medium of a chosen body of citizens." Representatives chosen by the people were wiser and more deliberate than the people themselves in mass assemblage. Hamilton frankly anticipated a kind of syndical paternalism in which the wealthy and dominant members of every trade or industry would represent the others in politics. Merchants, for example, were "the natural representatives" of their employees and of the mechanics and artisans they dealt with. Hamilton expected that Congress, "with too few exceptions to have any influence on the spirit of the government, will be composed of landholders, merchants, and men of the learned professions."

The third advantage of the government the Fathers were designing was pointed out most elaborately by John Adams in the first volume of his *Defence of the Constitutions of Government of the United States of America,* which reached Philadelphia while the Convention was in session and was cited with approval by several delegates.[2] Adams believed that the aristocracy and the democracy must be made to neutralize each other. Each element should be given its own house of the legislature, and over both houses there should be set a capable, strong, and impartial executive armed with the veto power. This split assembly would contain within itself an organic check and would be capable of self-control under the governance of the executive. The whole system was to be capped by an independent judiciary. The inevitable tendency of the rich and the poor to plunder each other would be kept in hand.

III

It is ironical that the Constitution, which Americans venerate so deeply, is based upon a political theory that at one crucial point stands in direct antithesis to the mainstream of American democratic faith. Modern

---

2. "Mr. Adams' book," wrote Benjamin Rush, often in the company of the delegates, "has diffused such excellent principles among us that there is little doubt of our adopting a vigorous and compounded Federal Legislature. Our illustrious Minister in this gift to his country has done us more service than if he had obtained alliances for us with all the nations of Europe."

American folklore assumes that democracy and liberty are all but identical, and when democratic writers take the trouble to make the distinction, they usually assume that democracy is necessary to liberty. But the Founding Fathers thought that the liberty with which they were most concerned was menaced by democracy. In their minds liberty was linked not to democracy but to property.

What did the Fathers mean by liberty? What did Jay mean when he spoke of "the charms of liberty"? Or Madison when he declared that to destroy liberty in order to destroy factions would be a remedy worse than the disease? Certainly the men who met at Philadelphia were not interested in extending liberty to those classes in America, the Negro slaves and the indentured servants, who were most in need of it, for slavery was recognized in the organic structure of the Constitution and indentured servitude was no concern of the Convention. Nor was the regard of the delegates for civil liberties any too tender. It was the opponents of the Constitution who were most active in demanding such vital liberties as freedom of religion, freedom of speech and press, jury trial, due process, and protection from "unreasonable searches and seizures." These guarantees had to be incorporated in the first ten amendments because the Convention neglected to put them in the original document. Turning to economic issues, it was not freedom of trade in the modern sense that the Fathers were striving for. Although they did not believe in impeding trade unnecessarily, they felt that failure to regulate it was one of the central weaknesses of the Articles of Confederation, and they stood closer to the mercantilists than to Adam Smith. Again, liberty to them did not mean free access to the nation's unappropriated wealth. At least fourteen of them were land speculators.

They did not believe in the right of the squatter to occupy unused land, but rather in the right of the absentee owner or speculator to preempt it.

The liberties that the constitutionalists hoped to gain were chiefly negative. They wanted freedom from fiscal uncertainty and irregularities in the currency, from trade wars among the states, from economic discrimination by more powerful foreign governments, from attacks on the creditor class or on property, from popular insurrection. They aimed to create a government that would act as an honest broker among a variety of propertied interests, giving them all protection from their common enemies and preventing any one of them from becoming too powerful. The Convention was a fraternity of types of absentee ownership. All property should be permitted to have its proportionate voice in government. Individual property interests might have to be sacrificed at times, but only for the community of propertied interests. Freedom for property would result in liberty for men—perhaps not for all men, but at least for all worthy men.[3] Because men have different faculties and abilities, the Fathers believed, they acquire different amounts of property. To protect property is only to pro-

3. The Fathers probably would have accepted the argument of the Declaration of Independence that "all men are created equal," but only as a legal, not as a political or psychological proposition. Jefferson himself believed in the existence of "natural aristocrats," but he thought they were likely to appear in any class of society. However, for those who interpreted the natural-rights philosophy more conservatively than he, the idea that all men are equal did not mean that uneducated dirt farmers or grimy-handed ship calkers were in any sense the equals of the Schuylers, Washingtons, or Pinckneys. It meant only that British colonials had as much natural right to self-government as Britons at home, that the average American was the legal peer of the average Briton. Among the signers of the Constitution, it is worth noting, there were only six men who had also signed the Declaration of Independence.

tect men in the exercise of their natural faculties. Among
the many liberties, therefore, freedom to hold and dispose property is paramount. Democracy, unchecked rule
by the masses, is sure to bring arbitrary redistribution
of property, destroying the very essence of liberty.

The Fathers' conception of democracy, shaped by
their practical experience with the aggressive dirt farmers in the American states and the urban mobs of the
Revolutionary period, was supplemented by their reading in history and political science. Fear of what Madison called "the superior force of an interested and over-
bearing majority" was the dominant emotion aroused
by their study of historical examples. The chief examples
of republics were among the city-states of antiquity,
medieval Europe, and early modern times. Now, the
history of these republics—a history, as Hamilton said,
"of perpetual vibration between the extremes of tyranny
and anarchy"—was alarming. Further, most of the men
who had overthrown the liberties of republics had "begun their career by paying an obsequious court to the
people; commencing demagogues and ending tyrants."

All the constitutional devices that the Fathers praised
in their writings were attempts to guarantee the future
of the United States against the "turbulent" political
cycles of previous republics. By "democracy," they
meant a system of government which directly expressed
the will of the majority of the people, usually through
such an assemblage of the people as was possible in the
small area of the city-state.

A cardinal tenet in the faith of the men who made the
Constitution was the belief that democracy can never be
more than a transitional stage in government, that it
always evolves into either a tyranny (the rule of the rich
demagogue who has patronized the mob) or an aristocracy (the original leaders of the democratic elements).

"Remember," wrote the dogmatic John Adams in one of his letters to John Taylor of Caroline, "democracy never lasts long. It soon wastes, exhausts, and murders itself. There never was a democracy yet that did not commit suicide." [4] Again:

If you give more than a share in the sovereignty to the democrats, that is, if you give them the command or preponderance in the . . . legislature, they will vote all property out of the hands of you aristocrats, and if they let you escape with your lives, it will be more humanity, consideration, and generosity than any triumphant democracy ever displayed since the creation. And what will follow? The aristocracy among the democrats will take your places, and treat their fellows as severely and sternly as you have treated them.

Government, thought the Fathers, is based on property. Men who have no property lack the necessary stake in an orderly society to make stable or reliable citizens. Dread of the propertyless masses of the towns was all but universal. George Washington, Gouverneur Morris, John Dickinson, and James Madison spoke of their anxieties about the urban working class that might arise some time in the future—"men without property and principle," as Dickinson described them—and even the democratic Jefferson shared this prejudice. Madison, stating the problem, came close to anticipating the modern threats to conservative republicanism from both communism and fascism:

---

4. Taylor labored to confute Adams, but in 1814, after many discouraging years in American politics, he conceded a great part of Adams's case: "All parties, however loyal to principles at first, degenerate into aristocracies of interest at last; and unless a nation is capable of discerning the point where integrity ends and fraud begins, popular parties are among the surest modes of introducing an aristocracy."

In future times, a great majority of the people will not only be without landed but any other sort of property. These will either combine, under the influence of their common situation—in which case the rights of property and the public liberty will not be secure in their hands—or, what is more probable, they will become the tools of opulence and ambition, in which case there will be equal danger on another side.

What encouraged the Fathers about their own era, however, was the broad dispersion of landed property. The small land-owning farmers had been troublesome in recent years, but there was a general conviction that under a properly made Constitution a *modus vivendi* could be worked out with them. The possession of moderate plots of property presumably gave them a sufficient stake in society to be safe and responsible citizens under the restraints of balanced government. Influence in government would be proportionate to property: merchants and great landholders would be dominant, but small property-owners would have an independent and far from negligible voice. It was "politic as well as just," said Madison, "that the interests and rights of every class should be duly represented and understood in the public councils," and John Adams declared that there could be "no free government without a democratical branch in the constitution."

The farming element already satisfied the property requirements for suffrage in most of the states, and the Fathers generally had no quarrel with their enfranchisement. But when they spoke of the necessity of founding government upon the consent of "the people," it was only these small property-holders that they had in mind. For example, the famous Virginia Bill of Rights, written by George Mason, explicitly defined those eligible for suffrage as all men "having sufficient evidence of permanent common interest with and attachment to the community"—which meant, in brief, sufficient property.

However, the original intention of the Fathers to admit the yeoman into an important but sharply limited partnership in affairs of state could not be perfectly realized. At the time the Constitution was made, Southern planters and Northern merchants were setting their differences aside in order to meet common dangers—from radicals within and more powerful nations without. After the Constitution was adopted, conflict between the ruling classes broke out anew, especially after powerful planters were offended by the favoritism of Hamilton's policies to Northern commercial interests. The planters turned to the farmers to form an agrarian alliance, and for more than half a century this powerful coalition embraced the bulk of the articulate interests of the country. As time went on, therefore, the mainstream of American political conviction deviated more and more from the antidemocratic position of the Constitution-makers. Yet, curiously, their general satisfaction with the Constitution together with their growing nationalism made Americans deeply reverent of the founding generation, with the result that as it grew stronger, this deviation was increasingly overlooked.

There is common agreement among modern critics that the debates over the Constitution were carried on at an intellectual level that is rare in politics, and that the Constitution itself is one of the world's masterpieces of practical statecraft. On other grounds there has been controversy. At the very beginning contemporary opponents of the Constitution foresaw an apocalyptic destruction of local government and popular institutions, while conservative Europeans of the old regime thought the young American Republic was a dangerous leftist experiment. Modern critical scholarship, which reached a high point in Charles A. Beard's *An Economic Interpretation of the Constitution of the United States,* started a new turn in the debate. The antagonism, long latent, between the philosophy of the Constitution and the philosophy of American democracy again came into the open. Professor Beard's work appeared in 1913 at the peak of the Progressive era, when the muckraking fever was still high; some readers tended to conclude from his findings that the Fathers were selfish reactionaries who do not deserve their high place in American esteem. Still more recently, other writers, inverting this logic, have used Beard's facts to praise the Fathers for their opposition to "democracy" and as an argument for returning again to the idea of a "republic."

In fact, the Fathers' image of themselves as moderate republicans standing between political extremes was quite accurate. They were impelled by class motives more than pietistic writers like to admit, but they were also controlled, as Professor Beard himself has recently emphasized, by a statesmanlike sense of moderation and a scrupulously republican philosophy. Any attempt, however, to tear their ideas out of the eighteenth-century context is sure to make them seem starkly reactionary. Consider, for example, the favorite maxim of John Jay: "The people who own the country ought to govern it." To the Fathers this was simply a swift axiomatic statement of the stake-in-society theory of political rights, a moderate conservative position under eighteenth-century conditions of property distribution in America. Under modern property relations this maxim demands a drastic restriction of the base of political power. A large portion of the modern middle class—and it is the strength of this class upon which balanced government depends—is propertyless; and the urban

proletariat, which the Fathers so greatly feared, is almost one half the population. Further, the separation
of ownership from control that has come with the corporation deprives Jay's maxim of twentieth-century
meaning even for many propertied people. The six hundred thousand stockholders of the American Telephone
& Telegraph Company not only do not acquire political
power by virtue of their stock-ownership, but they do
not even acquire economic power: they cannot control
their own company.

From a humanistic standpoint there is a serious dilemma in the philosophy of the Fathers, which derives
from their conception of man. They thought man was a
creature of rapacious self-interest, and yet they wanted
him to be free—free, in essence, to contend, to engage
in an umpired strife, to use property to get property.
They accepted the mercantile image of life as an eternal
battleground, and assumed the Hobbesian war of each
against all; they did not propose to put an end to this
war, but merely to stabilize it and make it less murderous. They had no hope and they offered none for any
ultimate organic change in the way men conduct themselves. The result was that while they thought self-
interest the most dangerous and unbrookable quality of
man, they necessarily underwrote it in trying to control
it. They succeeded in both respects: under the competitive capitalism of the nineteenth century America
continued to be an arena for various grasping and contending interests, and the federal government continued
to provide a stable and acceptable medium within
which they could contend; further, it usually showed
the wholesome bias on behalf of property which the Fathers expected. But no man who is as well abreast of
modern science as the Fathers were of eighteenth-century science believes any longer in unchanging human

nature. Modern humanistic thinkers who seek for a means by which society may transcend eternal conflict and rigid adherence to property rights as its integrating principles can expect no answer in the philosophy of balanced government as it was set down by the Constitution-makers of 1787.

CHAPTER II

THOMAS JEFFERSON:
THE ARISTOCRAT AS DEMOCRAT

❦

THE *sheep are happier of themselves, than under the care of the wolves.* THOMAS JEFFERSON

THE mythology that has grown up around Thomas Jefferson is as massive and imposing as any in American history. Although the bitterly prejudiced views of Federalist historians have never had wide acceptance, the stereotype perpetuated by such adherents of the Jeffersonian tradition as Claude Bowers and the late V. L. Parrington has been extremely popular. Jefferson has been pictured as a militant, crusading democrat, a Physiocrat who repudiated acquisitive capitalistic economics, a revolutionist who tore up the social fabric of Virginia in 1776, and the sponsor of a "Revolution of 1800" which destroyed Federalism root and branch. Although there is fact enough to give the color of truth to these notions, they have been torn down by shrewd Jefferson scholars like Charles A. Beard, Gilbert Chinard, and Albert J. Nock, and it is certainly not lack of good criticism that accounts for the dominant Jefferson legend. The issues of his time have been overdramatized, and Jefferson has been overdramatized with them.

It would have been strange if Jefferson had become

one of those bitter rebels who live by tearing up established orders and forcing social struggles to the issue. He was born into an eminent place in the Virginia aristocracy. Peter Jefferson, his father, was a self-made man, but through his mother, Jane Randolph, who came from the distinguished Virginia family, he had an assured social position. Peter Jefferson died in 1757, leaving his son, then fourteen, over 2,700 acres and a large number of bondsmen. During most of his mature life Thomas Jefferson owned about 10,000 acres and from one to two hundred Negroes. The leisure that made possible his great writings on human liberty was supported by the labors of three generations of slaves.

Jefferson was a benevolent slavemaster, and his feeling for the common people was doubtless affected by an ingrained habit of solicitude for the helpless dependents who supported him. He prided himself on not being overprotective, once writing Dupont that the difference between their affections for the people was that Dupont loved them as infants who must be nursed, while he loved them as adults who could govern themselves. But no aristocrat, reared in a society rent by such a gulf between rich and poor, learned and unlearned, could be quite the democrat Jefferson imagined himself. As Charles M. Wiltse puts it, "He remains always aloof from the masses, and if he claims equality for all men, it is not because he feels that men are equal, but because he reasons that they must be so." An element of gentle condescension is unmistakable in his democracy; its spirit is caught in one of his letters to Lafayette:

It will be a great comfort to you to know from your own inspection, the condition of all the provinces of your own country, and it will be interesting to them at some future day, to be known to you. This is, perhaps, the only moment of your life in which you can acquire that knowledge. And to do it most effectually, you must be absolutely incognito, you must ferret the people out of their hovels as I have done, look into their kettles, eat their bread, loll on their beds under pretence of resting yourself, but in fact, to find if they are soft. You will feel a sublime pleasure in the course of this investigation, and a sublimer one hereafter, when you shall be able to apply your knowledge to the softening of their beds, or the throwing of a morsel of meat into their kettle of vegetables.

Jefferson was educated at the College of William and Mary at Williamsburg, where in spite of his youth he was immediately accepted by the most brilliant and enlightened society. After graduation he fell into the expected pattern of the Virginia gentry, among whom political leadership was practically a social obligation. At twenty-four he was admitted to the bar, at twenty-six elected to a seat in the House of Burgesses, which he held for six years. At twenty-nine, a successful but unenthusiastic consulting lawyer, he married a young widow and settled at Monticello. His marriage brought large landholdings to add to his patrimony, but also a debt of four thousand pounds. Like many other Virginia planters, he developed from his own relations with British creditors a bilious view of the province's economic subordination to England and fell in with the anti-British group among the Burgesses. The ringing phrases he had learned from English republican philosophers began to take on more vivid meaning for him. In 1774 he wrote a bold tract applying the natural-rights doctrine to the colonial controversy, which won immediate attention throughout the colonies and gave him the reputation for literary craftsmanship that later made him the draftsman of the Declaration of Independence.

The Revolution found Jefferson in the prime of life and at the full flush of his reforming enthusiasm; during its first few years he did some of the most creative work of his life. Under his leadership the Virginia reformers abolished primogeniture and entail and laid the base for freedom of thought and religion by disestablishing the Anglican Church and forbidding legal or political disabilities for religious dissent. They also attempted, with paltry results, to found a good common-school system. Jefferson wrote the bills destroying primogeniture and entail, and on behalf of the bill for religious freedom drafted one of the most brilliant and trenchant pleas for free thought in the history of literature.

The accomplishments of this reform movement were considerable, but they have been subject to fantastic exaggeration by historians and biographers who look upon Jefferson and his colleagues as revolutionists putting through a sweeping program of social reform, destroying the Virginia aristocracy, and laying the foundations for democratic government. Even Jefferson, who was usually modest and accurate about his achievements, claimed too much when he said that these reforms "laid the axe" to the root of the Old Dominion's aristocracy. If the changes were actually so important, one would expect bitter resistance. The truth is that, with the exception of the bill for religious freedom (which, Jefferson testified, gave rise to "the severest contests in which I have ever been engaged"), the old institutions fell almost without a push. Jefferson wrote to Franklin that "this important transformation" was accomplished with the most remarkable ease; only "a half-dozen aristocratic gentlemen, agonizing under the loss of pre-eminence," had opposed it, and they "have been thought fitter objects of pity than of punishment."

The explanation of this "revolution by consent" is

simple: there was no revolution. Primogeniture in the full meaning of the word did not really exist in Virginia. It was never mandatory upon the landowner. It applied only when he died without leaving a will disposing of his land. It was not regularly practiced by the landed families of the Old Dominion, for Virginians usually did leave wills dividing their land among their sons, and sometimes even among their daughters. Entail was actually a nuisance to the aristocracy because it interfered with the sale of estates they often found inconvenient to hold. During the years before 1776 petition after petition came into the Virginia legislature from leading families asking that their lands be exempted from entail.

Much has been made by rapt biographers of Jefferson's interest in abolishing slavery at this time. As a member of a committee to revise the legal code, he did draft a law for gradual emancipation, but never presumed to introduce it. "It was found," he explained, "that the public mind would not bear the proposition. . . . Yet the day is not distant when it must bear and adopt it, or worse will follow." Trying to force through any law, however desirable, which "the public mind would not bear" would have been thoroughly uncharacteristic of Jefferson's pragmatic political temperament.[1]

After a most unhappy experience as war Governor of Virginia, Jefferson, at thirty-eight, was eager for permanent retirement from politics, but the death of his

---

1. Jefferson was characteristically circumspect about attacking slavery in his own state, but more aggressive in intercolonial affairs when he could expect Northern backing. Thus he included a bitter attack upon the slave trade in the Declaration of Independence—which was struck out—and tried to get slavery banned from the Northwest Territory in his Ordinance of 1784.

wife drove him away from Monticello and back into furiously active service for the Congress. From 1785 to 1789 he was American Minister to France, where his experience may have been crucial in determining the direction of his political thinking. While his friends at home were watching the failure of the Articles of Confederation, looking anxiously upon the political advances of the dirt farmers, and turning rightward in their politics, he was touring Europe, taking the measure of feudal and monarchical institutions, observing the bitter exploitation of the workers of England and the peasantry of France, and confirming his republicanism. Appalled at the extremes of wealth and misery in European countries, he found kings, nobles, and priests "an abandoned confederacy against the happiness of the mass of the people," saw in the royalty of Europe only "fools" and "idiots," and described the treatment of the English laboring classes in the bitterest language. Europe fortified his conviction that America, with its republican government, broad distribution of landed property, agrarian economy, and oceanic isolation, was the chosen spot of the earth. Although he found much to admire in the European common people, they too brought him back to the political superiority of America. A lifelong prejudice is summed up in a few words from one of his letters to Lafayette: "The yeomanry of the United States are not the *canaille* of Paris."

In France during the early days of the French Revolution, Jefferson was naturally consulted by the moderate leaders of its first phase. Once he committed the indiscretion of allowing Lafayette and a few friends to meet at his house. He promptly apologized to the French Foreign Minister, Montmorin; but Montmorin, who evidently understood Jefferson well, answered that he hoped Jefferson "would habitually assist at such confer-

ences, being sure I would be useful in moderating the
warmer spirits and promoting a wholesome and prac-
ticable reformation only." When the King showed the
first signs of a conciliatory state of mind, appearing in
public with the popular cockade on his head, Jefferson
concluded that the time had come for a compromise
with the crown. But the draft of terms which he gave
to his revolutionary friends was rejected—because it was
too moderate.

What of the notion that Jefferson was an impractical
visionary, that he was, as Charles Carroll of Carrollton
called him, "a theoretical and fanciful man"? There is a
sense in which this was true, but it has little to do with
his public activity or his cast of mind. He *was* fatally
generous, borrowed funds to give to beggars, enter-
tained with a lavishness far beyond the capacities of his
purse, and in his last years gave his declining fortunes
the *coup de grâce* by signing the note of a floundering
neighbor.

But did his mind run naturally to high abstractions?
Did he spend his spare moments on them? On the contrary, when he found time to write at length, he turned
his energies to such matter-of-fact projects as the ency-
clopedic *Notes on Virginia*, a parliamentary manual for
the use of the Senate, a study of Indian languages, and
his autobiography. He never attempted to write a systematic book of political theory—which was well, because he had no system and lacked the doctrinaire's compulsion to be consistent. Although he found time and
energy for everything from epistemology to the mechanical arts, it was the latter that interested him most.
He had an almost compulsive love of counting, observing, measuring. ("Not a sprig of grass shoots uninterest-
ing to me," he once wrote to his daughter.) His standard

of values was eminently practical. ("The greatest service which can be rendered any country is to add an useful plant to its culture.") He was the architect of his own home, ran his farm on a fairly self-sufficient basis, and made elaborate efficiency studies of his slaves' work. He invented a hempbeater, worked out the formula for a moldboard plow of least resistance, for which the French Institute of Agriculture of the Department of Seine-et-Oise gave him a prize, devised a leather buggy top, a swivel chair, and a dumbwaiter. He kept elaborate journals about the farms, gardens, social conditions, and natural phenomena he saw on his travels. Albert Jay Nock concludes that he "examined every useful tree and plant in western Europe and studied its cultivation." For long periods he kept daily thermometric and barometric readings. He was constantly studying new plows, steam engines, metronomes, thermometers, elevators, and the like, as well as the processing of butters and cheeses. He wrote a long essay for Congress on standards of weights and measures in the United States, and an excellent critique of the census returns, with detailed suggestions for collecting more minute information. On his travels he procured the plans of twelve large European cities, which he was able to lend L'Enfant to help him lay out the scheme of Washington. He conceived the American decimal system of coinage, demonstrating on this score his superiority to the financier Robert Morris. Such are the contributions to practical arts of this "theoretical and fanciful man."

What of the Jefferson who said that the tree of liberty must be watered periodically with the blood of tyrants, who thought that a rebellion every twenty years was an excellent thing, and who urged throughout his life that constitutions should be completely remade every twenty-five or thirty years? What of the Jefferson who was considered dangerous by so many conservative contemporaries, who was everywhere understood to be a strong-headed doctrinaire?

Jefferson was a complex person who must be measured in whole, not in part, in action as well as thought. There were deep ambiguities in his thinking, which made any effort at consistency impossible. Although Federalist historians have cited these ambiguities as evidence of a moral taint, a constitutional shiftiness of mind, they may in fact be traced to a continuously ambivalent personal and political history. He valued much more highly the achievements of his father, whom he intensely admired, than the high social status of his mother, whose influence he never acknowledged; but from the beginning he was aware of both the assurance of the aristocracy and the real merits and talents of men who came from unknown families. In his autobiography he remarked dryly of the Randolph genealogy: "They trace their pedigree far back in England and Scotland, to which let everyone ascribe the faith and merit he chooses." When he came to maturity, Jefferson was a slaveowner and yet a revolutionist, who could say that man's rights were "unalienable" at the very moment when he owned several dozen souls. All his life he circulated among men of wealth, learning, and distinction, and as befitted one who disliked acrimony he learned to accommodate himself to them—but he also absorbed the most liberal and questionable opinions of his age and associated on congenial terms with men like Thomas Paine and Joel Barlow. In American politics he became a leader of yeomen farmers—but also of great planters. He was the head of a popular faction that stood against the commercial interests—but it was also a propertied faction with acquisitive aspirations of its own. Well read in the best philosophical literature of his century, he accepted broad cosmopolitan ideas, but he was also an ardent American patriot. He was a pacifist in personal temperament and philosophy, a nationalist by training, and yet a Virginian with strong parochial loyalties. He wanted with all his heart to hold to the values of agrarian society, and yet he believed in progress. Add to all this the fact that he lived an unusually long life, saw many changes, and tried to adapt his views to changing circumstances.

Jefferson had warm impulses. His cosmopolitan mind refracted the most advanced and liberating ideas of his time. He believed in those ideas, and rephrased and reiterated them in language that has become classic; but he was not in the habit of breaking lances trying to fulfill them. The generous and emancipating thoughts for which his name is so justly praised are to be found almost entirely in his *private* correspondence; after he wrote the Declaration of Independence and the Virginia Statute for Religious Freedom he avoided expressing his more unacceptable ideas in public. He understood that in the workaday world of public activity his most lofty ideals were chiefly valuable to indicate the direction in which society should be guided. He never really expected them to be realized in his time and preferred to place his hopes in progress, in the promise that mankind would consummate his ideals in some magnificent future. ("Your taste is judicious," John Adams once taunted him, "in liking better the dreams of the future than the history of the past.")

Jefferson's practical activity was usually aimed at some kind of minimum program that could be achieved without keen conflict or great expenditure of energy. He hated vigorous controversy, shrank from asserting his principles when they would excite the anger of colleagues or neighbors. He tried to avoid a wide circulation of his *Notes on Virginia* because he did not want Virginians to read his bitter remarks on slavery and a few tart observations on the province's constitution. Jefferson did not lack courage—his futile embargo policy, carried out under bitter protest from every part of the country, proves that—but rather that hardihood of spirit which makes a political fight bearable. Although he had strong political prejudices and sometimes violent animosities, he did not enjoy power and could not bear publicity. He was acutely sensitive to criticism, admitting to Francis Hopkinson in 1789: "I find the pain of a little censure, even when it is unfounded, is more acute than the pleasure of much praise." Abnormally shy and troubled by a slight speech defect, he found it impossible to read his messages in person to Congress as Washington and Adams had done. He had not the temperament of an agitator, hardly even of a leader in the qualities that leadership requires under modern democracy. Not once did he deliver an exciting speech. His private life was one of enormous variety and interest, and there were many times when he would have been happy to desert public service to enjoy his farm, his family, and his books.

II

Jefferson's Federalist opponents feared, above all, power lodged in the majority. Jefferson feared power lodged anywhere else. In his First Inaugural Address he asked concerning the common observation "that man cannot be trusted with the government of himself": "Can he, then, be trusted with the government of others?" He would have agreed with Madison that power is "of

an encroaching nature," and he was sure that power
corrupts those who possess it. "If once the people become inattentive to the public affairs," he wrote Edward
Carrington from Paris, "you and I and Congress and As-
semblies, Judges and Governors, shall all become wolves.
It seems to be the law of our general nature, in spite of
individual exceptions."

Admitting that a majority will often decide public
questions wrongly, Jefferson argued that "the duperies
of the people are less injurious" than the self-interested
policies of kings, priests, and aristocrats. He refused to
be alarmed by popular uprisings like the Shays Rebellion. In the safety of his private corrrespondence he felt
free to say that "honest republican governments" should
be "so mild in their punishment of rebellions as not to
discourage them too much." "A little rebellion now and
then is a good thing, and as necessary in the political
world as storms in the physical." The people are not
always well informed, but it is better that they have mis-
conceptions that make them restless than that they be
lethargic—for lethargy in the people means death for
republics.

Again and again Jefferson urged that the people be
educated and informed through a broad common-
school system and a free press. Although he had small
faith in the power of republics to resist corruption and
decay, he hoped that mass education would stem this
degenerative process.[2] Education not only would give
stability and wisdom to the politics of a commonwealth,
but would widen opportunities, bring out the natural

2. In his Bill for the More General Diffusion of Knowledge
(1779) he declared that "experience hath shewn, that even
under the best forms [of government] those entrusted with power
have, in time, and by slow operations perverted it into
tyranny. . . ."

talents that could be found in abundance among the common people. Throughout Jefferson's life there runs this humane concern for "the pursuit of happiness," for the development of the individual without regard to limitations of class.

By and large, however, when Jefferson spoke warmly of the merits and abilities of "the people" he meant "the farmers." He did not see a town until he was almost eighteen, and he believed deeply that rural living and rural people are the wellspring of civic virtue and individual vitality, that farmers are the best social base of a democratic republic. "Those who labor in the earth are the chosen people of God, if ever he had a chosen people," he proclaimed in his *Notes on Virginia.* "Corruption of morals in the mass of cultivators is a phenomenon of which no age nor nation has furnished an example." [3]

. . . generally speaking, the proportion which the aggregate of the other classes of citizens bears in any State to that of its husbandmen, is the proportion of its unsound to its healthy parts, and is a good enough barometer

---

3. In 1787 he wrote: "I think our governments will remain virtuous for many centuries; as long as they remain chiefly agricultural; and this will be as long as there shall be vacant lands in any part of America. When they get piled upon one another in large cities, as in Europe, they will become corrupt as in Europe."

After he had observed the machinations of the Federalists, his faith in the husbandman's monopoly on civic virtue became even more rigid than before, and a shrill note rang through his letters: "Farmers, whose interests are entirely agricultural . . . are the true representatives of the great American interest, and are alone to be relied on for expressing the proper American sentiments."

In his belief that one economic class, the freeholding farmers, had more political virtue than the other orders, Jefferson made a significant breach in the abstract conception that human nature is everywhere the same, but he does not seem to have developed the implications of this insight.

whereby to measure its degree of corruption. While we
have lands to labor then, let us never wish to see our
citizens occupied at a work bench or twirling a distaff.
. . . Let our workshops remain in Europe.

The American economy, then, should be preserved in
its agricultural state. Manufacturers, cities, urban classes,
should be held at a minimum. So Jefferson believed, at
any rate, until the responsibilities of the White House
and the conduct of foreign policy caused him to modify
his views. He once went so far as to say that he hoped
the United States would remain, with respect to Europe,
on the same economic footing as China. Commerce he
would encourage—it supplied the needs of agriculture
—but this was the extent of his early concessions to the
urban classes.

Thus far Jefferson, with his faith in the farmers, his
distrust of the urban classes, and his belief in the long-
range value of rebellions and social disturbances, seems
at the opposite pole from the Constitution-makers—and
so he might have been if his political theory had been
elaborated into a coherent system. But he had more in
common with the conservative thinkers of his age than
is usually recognized. His differences with the political
theory of the Constitution-makers were differences of
emphasis, not of structure. He shared their primary
fears. He did not think that political constitutions could
safely rely on man's virtue. In a letter to Mann Page in
1795 he declared that he could not accept the idea of
the Rochefoucaulds and Montaignes that "fourteen out
of fifteen men are rogues." "*But I have always found
that rogues would be uppermost,* and I do not know
that the proportion is too strong for the higher orders
and for those who, rising above the swinish multitude,
always contrive to nestle themselves into the places of

power and profit." It was the upper, not the lower orders of society that he thought especially unregenerate—but it was Jefferson, too, who could use words like "canaille" and "swinish multitude."

Jefferson, of course, accepted the principle of balanced government and the idea that the people must be checked. "It is not by the consolidation, or concentration of powers, but by their distribution that good government is effected," he wrote in his autobiography. He designed a constitution for Virginia in 1776 which employed the principle of checks and balances and required property qualifications of voters.[4] Of the two houses of the legislature, only the lower was to be elected by the people: the senate was to be chosen by the house, as was the governor, so that two of the three parts of the lawmaking body were at one remove from the citizens. Five years later, criticizing the constitution that had been adopted by Virginia instead of his own, he complained primarily of its lack of checks: the Senate and the House of Delegates were too much alike because both were chosen by the voters in the same way, *The purpose of establishing different houses of legislation is to introduce the influence of different interests or different principles.*" He continued:

All the powers of government, legislative, executive, and judiciary, result to the legislative body. The concentrating these in the same hands is precisely the definition of despotic government. It will be no alleviation that

4. And yet in his *Notes on Virginia* he voiced his displeasure with the limited suffrage of the state: "The majority of the men in the State who pay and fight for its support, are unrepresented in the legislature, the roll of freeholders entitled to vote not including generally the half of those on the roll of the militia, or of the taxgatherers."

these powers will be exercised by a plurality of hands and not by a single one. One hundred and seventy-three despots would surely be as oppressive as one. . . . As little will it avail us that they are chosen by ourselves. An *elective despotism* was not the government we fought for, but one which should not only be founded on free principles, but in which the powers of government should be so divided and balanced among several bodies of magistracy, as that no one could transcend their legal limits without being effectually checked and restrained by the others.

This would have been accounted sound doctrine at the Philadelphia Convention of 1787. A government that does not divide and balance powers in a system of checks is precisely what Jefferson means by despotic; the fact that the governing body is chosen by the people does not qualify his complaint; such a government, without checks, is merely "an elective despotism." Jefferson, then, refused to accept simple majority rule, adopting instead the idea that "different interests or different principles" should be represented in government.

All this sounds close to the theories of Madison and Adams. In fact, Jefferson did not differ with them strongly enough to challenge their conservative writings of the constitutional period. In 1788 he wrote to Madison praising the *Federalist* as "the best commentary on the principles of government which ever was written." Two years later, advising his nephew Thomas Mann Randolph on a course of reading, Jefferson praised Locke's work as being "perfect as far as it goes," and then added: "Descending from theory to practice, there is no better book than the Federalist." In 1787 he told John Adams that he had read his *Defence* "with infinite satisfaction and improvement. It will do great good in America. Its learning and its good sense will, I hope, make it an institute for our politicians, old as well as young." [5]

When the text of the federal Constitution of 1787 reached him in France, Jefferson confessed to Adams that he was staggered at what had been attempted, but soon recovered his composure. He informed Madison that he saw many good features in it, but objected strongly to two things: the absence of a bill of rights (later included in the first ten amendments), and the eligibility of the president for more than one term. In the end he gave it a substantial endorsement: "It is a good canvas, on which some strokes only want retouching." His regard for it grew with the years.

As much as Madison or Morris, Jefferson disliked the idea of city mobs—"the panders of vice and the instruments by which the liberties of a country are generally overturned"—but he believed that they would not emerge in the calculable future because America's lands would be open to make substantial farmers of the ragged and discontented. In his First Inaugural he said that the land would last the American people "to the hundredth and thousandth generation"! The United States would be a nation of farmers, tilling their own soil, independent, informed, unexcitable, and incorruptible. Such a national destiny, he must have felt, would be secured by the Louisiana Purchase.

The future, then, would be founded on a propertied class in a propertied nation. Jefferson leaned strongly to the idea that a propertied interest in society is neces-

5. Later he also endorsed heartily John Taylor's *An Inquiry into the Principles and Policy of the Government of the United States* (1814), which was in large part a headlong assault on Adams's theories. This of course was after the Federalist-Republican antagonism had ripened.

sary to a stable political mentality. In 1800 he wrote a friend that he had always favored universal manhood suffrage; but this was one of those theoretical notions to which he was not firmly wedded. "Still I find some very honest men," he added, "who, thinking the possession of some property necessary to give due independence of mind, are for restraining the elective franchise to property." His 1776 draft of a constitution for Virginia had required that voters own either a freehold estate of twenty-five acres in the country or one fourth of an acre in town, or pay taxes within two years of the time of voting. Never did Jefferson try to introduce universal manhood suffrage anywhere.[6]

The outstanding characteristic of Jefferson's democracy is its close organic relation to the agrarian order of his time. It seems hardly enough to say that he thought that a nation of farmers, educated, informed, and blessed with free institutions, was the best suited to a democratic republic, without adding that he did not think any *other* kind of society a good risk to maintain republican government. In a nation of large cities, well-developed manufactures and commerce, and a numerous working class, popular republicanism would be an impossibility —or at best an improbability.

Certainly the balance of Jefferson's good society is a tenuous thing: the working class is corrupt; merchants are corrupt; speculators are corrupt; cities are "pestilen-

---

6. It is important to add, however, that in 1776 Jefferson proposed that Virginia grant fifty acres of land to every white of full age who had less than that amount. This would have made suffrage practically universal. It also illustrates his belief in broadening economic opportunities where free land made the policy possible, as well as the vital linkage in his mind between landed property and democracy. He was, at this time, more democratic in his conception of the economic *base* of government than in his conception of the *structure* of government.

tial"; only farmers are dependably good. Sunder human
nature from its proper or "natural" nourishment in the
cultivation of the soil and the ownership of real property, and he profoundly distrusts it. Sunder democracy
from the farm and how much more firmly does he believe in it than John Adams? Yet this is just what the re-
lentless advance of modern industrial capitalism has
done: it has sundered four fifths of society from the soil,
has separated the masses from their property, and has
built life increasingly on what Jefferson would have
called an artificial basis—in short, has gradually emptied
the practical content out of Jefferson's agrarian version
of democracy. This process had its earliest beginnings
during Jefferson's lifetime, and, as we shall see, he
yielded a good part of his agrarian prejudices (like the
pragmatic, undoctrinaire soul that he was) without sacrificing his democratic preferences. But although he
clung to his humane vision of democracy, he left it without the new economic rationale that it required.

III

In after years Jefferson declared that the struggle between his party and the Federalists was one between
those who cherished the people and those who distrusted them. But he had been associated with a number
of men like Elbridge Gerry, Pierce Butler, Charles
Pinckney, and Edmund Randolph who did not cherish
the people in the least, and the differences in abstract
principle were hardly intense enough to account for the
fierceness of the conflict or for the peculiar lines along
which it was drawn. Although democratically minded
Americans did stand with Jefferson, the line of division

was essentially between two kinds of property, not two kinds of philosophy.

The Federalists during Hamilton's service as Secretary of the Treasury had given the government a foundation of unashamed devotion to the mercantile and investing classes. Through his method of funding the national debt, through his national bank, and through all the subsidiary policies of the government, Hamilton subsidized those who invested in manufactures, commerce, and public securities, throwing as much of the tax burden as possible on planters and farmers. The landed interests, however, were in a majority, and it was only a matter of time before they could marshal themselves in a strong party of their own. Jefferson's party was formed to defend specific propertied interests rather than the abstract premises of democracy, and its policies were conceived and executed in the sober, moderate spirit that Jefferson's generation expected of propertied citizens when they entered the political arena.

When Jefferson was elected in 1800, the more naïve Federalists, frightened to the marrow by their own propaganda, imagined that the end of the world had come. Fisher Ames anticipated that he would soon scent "the loathsome steam of human victims offered in sacrifice." Among those who knew the President-elect, however, there was no such hysteria—especially not among insiders who had private knowledge of the circumstances under which he had been chosen.

The election of 1800 was unique in American history. Because no distinction had yet been made in the Constitution between ballots cast for presidential and vice-presidential candidates, Jefferson and his running mate, Aaron Burr, won the same number of votes in the electoral college. The tied contest was thrown into the

House of Representatives, where it fell to Federalist Congressmen to choose between two Republicans. To some this seemed merely a choice of executioners; others, looking upon Jefferson as their supreme enemy, gravitated naturally toward Burr. Not so Alexander Hamilton, who had long been Burr's political rival in New York. In a remarkable letter to a Federalist Representative, Hamilton gave a shrewd estimate of Jefferson's character. He admitted that his old foe's views were "tinctured with fanaticism; that he is too much in earnest with his democracy." But it is not true, he continued, in an appraisal that is as penetrating in substance as it is unfair in phrasing,

> that Jefferson is zealot enough to do anything in pursuance of his principles which will contravene his popularity or his interest. He is as likely as any man I know to temporize—to calculate what will be likely to promote his own reputation and advantage; and the probable result of such a temper is the preservation of systems, though originally opposed, which, being once established, could not be overturned without danger to the person who did it. To my mind a true estimate of Mr. Jefferson's character warrants the expectation of a temporizing rather than a violent system. . . . Add to this that there is no fair reason to suppose him capable of being corrupted, which is a security that he will not go beyond certain limits.

Not entirely satisfied with Hamilton's advice, Federalist leaders sought for assurance from Jefferson. The Virginian refused to commit himself in response to direct approach, but a friend who sounded him out informally was able to convey to the Federalists the comforting knowledge that Jefferson's intentions were moderate. That Jefferson abandoned any of his original plans, and in that sense bargained away any principles to win the office, is extremely unlikely; but when he entered the White House it was after satisfying the Federalists that he and they had come to some kind of understanding.

A little thought on the difficult position in which Jefferson now found himself should convince anyone that for a man of his moderate temperament there was small choice in fundamental policy. The Hamiltonian system, now in operation for twelve years, had become part of the American economy. The nation was faring well. To unscramble Hamilton's system of funding, banks, and revenues would precipitate a bitter struggle, widen the breach between the classes, and drive moderates out of the Republican ranks; it might bring a depression, perhaps even rend the Union. And when the strife was over, there would always be the need of coming to terms with the classes that carried on commerce and banking and manufactures. Further, even if the landed interests were charged with the burden of Hamilton's debts, there was always the probability that they were better off when the system was working smoothly than they would be after a ruinously successful assault upon it. Jefferson, in short, found himself in a position much like that of modern social-democratic statesmen who, upon attaining power, find themselves the managers of a going concern that they fear to disrupt. Just as they have been incapable of liquidating capitalism, so Jefferson found himself unable to keep it from growing and extending its sway over the agrarian masses. Instead he wisely confined himself to trimming carefully at the edges of the Hamiltonian system.

Jefferson's First Inaugural Address was a conciliatory document contrived to bind up the wounds of the bitter period from 1798 to 1800 and to attract moderate Federalists to his support. "We are all republicans—we are all federalists," he declared. Soon the President was writing to Dupont de Nemours in words that show how well Hamilton had taken his measure:

> When this government was first established, it was possible to have kept it going on true principles, but the contracted, English, half-lettered ideas of Hamilton destroyed that hope in the bud. We can pay off his debts in 15 years: but we can never get rid of his financial system. It mortifies me to be strengthening principles which I deem radically vicious, but this vice is entailed on us by the first error. In other parts of our government I hope we shall be able by degrees to introduce sound principles and make them habitual. What is practicable must often control what is pure theory.

Jefferson kept his promises to friends and enemies alike. So successfully did he whittle away at the Federalist machinery by reducing expenditures that he was able to abolish the hated excise duties that had stirred up the Whisky Rebellion and still make great inroads on the public debt. He tried hard to tame the federal judiciary —the last arm of the national government still under Federalist control—but to little effect. Through the Louisiana Purchase he widened the area for agrarian expansion. In 1811, two years after his terms were over, his party also allowed the First Bank of the United States to die upon the expiration of its charter.

But no attack was made upon other vital parts of the Hamiltonian system. No attempt was made to curb such abuses as speculation in public lands; nor did the well-organized Republican machines try hard to democratize the mechanics of government in the states or the nation. Limitations on the suffrage, for example, were left untouched. Professor Beard observes that the Republican states were "no more enamored of an equalitarian political democracy" than the Federalist states. Had Jefferson suggested a broad revision of the suffrage, many of his state leaders who had no use for theoretical democracy would have looked at him askance; if he had been the crusading democrat of Jeffersonian legend he could not have been so successful a machine leader.

Since his policies did not deviate too widely from those of the Federalists, Jefferson hoped to win over the moderates from their ranks and planned to use the patronage in doing so. "If we can hit on the true line of conduct which may conciliate the honest part of those who were called federalists," he wrote to Horatio Gates soon after taking office, "and do justice to those who have so long been excluded from [the patronage], I shall hope to be able to obliterate, or rather to unite the names of federalists and republicans."

In politics, then, the strategy was conciliation; in economics it was compromise. Soon the Republican machines began flirting with the financial interests they had sworn to oppose. Republican state legislatures issued charters liberally to local banks, which, in turn, tended to cleave to the Republican Party in politics. Jefferson gave his benediction to this process of mutual accommodation. When the Bank of Baltimore applied to the administration for assistance, he wrote to Secretary of the Treasury Albert Gallatin:

> It is certainly for the public good to keep all the banks competitors for our favors by a judicious distribution of them and thus to engage the individuals who belong to them in support of the reformed order of things or at least in an acquiescence under it.

And:

> . . . I am decidedly in favor of making all the banks Republican by sharing deposits among them in proportion

to the disposition they show. . . . It is material to the safety of Republicanism to detach the mercantile interest from its enemies and incorporate them into the body of its friends. A merchant is naturally a Republican, and can be otherwise only from a vitiated state of things.

John Adams, in the quiet of his retirement at Quincy, might have been amused to see a new elite, closely linked to the fiscal interests, emerging in the heart of the Republican Party, but the militant agrarian John Taylor was deeply discouraged. In 1811 he wrote:

. . . those who clearly discerned the injustice and im-policy of enriching and strengthening the federalists by bank or debt stock, at the publick expense, will seldom refuse to receive a similar sinecure. In short, a power in the individuals who compose legislatures, to fish up wealth from the people, by nets of their own weaving . . . will corrupt legislative, executive and judicial pub-lick servants, by whatever systems constituted.

The inability of the Republicans to follow a pure policy of democratic agrarianism was matched by their inability to fashion a positive theory of agrarian eco-nomics. The predominant strain in their economic think-ing was laissez-faire, their primary goal essentially nega-tive—to destroy the link between the federal govern-ment and the investing classes. Acute and observant, their economic writing was at its best in criticism, but it offered no guide to a specific agrarian program. They had no plan; indeed, they made a principle of planless-ness.

Jefferson has been described as a physiocrat by many writers—among them V. L. Parrington—but there is little more substance to this notion than there is to the preposterous idea that he was influenced chiefly by

French thought. He was naturally content to remain an eclectic in economics. "No one axiom," he wrote to J. B. Say in 1815, "can be laid down as wise and expedient for all times and circumstances." Their defense of free trade was responsible for whatever appeal the physiocrats had for Jefferson; but after he read *The Wealth of Nations* he became a convert to the doctrines of Adam Smith.[7]

Like other theorists of the "natural law" era, Jefferson was quite ready to believe that the "natural" operations of the system of self-seeking private enterprise were intrinsically beneficent and should not normally be disturbed by government. In his First Inaugural he called for "a wise and frugal government, which shall restrain men from injuring one another, *which shall leave them otherwise free to regulate their own pursuits of industry and improvement,* and shall not take from the mouth of labor the bread it has earned." [8] In a letter to Joseph Milligan, April 6, 1816, in which he discussed the proper limits of taxation, he concluded that the state ought not be aggressive in redistributing property:[9]

> To take from one, because it is thought his own industry and that of his fathers has acquired too much, in order to spare to others, who, or whose fathers have not exercised equal industry and skill, is to violate arbitrarily the first principle of association, "the *guarantee* to everyone

---

7. Ultimately he came to prefer J. B. Say's adaptations of Smith as more lucid and readable, and showed much admiration for the work of Destutt de Tracy.

8. In his Second Inaugural, when he listed the things government should do, he asserted that it should maintain "that state of property, equal or unequal, which results to every man from his own industry or that of his fathers."

9. He added that if an individual's wealth becomes so overgrown that it seems a danger to the State, the best corrective would not be discriminatory taxation but a law compelling equal inheritance in equal degree by all the heirs.

a free exercise of his industry and the fruits acquired by it."

John Taylor, perhaps the cleverest of the agrarian writers, likewise believed that "it is both wise and just to leave the distribution of property to industry and talents."

This conception of state policy was not anti-capitalist but anti-mercantilist. Jefferson and his followers had seen the unhappy effects of British governmental interference in American economic affairs, and they regarded Hamilton's system of state economic activity ("the contracted, English, half-lettered ideas of Hamilton") as merely a continuation at home of English economic ideas. Hamilton had set the government to helping the capitalists at the expense of the agrarians. The Jeffersonian response was not to call for a government that would help the agrarians at the expense of the capitalists, but simply for one that would let things alone. Where modern liberals have looked to government interference as a means of helping the poor, Jefferson, in common with other eighteenth-century liberals, thought of it chiefly as an unfair means of helping the rich through interest-bearing debts, taxation, tariffs, banks, privileges, and bounties. He concluded that the only necessary remedy under republican government would be to deprive the rich of these devices and restore freedom and equality through "natural" economic forces. Because he did not usually think of economic relationships as having an inherent taint of exploitation in them, he saw no necessity to call upon the state to counteract them. It was not the task of government to alter the economic order: the rich were not entitled to it and the poor would not find it necessary.

Jefferson rejected from his political philosophy the

idea that one man has any intrinsic superiority over another; but he implicitly and perhaps unwittingly took it back again when he accepted competitive laissez-faire economics with its assumption that, so long as men were equal in law, and government played no favorites, wealth would be distributed in accordance with "industry and skill." Such a philosophy seemed natural enough to American farmers and planters who were in their own rights entrepreneurs, businessmen, exporters, and often, in a small way, speculators with a weather eye on land values—men accustomed to stand on their own feet.

In due time, of course, Jeffersonian laissez-faire became the political economy of the most conservative thinkers in the country. Fifty years after Jefferson's death men like William Graham Sumner were writing sentences exactly like Jefferson's and John Taylor's to defend enterprising industrial capitalists and railroad barons from government regulation and reform. And one hundred years after the Jeffersonians first challenged John Adams at the polls, William Jennings Bryan, leading the last stand of agrarianism as an independent political power, was still striving to give his cause the color of respectability by showing that, after all, the farmer too was a businessman!

IV

The practical conduct of foreign relations forced the Jeffersonians into a position no less frustrating than the maintenance of Hamilton's domestic system. In the East they found themselves almost as dependent on foreign commerce as were the sea traders of New England; their cheapest manufactured goods were bought abroad, and abroad their surplus was sold. In the West, where they looked about hungrily for new lands, fear of the Indians and of the closure of their trade outlet at New Orleans intensified their expansionist appetites. Expansion of their export market on the land and defense of it on the sea finally started them on a headlong retreat from Jeffersonian principles.

Jefferson himself was both a fierce patriot and a sincere pacifist. During the Napoleonic Wars, when England and France began to prey upon American commerce, he tried to retaliate by a pacifistic policy of economic coercion. In December 1807 Congress passed his drastic Embargo Act, which simply confined American ships to port. His aim was to bring both sides to terms by withholding food and other supplies. This was the one doctrinaire and impractical measure of his career, and it proved a miserable failure. The Embargo not only failed to force Britain and France to respect American rights on the high seas, but also brought economic paralysis to the trading cities of the Northeast and the farms and plantations of the West and South. Jefferson finally admitted that the fifteen months of its operation cost more than a war. At the close of his second term the Embargo was replaced by a Nonintercourse Act, which opened trade with the rest of Europe but continued the costly ban on England and France.

Although Jefferson's successor, James Madison, continued to be harried by the maritime controversy, it was expansionism—what John Randolph called "agrarian cupidity"—rather than free trade that in the end brought the War of 1812. Southern planters wanted the Floridas and Northern farmers wanted Canada. Jefferson, always an ardent expansionist, approved of both aims and accepted the popular clichés with which expansion was justified. ("The possession of Canada," he wrote Adams in the summer of 1812, "secures our women and children forever from the tomahawk and scalping knife, by removing those who excite them.") As Julius W. Pratt has shown, enthusiasm for war with England raged along the broad arc of the frontier; resistance to war was hottest in the old Federalist and mercantile sections.

But if the United States was to withdraw from Europe economically, as under Jefferson, or to lose its best market through war, as under Madison, it had to find a way of employing its energies and supplying its people with manufactured goods. Accordingly, capital, cut off from its normal investment outlet in overseas commerce, began to turn to manufacturing. The period of the Embargo and the War of 1812 proved to be the seedtime of American industrialism; Henry Adams remarked on the ironic fact that "American manufactures owed more to Jefferson than to northern statesmen who merely encouraged them after they were established."

Jefferson, of course, realized the immediate implications of his desire to pursue an independent economic course and as early as 1805 became a convert to the development of manufactures. "The spirit of manufacture has taken deep root among us," he wrote Dupont in 1809, "and its foundations are laid in too great expense to be abandoned." "Our enemy," he wailed to William Short in 1814, "has indeed the consolation of Satan on removing our first parents from Paradise: from a peaceable and agricultural nation he makes us a military and manufacturing one." To another he wrote: "We must now place the manufacturer by the side of the agriculturist." If the United States was to be peaceful, it must be self-sufficient, must end its dependence on foreign goods and overseas trade. The Napoleonic Wars destroyed the Jeffersonian dream of an agrarian commonwealth. Since Jeffersonian democracy, as embodied in measures of public policy, was entirely dependent upon the agrarian order, these wars also erased the practical distinction between Republicans and Federalists.

Manufactures, if they were to be maintained, needed tariffs, especially when British capitalists, hoping to crush their new competitors at once, began dumping goods in the American market at the close of the war. In 1816 the Republicans passed a much higher tariff than Hamilton's. They, not the Federalists, began the American protective system.

And war must be financed. Hard hit by the economic drain of military operations and the financial sabotage of the Northeast, the Republicans were confronted with a bitter dilemma: either they must go begging to the fiscal interests for support, or they must charter a new national bank to fill the vacuum they had created by letting Hamilton's bank expire. They chose the second course—and soon Republican newspapers were reprinting Alexander Hamilton's arguments in favor of the constitutionality of the First Bank of the United States! In vain did Jefferson rage in his letters against the banking system. A second bank, similar in structure to Hamilton's, was chartered by the Republicans in 1816. By the end of that year Jefferson's party had taken over the whole complex of Federalist policies—manufactures, bank, tariffs, army, navy, and all—and this under the administration of Jefferson's friend, neighbor, and political heir, James Madison. As Josiah Quincy complained, the Republicans had "out-Federalized Federalism." By 1820 they had driven the rival party completely off the field, but only at the cost of taking over its program. Federalism, Jefferson wrote to Albert Gallatin in 1823, "has changed its name and hidden itself among us . . . as strong as it has ever been since 1800." Nathaniel Macon, one of the last of the intransigent agrarians, lamented: "The opinions of Jefferson and those who were with him are forgot."

And Jefferson himself? He lived through his last years without bitterness or anger, certainly without a sense of defeat. His country, in spite of one short-lived depression, was growing and flourishing, and as he looked down upon it from his mountaintop he predicted hopefully that the process of civilization would continue to sweep across the continent from east to west "like a cloud of light." He busied himself answering his voluminous correspondence, interpreting for inquirers the history of his times, trading opinions with scientists and inventors, trying to steady his failing fortunes, and laying the foundations of the University of Virginia, which gave him special pride. He renewed his old friendship with John Adams, and once again argued with him the case of democracy. At the age of seventy-eight he wrote to the old man at Quincy: "I shall not die without a hope that light and liberty are on steady advance." When Adams asked if he would choose to live his life over again, he replied in the affirmative, at least for the greater part of it. "From twenty-five to sixty, I would say yes; and I might go further back, but not come lower down." "I enjoy good health," he went on, "I am happy in what is around me, yet I assure you I am ripe for leaving all, this year, this day, this hour. Nothing proves more than this that the Being who presides over the world is essentially benevolent."

Here speaks the antithesis of the tragic temperament. Through all Jefferson's work there runs like a fresh underground stream the deep conviction that all will turn out well, that life will somehow assert itself. Wherever he was, he managed to find it good, and in these last years he never felt the need of moving more than a few miles from Monticello. Life had always come more than halfway to meet him, just as visitors now came from everywhere in the Western World to find him out on his mountain. For him no defeat could ever be more than a temporary interruption in the smooth flow of things toward their beneficent end. It was not, after all, a system of economics or politics that he was leaving, not even a political party, but an imperishable faith expressed in imperishable rhetoric. It did not matter that his agrarianism was in retreat, that his particularism was falling into the hands of proslavery apologists whom he would have detested, that his individualism would become the doctrine of plutocrats and robber barons. His sense of values would survive. Men like Hamilton could argue that manufactures ought to be promoted because they would enable the nation to use the labor of women and children, "many of them at a tender age," but Jefferson was outraged at such a view of humanity. Hamilton schemed to get the children into factories; Jefferson planned school systems. While Hamilton valued institutions and abstractions, Jefferson valued people and found no wealth more important than life. If he had gone astray as to means, he had at least kept his eyes on his original end—the pursuit of happiness.

One of the last survivors among the founders, Jefferson lived to see himself become an object of veneration, and as his life ebbed out he might easily have observed with the dying Roman Emperor: "I feel myself becoming a god." But he had no desire that he and his contemporaries should become oracles to future generations. "The earth," he was fond of saying, "belongs to the living." The world changes, and truths cannot be embalmed.

Some men look at constitutions with sanctimonious reverence, and deem them like the ark of the covenant, too sacred to be touched. They ascribe to the preceding age a wisdom more than human, and suppose what they did to be beyond amendment. I knew that age well; I belonged to it and labored with it. It deserved well of its country. It was very like the present, but without the experience of the present; and forty years of experience in government is worth a century of book-reading; and this they would say themselves, were they to rise from the dead. I am certainly not an advocate for frequent and untried changes in laws and institutions. . . . But I know also, that laws and institutions must go hand in hand with the progress of the human mind. As that becomes more developed, more enlightened, as new discoveries are made, new truths disclosed, and manners and opinions change with the change of circumstances, institutions must advance also, and keep pace with the times. We might as well require a man to wear still the coat which fitted him when a boy, as civilized society to remain ever under the regime of their barbarous ancestors.

Two years before his death he wrote: "Nothing then is unchangeable but the inherent and unalienable rights of man."

CHAPTER III

ANDREW JACKSON AND THE RISE OF LIBERAL CAPITALISM

❦

COULD *it really be urged that the framers of the constitution intended that our Government should become a government of brokers? If so, then the profits of this national brokers' shop must inure to the benefit of the whole and not to a few privileged monied capitalists to the utter rejection of the many.* ANDREW JACKSON

THE making of a democratic leader is not a simple process. Because Andrew Jackson came into prominence on the Tennessee frontier, he has often been set down as typical of the democratic frontiersman; but many patent facts about his life fit poorly with the stereotype. From the beginning of his career in Tennessee he considered himself to be and was accepted as an aristocrat, and his tastes, manners, and style of life were shaped accordingly. True, he could not spell, he lacked education and culture, but so did most of those who passed as aristocrats in the old Southwest during the 1790's and for long afterward; even many Virginians of the passing generation—George Washington among them—spelled no better. Since Virginians and Carolinians of the upper crust seldom migrated, the Southwestern aristocracy came mainly from middle- or lower-class migrants who had prospered and acquired a certain half-shod elegance. Jackson, the mid-Tennessee nabob, was typical, not of the Southwest's coonskin democrats, but of its peculiar blend of pioneer and aristocrat.

Jackson was born in 1767 on a little farm in the Carolinas some months after the death of his father. He enlisted in the Revolution at thirteen, was captured and mutilated by British troops at fourteen, and lost his entire family in the war when one brother was killed, another succumbed to smallpox in prison, and his mother was carried off by "prison fever" while nursing captured American militiamen. From his family he inherited a farm-size plot of land in North Carolina, from the Revolution a savage and implacable patriotism. For six months Jackson was apprenticed to a saddler. Then, although his own schooling had been slight and irregular, he turned for a brief spell to school-teaching. When a relative in Ireland left him a legacy of over three hundred pounds, he moved to Charleston, where, still in his teens, he aped the manners of the seaboard gentry and developed a taste for gambling, horses, and cock-fighting. When he was not playing cards or casting dice for the rent with his landlord, Jackson studied law. At twenty, knowing little about jurisprudence but a great deal about making his own way, he was admitted to the bar of North Carolina. A year later, tradition says, he turned up in Jonesboro, Tennessee, owning two horses, a pack of foxhounds, and a Negro girl.

Before long Jackson made what he intended to be a brief visit to the growing settlement of Nashville. The one established lawyer in the vicinity was retained by a syndicate of debtors, leaving creditors legally helpless. Jackson went to work for the creditors, collected handsome fees, and earned the gratitude and friendship of local merchants and moneylenders. From a fellow Carolina law student he also accepted an appointment as

public solicitor. He soon fell in with the machine of
William Blount, a powerful territorial land speculator
and political patron, and began to consolidate his position among the budding aristocrats, the owners of slaves
and horses, the holders of offices and titles. With his
salary and fees he began to buy land and Negroes.

Thus far Jackson's story was by no means unusual, for
the one-generation aristocrat was a common product of
the emerging South.[1] Because of the ease and rapidity
with which the shrewd and enterprising farmer might
become a leader of the community, and hence a gentleman, during the decades when the cotton economy was
expanding into the uplands, the upper classes of the
Southwest came to combine the qualities of the frontier
roughnecks and the landed gentry. The sportsmanlike,
lawless, individualistic, quick-tempered, brawling nature
of the first was soon sublimated into the courtly, sentimental, unreflective, touchy spirit of the second.
As slaveholding, horsemanship, patriarchal dignities,
money, and the deference of the community deepened
the ex-frontiersman's sense of pride, the habit of command was added and the transformation was complete.
The difference between the frontiersman's readiness to
fight and the planter's readiness to defend his "honor" is
not so much a difference of temperament as of method,
and there is no better exemplar of the fact than Jackson.
It is not recorded that the master of the Hermitage, a justice in the state courts and a major general of the militia,
ever engaged in a brawl—although one encounter with
the Bentons has so been called—or had a wrestling
match such as a commoner like Abraham Lincoln enjoyed on the Illinois frontier. Nor did it occur to Jackson

1. There is a superb account of these emergent aristocrats in
W. J. Cash's *The Mind of the South*, pp. 14–17.

to use his fists, although it is true that he threatened at least one social inferior with a caning. Insulted by anyone who technically qualified as a gentleman, he resorted to the code duello; his quarrels are classic in the history of that institution in the South. Charles Dickinson insulted Jackson over a horse race in 1806, and went to his grave for it; and Jackson carried from the encounter a bullet close to his heart. The same violent, self-assertive subjectivism of the duelist can be found in Old Hickory's conduct as a public man. "I have an opinion of my own on all subjects," he wrote in 1821, "and when that opinion is formed I persue it *publickly*, regardless of who goes with me." Historians have never been certain how much his policies were motivated by public considerations and how much by private animosities.

Yet in his calmer moods Jackson's manner ripened quickly into gentleness and gravity. Measured against the picture of the "cotton snob" painted by more than one sympathetic observer of the Old South, where, as F. L. Olmsted put it, "the farce of the vulgar rich" was played over and over again, Jackson was a man of gentility and integrity. In 1824 Daniel Webster could say of him: "General Jackson's manners are more presidential than those of any of the candidates." Mrs. Trollope, who admitted finding precious few gentlemen in America, saw him on his way to Washington in 1829 and reported that he "wore his hair carelessly but not ungracefully arranged, and in spite of his harsh, gaunt features looked like a gentleman and a soldier." With the common citizen he had a patient and gracious air.

The frontier, democratic in spirit and in forms of government, was nevertheless not given to leveling equalitarianism. The ideal of frontier society, as Frederick Jackson Turner has remarked, was the self-made man. And the self-made man generally received a measure of casual deference from the coonskin element, which itself was constantly generating new candidates for the local aristocracies. Keen class antagonisms were not typical of frontier politics, and class struggles did not flourish in a state like Tennessee until the frontier stage was about over.[2] The task of fighting the Indians gave all classes a common bond and produced popular heroes among the upper ranks. The cotton economy, as it spread, also brought its own insurance against bitter antagonisms, for the presence of a submerged class of slaves gave the humbler whites a sense of status and all whites a community of interest. Frontiersmen may have resented alien Eastern aristocrats—as Jackson did himself—but felt otherwise about those bred in their own community, as they thought, out of competitive skill rather than privilege. Even in those states and territories where suffrage was broadly exercised, men who owned and speculated in land and had money in the bank were often accepted as natural leaders, and political offices fell to them like ripe fruit. Such beneficiaries of popular confidence developed a stronger faith in the wisdom and justice of popular decisions than did the gentlemen of the older seaboard states, where class lines were no longer fluid and social struggles had venerable histories. A man like Jackson who had been on the conservative side of economic issues in Tennessee could become the leader of a national democratic movement without feeling guilty of any inconsistency. When we find a planter aristocrat of this breed expressing absolute confidence

2. Thomas Perkins Abernethy points out that in Tennessee during the 1790's "no strong and universal antagonism existed . . . between the rich and the poor. In fact, political office was rarely sought even on the frontier by any but the natural leaders of society, and they secured the suffrage of their neighbors by reason of their prestige, without resorting to electioneering methods."

in popular judgment, it is unfair to dismiss him as a demagogue. He became a favorite of the people, and might easily come to believe that the people chose well.

Offices, chiefly appointive, came quickly and easily to Jackson in the territory and youthful state of Tennessee. He was a solicitor at twenty-two, United States Attorney at twenty-three, a Congressman at twenty-nine, a United States Senator at thirty, and justice of the Supreme Court of Tennessee at thirty-one—all this without particularly strong political ambitions, for he applied himself casually to all these offices except the judgeship and resigned them readily after brief tenure. He accepted them, it seems clear, more as symbols of status than as means of advancement. Jackson's persistent land speculations, business ventures, and military operations suggest that he aspired more urgently to have wealth and military glory than political power.

It was, in fact, his achievements as a fighter of Indians and Englishmen that brought Jackson his national popularity.

Jackson's victory in January 1815 over the British forces besieging New Orleans, the crowning triumph of his military career, made him a national hero almost overnight. Americans had already developed their passion for victorious generals in politics. The hero of New Orleans was instantly acclaimed as another Washington, and in 1817 the first campaign biography appeared. But Jackson soon experienced severe political criticism for the conduct of his postwar campaigns in Florida, and he feared the effect of political prominence on his domestic happiness; at first he was slow to rise to the bait of presidential ambition. "I am wearied with public life," he wrote President Monroe in 1821. "I have been accused of acts I never committed, of crimes I never thought of." When a New York newspaper editor commented on the ambition of his friends to put him in the White House, the general grew impatient. "No sir," he exclaimed. "I know what I am fit for. I can command a body of men in a rough way: but I am not fit to be President."

II

The rise of Andrew Jackson marked a new turn in the development of American political institutions. During the period from 1812 to 1828 the two-party system disappeared and personal, local, and sectional conflicts replaced broad differences over public policy as the central fact in national politics. As the presidency declined from its heights under the leadership of Washington and Jefferson, the contest for the presidential seat resolved into a scramble of local and sectional princelings for the position of heir apparent. The Virginia dynasty's practice of elevating the forthcoming President through the vice-presidency or cabinet seemed to have become a set pattern. Presidential nominations, made by party caucuses in Congress, were remote from the popular will, and since the elections of 1816 and 1820 were virtually uncontested, nomination by "King Caucus" was equivalent to being chosen President. Since the days of Jefferson there had been no major turnover in the staff of officeholders, whose members were becoming encrusted in their posts.

However, the people, the propertyless masses, were beginning, at first quietly and almost unobtrusively, to enter politics. Between 1812 and 1821 six western states entered the Union with constitutions providing for universal white manhood suffrage or a close approximation,

and between 1810 and 1821 four of the older states substantially dropped property qualifications for voters.[3] As
poor farmers and workers gained the ballot, there developed a type of politician that had existed only in embryo
in the Jeffersonian period—the technician of mass leadership, the caterer to mass sentiment; it was a coterie of
such men in all parts of the country that converged upon
the prominent figure of Jackson between 1815 and 1824.
Generally subordinated in the political corporations and
remote from the choicest spoils, these leaders encouraged the common feeling that popular will should control the choice of public officers and the formation of
public policy. They directed popular resentment of
closed political corporations against the caucus system,
which they branded as a flagrant usurpation of the rights
of the people, and spread the conviction that politics and
administration must be taken from the hands of a social
elite or a body of bureaucratic specialists and opened
to mass participation. Success through politics, it was
implied, must become a legitimate aspiration of the
many.[4] Jackson expressed the philosophy of this movement in his first annual message to Congress, December
1829, when he confidently asserted:

---

3. In 1824, the first election on which we have statistics, there
were only 355,000 voters, chiefly because the triumph of a particular candidate—e.g., Jackson in Tennessee and Pennsylvania,
Adams in Massachusetts, Crawford in Virginia—was so taken for
granted in most states that voters lost interest. By 1828, when
interest was greatly heightened, 1,155,000 voted. Between 1828
and 1848 the vote trebled, although the population did not quite
double.

4. Jackson wrote to an editor of the Richmond *Enquirer* in
1829: "The road to office and preferment, being accessible alike
to the rich and poor, the farmer and the printer, honesty, probity,
and capability constituting the sole and exclusive test will, I am
persuaded, have the happiest tendency to preserve, unimpaired,
freedom of action."

The duties of all public offices are, or at least admit of being made, so plain and simple that men of intelligence may readily qualify themselves for their performance, and I can not but believe that more is lost by the long continuance of men in office than is generally to be gained by their experience. . . . In a country where offices are created solely for the benefit of the people no one man has any more intrinsic right to official station than another.

Rotation in office, he concluded, constituted a "leading principle in the Republican creed."

The trend toward popular activity in politics was heightened by the panic of 1819, which set class against class for the first time since the Jeffersonian era. A result of rapid expansion, speculation, and wildcat banking, the panic and ensuing depression fell heavily upon all parts of the country, but especially upon the South and West, where men had thrown all their resources into reckless buying of land. The banks, which had grossly overextended themselves, were forced to press their debtors to the wall, and through the process of foreclosure the national bank particularly became a great absentee owner of Western and Southern property. "All the flourishing cities of the West," complained Thomas Hart Benton, "are mortgaged to this money power. They may be devoured by it at any moment. They are in the jaws of the monster!" This alien power was resented with particular intensity in the West, where, as the New York *American* put it, "a wild son of Tennessee who has been with Jackson could ill brook that his bit of land, perhaps his rifle, should be torn from him by a neighboring shopkeeper, that the proceeds may travel eastward, where the 'sceptre' of money has fixed itself." The panic brought a cruel awakening for thousands who had hoped to become rich. John C. Calhoun, talking with

John Quincy Adams in the spring of 1820, observed that the last two years had produced "an immense revolution of fortunes in every part of the Union, enormous multitudes in deep distress, and a general mass of disaffection to the Government not concentrated in any particular direction, but ready to seize upon any event and looking out anywhere for a leader."

Calhoun's "general mass of disaffection" was not sufficiently concentrated to prevent the re-election, unopposed, of President Monroe in 1820 in the absence of a national opposition party; but it soon transformed politics in many states. Debtors rushed into politics to defend themselves, and secured moratoriums and relief laws from the legislatures of several Western states. State legislatures, under pressure from local banking interests, waged tax wars against the Bank of the United States. A popular demand arose for laws to prevent imprisonment for debt, for a national bankruptcy law, and for new tariff and public-land policies. For the first time many Americans thought of politics as having an intimate relation to their welfare. Against this background Jackson's star rose. But, curiously, the beneficiary of this movement not only failed to encourage it, but even disapproved. The story of his evolution as a national democratic leader is a strange paradox.

North Carolina, the scene of Jackson's childhood, had been a Jeffersonian stronghold, and Jackson was nurtured on Jeffersonian ideas. In 1796 and 1800 the young Tennessean voted for the sage of Monticello. Except for his nationalism, Jackson's politics chiefly resembled agrarian Republicanism of the old school, which was opposed to banks, public debts, paper money, high tariffs, and federal internal improvements. When the

Burr trial and Jefferson's pacificism disillusioned him with Jefferson, Jackson did not become a convert to Federalism but rather adhered to the Randolph-Macon school of intransigent Republicans.

Jackson's personal affairs shed much light on his ambiguous political evolution from 1796 to 1828. An event of 1796 that had a disastrous effect on his fortunes may have sown in him the seeds of that keen dislike of the Eastern money power and "paper system" which flowered during his presidency. Jackson had gone to Philadelphia to sell several thousand acres of land to a rich merchant and speculator, David Allison; he accepted notes from Allison, which he endorsed and promptly used to pay for supplies he planned to use in opening a general-merchandise store in Nashville. Allison failed, and defaulted on his notes; Jackson became liable. In order to pay the notes as they fell due, he was forced to retrench, give up the estate on which he lived, move to a smaller one built of logs, and sell many of his slaves. Subsequently his store enterprise turned out badly and he was obliged to sell out to his partners. Jackson seems never to have whined about his misfortune, but he lived for nineteen years in its shadow, remaining in debt from 1796 to 1815, when at last his military pay and allowances brought him into the clear. In the fall of 1815 he had a cash balance of over twenty-two thousand dollars at the Nashville bank, was again heavily committed in land speculations, and was building the fine new estate that has become famous as the Hermitage. Just at this time, when he was so vulnerable, the panic of 1819 struck.

The general distress of Tennessee debtors led, as in many other places, to a movement for relief. Felix Grundy, elected to the state Senate on a "relief" platform, brought forth a proposal to establish a state loan office to help debtors out of the state treasury.[5] Creditors who refused to accept notes of the loan bank in payment of debts would have their collections suspended for two years. Jackson's own obligations forced him to press his debtors hard, and he instituted a single lawsuit against one hundred and twenty-nine of them at once. One of the few men in middle Tennessee to stand against Grundy's relief program, he sent a protest to the state legislature, which was rejected on the ground that its language was disrespectful. Having learned from the Allison episode to feel for the luckless entrepreneur, Jackson was now learning to see things from the standpoint of the local moneyed class. The emergence of class conflict in Tennessee found him squarely on the side of the haves. In 1821, when General William Carroll ran for the governorship of the state on a democratic economic program, Jackson supported Carroll's opponent, Colonel Edward Ward, a wealthy planter who had joined Jackson in fighting Grundy's scheme. Carroll was elected, and proceeded to put through a program of tax revision and constitutional and humanitarian reform, which has many elements of what historians call "Jacksonian" democracy. At the moment when Jackson was pitting himself against Carroll in Tennessee, his friends were bringing him forward as a presidential candidate. None of this prevented Grundy and Carroll from later joining the Jackson bandwagon.

Had Jackson's record on popular economic reform been a matter of primary importance, he might never have been President. But by 1824, when he first accepted a presidential nomination, prosperity had returned, hos-

---

5. Grundy's history makes it clear that he represented what may be called entrepreneurial rather than lower-class radicalism. In 1818 he was a leader in a movement to bring a branch of the second United States Bank to Nashville.

tility to banks and creditors had abated, and breaking up established political machines seemed more important to the parvenu politician and the common citizen. As chief "issues" of the campaign the caucus system shared honors with the defense of New Orleans.[6] An outsider to the Congressional machines, a man of humble birth whose popularity was based on military achievement and whose attitude toward economic questions was unknown and of little interest to the average voter, Jackson had a considerable edge with the new electorate.

The consequences of the campaign of 1824 settled all doubt in Jackson's mind about the presidency. Far stronger in the popular vote than any of his three rivals, John Quincy Adams, Clay, and Crawford, he still fell short of the necessary majority in the electoral college, and the election was thrown into the House of Representatives. There the position of Clay became decisive, and Clay threw his support to Adams. Subsequently, when President Adams named Clay his Secretary of State, a bitter cry went up from the Jackson following. Jackson himself was easily persuaded that Clay and Adams had been guilty of a "corrupt bargain" and determined to retake from Adams what he felt was rightfully his. The campaign of 1828 began almost immediately with Adams's administration. For four years the President, a man of monumental rectitude but a career politician of the dying order par excellence, was hounded by the corrupt-bargain charge and subjected by the Jackson professionals to a skillful campaign of vilification, which culminated in the election of 1828. In Jackson's second presidential campaign the bank was hardly mentioned.

---

6. Actually only one of the four candidates, William H. Crawford, was nominated by the customary Congressional caucus; the others were nominated by state legislatures.

The tariff was played for what it was worth where men cared especially about it; but a series of demagogic charges about Adams's alleged monarchist, aristocratic, and bureaucratic prejudices served the Jackson managers for issues. Jackson got 647,000 votes, Adams 508,-000.

The election of 1828 was not an uprising of the West against the East nor a triumph of the frontier: outside of New England and its colonized areas in the West, Federalist Delaware, New Jersey, and Maryland, Jackson swept the country. Nor was his election a mandate for economic reform; no financial changes, no crusades against the national bank, were promised. The main themes of Jacksonian democracy thus far were militant nationalism and equal access to office. Jackson's election was more a result than a cause of the rise of democracy, and the "revolution of 1828" more an overturn of personnel than of ideas or programs. Up to the time of his inauguration Jackson had contributed neither a thought nor a deed to the democratic movement, and he was elected without a platform. So far as he can be said to have had a popular mandate, it was to be different from what the people imagined Adams had been and to give expression to their unformulated wishes and aspirations. This mandate Jackson was prepared to obey. Democrat and aristocrat, failure and success, debtor and creditor, he had had a varied and uneven history, which made it possible for him to see public questions from more than one perspective. He was a simple, emotional, and unreflective man with a strong sense of loyalty to personal friends and political supporters; he swung to the democratic camp when the democratic camp swung to him.

III

For those who have lived through the era of Franklin D. Roosevelt it is natural to see in Jacksonian democracy an earlier version of the New Deal, for the two periods have many superficial points in common. The Jacksonian movement and the New Deal were both struggles of large sections of the community against a business elite and its allies. There is a suggestive analogy between Nicholas Biddle's political associates and the "economic royalists" of the Liberty League, and, on the other side, between the two dynamic landed aristocrats who led the popular parties. Roosevelt himself did not fail to see the resemblance and exploit it.

But the two movements differed in a critical respect: the New Deal was frankly based upon the premise that economic expansion had come to an end and economic opportunities were disappearing; it attempted to cope with the situation by establishing governmental ascendancy over the affairs of business. The Jacksonian movement grew out of expanding opportunities and a common desire to enlarge these opportunities still further by removing restrictions and privileges that had their origin in acts of government; thus, with some qualifications, it was essentially a movement of laissez-faire, an attempt to divorce government and business. It is commonly recognized in American historical folklore that the Jackson movement was a phase in the expansion of democracy, but it is too little appreciated that it was also a phase in the expansion of liberated capitalism. While in the New Deal the democratic reformers were driven to challenge many assumptions of traditional

American capitalism, in the Jacksonian period the democratic upsurge was closely linked to the ambitions of the small capitalist.

To understand Jacksonian democracy it is necessary to re-create the social complexion of the United States in the 1830's. Although industrialism had begun to take root, this was still a nation of farms and small towns, which in 1830 found only one of every fifteen citizens living in cities of over 8,000. Outside the South, a sweeping majority of the people were independent property-owners. Factories had been growing in some areas, but industry was not yet concentrated in the factory system; much production was carried out in little units in which the employer was like a master craftsman supervising his apprentices. The development of transportation made it possible to extend trade over large areas, which resulted in a delay in collections and increased the dependence of business upon banks for credit facilities. The merchant capitalist found it easier to get the necessary credits than humbler masters and minor entrepreneurs, but the hope of growing more prosperous remained intensely alive in the breast of the small manufacturer and the skilled craftsman.

The flowering of manufacturing in the East, the rapid settlement of the West, gave to the spirit of enterprise a large measure of fulfillment. The typical American was an expectant capitalist, a hardworking, ambitious person for whom enterprise was a kind of religion, and everywhere he found conditions that encouraged him to extend himself. Francis J. Grund, an immigrant who described American social conditions in 1836, reported:

Business is the very soul of an American: he pursues it, not as a means of procuring for himself and his family the necessary comforts of life, but as the fountain of all human felicity. . . . It is as if all America were but one gigantic workshop, over the entrance of which there is the blazing inscription, "No admission here, except on business."

More than one type of American, caught up in this surge of ambition, had reason to be dissatisfied with the United States Bank. Some farmers were more interested in the speculative values of their lands than in their agricultural yield. Operators of wildcat banks in the South and West and speculators who depended upon wildcat loans shared the farmers' dislike of Biddle's bank for restraining credit inflation. In the East some of the heads of strong, sound state banks were jealous of the privileged position of the national bank—particularly the bankers of New York City, who resented the financial supremacy that the bank brought to Philadelphia.[7] In Eastern cities the bank was also widely disliked by workers, craftsmen, shopkeepers, and small business people. Labor was hard hit by the rising cost of living, and in many cases the workmen's agitation was directed not so much against their immediate employers as against the credit and currency system. Small business and working men felt that banks restricted competition and prevented new men from entering upon the avenues of enterprise.[8]

---

7. State-bank men were prominent in Jackson's councils. Roger Brooke Taney had been a lawyer for and stockholder in the Union Bank of Maryland. Two key members of the kitchen cabinet, Amos Kendall and Francis Preston Blair, were recruits from the famous relief war in Kentucky, and the former had been president of the Commonwealth Bank of Kentucky.

8. Workingmen had a special grievance against banks. Employers often paid them in the notes of distant or suspected banks, which circulated below par value. They were thus defrauded of a portion of their pay. Although the United States Bank was not responsible for such practices, it had to share in the general odium

The prevalent method of granting corporation charters in the states was a source of enormous resentment. The states did not have general laws governing incorporation.[9] Since banks and other profit-making businesses that wished to incorporate had to apply to state legislatures for individual acts of incorporation, the way was left open for favoritism and corruption. Very often the corporation charters granted by the legislatures were, or were construed to be, monopolies. Men whose capital or influence was too small to gain charters from the lawmakers were barred from such profitable and strategic lines of corporate enterprise as banks, bridges, railroads, turnpikes, and ferries. The practice was looked upon as an artificial closure of opportunity: laborers often blamed it for the high price of necessities.[10] The practice of granting economic privileges was also considered a threat to popular government. Jackson, explaining in one of his presidential messages why "the planter, the farmer, the mechanic, and the laborer" were "in constant danger of losing their fair interest in the Government," had a standard answer: "The mischief

---

that attached to banks. "I was not long in discovering," remembered the Whig politician Thurlow Weed, "that it was easy to enlist the laboring classes against a 'monster bank' or 'monied aristocracy.' . . . The bank issue 'hung like a millstone' about our necks."

9. There were exceptions. New York in 1811 and Connecticut in 1817 adopted laws permitting general incorporation for certain types of manufacturing enterprises.

10. "We cannot pass the bounds of the city," complained one of the left-wing Jacksonian leaders in New York, "without paying tribute to monopoly; our bread, our meat, our vegetables, our fuel, all, all pay tribute to monopolists." William Leggett of the New York *Post* declared: "Not a road can be opened, not a bridge can be built, not a canal can be dug, but a charter of exclusive privileges must be granted for the purpose. . . . The bargaining and trucking away chartered privileges is the whole business of our lawmakers."

springs from the power which the moneyed interest derives from a paper currency, which they are able to control, from the multitude of corporations with exclusive privileges which they have succeeded in obtaining in the different States."

Among all the exclusive privileged monopolies in the country the Bank of the United States was the largest, the best-known, and the most powerful. It became a symbol for all the others, and the burden of many grievances for which it was not really responsible fell upon it. As a national institution it was doubly vulnerable: it was blamed by Western inflationists for deflationary policies and by Eastern hard-money men for inflation. One certain accomplishment of Jackson's war on the bank was to discharge the aggressions of citizens who felt injured by economic privilege.

Jackson himself was by no means unfamiliar with the entrepreneurial impulse that gave Jacksonian democracy so much of its freshness and vitality. An enterpriser of middling success, he could spontaneously see things from the standpoint of the typical American who was eager for advancement in the democratic game of competition—the master mechanic who aspired to open his own shop, the planter or farmer who speculated in land, the lawyer who hoped to be a judge, the local politician who wanted to go to Congress, the grocer who would be a merchant. He had entered the scramble himself in a variety of lines, as a professional man, a merchant, a land speculator, a planter, an office-holder, and a military chieftain. He understood the old Jeffersonian's bias against overgrown government machinery, the Westerner's resentment of the entrenched East, the new politician's dislike of the old bureaucracy, and the aspiring citizen's hatred of privilege. Years before his presidency, he recalled, when a few Tennesseans proposed in 1817 to bring a branch of the bank to Nashville, he had opposed it on the ground that the bank "would drain the state of its specie to the amount of its profits for the support and prosperity of other places, and the Lords, Dukes, and Ladies of foreign countries who held the greater part of its stock—no individual but one in our state owning any of its stock." In 1827, when a branch of the bank was finally created at Nashville, and its agent, General Thomas Cadwalader, coyly hinted to Jackson that its patronage could be turned over to the Jackson party, he was rebuffed.

Looking at the bank from the White House, Jackson saw an instrument of great privilege and power ruled by a man of uncommon force and intelligence. As a fiscal agency it was comparable in magnitude to the government itself. It issued about one fourth of the country's bank paper; because of its power over the discounts of innumerable smaller banks, especially in the West and South, it was the only central instrument in the United States that could affect the volume of credit. A private agency performing a major public function, it was yet substantially free of government control.[11] As Hezekiah Niles put it, the bank had "more power than we would grant to any set of men unless responsible to the people." Nicholas Biddle, boasting of the forbearance with which he ran the bank, once stated in a Congressional investigation that there were "very few banks which might not have been destroyed by an exertion of the powers of the Bank." "As to mere power," he wrote to Thomas Cooper in 1837, "I have been for years in the daily exercise of

---

11. Five of its twenty-five directors were appointed by the federal government. Nicholas Biddle, who actually ran the bank without interference, was one of the government directors; before the bank controversy began, his appointment had been renewed by Jackson himself.

more personal authority than any President habitually enjoys." Understandably the bank's critics regarded it as a potential menace to democratic institutions.

As an economic instrument, there was a great deal to be said for the bank. Under Biddle it had done a creditable job in stabilizing the currency and holding in check inflationary pressure from the wildcatters. Before Jackson's election Biddle had also been concerned to keep the bank out of partisan politics and, as he wrote Webster, "bring it down to its true business character as a Counting House." But the bank inspired too many animosities to stay out of political life. After 1829 it had large loans outstanding to a great number of prominent politicians and influential newspaper editors, and Biddle was well aware how great its power would be if it should be employed directly in corruption. "I can remove all the constitutional scruples in the District of Columbia," he arrogantly informed a correspondent in 1833. "Half a dozen Presidencies—a dozen Cashierships —fifty Clerkships—a hundred Directorships—to worthy friends who have no character and no money."

Since the bank's charter was to expire in 1836, and since a second term for Jackson was probable, it seemed necessary that a renewal of the charter be secured under Jackson. Biddle attempted at first to be conciliatory, made earnest efforts to answer Jackson's grievances against the bank, appointed Jacksonian politicians to several branch directorships, and sent the President a not ungenerous proposal for assistance in discharging the government's indebtedness in return for recharter. Yet in the fall or winter of 1829–30, when Biddle and Jackson had an amicable interview, the general frankly said: "I do not dislike your Bank any more than all banks. But ever since I read the history of the South Sea bubble I have been afraid of banks." By December

1830, when Jackson questioned the bank's expediency and constitutionality, it was clear that he would not consent to renew its life. Biddle, reluctantly, uncertainly, and under prodding from Whig politicians, decided in the summer of 1832 to ask Congress for recharter before the presidential election. "The bank," said Jackson to Van Buren, "is trying to kill me, *but I will kill it!*" To the frontier duelist the issue had instantly become personal.

Jackson lost no time in returning the recharter bill to Congress with his[12] famous veto message, described by Biddle as "a manifesto of anarchy, such as Marat and Robespierre might have issued to the mob." The body of the message was an argument against the bank's constitutionality. The social indictment of the bank was inclusive: it was a monopoly, a grant of exclusive privilege; the whole American people were excluded from competition in the sale of the privilege, and the government thus received less than it was worth; a fourth of the bank's stock was held by foreigners, the rest by "a few hundred of our citizens, chiefly of the richest class"; it was a menace to the country's liberty and independence. At the end the President launched into a forthright statement of the social philosophy of the Jacksonian movement:

It is to be regretted that the rich and powerful too often bend the acts of government to their selfish purposes. Distinctions in society will always exist under every just government. Equality of talents, of education, or of wealth cannot be produced by human institutions. In the full enjoyment of the gifts of Heaven and the fruits of superior

---

12. The message was composed with the assistance of Amos Kendall, Andrew J. Donelson, Roger B. Taney, and Levi Woodbury.

industry, economy, and virtue, every man is equally entitled to protection by law; but when the laws undertake
to add to these natural and just advantages artificial distinctions, to grant titles, gratuities, and exclusive privileges, to make the rich richer and the potent more powerful, the humble members of society—the farmers, mechanics, and laborers—who have neither the time nor the
means of securing like favors to themselves, have a right
to complain of the injustice of their Government. There
are no necessary evils in government. Its evils exist only in
its abuses. If it would confine itself to equal protection,
and, as Heaven does its rains, shower its favors alike on the
high and the low, the rich and the poor, it would be an
unqualified blessing.

Certainly this is not the philosophy of a radical leveling movement that proposes to uproot property or to
reconstruct society along drastically different lines. It
proceeds upon no Utopian premises—full equality is
impossible, "distinctions will always exist," and reward
should rightly go to "superior industry, economy, and
virtue." What is demanded is only the classic bourgeois
ideal, equality before the law, the restriction of government to equal protection of its citizens. This is the philosophy of a rising middle class; its aim is not to throttle
but to liberate business, to open every possible pathway
for the creative enterprise of the people. Although the
Jacksonian leaders were more aggressive than the Jeffersonians in their crusades against monopoly and "the
paper system," it is evident that the core of their philosophy was the same: both aimed to take the grip of gov-
ernment-granted privileges off the natural economic
order.[13] It was no coincidence that Jacksonians like

---

13. This was the position not only of the regular Jacksonians
but also of the more "radical" Locofoco school. For example,
William Leggett, who was considered to be a hound of anarchy

William Leggett and Thomas Hart Benton still vener-
ated John Taylor, a thinker of what Jackson affection-
ately called "the old republican school."

IV

Pursuing the bank war to its conclusion, Jackson
found defeat in victory. Re-elected overwhelmingly on
the bank issue in 1832, he soon removed all United
States funds from the bank. Biddle, in the course of a
fight to get the federal deposits back, brought about a
short-lived but severe depression through restriction of
credit, which ended only when the business community
itself rebelled. No sooner did this artificial depression
end than an inflationary movement began. The federal
deposits that Jackson had taken from Biddle were made

---

by New York conservatives, believed implicitly in free trade and
was extremely solicitous of the rights of property when divorced
from special privilege. He looked upon a general law of incorporation as "the very measure to enable poor men to compete
with rich." "My creed," said Isaac Smith, a prominent Locofoco
candidate, "is to leave commercial men to manage their own affairs." And Martin Van Buren: "I have ever advocated . . .
limiting the interference of the Government in the business concerns of the People to cases of actual necessity, and [have been]
an enemy to monopoly in any form." "The people, the democracy," asserted Ely Moore, the New York labor leader, "contend
for no measure that does not hold out to individual enterprise
proper motives for exertion." William Gouge, the most popular
economic writer of the period, declared that his hard-money
policy would mold a society in which "the operation of the
natural and just causes of wealth and poverty will no longer be
inverted, but . . . each cause will operate in its natural and
just order, and produce its natural and just effect—wealth becoming the reward of industry, frugality, skill, prudence, and
enterprise, and poverty the punishment of few except the indolent
and prodigal."

available to several dozen state banks; these promptly used their new resources to start a credit boom, which broke disastrously in 1837. This had been no part of Jackson's original intention, nor that of his hard-money followers. "I did not join in putting down the Bank of the United States," complained Thomas Hart Benton, "to put up a wilderness of local banks." By destroying Biddle's bank Jackson had taken away the only effective restraint on the wildcatters, and by distributing the deposits had enlarged the capital in the hands of inflationists. He was opposed to both privilege and inflation, but in warring on one he had succeeded only in releasing the other. In killing the bank he had strangled a potential threat to democratic government, but at an unnecessarily high cost. He had caused Biddle to create one depression and the pet banks to aggravate a second, and he had left the nation committed to a currency and credit system even more inadequate than the one he had inherited.

Biddle, from 1823, when he took control of the bank, to 1833, when removal of the deposits provoked him to outrageous retaliation, had followed a policy of gradual, controlled credit expansion, which was well adapted to the needs of the growing American economy. Had Jackson not yielded to archaic hard-money theories on one hand and the pressure of interested inflationary groups on the other,[14] it might have been possible—and it

---

14. There was a division of purpose among those who supported the bank war. The hard-money theorists wanted to reduce all banks to the functions of discount and deposit and deny them the right to issue currency notes; they believed that overissue of bank notes was an essential cause of booms and depressions. The inflationary groups, including many state banks, objected to the Bank of the United States because it restrained note issues. Caught between these two forces, Jackson pursued an incon-

would have been far wiser—for him to have made a deal with Biddle, trading recharter of the bank for more adequate government control of the bank's affairs. It would have been possible to safeguard democratic institutions without such financial havoc but the Jacksonians were caught between their hostility to the bank and their unwillingness to supplant it with adequate federal control of credit. The popular hatred of privilege and the dominant laissez-faire ideology made an unhappy combination.

The bank war flared up, died, and was forgotten, its permanent results negative rather than positive. But the struggle against corporate privileges which it symbolized was waged on a much wider front. In the states this struggle bore fruit in a series of general incorporation acts, beginning with Connecticut's in 1837 and spreading to the other states in the two decades before the Civil War. By opening the process of incorporation to all comers who could meet state requirements, legislators progressively sundered the concept of the corporate form of business from its association with monopoly privilege and for many decades made it an element in the growth of free enterprise—a contribution to the development of American business that can hardly be overestimated. The same was done for banking. In 1838 New York, the center of the Locofoco agitation against bank monopolies, passed a free banking law that permitted banking associations to operate under general rules without applying for specific acts of incorporation.

---

sistent policy. Deposit of federal funds with state banks pleased the inflationists. The Specie Circular and the Independent Treasury policy adopted under Jackson's successor, Van Buren, was more consonant with the views of the hard-money faction.

A precedent for similar laws in other states, it has been described by one authority, Bray Hammond, as "the most important event in American banking history."

While the state legislatures were writing Jacksonian ideals into the law of corporations, a Jacksonian Supreme Court under Chief Justice Taney was reading them into the clauses of the Constitution. Taney, appointed by Jackson in 1836, sat on the Court until his death in 1864, and during his long tenure the Court propagated the Jacksonian view of business without privilege. Professor Benjamin F. Wright, in his study of *The Contract Clause of the Constitution*, has pointed out that as a result of the Court's work under Taney the contract clause "was a more secure and broader base for the defense of property rights in 1864 than it had been in 1835." Taney's most startling case, as symbolic of the fight against privilege in the juridical sphere as the bank war had been in politics, was the Charles River Bridge case. The majority decision, prepared by Taney, which represented a long forward step in detaching from the corporation the stigma of monopoly, stands as a classic statement of the Jacksonian faith.

The Charles River Bridge had been erected in the 1780's by Harvard College and prominent Bostonians under a Massachusetts charter. As the population of Boston and Cambridge grew, business flourished, traffic mounted, and the par value of the bridge's stock shot upwards. A share bought in 1805 at $444 was worth $2,080 in 1814. Since a new bridge was badly needed, the state legislature in 1828 chartered another, the Warren Bridge, to be built very close to the original, and to be free after sufficient tolls were collected to pay for its construction. Anxious to prevent a development that would destroy the value of their stock, the proprietors of the older bridge attempted to restrain the new builders from erecting the Warren Bridge. When Taney began sitting as Chief Justice in 1837, the issue was still pending before the Supreme Court. The case clearly involved a conflict between vested rights on one side and new entrepreneurs and the rest of the community on the other. Four distinguished Massachusetts lawyers, including Daniel Webster, represented the promoters of the Charles River Bridge. They argued that the legislative grant to the original bridge company was a contract, and that implicit in such a ferry or bridge franchise was a promise on the part of the state not to break the contract by granting another competing franchise that would lower the value of the original.

The Court decided for the new bridge, five to two. Since the two dissenting justices, Story and Thompson, were holdovers from the pre-Jackson period and the five majority judges were all Jackson appointees, the decision may accurately be called a Jacksonian document. Story's dissent, which expressed horror at "speculative niceties or novelties" and invoked the interests of "every stockholder in every public enterprise of this sort throughout the country," was reasoned in the language of entrenched capital, of monopoly investors who abhorred risk. Taney's majority decision was a plea for the public interest, for technological progress and fresh enterprise.[15]

The object of all government, Taney asserted, is to promote the happiness and prosperity of the community, and it could never be assumed that a government intended to curtail its own powers in this respect. "And in

---

15. Taney's moderate and balanced view of state policy toward corporations is most clearly brought out by his deft decision in *Bank of Augusta* v. *Earle* (1839). For this and his continuing friendliness to the non-monopoly corporation, see Carl Brent Swisher's *Roger B. Taney*, Chapter xviii.

a country like ours, free, active, and enterprising, continually advancing in numbers and wealth," new channels of communication and travel are continually found necessary; an abandonment of the state's power to facilitate new developments should not be construed from contracts that do not contain an explicit statement of such intent.

What would happen, Taney asked, if the idea of an implied monopoly in charters should be sustained by the Court? What would become of the numerous railroads established on the same line of travel with old turnpike companies? He thought he knew: if these old corporations were given an "undefined property in a line of travelling," they would awaken from their sleep and call upon the Court to put down new improvements to protect their vested interests. The "millions of property" that had been invested in railroads and canals upon lines of travel once occupied by turnpike corporations would be endangered. Until obsolete claims were settled, the community would be deprived of the benefits of invention enjoyed by every other part of the civilized world. The rights of property, Taney conceded, should be "sacredly guarded," but "we must not forget that the community also have rights, and that the happiness and well being of every citizen depends upon their faithful preservation."

To the Whig press and conservative lawyers like Kent and Story this opinion appeared as another "manifesto of anarchy," comparable to Jackson's bank veto message. In fact, as Charles Warren observes in his history of the Court, it gave encouragement to "all business men who contemplated investments of capital in new corporate enterprise and who were relieved against claims of monopoly concealed in ambiguous clauses of old charters."

In the Congressional session of 1823–4, at the beginning of the Jackson era, Daniel Webster had observed: "Society is full of excitement: competition comes in place of monopoly; and intelligence and industry ask only for fair play and an open field." No friend of Jacksonian democracy expressed more accurately than this opponent the historic significance of the Jackson movement. With Old Hickory's election a fluid economic and social system broke the bonds of a fixed and stratified political order. Originally a fight against political privilege, the Jacksonian movement had broadened into a fight against economic privilege, rallying to its support a host of "rural capitalists and village entrepreneurs." When Jackson left office he was the hero of the lower and middling elements of American society who believed in expanding opportunity through equal rights, and by the time of his death in 1845 the "excitement" Webster had noticed had left a deep and lasting mark upon the nation. "This," exulted Calvin Colton, "is a country of self-made men, than which there can be no better in any state of society."

CHAPTER IV

JOHN C. CALHOUN:
THE MARX OF THE MASTER CLASS

❦

IT WOULD *be well for those interested to reflect whether
there now exists, or ever has existed, a wealthy and civilized
community in which one portion did not live on the labor of
another; and whether the form in which slavery exists in the
South is not but one modification of this universal condition.
. . . Let those who are interested remember that labor is
the only source of wealth, and how small a portion of it, in all
old and civilized countries, even the best governed, is left to
those by whose labor wealth is created.*   JOHN C. CALHOUN

JACKSON led through force of personality, not intellect;
his successors in the White House were remarkable for
neither, and yielded pre-eminence to Congressional politicians. Of the three greatest, Clay, Webster, and Calhoun, the last showed the most striking mind. His problem, that of defending a minority interest in a democracy, offered the toughest challenge to fresh thinking.

As nationalists closely allied with capitalistic interests,
Clay and Webster could both use the ideas of the
Founding Fathers as they were transmitted through the
Federalist tradition. Clay, content to leave theoretical
elaboration of his "American system" to economists like
Mathew Carey and Hezekiah Niles, never presumed to
be a thinker, and his greatest contribution to the political

art was to demonstrate how a Hamiltonian program could gain strength by an admixture of the Jeffersonian spirit. Webster, who was satisfied, on the whole, to follow the conservative republicanism of the Fathers, is rightly remembered best as the quasi-official rhapsodist of American nationalism. He felt no need to attempt a new synthesis for his own time.

Calhoun, representing a conscious minority with special problems, brought new variations into American political thinking. Although his concepts of nullification and the concurrent voice have little more than antiquarian interest for the twentieth-century mind, he also set forth a system of social analysis that is worthy of considerable respect. Calhoun was one of a few Amercans of his age—Richard Hildreth and Orestes Brownson were others—who had a keen sense for social structure and class forces. Before Karl Marx published the *Communist Manifesto,* Calhoun laid down an analysis of American politics and the sectional struggle which foreshadowed some of the seminal ideas of Marx's system. A brilliant if narrow dialectician, probably the last American statesman to do any primary political thinking, he placed the central ideas of "scientific" socialism in an inverted framework of moral values and produced an arresting defense of reaction, a sort of intellectual Black Mass.

Calhoun was born in 1782 into a Scotch-Irish family that had entered the colonies in Pennsylvania and migrated to the Southern back country in the middle of the century. His paternal grandmother had been killed by Indians on the frontier in 1760 and his mother's brother, John Caldwell, after whom he was named, had been murdered by Tories during the Revolution. Patrick Calhoun, his father, acquired over thirty slaves in an area where slaves were rare, became a prominent citizen of the South Carolina hinterland and a member of the state legislature, and opposed the federal Constitution. When John was fourteen, Patrick died. The boy was tutored for a time by his brother-in-law, Moses Waddel, soon to become one of the South's outstanding educators; he graduated from Yale in 1804, studied law at Tapping Reeve's famous school in Litchfield, and joined the Carolina bar.

Calhoun's warmest attachment during these years, and perhaps all his life, was to an older woman, Floride Bonneau Calhoun, his father's cousin by marriage. After years of close friendship and constant correspondence, he married her eighteen-year-old daughter, whose name was also Floride. It was customary for a bride to keep control of her own fortune, but the young planter indelicately insisted that she place her property in his hands. It was so arranged. Besides these extensive landholdings, the connection brought Calhoun an assured position among gentlefolk of the seaboard.

In 1808, three years before his marriage and shortly after his admission to the bar, Calhoun was elected to the South Carolina legislature. In 1810 he was elected to Congress, where he promptly became a leader among the young "war hawks." When the war with Britain began, he became the foremost advocate of war appropriations, and for fifteen years he remained the most ardent worker for national unity and national power. He was for more troops, more funds, for manufactures, federal roads, a higher tariff, and a new national bank. Impatient with "refined arguments on the Constitution," he waved all constitutional objections aside. In 1817 he became Secretary of War in James Monroe's Cabinet and put through an ambitious program of fortifications and administrative improvement. John Quincy Adams, his colleague in the Cabinet, wrote in his diary that Calhoun was

> a man of fair and candid mind, of honorable principles, of clear and quick understanding, of cool self-possession, of enlarged philosophic views, and of ardent patriotism. He is above all sectional and factional prejudices more than any other statesman of this Union with whom I have ever acted.

Calhoun took a conciliatory view of sectional issues. When the question of slavery first appeared in the controversy over Missouri, he stood for moderation. "We to the South ought not to assent easily to the belief that there is a conspiracy either against our property or just weight in the Union," he wrote to a friend, adding that he favored supporting such measures and men "without a regard to sections, as are best calculated to advance the general interest." One must agree with William E. Dodd: Calhoun's whole early life as a public man had been built upon nationalism, and at heart he remained a Unionist as well as a Southerner. What he wanted was not for the South to leave the Union, but to dominate it. Even as late as 1838 he cautioned his daughter against the disunionist school of thought. "Those who make it up, do not think of the difficulty involved in the word; how many bleeding [pores] must be taken up on passing the knife of separation through a body politic. . . . *We must remember, it is the most difficult process in the world to make two people of one.*"

Changes at home converted the reluctant Calhoun from a nationalist to a sectionalist. As the cotton economy spread, South Carolina became entirely a staple-growing state. Her planters, working exhausted land,

and hard pressed to compete with the fresh soil of the interior, found it impossible to submit quietly any longer to the exactions of the protective tariff. Before long a fiery local group of statesmen made it impossible for any politician to stay in business who did not take a strong stand for sectional interests.

Calhoun, who aspired to be much more than a regional leader, managed for some years to soft-pedal his swing to a sectional position. His initial strategy was to make an alliance with the Jackson supporters in the hope that Jackson, himself a Southern planter and an old Republican, would pursue policies favorable to the South and eventually pass the presidency on to Calhoun. Then Calhoun would cement an alliance between the agrarian South and West against the capitalistic East. Both in 1824, when Jackson was defeated by the Clay-Adams bargain, and in 1828, when he was elected, Calhoun was his vice-presidential running mate.[1]

During the campaign of 1828 the exorbitant Tariff of Abominations became law, and Calhoun wrote his first great document on the sectional question, the *Exposition and Protest*, the authorship of which remained secret for some time for political reasons.[2] Denouncing the tariff bitterly, Calhoun declared: "We are the serfs of the system." After giving an impressive analysis of the costs of the tariff to the plantation economy, he came to political remedies. "No government based on the naked principle that the majority ought to govern, however true the maxim in its proper sense, and under proper re-

---

1. Because of the unusual circumstances of the election of 1824, Calhoun became Vice President although Jackson was defeated.

2. Calhoun's report was not officially adopted, but because the lower house of the Carolina legislature ordered a printing of five thousand copies, it was generally taken as an official statement.

strictions, can preserve its liberty even for a single generation." Only those governments which provide checks on power, "which limit and restrain within proper bounds the power of the majority," have had a prolonged and happy existence. Seeking for some constitutional means, short of secession, of resisting the majority, Calhoun seized upon the idea of state nullification. The powers of sovereignty, he contended, belonged of right entirely to the several states and were only delegated, in part, to the federal government. Therefore the right of judging whether measures of policy were infractions of their rights under the Constitution belonged to the states. When a state convention, called for the purpose, decided that constitutional rights were violated by any statute, the state had a right to declare the law null and void within its boundaries and refuse to permit its enforcement there. Nullification would be binding on both the citizens of the state and the federal government. The *Exposition* closed with the hope that Jackson would be elected and would make a practical test of nullification unnecessary.

Calhoun and the South were soon disappointed with Old Hickory. Personal grievances—among them Jackson's discovery that Calhoun as Secretary of War had wanted to repudiate his free and easy conduct in the Seminole campaign—caused the general to break with the Carolinian. The final breach came during the nullification crisis of 1832, when Jackson turned all his wrath upon South Carolina and incontinently threatened to hang Calhoun. At its close Calhoun, having resigned from the vice-presidency, sat in the Senate for his state, planning to join the anti-Jackson coalition, and militant Southerners were thinking about new ways of stemming Northern capital. Calhoun's trajectory toward the presidency had been forcibly deflected. Henceforth his life became a long polemical exercise, his career a series of maneuvers to defend the South and propel himself into the White House. Nourished on ambition and antagonism, he grew harder, more resolute, and more ingenious.

II

Charleston was the great cultural center of the Old South, a city with a flavor of its own and an air of cosmopolitan taste and breeding, and Charleston was the one part of South Carolina for which Calhoun had no use. He hated the life of ease and relaxation enjoyed by the absentee planters who were the mainstay of its social and cultural distinction. In 1807, when malaria was ravaging the city, he wrote to Floride Bonneau Calhoun with ill-disguised relish that every newspaper brought a long list of deaths. This, he thought, was due far less to the climate of the place than to "the misconduct of the inhabitants; and may be considered as a curse for their intemperance and debaucheries."

Debaucheries of any kind Calhoun was never accused of. There is no record that he ever read or tried to write poetry, although there is a traditional gibe to the effect that he once began a poem with "Whereas," and stopped. Once in his life he read a novel—this at the request of a lady who asked for his judgment on it. A friend, Mary Bates, observed that she "never heard him utter a jest," and Daniel Webster in his eulogy said he had never known a man "who wasted less of life in what is called recreation, or employed less of it in any pursuits not immediately connected with the discharge of his duty." Duty is the word, for duty was the demonic force in Calhoun. "I hold the duties of life to be greater than life itself," he once wrote. ". . . I regard this life very much as a struggle against evil, and that to him who acts on proper principle, the reward is in the struggle more than in victory itself, although that greatly enhances it." In adult life to relax and play are in a certain sense to return to the unrestrained spirits of childhood. There is reason to believe that Calhoun was one of those people who have had no childhood to return to. This, perhaps, was what Harriet Martineau sensed when she said that he seemed never to have been born. His political lieutenant, James H. Hammond, remarked after his death: "Mr. Calhoun had no youth, to our knowledge. He sprang into the arena like Minerva from the head of Jove, fully grown and clothed in armor: a man every inch himself, and able to contend with any other man."

For men whom he took seriously, this white-hot intensity was difficult to bear. Senator Dixon Lewis of Alabama, who weighed four hundred and thirty pounds and found relaxation a natural necessity, once wrote to Calhoun's friend Richard K. Crallé during an election year:

> Calhoun is now my principal associate, and he is too intelligent, too industrious, too intent on the struggle of politics to suit me except as an occasional companion. There is no *relaxation* with him. On the contrary, when I seek relaxation with him, he screws me only the higher in some sort of excitement.

Judge Prioleau, when he first met Calhoun, told an inquirer he hoped never to see him again. For three hours he had been trying to follow Calhoun's dialectic "through heaven and earth," and he was exhausted with the effort. "I hate a man who makes me think so much

. . . and I hate a man who makes me feel my own inferiority." Calhoun seldom made himself congenial. He once admitted that he was almost a stranger five miles from his home, and we can be sure that his political popularity was not personal, but abstract. Nor is there any reason to believe that he often felt lonesome, except for his family. He loved an audience, but he did not especially care for company. He enjoyed spending long hours in solitary thought.

Colleagues in the Senate who were used to the harangues of this tall, gaunt, sickly man with his traplike mouth and harsh voice, suited, as someone said, to a professor of mathematics, respected him deeply for his extraordinary mind and his unquestionable integrity, but found him on occasion just a bit ludicrous. Clay has left a memorable caricature of him—"tall, careworn, with furrowed brow, haggard and intensely gazing, looking as if he were dissecting the last abstraction which sprung from metaphysician's brain, and muttering to himself, in half-uttered tones, 'This is indeed a real crisis.' "

There is testimony to Calhoun's gentleness and charm, to the winning quality of his very seriousness at times. "He talked," reports one admirer, "on the most abstruse subjects with the guileless simplicity of a prattling child." Benjamin F. Perry, a bitter political opponent, testified to his kindness, but observed: "He liked very much to talk of himself." He saved his charm and indulgence particularly for women and children, whose world, one imagines, he considered to be a world entirely apart from the serious things of life. There is a brief and touching picture of him at his daughter's wedding removing the ornaments of a cake to save them for a little child. It is easy enough to believe that he never spoke impatiently to any member of his family, for he could always discharge his aggressions upon a senator. And two of the most effective characterizations have been left by women: it was Harriet Martineau who called him "the cast iron man who looks as if he had never been born, and could never be extinguished," and Varina Howell Davis who described him as "a mental and moral abstraction."

It would be interesting to know what Mrs. John C. Calhoun thought of him. That he was devoted to her one can readily imagine, but devotion in a man like Calhoun is not an ordinary man's devotion. When he was thinking of marrying her, he wrote to her mother: "After a careful examination, I find none but those qualities in her character which are suited to me." In the course of their exemplary married life she bore him nine children, whom he treated with paternal tenderness. But there survives a curious letter written to his cherished mother-in-law on the death of his first-born daughter in her second year of life, which reads in part:

> So fixed in sorrow is her distressed mother that every topick of consolation which I attempt to offer but seems to grieve her the more. It is in vain I tell her it is the lot of humanity; that almost all parents have suffered equal calamity; that Providence may have intended it in kindness to her and ourselves, as no one can say what, had she lived, would have been her condition, whether it would have been happy or miserable; and above all we have the consolation to know that she is far more happy than she could be here with us. She thinks only of her dear child; and recalls to her mind every thing that made her interesting, thus furnishing additional food for her grief.

Here surely is a man who lived by abstractions; it is amazing, and a little pathetic, that he sought to make his business the management of human affairs.

Calhoun had a touching faith in his ability to catch life in logic. His political reasoning, like so many phases of his personal life, was a series of syllogisms. Given a premise, he could do wonders, but at times he showed a fantastic lack of judgment in choosing his premises, and he was often guilty of terrible logic-chopping.[3] His trust in logic led to an almost insane self-confidence. "Whether it be too great confidence in my own opinion I cannot say," he once wrote, "but what I think I see, I see with so much apparent clearness as not to leave me a choice to pursue any other course, which has always given me the impression that I acted with the force of destiny." "In looking back," he wrote to Duff Green six years before his death, "I see nothing to regret and little to correct."

That all Calhoun's ability and intensity were focused on making himself President was the accepted view of his contemporaries, friend and foe, and has not been denied by his friendliest biographers. But he himself never acknowledged or understood it. "I am no aspirant —never have been," he declared fervently to the Senate in 1847. "I would not turn on my heel for the Presidency." On this score he thought himself "the most misunderstood man in the world." A certain relative purity of motive, however, must be credited to him. He was not primarily an opportunist. He generally sought

---

3. Typical of Calhoun at his worst was his assault on the philosophy of the Declaration of Independence, which he read as "all men are born free and equal": "Taking the proposition literally . . . there is not a word of truth in it. It begins with 'all men are born,' which is utterly untrue. Men are not born. Infants are born. They grow to be men. . . . They are not born free. While infants they are incapable of freedom. . . ." Anyone whose introduction to Calhoun came through such portions of his work would find it hard to believe that he had sound and trenchant criticisms of the natural-rights philosophy, and yet he did.

to advance himself on the basis of some coherent and well-stated body of principles in which he actually believed. It was quite in keeping that he could on occasion be devious with individual men—as he was with Jackson for years—but not with ideas. His scruples about money were matched only by those of Adams, and might have been held up as an example to Webster. He supported a large family—seven of the nine children survived to adulthood—on his declining plantation enterprises, and sincerely professed his indifference to money-making. In 1845 he applied to Webster's rich Boston patron, Abbott Lawrence, for a loan of thirty thousand dollars, and when Lawrence replied in language suggesting that for a man of Calhoun's personal eminence he might be generous beyond the call of commercial duty, Calhoun withdrew his request in a letter of supreme dignity.

Calhoun's failure to understand that politics works through people and requires sustained personal loyalty as well as fidelity to ideas was resented by his followers and partisans. James H. Hammond once complained that the leader was "always buying over enemies and never looks after friends." Again: "He marches and countermarches all who follow him until after having broken from the bulk of his followers he breaks from his friends one by one and expends them in breaking down his late associates—so all ends in ruin." Rhett and Hammond both agreed that he was too unyielding and impersonal to be a great party leader. As Rhett put it, "he understood principles . . . but he did not understand how best to control and use . . . man."

Calhoun, of course, was a slavemaster, and his view of himself in this capacity was what might be expected: "My character as a master is, I trust, unimpeachable, as I hope it is in all the other relations of life." He looked upon his relation to his slaves, he asserted, "in the double capacity of master and guardian." His neighbors testified that he was kind to them, and by the lights of his section and class there is little reason to doubt it. But the only record of his relation to a slave suggests that kindness to slaves was a mixed quality in the South. In 1831 a house servant, Aleck, committed some offense to Mrs. Calhoun for which she promised a severe whipping, and he ran away. When he was caught in Abbeville a few days later, Calhoun left instructions with a friend:

> I wish you would have him lodged in jail for one week, to be fed on bread and water, and to employ some one for me to give him 30 lashes well laid on at the end of the time. . . . I deem it necessary to our proper security to prevent the formation of the habit of running away, and I think it better to punish him before his return home than afterwards.

The case of Aleck and the "thirty lashes well laid on" does more for our understanding of the problem of majorities and minorities than all Calhoun's dialectics on nullification and the concurrent majority.

III

In 1788 Patrick Henry, arguing against the federal Constitution, asked: "How can the Southern members prevent the adoption of the most oppressive mode of taxation in the Southern States, as there is a majority of the Northern States?" This anxiety about the North's majority ripened like the flora of the Southern swamplands. As the years went by, the South grew, but the North grew faster. In 1790, when Calhoun was eight

years old, populations North and South were practically
equal. By 1850, the year of his death, the North's was
13,527,000, the South's only 9,612,000. This preponderance was reflected in Congress. Although Southern politicians held a disproportionate number of executive
offices, federal policy continued to favor Northern capital, and Southern wealth funneled into the pockets of
Northern shippers, bankers, and manufacturers. Of
course, the greater part of the drain of Southern resources was the inevitable result of a relationship between a capitalistic community and an agrarian one
that did little of its own shipping, banking, or manufacturing. But a considerable portion too came from what
Southerners considered an "artificial" governmental in-
trusion—the protective tariff. It was tariffs, not slavery,
that first made the South militant. Planters were understandably resentful as the wealth of the Southern fields,
created by the hard labor of the men, women, and children they owned, seemed to be slipping away from
them. "All we want to be rich is to let us have what we
make," said Calhoun.

Southern leaders began to wonder where all this was
going to stop. Given its initial advantage, what was to
prevent the North from using the federal government to
increase the span between the political power of the sections still further, and then, presuming upon the South's
growing weakness, from pushing exploitation to outrageous and unbearable extremes? Humiliated by their
comparative economic backwardness, frightened at its
political implications, made uneasy by the world's condemnation of their "peculiar institution," Southern leaders reacted with the most intense and exaggerated anxiety to every fluctuation in the balance of sectional
power. How to maintain this balance was Calhoun's
central problem, and for twenty-two years his terrible

and unrelenting intensity hung upon it. "The South," he lamented as early as 1831, ". . . is a fixed and hopeless minority," and five years later he declared in significant hyperbole on the floor of the Senate: "We are here but a handful in the midst of an overwhelming majority." In 1833, speaking on the Force Bill, he saw the South confronted with "a system of hostile legislation . . . an oppressive and unequal imposition of taxes . . . unequal and profuse appropriations . . . rendering the entire labor and capital of the weaker interest subordinate to the stronger."

After 1830, when abolitionism began to be heard, the South's revolt was directed increasingly against this alleged menace. There is little point in debating whether fear of abolition or fear of further economic exploitation was more important in stimulating Southern militancy and turning the Southern mind toward secession. The North, if the balance of power turned completely in its favor, could both reduce the planter class to economic bondage and emancipate its slaves. Southern leaders therefore concentrated on fighting for the sectional equilibrium without making any artificial distinctions about their reasons. As Calhoun put it in 1844, "plunder and agitation" were "kindred and hostile measures." "While the tariff takes from us the proceeds of our labor, abolition strikes at the labor itself."

Of course, voluntary emancipation was out of the question. To understand the mind of the Old South it is necessary to realize that emancipation meant not merely the replacement of slave labor by hired labor, but the loss of white supremacy, the overthrow of the caste system—in brief, the end of a civilization. Although Calhoun once condemned the slave trade as an "odious traffic," there is no evidence that he ever shared the Jeffersonian view of slavery, widespread in the South during his youth, that slavery was a necessary but temporary evil. During a conversation with John Quincy Adams in 1820 he revealed how implicitly he accepted the caste premises of slavery. Adams spoke of equality, of the dignity and worth of human life. Calhoun granted that Adams's beliefs were "just and noble," but added in a matter-of-fact way that in the South they were applied only to white men. Slavery, he said, was "the best guarantee to equality among the whites. It produced an unvarying level among them . . . did not even admit of inequalities, by which one white man could domineer over another."

Calhoun was the first Southern statesman of primary eminence to say openly in Congress what almost all the white South had come to feel. Slavery, he affirmed in the Senate in 1837, "is, instead of an evil, a good—a positive good." By this he did not mean to imply that slavery was always better than free labor relations, but simply that it was the best relation between blacks and whites. Slavery had done much for the Negro, he argued. "In few countries so much is left to the share of the laborer, and so little exacted from him, or . . . more kind attention paid to him in sickness or infirmities of age." His condition is greatly superior to that of poorhouse inmates in the more civilized portions of Europe. As for the political aspect of slavery, "I fearlessly assert that the existing relation between the two races in the South . . . forms the most solid and durable foundation on which to rear free and stable institutions."

The South thought of emancipation as an apocalyptic catastrophe. In a manifesto prepared in 1849 Calhoun portrayed a series of devices by which he thought abolitionists would gradually undermine slavery until at last the North could "monopolize all the territories," add a sufficient number of states to give her three fourths of the whole, and then pass an emancipation amendment. The disaster would not stop with this. Since the two races "cannot live together in peace, or harmony, or to their mutual advantage, except in their present relation," one or the other must dominate. After emancipation the ex-slaves would be raised "to a political and social equality with their former owners, by giving them the right of voting and holding public offices under the Federal Government." They would become political associates of their Northern friends, acting with them uniformly, "holding the white race at the South in complete subjection." The blacks and the profligate whites that might unite with them would become the principal recipients of federal offices and patronage and would "be raised above the whites of the South in the political and social scale." The only resort of the former master race would be to abandon the homes of its ancestors and leave the country to the Negroes.[4]

Faced with such peril, the South should be content with nothing less than the most extreme militancy, stand firm, meet the enemy on the frontier, rather than wait till she grew weaker. Anything less than decisive victory was unthinkable. "What! acknowledged inferiority! The surrender of life is nothing to sinking down into acknowledged inferiority!"

It was one of Calhoun's merits that in spite of his saturation in the lore of constitutional argument he was not satisfied with a purely formal or constitutional interpretation of the sectional controversy, but went beyond it to translate the balance of sections into a balance of classes. Although he did not have a complete theory of history,

4. Setting aside its valuations and demagogic language, Calhoun's forecast bears a strong resemblance to the plans actually adopted by the Radical Republicans during Reconstruction.

he saw class struggle and exploitation in every epoch of human development. He was sure that "there never has yet existed a wealthy and civilized society in which one portion of the community did not, in point of fact, live on the labor of the other." It would not be too difficult "to trace out the various devices by which the wealth of all civilized communities has been so unequally divided, and to show by what means so small a share has been allotted to those by whose labor it was produced, and so large a share to the non-producing classes." Concerning one such device he had no doubts; the tariff was a certain means of making "the poor poorer and the rich richer." As early as 1828 he wrote of the tariff system in his *Exposition and Protest*:

> After we [the planters] are exhausted, the contest will be between the capitalist and operatives [workers]; for into these two classes it must, ultimately, divide society. The issue of the struggle here must be the same as it has been in Europe. Under the operation of the system, wages must sink more rapidly than the prices of the necessaries of life, till the operatives will be reduced to the lowest point, —when the portion of the products of their labor left to them, will be barely sufficient to preserve existence.

In his *Disquisition on Government* Calhoun predicted that as the community develops in wealth and population, "the difference between the rich and poor will become more strongly marked," and the proportion of "ignorant and dependent" people will increase. Then "the tendency to conflict between them will become stronger; and, as the poor and dependent become more numerous in proportion there will be, in governments of the numerical majority, no want of leaders among the wealthy and ambitious, to excite and direct them in their efforts to obtain the control."

Such arguments were not merely for public consumption. In 1831 a friend recorded a conversation in which Calhoun "spoke of the tendency of Capital to destroy and absorb the property of society and produce a collision between itself and operatives." "The capitalist owns the instruments of labor," Calhoun once told Albert Brisbane, "and he seeks to draw out of labor all the profits, leaving the laborer to shift for himself in age and disease." In 1837 he wrote to Hammond that he had had "no conception that the lower class had made such great progress to equality and independence" as Hammond had reported. "Modern society seems to me to be rushing to some new and untried condition." "What I dread," he confessed to his daughter Anna in 1846, "is that progress in political science falls far short of progress in that which relates to matter, and which may lead to convulsions and revolutions, that may retard, or even arrest the former." During the peak of the Jacksonian bank war he wrote to his son James that the views of many people in the North were inclining toward Southern conceptions. They feared not only Jackson's power, but "the needy and corrupt in their own section. They begin to feel what I have long foreseen, that they have more to fear from their own people than we from our slaves."

In such characteristic utterances there is discernible a rough parallel to several ideas that were later elaborated and refined by Marx: the idea of pervasive exploitation and class struggle in history; a labor theory of value and of a surplus appropriated by the capitalists; the concentration of capital under capitalistic production; the fall of working-class conditions to the level of subsistence; the growing revolt of the laboring class against the capitalists; the prediction of social revolution. The difference was that Calhoun proposed that no revolution should be allowed to take place. To forestall it he suggested consistently—over a period of years—what Richard Current has called "planter-capitalist collaboration against the class enemy." In such a collaboration the South, with its superior social stability, had much to offer as a conservative force. In return, the conservative elements in the North should be willing to hold down abolitionist agitation; and they would do well to realize that an overthrow of slavery in the South would prepare the ground for social revolution in the North.

> There is and always has been [he said in the Senate] in an advanced stage of wealth and civilization, a conflict between labor and capital. The condition of society in the South exempts us from the disorders and dangers resulting from this conflict; and which explains why it is that the political condition of the slave-holding states has been so much more stable and quiet than that of the North. . . . The experience of the next generation will fully test how vastly more favorable our condition of society is to that of other sections for free and stable institutions, provided we are not disturbed by the interference of others, or shall . . . resist promptly and successfully such interference.

On January 9, 1838 Calhoun explained further why it was impossible in the South for the conflict "between labor and capital" to take place, "which makes it so difficult to establish and maintain free institutions in all wealthy and highly civilized nations where such institutions as ours do not exist." It was because the Southern states were an aggregate of communities, not of individuals. "Every plantation is a little community, with the master at its head, who concentrates in himself the united interests of capital and labor, of which he is the common representative." In the Southern states labor and capital are "equally represented and perfectly harmonized." In the Union as a whole, the South, accordingly, becomes

> the balance of the system; the great conservative power, which prevents other portions, less fortunately constituted, from rushing into conflict. In this tendency to conflict in the North, between labor and capital, which is constantly on the increase, the weight of the South has been and ever will be found on the conservative side; against the aggression of one or the other side, whichever may tend to disturb the equilibrium of our political system.

In 1836 Calhoun had pointed out to "the sober and considerate" Northerners

> who have a deep stake in the existing institutions of the country that the assaults which are now directed against the institutions of the Southern States may be very easily directed against those which uphold their own property and security. A very slight modification of the arguments used against the institutions [of the South] would make them equally effectual against the institutions of the North, including banking, in which so vast an amount of its property and capital is invested.

In 1847 he again reminded Northern conservatives how much interest they had "in upholding and preserving the equilibrium of the slaveholding states." "Let gentlemen then be warned that while warring on us, they are warring on themselves." Two years later he added that the North, without the South, "would have no central point of union, to bind its various and conflicting interests together; and would . . . be subject to all the agitations and conflicts growing out of the divisions of wealth and poverty." All these warnings were merely the consequence of a longstanding conviction which Calhoun had expressed to Josiah Quincy that "the interests of the *gentlemen* of the North and of the South are identical." The Carolinian had no serious expectation that his appeals and predictions would change Northern public opinion, but he hoped that events might. Growing discontent among the masses might drive Northern conservatives into the arms of the planters, but as he confessed to Duff Green in 1835, whether the intelligence of the North would see the situation "in time to save themselves and the institutions of the Country God only knows."

Calhoun had an ingenious solution for the sectional problem: in return for the South's services as a balance wheel against labor agitation, the solid elements in the North should join her in a common front against all agitation of the slavery issue. His program for the tariff problem was best expressed in a letter to Abbott Lawrence in 1845: Northern manufacturers should join the planters in producing for the export market. At best it would be impossible for manufacturers to attain prosperity in the home market alone; "the great point is to get possession of the foreign market," and for that the high-duty tariff is nothing but an obstruction. The North should emulate English manufacturers by lowering duties, importing cheap raw materials, and competing aggressively for foreign trade. "When that is accomplished all conflict between the planter and the manufacturer would cease."

IV

During the last seven years of Calhoun's life the sectional conflict centered more and more on the acquisition of new territory and its division between slave and free society. Nullification had failed for lack of unity within the South. The alliance with the West was unstable and uncertain. The proposed alliance with Northern capital Calhoun could not bring about. Hence the problem of defense turned increasingly upon the attempt to acquire new slavery in Texas, Mexico, and the vast area wrested from Mexico by war, and keeping the North from taking the West for free labor.

Calhoun's interest in Texas was defensive in intent, but exorbitantly aggressive in form. Great Britain, eager for a new market and an independent source of cotton, was encouraging Texas to remain independent by offering financial aid and protection. During 1843, when Lord Brougham and Lord Aberdeen both openly confessed Britain's intent to foster abolition along with national independence in Texas, Calhoun, then Secretary of State, stepped forward in alarm to link the annexation issue with a thoroughgoing defense of slavery. Southerners feared that another refuge for fugitive slaves and the example of an independent, free-labor cotton-producing country on their border would be a grave menace to their social structure. Britain, Calhoun frankly told the British Minister, was trying to destroy in Texas an institution "essential to the peace, safety, and prosperity of the United States"! In 1844 he published an interpretation of Britain's motives. Having freed the slaves in her own colonial empire, he charged, she had lost ground in world production of tropical products, including cotton, had endangered the investment in her empire, and had reduced it to far poorer condition than such areas as the Southern United States and Brazil, where slavery survived. Britain, in her effort "to regain and keep a superiority in tropical cultivation, commerce, and influence," was desperately trying to "cripple or destroy the productions of her successful rivals" by undermining their superior labor system.

Ardent as he had been for annexation of Texas, Calhoun was frightened during the war with Mexico by sentiment in the South for conquest and annexation of all Mexico. If Mexico were taken, he feared that the necessity of controlling her would give the executive tremendous powers and vast patronage, bring about precisely the centralization of federal power that he so feared, and finally destroy the constitutional system. He predicted that conflict between North and South over disposition of the acquired territory might easily disrupt the Union. "Mexico is for us the forbidden fruit; the penalty of eating it would be to subject our institutions to political death."

In 1846 the introduction of the Wilmot Proviso, which banned slavery from all territory to be taken from Mexico, excited the South as nothing had before. Calhoun felt that it involved a matter of abstract right upon which no compromise should be considered, even though it was unlikely that slavery would go into the territories in question. In December he told President Polk that he "did not desire to extend slavery," that it would "probably never exist" in California and New Mexico. Still he would vote against any treaty that included the Wilmot Proviso, because "it would involve a principle." [5]

Calhoun became obsessed with the North's tendency to "monopolize" the territories for free labor. In 1847, when Iowa had entered the Union and Wisconsin was ready for statehood, he expressed his fear that the terri-

---

5. This was not his view alone. "It cannot be a slave country," wrote Robert Toombs to J. J. Crittenden, January 22, 1849. "We have only the point of honor to save . . . and [to] rescue the country from all danger of agitation."

tories would yield twelve or fifteen more free states. The South was fast losing that parity in the Senate which was its final stronghold of equality in the federal government. In March of that year he called for a united Southern party to force a showdown on Southern rights. In his last great speech, which was read to the Senate for him because he was dying, he declared with finality that the balance of power had already been lost. The South no longer had "any adequate means of protecting itself against . . . encroachment and oppression." Reviewing the growth of Northern preponderance, the exploitation of the South, and the progressive disintegration of the moral bonds of Union, Calhoun warned that the nation could be saved only by conceding to the South an equal right in the newly acquired Western territory[6] and amending the Constitution to restore to her the power of self-protection that she had had before the sectional balance was destroyed.

An amendment to the Constitution would be a guarantee of equality to the South. Calhoun demanded that this guarantee should take the form of the concurrent majority, which was the king pin in his political system. All through his sectional phase Calhoun had been preaching for the concurrent majority. He expressed it as early as 1833 in his speech on the Force Bill and last formulated it in the *Disquisition on Government,* published after his death. Government by numerical majorities, he always insisted, was inherently unstable; he proposed to replace it with what he called government by the whole community—that is, a government that would organically represent both majority and minority. So-

6. It is not certain whether Calhoun had changed his mind about not expecting slavery to go into the territory, as he had admitted to Polk, or whether he still considered that the mere victory on principle was of that much importance.

ciety should not be governed by counting heads but by considering the great economic interests, the geographical and functional units, of the nation. In order to prevent the plunder of a minority interest by a majority interest, each must be given an appropriate organ in the constitutional structure which would provide it with "either a concurrent voice in making and executing the laws or a veto on their execution." Only by such a device can the "different interests, orders, classes, or portions" of the community be protected, "and all conflict and struggle between them prevented." [7]

Time had persuaded Calhoun that a dual executive would be the best means of employing the concurrent majority in the United States. The nation should have two presidents, each representing one of the two great sections, each having a veto power over acts of Congress. No measure could pass that did not win the approval of the political agents of both sections. The equality between sections that had existed at the beginning of the government would thus be restored.

---

7. The concurrent majority was actually operative in South Carolina from the time of Calhoun's entrance into politics, when apportionment of the state legislature was so arranged as to give one house to the seaboard plantation area and the other to the upcountry farmers. William A. Schaper has pointed out, however, that the concurrent-majority principle could work there because the minority, the planters, kept possession of power "until it had won over the majority to its interests and its institutions."

Some Southerners hoped that since the South had a faction in both major parties, she could exercise an informal equivalent of the concurrent majority within the bisectional party system rather than the Constitution itself. This plan worked for some time, but Calhoun had no faith in it for the long run. He argued that parties must ultimately partake "more or less of a sectional character," a tendency that would grow stronger with the passage of time. And if parties became sectional, the concurrent voice could be found only in a formal constitutional amendment.

Calhoun's analysis of American political tensions certainly ranks among the most impressive intellectual achievements of American statesmen. Far in advance of the event, he forecast an alliance between Northern conservatives and Southern reactionaries, which has become one of the most formidable aspects of American politics. The South, its caste system essentially intact, has proved to be for an entire century more resistant to change than the North, its influence steadily exerted to retard serious reform and to curb the power of Northern labor. Caste prejudice and political conservatism have made the South a major stronghold of American capitalism.

But prescient and ingenious as Calhoun was, he made critical miscalculations for the sectional struggle of his own time. He had a remarkable sense for the direction of social evolution, but failed to measure its velocity. His fatal mistake was to conclude that the conflict between labor and capital would come to a head before the conflict between capital and the Southern planter. Marx out of optimism and Calhoun out of pessimism both overestimated the revolutionary capacities of the working class. It was far easier to reconcile the Northern masses to the profit system than Calhoun would ever admit. He failed to see that the expanding Northern free society, by offering broad opportunities to the lower and middle classes, provided itself with a precious safety valve for popular discontents. He also failed to see that the very restlessness which he considered the North's weakness was also a secret of its strength. "The main spring to progress," he realized, "is the desire of individuals to better their condition," but he could not admit how much more intensely free society stimulated that essential desire in its working population than his cherished slave system with its "thirty lashes well laid on."

Calhoun, in brief, failed to appreciate the staying power of capitalism. At the very time when it was swinging into its period of most hectic growth he spoke as though it had already gone into decline. The stirrings of the Jackson era particularly misled him; mass discontent, which gained further opportunities for the common man in business and politics, and thus did so much in the long run to strengthen capitalism, he misread as the beginning of a revolutionary upsurge. Calhoun was, after all, an intense reactionary, and to the reactionary ear every whispered criticism of the elite classes has always sounded like the opening shot of an uprising.

Calhoun's social analysis lacked the rough pragmatic resemblance to immediate reality that any analysis must have if it is to be translated into successful political strategy. He never did find a large capitalist group in the North that would see the situation as he did. Although he joined the Whig Party for a few years after his disappointment with Jackson, a long-term alliance with such firm spokesmen of capitalist tariff economics as Clay and Webster was unthinkable. Under the Van Buren administration he returned to the Democratic fold on the subtreasury issue, and there he remained. During the late thirties, while he was still appealing to Northern conservatives to join hands with the planters, he admitted that the Whig Party, the party most attractive to Northern capital, was more difficult than the Democrats on both the tariff and abolition.

Ironically, for a long time Northern labor was ideologically closer than Northern capital to the planters. The workers had little sympathy for abolitionism, but responded with interest when Southern politicians unleashed periodic assaults on Northern wage slavery. When Francis W. Pickens, one of Calhoun's own lieutenants, rose in the House in the fall of 1837 to point out that the planters stood in relation to Northern capital "precisely in the same situation as the laborer of the North" and that they were "the only class of capitalists . . . which, as a class, are identified with the laborers of the country," Ely Moore, a labor spokesman, endorsed his position. And eight years after Calhoun's death, when James H. Hammond lashed out in a famous speech against "wage slavery," he received many letters of thanks from Northern workers for exposing their condition. Calhoun himself, organizing his presidential drive between 1842 and 1844, found strong support among many members of the former left wing of Northern democracy. Fitzwilliam Byrdsall, ardent democrat and historian of the Locofocos, wrote to him from New York City that "the radical portion of the Democratic party here, to whom free suffrage is dear and sacred, is the very portion most favorable to you." Calhoun had not long before expected this sort of man to frighten the capitalists into the arms of the planters!

The essence of Calhoun's mistake as a practical statesman was that he tried to achieve a static solution for a dynamic situation. The North, stimulated by invention and industry and strengthened by a tide of immigration, was growing in population and wealth, filling the West, and building railroads that bound East and West together. No concurrent majority, nor any other principle embodied in a parchment, could stem the tide that was measured every ten years in the census returns. William H. Seward touched upon the South's central weakness in his speech of March 11, 1850, when he observed that what the Southerners wanted was "a *political* equilibrium. Every political equilibrium requires a physical equilibrium to rest upon, and is valueless without it." In the face of all realities, the Southerners kept demanding that equality of territory and approximate equality of populations be maintained. "And this," taunted Seward, "must be perpetual!"

Moreover, the Calhoun dialectic was so starkly reactionary in its implications that it became self-defeating. There was disaster even for the South in the premise that every civilized society must be built upon a submerged and exploited labor force—what Hammond called a "mud-sill" class. *If* there must always be a submerged and exploited class at the base of society, and *if* the Southern slaves, as such a class, were better off than Northern free workers, and *if* slavery was the safest and most durable base on which to found political institutions, then there seemed to be no reason why *all* workers, white or black, industrial or agrarian, should not be slave rather than free. Calhoun shrank from this conclusion, but some Southerners did not. George Fitzhugh won himself quite a reputation in the fifties arguing along these lines. The fact that some Southerners, however few, followed Fitzhugh was an excellent one for Northern politicians to use to rouse freemen, especially those who were indifferent to the moral aspects of slavery, to take a stand against the spread of the institution.

Calhoun could see and expound very plausibly every weakness of Northern society, but his position forced him to close his eyes to the vulnerability of the South. Strong as he was on logical coherence, he had not the most elementary moral consistency. Here it is hard to follow those who, like Professor Wiltse, find in him "the supreme champion of minority rights and interests everywhere." It is true that Calhoun superbly formulated the problem of the relation between majorities and minorities, and his work at this point may have the permanent significance for political theory that is often ascribed to it. But how can the same value be assigned to his practical solutions? Not in the slightest was he concerned with minority rights as they are chiefly of interest to the modern liberal mind—the rights of dissenters to express unorthodox opinions, of the individual conscience against the State, least of all of ethnic minorities. At bottom he was not interested in any minority that was not a propertied minority. The concurrent majority itself was a device without relevance to the protection of dissent, but designed specifically to protect a vested interest of considerable power. Even within the South Calhoun had not the slightest desire to protect intellectual minorities, critics, and dissenters. Professor Clement Eaton, in his *Freedom of Thought in the Old South,* places him first among those politicians who "created stereotypes in the minds of the Southern people that produced intolerance." Finally, it was minority privileges rather than rights that he really proposed to protect. He wanted to give to the minority not merely a proportionate but an *equal* voice with the majority in determining public policy. He would have found incomprehensible the statement of William H. Roane, of Virginia, that he had "never thought that [minorities] had any other *Right* than that of freely, peaceably, & *legally* converting themselves into a *majority* whenever they can." This elementary right Calhoun was prompt to deny to any minority, North or South, that disagreed with him on any vital question. In fact, his first great speeches on the slavery question were prompted by his attempt to deny the right of petition to a minority.

Calhoun was a minority spokesman in a democracy, a particularist in an age of nationalism, a slaveholder in an age of advancing liberties, and an agrarian in a furiously capitalistic country. Quite understandably he developed a certain perversity of mind. It became his peculiar faculty, the faculty of a brilliant but highly abstract and isolated intellect, to see things that other men never dreamt of and to deny what was under his nose, to forecast with uncanny insight several major trends of the future and remain all but oblivious of the actualities of the present. His weakness was to be inhumanly schematic and logical, which is only to say that he thought as he lived. His mind, in a sense, was *too* masterful—it imposed itself upon realities. The great human, emotional, moral complexities of the world escaped him because he had no private training for them, had not even the talent for friendship, in which he might have been schooled. It was easier for him to imagine, for example, that the South had produced upon its slave base a better culture than the North because he had no culture himself, only a quick and muscular mode of thought. It may stand as a token of Calhoun's place in the South's history that when he did find culture there, at Charleston, he wished a plague on it.

CHAPTER V

ABRAHAM LINCOLN AND THE
SELF-MADE MYTH

❦

I HAPPEN, *temporarily, to occupy this White House. I am a living witness that any one of your children may look to come here as my father's child has.* ABRAHAM LINCOLN to the 166th Ohio Regiment

HIS *ambition was a little engine that knew no rest.*
WILLIAM H. HERNDON

THE Lincoln legend has come to have a hold on the American imagination that defies comparison with anything else in political mythology. Here is a drama in which a great man shoulders the torment and moral burdens of a blundering and sinful people, suffers for them, and redeems them with hallowed Christian virtues—"malice toward none and charity for all"—and is destroyed at the pitch of his success. The worldly-wise John Hay, who knew him about as well as he permitted himself to be known, called him "the greatest character since Christ," a comparison one cannot imagine being made of any other political figure of modern times.

If the Lincoln legend gathers strength from its similarity to the Christian theme of vicarious atonement and redemption, there is still another strain in American experience that it represents equally well. Although his

métier was politics and not business, Lincoln was a preeminent example of that self-help which Americans have
always so admired. He was not, of course, the first eminent American politician who could claim humble origins, nor the first to exploit them. But few have been
able to point to such a sudden ascent from relative obscurity to high eminence; none has maintained so completely while scaling the heights the aspect of extreme
simplicity; and none has combined with the attainment
of success and power such an intense awareness of humanity and moral responsibility. It was precisely in his
attainments as a common man that Lincoln felt himself
to be remarkable, and in this light that he interpreted to
the world the significance of his career. Keenly aware of
his role as the exemplar of the self-made man, he played
the part with an intense and poignant consistency that
gives his performance the quality of a high art. The first
author of the Lincoln legend and the greatest of the
Lincoln dramatists was Lincoln himself.

Lincoln's simplicity was very real. He called his wife
"mother," received distinguished guests in shirtsleeves,
and once during his presidency hailed a soldier out of
the ranks with the cry: "Bub! Bub!" But he was also a
complex man, easily complex enough to know the value
of his own simplicity. With his morbid compulsion for
honesty he was too modest to pose coarsely and blatantly
as a Henry Clay or James G. Blaine might pose. (When
an 1860 campaign document announced that he was a
reader of Plutarch, he sat down at once to validate the
claim by reading the *Lives*.) But he did develop a political personality by intensifying qualities he actually possessed.

Even during his early days in politics, when his
speeches were full of conventional platform bombast,
Lincoln seldom failed to strike the humble manner that

was peculiarly his. "I was born and have ever remained,"
he said in his first extended campaign speech, "in the
most humble walks of life. I have no popular relations or
friends to recommend me." Thereafter he always
sounded the theme. "I presume you all know who I am
—I am humble Abraham Lincoln. . . . If elected I
shall be thankful; if not it will be all the same." Opponents at times grew impatient with his self-derogation
("my poor, lean, lank face") and a Democratic journal
once called him a Uriah Heep. But self-conscious as the
device was, and coupled even as it was with a secret
confidence that Hay called "intellectual arrogance,"
there was still no imposture in it. It corresponded to Lincoln's own image of himself, which placed him with the
poor, the aged, and the forgotten. In a letter to Herndon
that was certainly not meant to impress any constituency, Lincoln, near his thirty-ninth birthday, referred
to "my old, withered, dry eyes."

There was always this pathos in his plainness, his
lack of external grace. "He is," said one of Mrs. Lincoln's
friends, "the *ungodliest* man you ever saw." His colleagues, however, recognized in this a possible political
asset and transmuted it into one of the most successful
of all political symbols—the hard-fisted rail-splitter. At
a Republican meeting in 1860 John Hanks and another
old pioneer appeared carrying fence rails labeled: "Two
rails from a lot made by Abraham Lincoln and John
Hanks in the Sangamon Bottom in the year 1830." And
Lincoln, with his usual candor, confessed that he had no
idea whether these were the same rails, but he was sure
he had actually split rails every bit as good. The time
was to come when little Tad could say: "Everybody in
this world knows Pa used to split rails."

Humility belongs with mercy among the cardinal
Christian virtues. "Blessed are the meek, for they shall

inherit the earth." But the demands of Christianity and the success myth are incompatible. The competitive society out of which the success myth and the self-made man have grown may accept the Christian virtues in principle but can hardly observe them in practice. The motivating force in the mythology of success is ambition, which is closely akin to the cardinal Christian sin of pride. In a world that works through ambition and self-help, while inculcating an ethic that looks upon their results with disdain, how can an earnest man, a public figure living in a time of crisis, gratify his aspirations and yet remain morally whole? If he is, like Lincoln, a man of private religious intensity, the stage is set for high tragedy.

II

The clue to much that is vital in Lincoln's thought and character lies in the fact that he was thoroughly and completely the politician, by preference and by training. It is difficult to think of any man of comparable stature whose life was so fully absorbed into his political being. Lincoln plunged into politics almost at the beginning of his adult life and was never occupied in any other career except for a brief period when an unfavorable turn in the political situation forced him back to his law practice. His life was one of caucuses and conventions, party circulars and speeches, requests, recommendations, stratagems, schemes, and ambitions. "It was in the world of politics that he lived," wrote Herndon after his death. "Politics were his life, newspapers his food, and his great ambition his motive power."

Like his father, Lincoln was physically lazy even as a

youth, but unlike him had an active forensic mind. When
only fifteen he was often on stumps and fences making
political speeches, from which his father had to haul
him back to his chores. He was fond of listening to lawyers' arguments and occupying his mind with them.
Herndon testifies that "He read specially for a special
object and thought things useless unless they could be
of utility, use, practice, etc." [1] When Lincoln read he
preferred to read aloud. Once when Herndon asked him
about it he answered: "I catch the idea by two senses,
for when I read aloud I *hear* what is read and I see it
. . . and I remember it better, if I do not understand it
better." These are the reading habits of a man who is
preparing for the platform.

For a youth with such mental habits—and one who
had no business talents in the narrower sense—the greatest opportunities on the Illinois prairies were in the
ministry, law, or politics. Lincoln, who had read Paine
and Volney, was too unorthodox in theology for the
ministry, and law and politics it proved to be. But politics was first: at twenty-three, only seven months after
coming to the little Illinois community of New Salem,
he was running for office. Previously he had worked only
at odd jobs as ferry man, surveyor, postmaster, storekeeper, rail-splitter, farm hand, and the like; and now,
without any other preparation, he was looking for election to the state legislature. He was not chosen, but two
years later, in 1834, Sangamon County sent him to the
lower house. Not until his first term had almost ended

---

1. For years Herndon kept on their office table the *Westminster
Review,* the *Edinburgh Review,* other English periodicals, the
works of Darwin, Spencer, and other English writers. He had
little success in interesting Lincoln. "Occasionally he would
snatch one up and peruse it for a little while, but he soon threw
it down with the suggestion that it was entirely too heavy for an
ordinary mind to digest."

was he sufficiently qualified as a lawyer to be admitted to the state bar.

From this time to the end of his life—except for the years between 1849 and 1854, when his political prospects were discouraging—Lincoln was busy either as officeholder or office-seeker. In the summer of 1860, for a friend who wanted to prepare a campaign biography, he wrote in the third person a short sketch of his political life up to that time: 1832—defeated in an attempt to be elected to the legislature; 1834—elected to the legislature "by the highest vote cast for any candidate"; 1836, 1838, 1840—re-elected; 1838 and 1840—chosen by his party as its candidate for Speaker of the Illinois House of Representatives, but not elected; 1840 and 1844—placed on Harrison and Clay electoral tickets "and spent much time and labor in both those canvasses"; 1846—elected to Congress; 1848—campaign worker for Zachary Taylor, speaking in Maryland and Massachusetts, and "canvassing quite fully his own district in Illinois, which was followed by a majority in the district of over 1500 for General Taylor"; 1852—placed on Winfield Scott's electoral ticket, "but owing to the hopelessness of the cause in Illinois he did less than in previous presidential canvasses"; 1854—". . . his profession had almost superseded the thought of politics in his mind, when the repeal of the Missouri Compromise aroused him as he had never been before"; 1856—"made over fifty speeches" in the campaign for Frémont; prominently mentioned in the Republican national convention for the vice-presidential nomination. . . .

The rest of the story is familiar enough.

As a politician Lincoln was no maverick. On the bank question, on internal improvements, on the Mexican War (even at his own political expense), on the tariff, he was

always a firm, orthodox Whig. He early became a party
wheelhorse, a member of the Illinois State Whig Committee, and in the legislature a Whig floor leader. As
Lord Charnwood puts it, "The somewhat unholy business of party management was at first attractive to him."
It was during this period that he learned the deliberate
and responsible opportunism that later was so characteristic of his statecraft.

In 1848, when he was still in Congress, Lincoln threw
in his lot with the shrewd Whig leaders who preferred
the ill-equipped but available Zachary Taylor to the
party's elder statesman, Henry Clay, as presidential candidate. During the campaign he defended Taylor's
equivocations by saying that, far from having no principles, Taylor stood for the highest of principles—"allowing the people to do as they please with their own
business." Lincoln himself, because of an agreement to
rotate the candidacy for his seat, did not run for re-election to Congress; had he done so, defeat would have
been certain. When he tried to get an appointment to the
General Land Office he was turned down; a less appealing offer of the Secretaryship of Oregon Territory he
declined. For a while it seemed that his political career
had come to an end. Thoroughly humbled by his de-
pressing obscurity in Congress, he turned with reluctance to the law, overcome by a melancholy "so profound," says Beveridge, "that the depths of it cannot be
sounded or estimated by normal minds. Certainly political disappointment had something to do with his de-
spondency." His ambitions were directed toward public
life; he had no legal aspirations, lucrative though his
practice was. Years later, when the two were preparing
their study of him, Herndon objected to Jesse Weik's
desire to stress Lincoln's legal eminence: "How are you

going to make a *great* lawyer out of Lincoln? His soul was afire with its own ambition and that was not law."

The repeal of the Missouri Compromise in 1854, which started the dissolution of both major parties and created a fluid political situation, once again aroused Lincoln's hopes. For some time he seems to have thought of the slavery-extension issue as a means of revivifying the Whig Party, which he found it hard to abandon. For two years after the Republicans had formed local and state organizations in the Northwest he refused to join them, and even while supporting their candidate, Frémont, in 1856 he carefully avoided speaking of himself or his colleagues as Republicans. In the fall of 1854, hungering for the Senatorial nomination and fearing to offend numerous old-line Whigs in Illinois, he fled from Springfield on Herndon's advice to avoid attending a Republican state convention there. One of his most terrible fits of melancholy overcame him when he failed to get the nomination the following year. "That man," says Herndon (whose adoration of Lincoln assures us we are listening to no hostile critic), "who thinks Lincoln calmly gathered his robes about him, waiting for the people to call him, has a very erroneous knowledge of Lincoln. He was always calculating and planning ahead. His ambition was a little engine that knew no rest." With all his quiet passion Lincoln had sought to rise in life, to make something of himself through his own honest efforts. It was this typically American impulse that dominated him through the long course of his career before he became interested in the slavery question. It was his understanding of this impulse that guided his political thought.

III

If historical epochs are judged by the opportunities they offer talented men to rise from the ranks to places of wealth, power, and prestige, the period during which Lincoln grew up was among the greatest in history, and among all places such opportunities were most available in the fresh territory north and west of the Ohio River—the Valley of Democracy.

Abraham Lincoln was nineteen years old when Andrew Jackson was elected President. Like most of the poor in his part of the country, Thomas Lincoln was a Jacksonian Democrat, and his son at first accepted his politics. But some time during his eighteenth or nineteenth year Abraham went through a political conversion, became a National Republican, and cast his first vote, in 1832, for Henry Clay.

The National Republican (later Whig) Party was the party of internal improvements, stable currency, and conservative banking; Lincoln lived in a country that needed all three. Doubtless there were also personal factors in his decision. If the Democrats spoke more emphatically about the equality of man, the Whigs, even in the West, had the most imposing and affluent men. That an ambitious youth should look to the more solid citizens of his community for political guidance was natural and expedient; the men Lincoln most respected in the Indiana town of his boyhood were National Republicans, great admirers of Henry Clay; and as Dennis Hanks mournfully recalled, Lincoln himself "allways Loved Hen Clay's speaches." With one exception, John Hanks, who turned Republican in 1860, Abraham was the only member of the Lincoln or Hanks families who deserted the Democratic Party.

After a few years of stagnation Lincoln advanced with the utmost rapidity in his middle twenties. While many of the stories about the hardships of his youth celebrated in Lincoln legendry are true, it is noteworthy that success came to him suddenly and at a rather early age. At twenty-four he was utterly obscure. At twenty-eight he was the leader of his party in the Illinois House of Representatives, renowned as the winner of the fight to bring the state capital to Springfield, extremely popular in both Sangamon County and the capital itself, and partner of one of the ablest lawyers in the state. Of his first years in Springfield Herndon writes: "No man ever had an easier time of it in his early days than Lincoln. He had . . . influential and financial friends to help him; they almost fought each other for the privilege of assisting Lincoln. . . . Lincoln was a pet . . . in this city." And, adds Herndon, "he deserved it." Success of this sort eases and fattens smaller men; for more restless souls it is a form of poison.

Like his "influential and financial friends," Lincoln belonged to the party of rank and privilege; it exacted a price from him. In time he was to marry into the family circle of Ninian Edwards, of whom it was once observed that he was "naturally and constitutionally an aristocrat and . . . hated democracy . . . as the devil is said to hate holy water." Lincoln's connection with such a tribe could only spur his loyalty to the democratic ways in which he had been brought up; he never did "belong," and Mary Todd's attitude toward him as a social creature was always disdainful.

In a letter written in 1858, discussing the growth of the Republican Party, he observed: "Much of the plain old Democracy is with us, while nearly all the old exclusive silk-stocking Whiggery is against us. I don't mean all the Old Whig party, but nearly all of the nice exclusive sort." Lincoln's keen sense of not belonging to the "nice exclusive sort" was a distinct political asset. Throughout his early career, no doubt, it enabled him to speak with sincerity for Jeffersonian principles while supporting Hamiltonian measures. For public and private reasons alike he was touchy about attempts to link him with the aristocrats because of his Whig affiliations, and once complained bitterly at being incongruously "put down here as the candidate of pride, wealth, and aristocratic family distinction."

And yet it was true that the young Lincoln fell short of being an outspoken democrat. In the social climate of Illinois he ranked as a moderate conservative. Running for re-election to the legislature in 1836, he submitted to a newspaper a statement of his views which included the following: "I go for all sharing the privileges of the government who assist in bearing its burdens. Consequently I go for admitting all whites to the right of suffrage who pay taxes or bear arms (by no means excluding females)." Now, the Illinois Constitution of 1818 had already granted the suffrage to all white male inhabitants of twenty-one or over without further qualification, so that Lincoln's proposal actually involved a step backward.[2]

Lincoln's democracy was not broad enough to transcend color lines, but on this score it had more latitude than the democracy professed by many of his neighbors

2. The parenthetic inclusion of women was bold enough, however, assuming that Lincoln expected to be taken seriously. The words were written twelve years before the first Women's Rights Convention met at Seneca Falls, and even then, when Elizabeth Cady Stanton proposed to include suffrage among other demands, her colleague, the Quakeress Lucretia Mott, had chided: "Elizabeth, thee will make us ridiculous."

and contemporaries. One of the extraordinary things about his strangely involved personality is the contrast between his circumspectness in practical politics wherever the Negro was concerned, and his penetration of the logic of the proslavery argument, which he answered with exceptional insight. His keen onslaughts against slavery, in fact, carry the conviction of a man of far greater moral force than the pre-presidential Lincoln ever revealed in action. After 1854, when he renewed his study of the slavery question, Lincoln was particularly acute in showing that the logic of the defenders of slavery was profoundly undemocratic, not only in reference to the Southern scene, but for human relations everywhere. The essence of his position was that the principle of exclusion has no inner check; that arbitrarily barring one minority from the exercise of its rights can be both a precedent and a moral sanction for barring another, and that it creates a frame of mind from which no one can expect justice or security. "I am not a Know-nothing," he wrote to Speed:

> How could I be? How can anyone who abhors the oppression of Negroes be in favor of degrading classes of white people? Our progress in degeneracy appears to me to be pretty rapid. As a nation we began by declaring that "all men are created equal." We now practically read it "all men are created equal except negroes." When the Know-nothings get control, it will read "all men are created equal, except negroes and foreigners and Catholics." When it comes to this, I shall prefer emigrating to some country where they make no pretence of loving liberty,—to Russia, for instance, where despotism can be taken pure, and without the base alloy of hypocrisy.

In Lincoln's eyes the Declaration of Independence thus becomes once again what it had been to Jefferson—

not merely a formal theory of rights, but an instrument of democracy. It was to Jefferson that Lincoln looked as the source of his political inspiration, Jefferson whom he described as "the most distinguished politician of our history." "The principles of Jefferson are the definitions and axioms of free society," he declared in 1859. "The Jefferson party," he wrote privately at about the same time, "was formed upon its supposed superior devotion to the rights of men, holding the rights of property to be secondary only, and greatly inferior." The Democratic Party, he charged, had abandoned Jeffersonian tradition by taking the position that one man's liberty was absolutely nothing when it conflicted with another man's property. "Republicans," he added, in an utterly characteristic sentence which ought to be well remembered, "are for both the man and the dollar, but in case of conflict the man before the dollar." There is self-portraiture in the remark: one sees the moral idealism of the man; it is there, unquestionably, but he hopes that the world will never force it to obtrude itself.

The Declaration of Independence was not only the primary article of Lincoln's creed; it provided his most formidable political ammunition. And yet in the end it was the Declaration that he could not make a consistent part of his living work. The Declaration was a revolutionary document, and this too Lincoln accepted. One of his early public statements declares:

> Any people anywhere being inclined and having the power have the right to rise up and shake off the existing government, and form a new one that suits them better. This is a most valuable, a most sacred right—a right which we hope and believe is to liberate the world.

Having said so much, he did not stop:

Any portion of such people that can may revolutionize and make their own of so much territory as they inhabit. More than this, *a majority of any portion of such people may revolutionize, putting down a minority, intermingled with or near about them,* who may oppose this movement. Such a minority was precisely the case of the Tories of our own revolution. It is a quality of revolutions not to go by old lines or old laws; but to break up both, and make new ones.

The principle is reiterated with firmness in the First Inaugural Address.

So Lincoln, the revolutionary theorist. There was another Lincoln who had a lawyer-like feeling for the niceties of established rules and a nationalist's reverence for constitutional sanction. This Lincoln always publicly condemned the abolitionists who fought slavery by extraconstitutional means—and condemned also the mobs who deprived them of their right of free speech and free press. This Lincoln, even before he was thirty, warned the young men of Springfield that disrespect for legal observances might destroy free institutions in America, and urged them to let reverence for the laws "become the political religion of the nation." This Lincoln suppressed secession and refused to acknowledge that the right of revolution he had so boldly accepted belonged to the South. The same Lincoln, as we shall see, refused almost to the last minute even to suppress rebellion by revolutionary means. The contradiction is not peculiar to Lincoln; Anglo-Saxon history is full of it.

As an economic thinker, Lincoln had a passion for the great average. Thoroughly middle-class in his ideas, he spoke for those millions of Americans who had begun their lives as hired workers—as farm hands, clerks,

teachers, mechanics, flatboat men, and rail-splitters—and
had passed into the ranks of landed farmers, prosperous
grocers, lawyers, merchants, physicians, and politicians.
Theirs were the traditional ideals of the Protestant ethic:
hard work, frugality, temperance, and a touch of ability
applied long and hard enough would lift a man into the
propertied or professional class and give him independence and respect if not wealth and prestige. Failure to
rise in the economic scale was generally viewed as a
fault in the individual, not in society. It was the outward
sign of an inward lack of grace—of idleness, indulgence,
waste, or incapacity.

This conception of the competitive world was by no
means so inaccurate in Lincoln's day as it has long since
become; neither was it so conservative as time has made
it. It was the legitimate inheritance of Jacksonian democracy. It was the belief not only of those who had arrived
but also of those who were pushing their way to the top.
If it was intensely and at times inhumanly individualistic, it also defied aristocracy and class distinction. Lincoln's life was a dramatization of it in the sphere of politics as, say, Carnegie's was in business. His own rather
conventional version of the self-help ideology[3] is expressed with some charm in a letter written to his feck-
less stepbrother, John D. Johnston, in 1851:

-----

3. William C. Howells, father of the novelist, wrote in an
Ohio newspaper shortly before Lincoln's inauguration as President that he and his wife represented "the western type of
Americans." "The White House," he said, "has never been occupied by better representatives of the bourgoise [sic] or citizen
class of people, than it will be after the 4th proximo. If the idea
represented by these people can only be allowed to prevail in
this government, all will be well. Under such a rule, the
practical individual man, who respects himself and regards the rights of
others will grow to just proportions."

Your request for eighty dollars I do not think it best to comply with now. At the various times when I have helped you a little you have said to me, "We can get along very well now"; but in a very short time I find you in the same difficulty again. Now, this can only happen by some defect in your conduct. What that defect is, I think I know. You are not lazy, and still you are an idler. I doubt whether, since I saw you, you have done a good whole day's work in any one day. You do not very much dislike to work, and still you do not work much, merely because it does not seem to you that you could get much for it. This habit of uselessly wasting time is the whole difficulty.

Lincoln advised Johnston to leave his farm in charge of his family and go to work for wages.

I now promise you, that for every dollar you will, between this and the first of May, get for your own labor . . . I will then give you one other dollar. . . . Now if you will do this, you will soon be out of debt, and, what is better, you will have a habit that will keep you from getting in ' debt again. . . . You have always been kind to me, and I do not mean to be unkind to you. On the contrary, if you will but follow my advice, you will find it worth more than eighty times eighty dollars to you.

Given the chance for the frugal, the industrious, and the able—for the Abraham Lincolns if not the John D. Johnstons—to assert themselves, society would never be divided along fixed lines. There would be no eternal mud-sill class. "There is no permanent class of hired laborers among us," Lincoln declared in a public address. "Twenty-five years ago I was a hired laborer. The hired laborer of yesterday labors on his own account today, and will hire others to labor for him tomorrow.

Advancement—improvement in condition—is the order of things in a society of equals." For Lincoln the vital test of a democracy was economic—its ability to provide opportunities for social ascent to those born in its lower ranks. This belief in opportunity for the self-made man is the key to his entire career; it explains his public appeal; it is the core of his criticism of slavery.

There is a strong pro-labor strain in all of Lincoln's utterances from the beginning to the end of his career. Perhaps the most sweeping of his words, and certainly the least equivocal, were penned in 1847. "Inasmuch as most good things are produced by labor," he began,

> it follows that all such things of right belong to those whose labor has produced them. But it has so happened, in all ages of the world, that some have labored, and others have without labor enjoyed a large proportion of the fruits. This is wrong and should not continue. To secure to each laborer the whole product of his labor, or as nearly as possible, is a worthy object of any good government.

This reads like a passage from a socialist argument. But its context is significant; the statement was neither a preface to an attack upon private property nor an argument for redistributing the world's goods—it was part of a firm defense of the protective tariff!

In Lincoln's day, especially in the more primitive communities of his formative years, the laborer had not yet been fully separated from his tools. The rights of labor still were closely associated in the fashion of Locke and Jefferson with the right of the laborer to retain his own product; when men talked about the sacredness of labor, they were often talking in veiled terms about the right to own. These ideas, which belonged to the age of craftsmanship rather than industrialism, Lincoln carried into the modern industrial scene. The result is a quaint equivocation, worth observing carefully because it pictures the state of mind of a man living half in one economy and half in another and wishing to do justice to every interest. In 1860, when Lincoln was stumping about the country before the Republican convention, he turned up at New Haven, where shoemakers were on strike. The Democrats had charged Republican agitators with responsibility for the strike, and Lincoln met them head-on:

> . . . I am glad to see that a system of labor prevails in New England under which laborers can strike when they want to, where they are not obliged to work under all circumstances, and are not tied down and obliged to labor whether you pay them or not! I like the system which lets a man quit when he wants to, and wish it might prevail everywhere. One of the reasons why I am opposed to slavery is just here. What is the true condition of the laborer? I take it that it is best for all to leave each man free to acquire property as fast as he can. Some will get wealthy. I don't believe in a law to prevent a man from getting rich; it would do more harm than good. So while we do not propose any war upon capital, we do wish to allow the humblest man an equal chance to get rich with everybody else. When one starts poor, as most do in the race of life, free society is such that he knows he can better his condition; he knows that there is no fixed condition of labor for his whole life. . . . That is the true system.

If there was a flaw in all this, it was one that Lincoln was never forced to meet. Had he lived to seventy, he would have seen the generation brought up on self-help come into its own, build oppressive business corporations, and begin to close off those treasured opportunities for the little man. Further, he would have seen his own party become the jackal of the vested interests, placing the dollar far, far ahead of the man. He himself presided over the social revolution that destroyed the simple equalitarian order of the 1840's, corrupted what remained of its values, and caricatured its ideals. Booth's bullet, indeed, saved him from something worse than embroilment with the radicals over Reconstruction. It confined his life to the happier age that Lincoln understood—which unwittingly he helped to destroy—the age that gave sanction to the honest compromises of his thought.

IV

A story about Abraham Lincoln's second trip to New Orleans when he was twenty-one holds an important place in the Lincoln legend. According to John Hanks, when Lincoln went with his companions to a slave market they saw a handsome mulatto girl being sold on the block, and "the iron entered his soul"; he swore that if he ever got a chance he would hit slavery "and hit it hard." The implication is clear: Lincoln was half abolitionist and the Emancipation Proclamation was a fulfillment of that young promise. But the authenticity of the tale is suspect among Lincoln scholars. John Hanks recalled it thirty-five years afterward as a personal witness, whereas, according to Lincoln, Hanks had not gone beyond St. Louis on the journey. Beveridge observes that Lincoln himself apparently never spoke of the alleged incident publicly or privately,[4] and that for twenty years afterward he showed little concern over slavery. We know that he refused to denounce the Fugitive Slave Law, viciously unfair though it was, even to free Negroes charged as runaways. ("I confess I hate to see the poor creatures hunted down," he wrote to Speed, ". . . but I bite my lips and keep quiet.")

His later career as an opponent of slavery extension must be interpreted in the light of his earlier public indifference to the question. Always moderately hostile to the South's "peculiar institution," he quieted himself with the comfortable thought that it was destined very gradually to disappear. Only after the Kansas-Nebraska Act breathed political life into the slavery issue did he seize upon it as a subject for agitation; only then did he attack it openly. His attitude was based on justice tempered by expediency—or perhaps more accurately, expediency tempered by justice.

Lincoln was by birth a Southerner, a Kentuckian; both his parents were Virginians. His father had served on the slave patrol of Hardin County. The Lincoln family was one of thousands that in the early decades of the nineteenth century had moved from the Southern states, particularly Virginia, Kentucky, and Tennessee, into the Valley of Democracy, and peopled the southern parts of Ohio, Indiana, and Illinois.

During his boyhood days in Indiana and Illinois Lincoln lived in communities where slaves were rare or un-

---

4. Herndon, however, attested that he heard Lincoln refer to having seen slaves on sale. *Herndon's Life of Lincoln* (Angle ed., 1930), p. 64. In a letter to Alexander H. Stephens, January 19, 1860, Lincoln wrote: "When a boy I went to New Orleans in a flat boat and there I saw slavery and slave markets as I have never seen them in Kentucky, and I heard worse of the Red River plantations."

known, and the problem was not thrust upon him. The prevailing attitude toward Negroes in Illinois was intensely hostile. Severe laws against free Negroes and runaway slaves were in force when Lincoln went to the Springfield legislature, and there is no evidence of any popular movement to liberalize them. Lincoln's experiences with slavery on his journeys to New Orleans in 1828 and 1831 do not seem to have made an impression vivid enough to change his conduct. Always privately compassionate, in his public career and his legal practice he never made himself the advocate of unpopular reform movements.

While Lincoln was serving his second term in the Illinois legislature the slavery question was discussed throughout the country. Garrison had begun his agitation, and petitions to abolish slavery in the District of Columbia had begun to pour in upon Congress. State legislatures began to express themselves upon the matter. The Illinois legislature turned the subject over to a joint committee, of which Lincoln and his Sangamon County colleague, Dan Stone, were members. At twenty-eight Lincoln thus had occasion to review the whole slavery question on both sides. The committee reported proslavery resolutions, presently adopted, which praised the beneficent effects of white civilization upon African natives, cited the wretchedness of emancipated Negroes as proof of the folly of freedom, and denounced abolitionists.

Lincoln voted against these resolutions. Six weeks later—the delay resulted from a desire to alienate no one from the cause that then stood closest to his heart, the removal of the state capital from Vandalia to Springfield —he and Stone embodied their own opinions in a resolution that was entered in the Journal of the House and promptly forgotten. It read in part: "They [Lincoln and

Stone] believe that the institution of slavery is founded
on injustice and bad policy, but that the promulgation
of abolition doctrines tends to increase rather than abate
its evils." (Which means, the later Lincoln might have
said, that slavery is wrong but that proposing to do away
with it is also wrong because it makes slavery worse.)
They went on to say that while the Constitution does
not permit Congress to abolish slavery in the states, Congress can do so in the District of Columbia—*but* this
power should not be exercised unless at "the request of
the people of the District." This statement breathes the
fire of an uncompromising insistence upon moderation.
Let it be noted, however, that it did represent a point
of view faintly to the left of prevailing opinion. Lincoln
had gone on record as saying not merely that slavery was
"bad policy" but even that it was unjust; but he had done
so without jeopardizing his all-important project to
transfer the state capital to Springfield.

In 1845, not long before he entered Congress, Lincoln
again had occasion to express himself on slavery, this
time in a carefully phrased private letter to a political
supporter who happened to be an abolitionist.

> I hold it a paramount duty of us in the free States, due
> to the Union of the States, and perhaps to liberty itself
> (paradox though it may seem), to let the slavery of the
> other states alone; while, on the other hand, I hold it to
> be equally clear that we should never knowingly lend
> ourselves, directly or indirectly, to prevent that slavery
> from dying a natural death—to find new places for it to
> live in, when it can not longer exist in the old.

Throughout his political career he consistently held to
this position.

After he had become a lame-duck Congressman, Lincoln introduced into Congress in January 1849 a resolu-

tion to instruct the Committee on the District of Columbia to report a bill abolishing slavery in the District. The bill provided that children born of slave mothers after January 1, 1850 should be freed and supported by their mothers' owners until of a certain age. District slaveholders who wanted to emancipate their slaves were to be compensated from the federal Treasury. Lincoln himself added a section requiring the municipal authorities of Washington and Georgetown to provide "active and efficient means" of arresting and restoring to their owners all fugitive slaves escaping into the District. (This was six years before he confessed that he hated "to see the poor creatures hunted down.") Years later, recalling this fugitive-slave provision, Wendell Phillips referred to Lincoln somewhat unfairly as "that slavehound from Illinois." The bill itself, although not passed, gave rise to a spirited debate on the morality of slavery, in which Lincoln took no part.

When Lincoln returned to active politics the slavery issue had come to occupy the central position on the American scene. Stephen Douglas and some of his colleagues in Congress had secured the passage of the Kansas-Nebraska Act, which, by opening some new territory, formally at least, to slavery, repealed the part of the thirty-four-year-old Missouri Compromise that barred slavery from territory north of 36°30'. The measure provoked a howl of opposition in the North and split Douglas's party. The Republican Party, built on opposition to the extension of slavery, began to emerge in small communities in the Northwest. Lincoln's ambitions and interests were aroused, and he proceeded to rehabilitate his political fortunes.

His strategy was simple and forceful. He carefully avoided issues like the tariff, internal improvements, the

Know-Nothing mania, or prohibitionism, each of which would alienate important groups of voters. He took pains in all his speeches to stress that he was not an abolitionist and at the same time to stand on the sole program of opposing the extension of slavery. On October 4, 1854, at the age of forty-five, Lincoln *for the first time in his life* denounced slavery in public. In his speech delivered in the Hall of Representatives at Springfield (and later repeated at Peoria) he declared that he hated the current zeal for the spread of slavery: "I hate it because of the monstrous injustice of slavery itself." He went on to say that he had no prejudice against the people of the South. He appreciated their argument that it would be difficult to get rid of the institution "in any satisfactory way." "I surely will not blame them for not doing what I should not know how to do myself. If all earthly power were given me, I should not know what to do as to the existing institution. My first impulse would be to free all the slaves and send them to Liberia, to their own native land." But immediate colonization, he added, is manifestly impossible. The slaves might be freed and kept "among us as underlings." Would this really better their condition?

> What next? Free them, and make them politically and socially our equals. *My own feelings will not admit of this,* and if mine would, we well know that those of the great mass of whites will not. Whether this feeling accords with justice and sound judgment is not the sole question, if indeed it is any part of it. A universal feeling, whether well or ill founded, cannot be safely disregarded.[5]

---

5. Later, in the debate at Ottawa, Illinois, Lincoln repeated a larger passage containing this statement, and added: "this is the true complexion of all I have said in regard to the institution of slavery and the black race."

And yet nothing could justify an attempt to carry slavery into territories now free, Lincoln emphasized. For slavery is unquestionably wrong. "The great mass of mankind," he said at Peoria, "consider slavery a great moral wrong. [This feeling] lies at the very foundation of their sense of justice, and it cannot be trifled with. . . . No statesman can safely disregard it." The last sentence was the key to Lincoln's growing radicalism. As a practical politician he was naturally very much concerned about those public sentiments which no statesman can safely disregard. It was impossible, he had learned, safely to disregard either the feeling that slavery is a moral wrong or the feeling—held by an even larger portion of the public—that Negroes must not be given political and social equality.

He had now struck the core of the Republican problem in the Northwest: how to find a formula to reconcile the two opposing points of view held by great numbers of white people in the North. Lincoln's success in 1860 was due in no small part to his ability to bridge the gap, a performance that entitles him to a place among the world's great political propagandists.

To comprehend Lincoln's strategy we must keep one salient fact in mind: the abolitionists and their humanitarian sympathizers in the nation at large and particularly in the Northwest, the seat of Lincoln's strength, although numerous enough to hold the balance of power, were far too few to make a successful political party. Most of the white people of the Northwest, moreover, were in fact not only not abolitionists, but actually—and here is the core of the matter—Negrophobes. They feared and detested the very thought of living side by side with large numbers of Negroes in their own states, to say nothing of competing with their labor. Hence the severe laws against free Negroes, for example in Lincoln's Illinois.[6] Amid all the agitation in Kansas over making the territory a free state, the conduct of the majority of Republicans there was colored far more by self-interest than by moral principle. In their so-called Topeka Constitution the Kansas Republicans *forbade free Negroes even to come into the state*, and gave only to whites and Indians the right to vote. It was not bondage that troubled them—it was the Negro, free or slave. Again and again the Republican press of the Northwest referred to the Republican Party as the "White Man's Party." The motto of the leading Republican paper of Missouri, Frank Blair's *Daily Missouri Democrat*, was "White Men for Missouri and Missouri for White Men." Nothing could be more devastating to the contention that the early Republican Party in the Northwest was built upon moral principle. At the party convention of 1860 a plank endorsing the Declaration of Independence was almost hissed down and was saved only by the threat of a bolt by the antislavery element.

If the Republicans were to succeed in the strategic Northwest, how were they to win the support of both Negrophobes and antislavery men? Merely to insist that slavery was an evil would sound like abolitionism and offend the Negrophobes. Yet pitching their opposition to slavery extension on too low a moral level might lose the valued support of the humanitarians. Lincoln, perhaps

---

6. The Illinois constitutional convention of 1847 had adopted and submitted to a popular referendum a provision that instructed the legislature to pass laws prohibiting the immigration of colored persons. It was ratified by a vote of 50,261 to 21,297. If this vote can be taken as an index, the Negrophobes outnumbered their opponents by more than two to one. In 1853 the state was in effect legally closed to Negro immigration, free or slave. A Negro who entered in violation of the law was to be fined exorbitantly, and if unable to pay the fine could be sold into service. None of the states of the Northwest allowed Negro suffrage.

borrowing from the old free-soil ideology, had the right formula and exploited it. He first hinted at it in the Peoria speech:

> The whole nation is interested that the best use shall be made of these Territories. *We want them for homes of free white people. This they cannot be, to any considerable extent, if slavery shall be planted within them.* Slave States are places for poor white people to remove from, not to remove to. New free States are the places for poor people to go to, and better their condition. For this use the nation needs these Territories.

The full possibilities of this line first became clear in Lincoln's "lost" Bloomington speech, delivered at a Republican state convention in May 1856. There, according to the report of one of his colleagues at the Illinois bar, Lincoln warned that Douglas and his followers would frighten men away from the very idea of freedom with their incessant mouthing of the red-herring epithet: "Abolitionist!" "If that trick should succeed," he is reported to have said,[7] "if free negroes should be made *things,* how long, think you, before they will begin to make *things* out of poor white men?"

Here was the answer to the Republican problem. Negrophobes and abolitionists alike could understand this threat; if freedom should be broken down they might themselves have to compete with the labor of slaves in the then free states—or might even be reduced to bondage along with the blacks! Here was an argument that could strike a responsive chord in the nervous system of every Northern man, farmer or worker, abolitionist or racist: *if a stop was not put somewhere upon*

---

7. The only existing version of this speech is not a verbatim report.

*the spread of slavery, the institution would become
nation-wide.*[8] Here, too, is the practical significance of
the repeated statements Lincoln made in favor of labor
at this time. Lincoln took the slavery question out of the
realm of moral and legal dispute and, by dramatizing it
in terms of free labor's self-interest, gave it a universal
appeal. To please the abolitionists he kept saying that
slavery was an evil thing; but for the material benefit of
all Northern white men he opposed its further extension.

The importance of this argument becomes increasingly clear when it is realized that Lincoln used it in
every one of his recorded speeches from 1854 until he

---

8. Stephen A. Douglas's appeal to this fear was as strong as
Lincoln's: "Do you desire to turn this beautiful State into a
free Negro colony in order that when Missouri abolishes slavery
she can send one hundred thousand emancipated slaves into
Illinois to become citizens and voters, on an equality with yourselves?" But Douglas had no comparable appeal to antislavery
sentiment, and Lincoln was able to exploit the fact.

The conception that slavery was a menace to free labor
throughout the nation was by no means new, nor peculiar to
Lincoln. At the time of the Mexican War, Lowell had made
Hosea Biglow say:

> Wy, it's jest ez clear ez figgers,
>   Clear ez one an' one make two,
> Chaps that make black slaves o' niggers
>   Want to make white slaves o' you.

Seward, in his "Irrepressible Conflict" speech, delivered four
months after Lincoln's "House Divided" speech, declared: "The
United States must and will, sooner or later, become either entirely
a slaveholding nation or entirely a free-labor nation. Either the
cotton and rice-fields of South Carolina and the sugar plantations
of Louisiana will ultimately be tilled by free labor, and Charleston and New Orleans become marts for legitimate merchandise
alone, or else the rye-fields and wheat-fields of Massachusetts and
New York must again be surrendered by their farmers to slave
culture and to the production of slaves, and Boston and New
York become once more markets for trade in the bodies and souls
of men." But largely because Lincoln was considered more
conservative than Seward on the slavery question he was chosen
for the party nomination in 1860.

became the President-elect. He once declared in Kansas that preventing slavery from becoming a nation-wide institution "is *the purpose* of this organization [the Republican Party]." The argument had a great allure too for the immigrants who were moving in such great numbers into the Northwest. Speaking at Alton, in the heart of a county where more than fifty per cent of the population was foreign-born, Lincoln went out of his way to make it clear that he favored keeping the territories open not only for native Americans, "but as an outlet for *free white people* everywhere, the world over—in which Hans, and Baptiste, and Patrick, and all other men from all the world, may find new homes and better their condition in life."

During the debates with Douglas, Lincoln dwelt on the theme again and again, and added the charge that Douglas himself was involved in a Democratic "conspiracy . . . for the sole purpose of nationalizing slavery." [9] Douglas and the Supreme Court (which a year before had handed down the Dred Scott decision) would soon have the American people "working in the traces that tend to make this one universal slave nation." Chief Justice Taney had declared that Congress did not have the constitutional power to exclude slavery from the territories. The next step, said Lincoln, would be

> another Supreme Court decision, declaring that the Constitution of the United States does not permit a *State* to exclude slavery from its limits. . . . We shall lie down pleasantly, dreaming that the people of Missouri are on the verge of making their State free; and we shall awake to the reality instead, that the Supreme Court has made Illinois a slave State.

9. Historians have dismissed these charges as untrue. Lincoln admitted that they were based on circumstantial evidence.

So also the theme of the "House Divided" speech:

> I do not expect the Union to be dissolved—I do not ex-
> pect the House to fall—but I do expect it to cease to
> be divided. It will become all one thing or all the other.
> Either the opponents of slavery will arrest the further
> spread of it, and place it where the public mind shall rest
> in the belief that it is in the course of ultimate extinction;
> or its advocates will push it forward, till it shall become
> alike lawful in all the States, old as well as new, North as
> well as South.
> Have we no tendency to the latter condition? [10]

The last sentence is invariably omitted when this passage is quoted, perhaps because from a literary standpoint it is anticlimactic. But in Lincoln's mind—and, one
may guess, in the minds of those who heard him—it
was not anticlimactic, but essential. Lincoln was *not* emphasizing the necessity for abolition of slavery in the
near future; he was emphasizing the immediate "danger"
that slavery would become a nation-wide American in-

---

10. Lincoln is reported to have said to political friends of the
"House Divided" utterance: "I would rather be defeated with this
expression in my speech, and uphold it and discuss it before the
people,. than be victorious without it." (Herndon refused to believe it would harm him politically, assuring: "It will make you
President.") It would probably be truer to say that Lincoln was
making the great gamble of his career at this point than to say
that he was sacrificing his political prospects for a principle. He
had had his experience with pettifogging politics of the timid sort
during his Congressional phase, and it had led only to disaster.
When Joseph Medill asked Lincoln in 1862 why he had delivered "that radical speech," Lincoln answered: "Well, after
you fellows had got me into that mess and begun tempting me
with offers of the Presidency, I began to think and I made up my
mind that the next President of the United States would need to
have a stronger anti-slavery platform than mine. So I concluded
to say something." Then Lincoln asked Medill to promise not to
to repeat his answer to others.

stitution if its geographical spread were not severely restricted at once.

Once this "House Divided" speech had been made, Lincoln had to spend a great deal of time explaining it, proving that he was not an abolitionist. These efforts, together with his strategy of appealing to abolitionists and Negrophobes at once, involved him in embarrassing contradictions. In northern Illinois he spoke in one vein before abolition-minded audiences, but farther south, where settlers of Southern extraction were dominant, he spoke in another. It is instructive to compare what he said about the Negro in Chicago with what he said in Charleston.

Chicago, July 10, 1858:

> Let us discard all this quibbling about this man and the other man, this race and that race and the other race being inferior, and therefore they must be placed in an inferior position. Let us discard all these things, and unite as one people throughout this land, until we shall once more stand up declaring that all men are created equal.

Charleston, September 18, 1858:

> I will say, then, that I am not, nor ever have been, in favor of bringing about in any way the social and political equality of the white and black races [applause]: that I am not, nor ever have been, in favor of making voters or jurors of negroes, nor of qualifying them to hold office, nor to intermarry with white people. . . .
>
> And inasmuch as they cannot so live, while they do remain together there must be the position of superior and inferior, and I as much as any other man am in favor of having the superior position assigned to the white race.

It is not easy to decide whether the true Lincoln is the one who spoke in Chicago or the one who spoke in

Charleston. Possibly the man devoutly believed each of the utterances at the time he delivered it; possibly his mind too was a house divided against itself. In any case it is easy to see in all this the behavior of a professional politician looking for votes.[11]

Douglas did what he could to use Lincoln's inconsistency against him. At Galesburg, with his opponent sitting on the platform behind him, he proclaimed: "I would despise myself if I thought that I was procuring your votes by concealing my opinions, and by avowing one set of principles in one part of the state, and a different set in another." Confronted by Douglas with these clashing utterances from his Chicago and Charleston speeches, Lincoln repiled: "I have not supposed and do not now suppose, that there is any conflict whatever between them."

But this was politics—the premium was on strategy, not intellectual consistency—and the effectiveness of Lincoln's campaign is beyond dispute. In the ensuing elections the Republican candidates carried a majority

11. Lincoln was fond of asserting that the Declaration of Independence, when it said that all men are created equal, included the Negro. He believed the Negro was probably inferior to the white man, he kept repeating, but in his right to eat, without anyone's leave, the bread he earned by his own labor, the Negro was the equal of any white man. Still he was opposed to citizenship for the Negro. How any man could be expected to defend his right to enjoy the fruits of his labor without having the power to defend it through his vote, Lincoln did not say. In his Peoria speech he had himself said: "No man is good enough to govern another man, without that man's consent." In one of his magnificent private memoranda on slavery Lincoln argued that anyone who defends the moral right of slavery creates an ethic by which his own enslavement may be justified. ("Fragment on Slavery," 1854.) But the same reasoning also applies to anyone who would deny the Negro citizenship. It is impossible to avoid the conclusion that so far as the Negro was concerned, Lincoln could not escape the moral insensitivity that is characteristic of the average white American.

of the voters and elected their state officers for the first time. Douglas returned to the Senate only because the Democrats, who had skillfully gerrymandered the election districts, still held their majority in the state legislature. Lincoln had contributed greatly to welding old-line Whigs and antislavery men into an effective party, and his reputation was growing by leaps and bounds. What he had done was to pick out an issue—the alleged plan to extend slavery, the alleged danger that it would spread throughout the nation—which would turn attention from the disintegrating forces in the Republican Party to the great integrating force. He was keenly aware that the party was built out of extremely heterogeneous elements, frankly speaking of it in his "House Divided" speech as composed of "strange, discordant, and even hostile elements." In addition to abolitionists and Negrophobes, it united high- and low-tariff men, hard- and soft-money men, former Whigs and former Democrats embittered by old political fights, Maine-law prohibitionists and German tipplers, Know-Nothings and immigrants. Lincoln's was the masterful diplomacy to hold such a coalition together, carry it into power, and with it win a war.

Lincoln may have become involved in a gross inconsistency over slavery and the Negro, but this was incidental to his main concern. Never much troubled about the Negro, he had always been most deeply interested in the fate of free republicanism and its bearing upon the welfare of the common white man with whom he identified himself. On this count there was an underlying coherence in the logic of his career. His thesis that slavery might become national, although probably without factual foundation,[12] was a clever dialectical inversion of a challenge to the freedom of the common white man set forth by the most extreme Southern advocate of slavery. George Fitzhugh, a Virginia lawyer, had written and published a volume in 1854 entitled *Sociology for the South,* in which he carried to its logical conclusion the proslavery argument laid down by men like Calhoun. These men had said that Northern industrialism was brutal in its treatment of free labor, while Southern slavery was relatively kind to the Negro. Fitzhugh insisted that since slavery is the best condition for labor, all

---

12. Historians are in general agreement with such contemporaries of Lincoln as Clay, Webster, Douglas, and Hammond that the natural limits of slavery expansion in the continental United States had already been reached. But even if slavery had spread into new territories, it hardly follows that it would have spread into the free states of the North.

As to the territories, if natural causes were not sufficient to keep slavery from going there, Douglas's popular sovereignty probably would have done so. The free population of the North was expanding far more rapidly than the South's population, and it was much more mobile. Many Republicans accepted Douglas's assurances that slavery would be kept out of the territories by action of local settlers alone. After Douglas split with the more Southern faction of the Democratic Party headed by President Buchanan, there was even a movement among Republicans to coalesce with him and offer him the presidential nomination in 1860 on a popular-sovereignty platform! Why, it was reasoned, should opponents of the extension of slavery try to exclude it from the territories by an act of Congress that would be a gratuitous insult to the South, if the same end could be served by letting geography and popular sovereignty have their way? Part of Lincoln's achievement in the Lincoln-Douglas debates was to taunt Douglas into statements that made him absolutely unpalatable to free-soil Republicans. But the supreme irony can be found in the fact that early in 1861 the Republicans in Congress gave their votes to measures organizing the territories of Colorado, Nevada, and Dakota *without prohibiting slavery.* After beating Douglas in 1860, they organized the territories along the pattern of his policy, not Lincoln's.

labor, black or white, should be owned by capital. "Slavery," Fitzhugh predicted, "will everywhere be abolished, or everywhere be re-instituted." Herndon had shown the volume to Lincoln, and Lincoln had read it with mounting anger and loathing. Although a half-dozen Southern papers had toyed with his thesis, Fitzhugh was not taken too seriously in the South, but Lincoln seized upon his ultra-reactionary ideas as a symbol.[13]

Even as early as 1856 the Republicans had been exploiting the theme of the menace of slavery to free labor. The party put out a campaign pamphlet entitled: *The New Democratic Doctrine: Slavery not to be confined to the Negro race, but to be made the universal condition of the laboring classes of society. The supporters of this doctrine vote for Buchanan.* Lincoln carefully cut out the following editorial from a Southern paper and pasted it in his campaign scrapbook:

Free society! We sicken of the name! What is it but a conglomeration of greasy mechanics, filthy operatives, small-fisted farmers, and moon-struck theorists? All the Northern and especially the New England states are devoid of society fitted for well bred gentlemen. The prevailing class one meets is that of mechanics struggling to be genteel, and small farmers who do their own drudgery; and yet are hardly fit for association with a southern gen-

---

13. Some of Lincoln's devices were a little sharp. A Springfield newspaper, the *Conservative,* opposed him and spoke in moderate language for acquiescence in extending slavery. Herndon, who knew the editor of the *Conservative,* once came upon an article in the Richmond *Enquirer* justifying slavery for both black and white laborers, à la Fitzhugh. Lincoln observed that it would be helpful if Illinois proslavery papers would take up such an extreme and vulnerable position. Herndon, with Lincoln's permission, induced the editor of the *Conservative* to reprint the *Enquirer*'s article with approval. The editor fell for the scheme and his paper was "almost ruined" as a result.

tleman's body servant. This is your free society which the northern hordes are endeavoring to extend to Kansas.

This was the direct antithesis of everything that Lincoln had been taught to believe—the equality of man, the dignity of labor, and the right to move upward in the social scale. It defied the beliefs of millions of free men in the North who, like Lincoln, were ambitious to move forward and believed that the most sacred thing free society could do was to give to the common man freedom and opportunity to make his own way. When Lincoln debated Douglas at Galesburg, Republican supporters carried a huge banner reading: "Small Fisted Farmers, Mud-sills of Society, Greasy Mechanics for A. Lincoln."

Flouting the aspirations of free labor cost the Southerners dear. The current of proslavery reaction had run its course, and it was somehow fitting that a man like Lincoln should use ideas like Fitzhugh's to destroy the Old South.

V

Before Lincoln took office the issues upon which he was elected had become obsolete. Seven states of the deep South had seceded. The great question was no longer slavery or freedom in the territories, but the nation itself. The Union, if it was to be maintained, as Lincoln, an ardent nationalist, thought it must, could be defended only by the sort of aggressive war that few Northerners wanted to wage. Psychologically on the defensive, the North had to be strategically on the offensive. One of Lincoln's most striking achievements was his tactical and ideological resolution of this difficulty.

By all rational calculation the Confederacy had much to lose and nothing to gain by war. Its strategic aim was merely to preserve itself as an independent state, an end that could be lost in war and achieved in peace. The North, on the other hand, once compromise and reconciliation had failed, had to wage a successful coercive war in order to restore the Union. Northern public opinion, which was in fierce agreement on the desirability of maintaining the Union, was reluctant to consider what saving the Union might cost. There was no more unanimity in the North on waging war to keep the Union than there had been in the South on seceding to destroy it. *Always there loomed the danger that an apparently unprovoked attack upon the Confederacy would alienate so many people in the Union and the world at large that it would hopelessly cripple the very cause for which the war would be fought.* Such an attack would certainly lose the support of the border states, still not withdrawn from the Union, which Lincoln was desperately eager to hold. He had deferred to this sentiment in his Inaugural Address, saying to the South: "The government will not assail you. You can have no conflict without being yourselves the aggressors."

And still there were the forts, the troublesome forts belonging to the government of the United States but located in Confederate territory. Particularly urgent was the problem of Fort Sumter, so placed in the mouth of Charleston harbor that it could hardly be reinforced without subjecting Union ships to the fire of Confederate batteries. Already Major Anderson's men there were running short of supplies and calling for help.

The situation had all the elements of a dilemma for both sides. But since Lincoln had to act first to save the fort from starvation, his was the initial problem. He had promised to maintain the Union, and protect, preserve, and defend the Constitution. It was now too late to restore the Union by compromise, because the Republican leaders, with his advice and consent, had rejected compromise in December.[14] To order Anderson to withdraw Fort Sumter's garrison at the demand of the Confederates was a tremendous concession, which Lincoln actually considered but rejected; it would be an implicit acknowledgment of the legality of secession, and the Union would, by his own recognition, be at an end; the moral stock of the Confederacy would go soaring. And yet a military assault to bring relief to the fort would be a dangerous expedient. If it failed, it would ruin the already diminished prestige of his administration; success or failure, it would be looked upon by peace advocates and the border states as wanton aggression. However, there was one way out: the Confederates themselves might bring matters to a head by attacking Sumter before Anderson should be forced by shortages to evacuate.

It was precisely such an attack that Lincoln's strategy brought about. On March 29, 1861 the Secretaries of War and the Navy were ordered to co-operate in preparing a relief expedition to move by sea on April 6. Governor Pickens of South Carolina was notified that an attempt would be made to supply Fort Sumter *"with provisions only,"* and not with arms, and was advised by Lincoln that "if such an attempt be not resisted, no

---

14. Always a good party man, Lincoln feared the Republican Party would disintegrate if it sacrificed the one principle its variegated supporters held in common. Compromise, he wrote Thurlow Weed, December 17, 1860, "would lose us everything we gain by the election . . . would be the end of us."

effort to throw in men, arms, or ammunition will be made without further notice, or [*sic*] in case of an attack upon the fort."

To Northern opinion such a relief expedition would seem innocent enough—bringing food to hungry men. But to the Confederacy it posed a double threat: force would be used *if* the attempt to provision the fort were resisted; and should it not be resisted, an indefinite occupation by Union forces could be expected, which would weaken the Confederate cause at home and sap its prestige abroad, where diplomatic recognition was so precious. Lincoln had now taken the burden of the dilemma from his own shoulders and forced it upon the Southerners. Now they must either attack the fort and accept the onus of striking the first blow, or face an indefinite and enervating occupation of Sumter by Anderson's soldiers. Could any supposedly sovereign government permit a foreign power to hold a fort dominating the trade of one of its few great harbors? As Professor James G. Randall has observed, the logic of secession demanded that the Confederates take the fort or that the Union abandon it.

Major Anderson refused a demand for prompt evacuation. Knowing that the Union relief fleet was approaching, the Confederates on the morning of April 12 began firing upon Sumter, and thus convicted themselves by an act of aggression. They had not only broken the Union, they had attacked it; and the reception of the deed at the North was everything that Lincoln could wish.

Lincoln's secretaries, Nicolay and Hay, observe in their monumental biography:

Abstractly it was enough that the Government was in the right. But to make the issue sure, he [Lincoln] determined that in addition the rebellion should be put in the wrong. . . . When he finally gave the order that the

fleet should sail he was master of the situation . . .
master if the rebels hesitated or repented, because they
would thereby forfeit their prestige with the South; master if they persisted, for he would then command a united
North.

Nicolay, in his *Outbreak of Rebellion,* asserted his belief that it was Lincoln's carefully matured purpose to
force rebellion to put itself flagrantly and fatally in the
wrong by attacking Fort Sumter. But there is even more
intimate evidence of Lincoln's intention. On July 3 the
newly appointed Senator from Illinois, Orville Browning
(chosen to replace Douglas, who had just died), called
upon Lincoln and held a conversation with him. Fortunately Browning kept a diary, and his entry for that
evening reads:

> He [Lincoln] told me that the very first thing placed
> in his hands after his inauguration was a letter from Majr.
> Anderson announcing the impossibility of defending or
> relieving Sumter. That he called the cabinet together and
> consulted Genl Scott—that Scott concurred with Ander-
> son, and the cabinet, with the exception of P M Genl
> Blair were for evacuating the Fort, and all the troubles
> and anxieties of his life had not equalled those which
> intervened between this time and the fall of Sumter. He
> himself conceived the idea, and proposed sending sup-
> plies, without an attempt to reinforce [,] giving notice of
> the fact to Gov Pickens of S. C. *The plan succeeded. They
> attacked Sumter—it fell, and thus, did more service than
> it otherwise could.*

If we may trust Browning, who was one of Lincoln's
friends, it was the Confederate attack and not the military success of the expedition that mattered most. In a
letter to Gustavus Vasa Fox, the extraordinary naval

officer who had led the relief attempt, Lincoln concluded, "You and I both anticipated that the cause of the country would be advanced by making the attempt to provision Fort Sumter, even if it should fail; and it is no small consolation now to feel that our anticipation is justified by the result."

This realistic bit of statecraft provides no reason for disparaging Lincoln, certainly not by those who hold that it was his legal and moral duty to defend the integrity of the Union by the most effective means at his command.[15] The Confederate attack made it possible to picture the war as a defensive one;[16] for some time it unified Northern sentiment. Who can say with certainty that the war could have been won on any other terms?

There was, for all this, a tremendous incongruity in Lincoln as a war leader. He did not want war; he wanted Union, and accepted war only when it seemed necessary to the Union. He had always been pre-eminently a man of peace. Probably the only time in his early political career when he seriously exposed himself by taking an unpopular stand on an important issue had been the

15. Professor Kenneth Stampp concludes in his admirable review of the Sumter incident: "Although Lincoln accepted the possibility of war, which, in retrospect at least, was the inevitable consequence of his strategy of defense . . . the burden rested not on Lincoln alone, but on the universal standards of statesmanship and on the whole concept of "national interest". . . . The fact remains that southern leaders shared with Lincoln the responsibility for a resort to force. They too preferred war to submission."

16. "They well knew," said Lincoln of the Confederates in his July message to Congress, "that the garrison in the fort could by no possibility commit aggression upon them. They knew—they were expressly notified—that the giving of bread to the few brave and hungry men of the garrison was all which would on that occasion be attempted, unless themselves, by resisting so much, should provoke more."

occasion of his opposition to the Mexican War. His speech before Congress in 1848 ridiculing his own participation in the Black Hawk War is one of the classics of American frontier humor.

Evidently he did not expect a long fight. His first call for 75,000 volunteers required a three months' enlistment. (These figures must have come back to haunt him: in four years the war took some 618,000 lives on both sides.) But it soon enough became clear that the struggle would not be brief or easy. In a short time it loomed up as one of the major crises of modern history. To Lincoln fell the task of interpreting it to his people and the world.

There need be no doubt as to how Lincoln saw the conflict; he had innumerable occasions to state his view of it to Congress, to the country, even to foreign workingmen. It was, of course, a war to preserve the Union; but the Union itself was a means to an end. The Union meant free popular government, "government of the people, by the people, for the people." [17] But popular government is something deeper and more valuable than a mere system of political organization: it is a system of social life that gives the common man a chance. Here Lincoln returns again to his favorite theme—the stupendous value to mankind of the free-labor system. "This," he asserts gravely in his first extended message to Congress,

> is essentially a people's contest. On the side of the Union it is a struggle for maintaining in the world that form and substance of a government whose leading object is to elevate the condition of men—to lift artificial weights

---

17. In conversation with John Hay, Lincoln said: "For my own part, I consider the first necessity that is upon us, is of proving that popular government is not an absurdity."

from all shoulders; to clear the paths of laudable pursuit for all; to afford all an unfettered start, and a fair chance in the race of life . . . this is the leading object of the government for whose existence we contend.

Such popular government has often been called an experiment, he went on, but two phases of the experiment have already been successfully concluded: the establishing and administering of it. There remains a final test—"its successful maintenance against a formidable internal attempt to overthrow it." The people must now demonstrate to the world that those who can fairly win an election can defeat a rebellion, and that the power of government which has been honestly lost by ballots cannot be won back by bullets. "Such will be a great lesson of peace: teaching men that what they cannot take by an election, neither can they take it by a war; teaching all the folly of being the beginners of a war."

Then there was his superb formulation of an everlasting problem of republican politics: "Must a government, of necessity, be too strong for the liberties of its own people, or too weak to maintain its own existence?"

Thus, skillfully, Lincoln inverted the main issue of the war to suit his purpose. What the North was waging, of course, was a war to save the Union by denying self-determination to the majority of Southern whites. But Lincoln, assisted by the blessed fact that the Confederates had struck the first blow, presented it as a war to defend not only Union but the sacred principles of popular rule and opportunity for the common man.

Here is a war aim couched in the language of Lincoln's old ideal, the language that had helped to make him President. Notice that while it is politically on the radical or "popular" side of the fight, it is historically conservative: it aims to preserve a long-established order that has well served the common man in the past. The Union is on the *defensive,* resisting "a war upon the rights of all working people." Sometimes Lincoln's language is frankly conservative. No men living, he insists, "are more worthy to be trusted than those who toil up from poverty. . . . Let them beware of *surrendering a political power which they already possess,* and which, if surrendered, will surely be used to close the door of advancement against such as they, and to fix *new* disabilities and burdens upon them, till all of liberty shall be lost." Again: "There is involved in this struggle the question whether your children and my children shall enjoy the privileges we have enjoyed."

Such being his conception of the meaning of the struggle, is it not understandable that Lincoln thinks in terms of restoring in its pristine simplicity that which has gone before? Is it not understandable that he sets for his cause no such revolutionary goal as destroying the South's social fabric? Bring the South back, save the Union, restore orderly government, establish the principle that force cannot win out, and do it with the least cost in lives and travail—there is the Lincoln program. The tremendous forces of social revolution storm about his head, and in the end he bows to them. But not without doubt and hesitation. Not even without a struggle against his own destiny to become the symbol of freedom.

VI

From the beginning, then, everything was subordinate to the cause of Union. In his Inaugural Address Lincoln repeated with pathetic vehemence his several earlier assurances that slavery would not be attacked in the states. He went farther. Congress had recently passed a constitutional amendment guaranteeing that the federal government would never interfere with slavery. Should the amendment be ratified by the states, it would nourish bondage for an epoch by fixing slavery fast in the constitutional structure of the nation. It would expressly make emancipation impossible except by voluntary action of the states severally. Although it was no part of his constitutional function, Lincoln did what he could to speed this amendment toward ratification by announcing that he considered it only an explicit statement of what was already implicit in the Constitution—"I have no objection to its being made express and irrevocable."

When war came, its goal was almost universally considered in the North to be as Lincoln declared it—to bring back the South *with slavery intact.* So general was this sentiment that when the aged John J. Crittenden of Kentucky introduced into Congress on the day after Bull Run a resolution declaring that the war was not being waged for conquest or subjugation nor to interfere with "the established institutions" of the seceded states, even Republicans of Jacobin leanings were afraid to vote against it. When Lincoln declared to Congress that he was determined not to allow the war to "degenerate into a violent and remorseless revolutionary struggle," he only voiced the initial opinion of a vast majority of Northerners. But before the war was eight months old, the House had significantly refused to re-enact the Crittenden resolution. Lincoln's mind would not change so readily.

As the conflict wore on, the difficulties of fighting a war against a slave power without fighting slavery became painfully evident. Fugitive slaves began to make their way into the Union lines. How were the generals to deal with them? In August 1861 the abolitionist General Frémont, sorely tried by guerrilla warfare in Missouri, declared martial law and proclaimed that all slaves of local owners resisting the United States were freemen. After failing to induce Frémont to revoke his proclamation voluntarily, Lincoln promptly countermanded it. Later he overruled an order of General David Hunter freeing slaves in Georgia, Florida, and South Carolina.

Antislavery men everywhere became impatient with this mode of conducting the war. They were fighting a power based on the labor of slaves, the greatest single wartime resource of the Confederacy. Not only did the administration refuse to issue an injunction to the slaves to free themselves and cease working for the secession cause, but it even withheld freedom from the blacks in those regions where its armies were penetrating the South. Fighting an attack upon the Constitution with the nicest constitutional methods had become preposterous.

Lincoln had genuine constitutional scruples, but his conservatism in everything pertaining to slavery was also dictated by political and strategic considerations. He was determined to hold the loyalty of the four border states, Maryland, Kentucky, Missouri, and Delaware, all of which were unwilling to participate in an antislavery crusade. The three larger states, as a glance at the map will show, were vital to Union strategy and to the safety of the capital itself. They were also contributing soldiers to the cause. Frémont's action, Lincoln reported, had had an extremely unfavorable effect on the Kentucky legislature, and in the field a whole company of volunteers upon hearing it had thrown down their arms and disbanded. Further, a great section of conservative Northern opinion was willing to fight for the Union but might refuse to support a war to free Negroes, and kept insisting that the war would become more bitter if the South saw that it was fighting avowed abolitionism. In everything he did, Lincoln had to reckon with the political potential of this sentiment, and he well understood its power, for it was of a piece with the old anti-Negro feeling he had always known in Illinois politics.

To become President, Lincoln had had to talk more radically on occasion than he actually felt; to be an effective President he was compelled to act more conservatively than he wanted. The Radicals raged against him with increasing bitterness, and concluded, as one of their representatives reported after an interview, that he had "no antislavery instincts." As the war lengthened, Radical sentiment became stronger. Lincoln was in no position to thrust aside the demands of the very element in the country that supported the war most wholeheartedly. Men who had never thought of attacking the South's peculiar institution before secession were now ready to destroy it in the most abrupt and ruthless way if by so doing they could hasten the end of the war. They argued that it was self-contradictory to fight the war without smashing slavery and with it the South's entire social structure. Calculating Republican leaders pointed out that to win the war without destroying the slave-owning class would only

> bring back the rebel States into full fellowship as members of the Union, with their full delegations in both Houses of Congress. They, with the pro-slavery conservatives of the border States and the Democrats of the Northern states, will control Congress. Republicans and Republican principles will be in the minority under law, and this latter state would be worse than the former—worse than war itself.

There was, then, a logic to social revolution that Lincoln was vainly trying to override. He proposed the impossible, as Harry Williams has remarked: "to conduct the war for the preservation of the status quo which had produced the war."

Lincoln surveyed the scene with his extraordinary brooding detachment, and waited. (He had, reported Charles Francis Adams, Jr., "a mild, dreamy, meditative eye, which one would scarcely expect to see in a successful chief magistrate in these days of the republic.") He listened to the protests and denunciations of the Radicals and their field agents throughout the country, and politely heard abolition delegations to the White House. Like a delicate barometer, he recorded the trend of pressures, and as the Radical pressure increased he moved toward the left. To those who did not know him, it seemed that he did so reluctantly. The Radicals watched his progress with grim satisfaction—with the feeling, as Wendell Phillips expressed it, that if Lincoln was able to grow, "it is because we have watered him." But it is significant that such a haughty and impatient abolitionist as Senator Charles Sumner developed a deep respect and affection for Lincoln. According to one report, Lincoln said one day to Sumner: "We'll fetch 'em; just give us a little time. . . . I should never have had votes enough to send me here, if the people had supposed I should try to use my veto power to upset slavery." To two famous Unitarian clergymen, William Ellery Channing and Moncure D. Conway, he observed that the masses of the people were concerned only about military success and remained indifferent to the Negro. He added: "We shall need all the anti-slavery feeling in the country and more; you can go home and try to bring the people to your views; and you may say anything you like about me, if that will help. Don't spare me!"

It was all in keeping with his profound fatalism. He had always believed—and in conversations at Springfield had often told Herndon of his faith—that events are governed (the words are Herndon's) "by certain irrefragable and irresistible laws, and that no prayers of ours could arrest their operation in the least . . . that what was to be would be inevitable." It was the conviction of a man without haste and without malice, but it was not the philosophy of a reformer. Back in Illinois, Douglas, knowing and respecting Lincoln, had been asked if he was not a weak man. No, replied the Little Giant, but "he is preeminently a man of the atmosphere that surrounds him." Looking back upon events in 1864, Lincoln could say with a profound modesty: "I claim not to have controlled events but confess plainly that events have controlled me." As the Radicals gained in strength, he conducted a brilliant strategic retreat toward a policy of freedom.

To say that Lincoln's approach to the slavery question was governed by his penchant for philosophic resignation is not to say that he had no policy of his own. His program flowed from his conception that his role was to be a moderator of extremes in public sentiment. It called for compensated emancipation (at first in the loyal border states) assisted by federal funds, to be followed at length by deportation and colonization of the freed Negroes. To a member of the Senate he wrote in 1862 that the cost of freeing with compensation all slaves in the four border states and the District of Columbia, at an average price of four hundred dollars per slave, would come to less than the cost of eighty-seven days of the war. Further, he believed that taking such action would shorten the war by more than eighty-seven days and "thus be an actual saving of expense." Despite the gross note of calculation at the end (one rescues 432,000 human beings from slavery and it turns out to be a saving of expense), the proposal was a reasonable and statesmanlike one, and it is incredible that the intransigence of all but one of the states involved should have consigned it to defeat.

The alternative idea of colonizing the Negroes abroad was and always had been pathetic. There had been in existence for a generation an active movement to colonize the slaves, but it had not sent out of the country more than the tiniest fraction of the annual increase of the slave population. By 1860 its fantastic character must have been evident to every American who was not determined to deceive himself. Nevertheless, when a deputation of colored men came to see Lincoln in the summer of 1862, he tried to persuade them to set up a colony in Central America, which, he said, stood on one of the world's highways and provided a country of "great natural resources and advantages." "If I could find twenty-five able-bodied men, with a mixture of women and children," he added, with marvelous naïveté, ". . . I could make a successful commencement."

Plainly Lincoln was, as always, thinking primarily of the free white worker: the Negro was secondary. The submerged whites of the South and the wage workers of the North feared the prospect of competing with the labor of liberated blacks. The venerable idea of deporting emancipated Negroes, fantastic though it was, grew logically out of a caste psychology in a competitive labor market. Lincoln assured Congress that emancipation would not lower wage standards of white labor even if the freedmen were not deported. But if they were deported, "enhanced wages to white labor is mathematically certain. . . . Reduce the supply of black labor by colonizing the black laborer out of the country, and by precisely so much you increase the demand for, and wages of, white labor."

In the summer of 1862 Congress passed a Confiscation Act providing that the slaves of all persons supporting the rebellion should be forever free. The Radicals had also proposed to make the measure retroactive and to provide for permanent forfeiture of the real estate of rebels. Lincoln was adamant about these features, and had no enthusiasm for the act in general, but finally signed a bill that had been modified according to his demands. Even with these concessions the Radicals had scored a triumph and forced Lincoln part way toward emancipation. He had prevented them from destroying the landed basis of the Southern aristocracy, but he had put his signature, however reluctantly, to a measure that freed the slaves of all persons found guilty of disloyalty; freed them on paper, at least, for the act was unenforceable during the war. It also guaranteed that escaped slaves would no longer be sent back to work for disloyal masters, and in this respect freed some slaves in reality.

When Lincoln at last determined, in July 1862, to move toward emancipation, it was only after all his other policies had failed. The Crittenden Resolution had been rejected, the border states had quashed his plan of compensated emancipation, his generals were still floundering, and he had already lost the support of great numbers of conservatives. The Proclamation became necessary to hold his remaining supporters and to forestall— so he believed—English recognition of the Confederacy. "I would save the Union," he wrote in answer to Horace Greeley's cry for emancipation. ". . . If I could save the Union without freeing any slave, I would do it; and if I could do it by freeing all the slaves, I would do it." In the end, freeing all the slaves seemed necessary.

It was evidently an unhappy frame of mind in which Lincoln resorted to the Emancipation Proclamation. "Things had gone from bad to worse," he told the artist F. B. Carpenter a year later, "until I felt that we had reached the end of our rope on the plan of operations we had been pursuing; that we had about played our last card, and must change our tactics, or lose the game. I now determined upon the adoption of the emancipation policy. . . ." The passage has a wretched tone: things had gone from bad to worse, and as a result the slaves were to be declared free!

The Emancipation Proclamation of January 1, 1863 had all the moral grandeur of a bill of lading. It contained no indictment of slavery, but simply based emancipation on "military necessity." It expressly omitted the loyal slave states from its terms. Finally, it did not in fact free any slaves. For it excluded by detailed enumeration from the sphere covered in the Proclamation all the counties in Virginia and parishes in Louisiana that were occupied by Union troops and into which the government actually had the power to bring freedom. It simply declared free all slaves in "the States and parts of States" where the people were in rebellion—that is to say, precisely where its effect could not reach.[18] Beyond its propaganda value the Proclamation added nothing to what Congress had already done in the Confiscation Act.

Seward remarked of the Proclamation: "We show our sympathy with slavery by emancipating the slaves where we cannot reach them and holding them in bondage where we can set them free." The London *Spectator*

18. There was also a cautious injunction to the "liberated" slaves "to abstain from all violence, unless in necessary self-defense," and another to "labor faithfully for reasonable wages." The latter has a sardonic ring.

gibed: "The principle is not that a human being cannot justly own another, but that he cannot own him unless he is loyal to the United States."

But the Proclamation was what it was because the average sentiments of the American Unionist of 1862 were what they were. Had the political strategy of the moment called for a momentous human document of the stature of the Declaration of Independence, Lincoln could have risen to the occasion. Perhaps the largest reasonable indictment of him is simply that in such matters he was a follower and not a leader of public opinion. It may be that there was in Lincoln something of the old Kentucky poor white, whose regard for the slaves was more akin to his feeling for tortured animals than it was to his feeling, say, for the common white man of the North. But it is only the intensity and not the genuineness of his antislavery sentiments that can be doubted. His conservatism arose in part from a sound sense for the pace of historical change. He knew that formal freedom for the Negro, coming suddenly and without preparation, would not be real freedom, and in this respect he understood the slavery question better than most of the Radicals, just as they had understood better than he the revolutionary dynamics of the war.

For all its limitations, the Emancipation Proclamation probably made genuine emancipation inevitable. In all but five of the states freedom was accomplished in fact through the thirteenth amendment. Lincoln's own part in the passing of this amendment was critical. He used all his influence to get the measure the necessary two-thirds vote in the House of Representatives, and it was finally carried by a margin of three votes. Without his influence the amendment might have been long delayed, though it is hardly conceivable that it could have been held off indefinitely. Such claim as he may have to be

remembered as an Emancipator perhaps rests more
justly on his behind-the-scenes activity for the thirteenth
amendment than on the Proclamation itself. It was the
Proclamation, however, that had psychological value,
and before the amendment was passed, Lincoln had already become the personal symbol of freedom. Believing that he was called only to conserve, he had turned
liberator in spite of himself:

*"I claim not to have controlled events but confess
plainly that events have controlled me."*

VII

Lincoln was shaken by the presidency. Back in Springfield, politics had been a sort of exhilarating game; but
in the White House, politics was power, and power was
responsibility. Never before had Lincoln held executive
office. In public life he had always been an insignificant
legislator whose votes were cast in concert with others
and whose decisions in themselves had neither finality
nor importance. As President he might consult others,
but innumerable grave decisions were in the end his
own, and with them came a burden of responsibility ter-
rifying in its dimensions.

Lincoln's rage for personal success, his external and
worldly ambition, was quieted when he entered the
White House, and he was at last left alone to reckon
with himself. To be confronted with the fruits of his victory only to find that it meant choosing between life and
death for others was immensely sobering. That Lincoln
should have shouldered the moral burden of the war was
characteristic of the high seriousness into which he had
grown since 1854; and it may be true, as Professor

Charles W. Ramsdell suggested, that he was stricken by an awareness of his own part in whipping up the crisis. This would go far to explain the desperation with which he issued pardons and the charity that he wanted to extend to the conquered South at the war's close. In one of his rare moments of self-revelation he is reported to have said: "Now I don't know what the soul is, but whatever it is, I know that it can humble itself." The great prose of the presidential years came from a soul that had been humbled. Lincoln's utter lack of personal malice during these years, his humane detachment, his tragic sense of life, have no parallel in political history.

"Lincoln," said Herndon, "is a man of heart—aye, as gentle as a woman's and as tender. . . ." Lincoln was moved by the wounded and dying men, moved as no one in a place of power can afford to be. He had won high office by means sometimes rugged, but once there, he found that he could not quite carry it off. For him it was impossible to drift into the habitual callousness of the sort of officialdom that sees men only as pawns to be shifted here and there and "expended" at the will of others. It was a symbolic thing that his office was so constantly open, that he made himself more accessible than any other chief executive in our history. "Men moving only in an official circle," he told Carpenter, "are apt to become merely official—not to say arbitrary—in their ideas, and are apter and apter with each passing day to forget that they only hold power in a representative capacity." Is it possible to recall anyone else in modern history who could exercise so much power and yet feel so slightly the private corruption that goes with it? Here, perhaps, is the best measure of Lincoln's personal eminence in the human calendar—that he was chastened and not intoxicated by power. It was almost apologetically that he remarked in response to a White

House serenade after his re-election that "So long as I have been here, I have not willingly planted a thorn in any man's bosom."

There were many thorns planted in *his* bosom. The criticism was hard to bear (perhaps hardest of all that from the abolitionists, which he knew had truth in it). There was still in him a sensitivity that the years of knock-about politics had not killed, the remarkable depths of which are suddenly illumined by a casual sentence written during one of the crueler outbursts of the opposition press. Reassuring the apologetic actor James Hackett, who had unwittingly aroused a storm of hostile laughter by publishing a confidential letter, Lincoln added that he was quite used to it: "I have received a great deal of ridicule without much malice; and have received a great deal of kindness, not quite free from ridicule."

The presidency was not something that could be enjoyed. Remembering its barrenness for him, one can believe that the life of Lincoln's soul was almost entirely without consummation. Sandburg remarks that there were thirty-one rooms in the White House and that Lincoln was not at home in any of them. This was the house for which he had sacrificed so much!

As the months passed, a deathly weariness settled over him. Once when Noah Brooks suggested that he rest, he replied: "I suppose it is good for the body. But the tired part of me is *inside* and out of reach." There had always been a part of him, inside and out of reach, that had looked upon his ambition with detachment and wondered if the game was worth the candle. Now he could see the truth of what he had long dimly known and perhaps hopefully suppressed—that for a man of sensitivity and compassion to exercise great powers in a time of crisis is a grim and agonizing thing. Instead of glory, he once said, he had found only "ashes and blood." This was, for him, the end product of that success myth by which he had lived and for which he had been so persuasive a spokesman. He had had his ambitions and fulfilled them, and met heartache in his triumph.

CHAPTER VI

WENDELL PHILLIPS:
THE PATRICIAN AS AGITATOR

❧

COLLEGE *bred men should be agitators to tear a question open and riddle it with light and to educate the moral sense of the masses.* WENDELL PHILLIPS

THE historical reputation of Wendell Phillips stands very low. With the single exception of V. L. Parrington, the standard writers have been handling him roughly for over forty years. Finding him useful chiefly as a foil to Abraham Lincoln, historians have stereotyped him as the wrongheaded radical of the Civil War crisis—an emotional person, lacking in responsibility, but quick to condemn those who had it, standing always for extremes that public opinion would not sustain, reckless, mischievous, and vindictive.

But conventional historians in condemning men like Phillips have used a double standard of political morality. Scholars know that the processes of politics normally involve exaggeration, mythmaking, and fierce animosities. In the pursuit of their ends the abolitionists were hardly more guilty of these things than the more conventional politicians were in theirs. Somehow the same historians who have been indulgent with men who exaggerated because they wanted to be elected

175

have been extremely severe with men who exaggerated because they wanted to free the slaves.

And Phillips is vulnerable. He was an agitator by profession, and the agitator is always vulnerable. Horace Greeley cleverly—but untruthfully—said of him that he was so lacking in largeness of views that "he cannot conceive of a tempest outside of a teapot." Dozens of irresponsible utterances can be combed out of his speeches. "The South," he once said, "is one great brothel, where half a million of women are flogged to prostitution," and the sentence has made its way into innumerable histories of the slavery controversy as an illustration of the abolitionist mentality.[1] The generation of historians that has condemned this as a distortion has also chosen to ignore the vital subject of miscegenation and the light it throws upon the slave system and its caste psychology. It is hard to say which distortion is the more serious, but the advantage in controversy will always rest with the academic historian who can fall back upon the pose of scholarly impartiality to substantiate his claims.

Phillips was in some ways more sophisticated than those who condemn him. Certainly he had attained a higher level of intellectual self-awareness. Both historians and agitators are makers of myths, a fact of which Phillips was intensely conscious, but while few historians of the slavery controversy have had a reasoned philosophy of history, Phillips had a reasoned philosophy of agitation. The work of the agitator, he saw, consists chiefly in talk; his function is not to make

---

1. The qualification with which Phillips's sentence ends: "or, worse still, are degraded to believe it honorable," is generally omitted when he is quoted.

laws or determine policy, but to influence the public mind in the interest of some large social transformation. His role in society is vastly different from the responsible politician's, and rightly so:

> The reformer is careless of numbers, disregards popularity, and deals only with ideas, conscience, and common sense. He feels, with Copernicus, that as God waited long for an interpreter, so he can wait for his followers. He neither expects nor is overanxious for immediate success. The politician dwells in an everlasting NOW. His motto is "Success"—his aim, votes. His object is not absolute right, but, like Solon's laws, as much right as the people will sanction. His office is not to instruct public opinion, but to represent it. Thus, in England, Cobden, the reformer, created sentiment, and Peel, the politician, stereotyped it into statutes.

The agitator is necessary to a republican commonwealth; he is the counterweight to sloth and indifference.

> Republics exist only on the tenure of being constantly agitated. The antislavery agitation is an important, nay, an essential part of the machinery of the state. . . . Every government is always growing corrupt. Every Secretary of State . . . is an enemy to the people of necessity, because the moment he joins the government, he gravitates against that popular agitation which is the life of a republic. A republic is nothing but a constant overflow of lava. . . . The republic which sinks to sleep, trusting to constitutions and machinery, to politicians and statesmen, for the safety of its liberties, never will have any.

Like many other Americans of his period, Phillips had an unconquerable faith in moral progress. He believed that he was living in an age of ideas—a democratic age, in which the ideas of the masses were the important thing. There was no higher office, he felt, than exercising the moral imagination necessary to mold the sentiments of the masses into the form most suitable for the next forward movement of history. "The people always mean right, and in the end they will have the right." The man who launches a sound argument for a just cause is certain to win in the long run. "The difficulty of the present day and with us is, we are bullied by institutions. . . . Stand on the pedestal of your own individual independence, summon these institutions about you, and judge them."

Phillips's career illustrates the principle that the agitator is likely to be a crisis thinker. In periods of relative social peace the agitator labors under intellectual as well as practical restraints, for he thinks in terms of the *ultimate potentialities* of social conflicts rather than the immediate compromises by which they are softened. His moral judgments are made from the standpoint of absolute values, with which the mass of men cannot comfortably live. But when a social crisis or revolutionary period at last matures, the sharp distinctions that govern the logical and doctrinaire mind of the agitator become at one with the realities, and he appears overnight to the people as a plausible and forceful thinker. The man who has maintained that all history is the history of class struggles and has appeared so wide of the mark in times of class collaboration may become a powerful leader when society is seething with unresolved class conflict; the man who has been vainly demanding the abolition of slavery for thirty years may become a vital figure when emancipation makes its appearance as a burning issue of practical politics. Such was the experience of Wendell Phillips: although he never held office, he became one of the most influential Americans during the few years after the fall of Fort Sumter.

Phillips is by far the most impressive of the abolitionists. Although he shared most of the foibles of the abolitionist movement, he was a keener observer and had a more flexible mind than most of his colleagues, and in the end he rose high above the intellectual limitations of Garrisonism. He was also the only major figure who combined in one career the abolition ferment of the prewar period with the labor movement of the postwar industrial epoch. When he began his agitations, he was steeped in the moral transcendentalism of the age of Emerson, Parker, and Thoreau; when he died, in 1884, he was a militant partisan of labor who spoke in the phrases—though he could never fully assimilate them—of economic realism. Often mistaken, he had often been utterly right when others were terribly wrong. A man of conscience and keen perceptivity, he represented the priceless provincial integrity that can be found in midcentury America wherever the seed of the Puritans had been sown.

The first of the Phillipses came to America in 1630; the family prospered through the generations, always producing large numbers of merchants and Congregational clergymen. Wendell's father, a wealthy lawyer with excellent mercantile connections, became the first Mayor of Boston under the city charter of 1821. Life gave the son everything a Boston boy could want— family, good looks, wealth, brains, and an education at the Boston Latin School and Harvard. At the university he was a social lion, a darling among the aristocrats; Thomas Wentworth Higginson recalled many years later that Phillips was the only undergraduate for whom the

family carriage was habitually sent out to Cambridge
on Saturday mornings to fetch him to Boston for Sun-
days. When Beacon Street turned its back on him for
joining the abolitionists, Phillips could indulge in the
snobbery of calling his detractors "men of no family."

In 1835, after a course of study at Harvard Law
School under Justice Joseph Story, Phillips opened a law
office in Court Street. It was then only four years since
William Lloyd Garrison had begun publishing the
Liberator. Respectable people, although they might express a genteel distaste for slavery, an institution peculiar to the South and long since disappeared from Massachusetts, would have nothing to do with Garrison; solid
citizens like Edward Everett could publicly express
pleasure at the capture of fugitive slaves. State and Milk
streets hummed with Southern trade.

One afternoon, not long after Phillips began his practice, a mob rushed down Court Street dragging Garrison
by a rope. When the lawyer ran to the street and inquired why the Boston regiment was not called out to
protect the victim, a bystander pointed out that most
of the regiment was in the crowd. Phillips, born within
sight of Bunker Hill and nurtured on the traditions of
the Revolution, was an intense Boston patriot, and this
violation of civil liberty in the old town revolted him.
He soon drew close to the abolition movement, and in
little more than a year married Anne Terry Greene,
daughter of a wealthy Boston shipper, a stern militant
among the early abolitionists. "My wife made me an
out and out abolitionist," he declared in later years,
"and she always preceded me in the adoption of the
various causes I have advocated." For a short time he
played only a small part in the abolition movement, but
this was enough to burn the bridges that bound him to
Beacon Street. He became an outcast to the Boston

aristocracy and lost his prospects as a lawyer. His family concluded that he was insane and thought seriously of putting him in an asylum.

In 1837, at the age of twenty-six, Phillips really found himself. Elijah Lovejoy, a newspaper editor, had been murdered by a mob in Alton, Illinois, for insisting upon his right to attack slavery. William Ellery Channing called a protest meeting at Faneuil Hall, and Phillips was standing among the crowd when Attorney General William Austin rose to defend the slayers of Lovejoy by comparing them to the mob that managed the Boston Tea Party. Nothing could have been better calculated to arouse the provincial patriot in Phillips. He leaped to the platform and denounced Austin in a remarkable extemporaneous speech which was cheered enthusiastically. He had felt his power over an audience, and it was natural now that he should throw himself wholeheartedly into abolitionist agitation.

Phillips was the most valuable acquisition of the New England abolitionists. He brought to the movement a good name, an ingratiating personality, a great talent for handling mobs and hecklers, and, above all, his voice. He was probably the most effective speaker of his time. Chauncey Depew, when over ninety, declared that he could recall hearing all the leading speakers from Clay and Webster to Woodrow Wilson, and that Phillips was the greatest. In casual intercourse not everyone found him an impressive man; Emerson even said that he had only a "platform existence." But if this was true, his platform personality at least was incomparably genuine. His manner, informal and direct in contrast to the pompous pedestal oratory that was so common, warmed his audiences. Listeners, sympathetically disposed, could achieve a feeling of identification with him that was impossible with formal orators like Webster and Edward Everett. As he himself said of Daniel O'Connell, his speech was effortless—"like picking up chips." Where other speakers indulged in long periods and complex metaphors, he understood the rhythms of speech best adapted to the needs of agitation. His talk was familiar, often homely, but his inspired passages throbbed with the heady moral rhetoric of transcendentalism, and grew nervous and staccato in their impassioned climaxes, sustained only by their continuous moral thunder and lightning. When he spoke, Emerson testified, "the whole air was full of splendors." "Phillips goes to the popular assembly as the others go to their library. Whilst he speaks, his mind feeds. Animal spirits, enthusiasm, insight, and decision." Speakers refused to follow him on the platform; if he were not last, everything would be anticlimax.

Phillips's own wealth, and his wife's, would have released him from the cramping necessity of sober work, but he turned his talents into money. Not long after joining the abolitionists, Phillips closed his law office and devoted himself to speaking and lecturing. His income from this source ranged from $10,000 to $15,000 a year; one of his standard lectures, called "The Lost Arts," which seems today in cold print a rather feeble performance—"not worth hearing" was his own judgment—was repeated over two thousand times from Portland to St. Louis and earned him by his estimate $150,000 over a period of forty-five years. He exerted pressure on lecture societies by charging high fees for his formal talks but speaking against slavery free of charge. Charity became a kind of vocation with him; his generosity was almost pathological. An old memorandum book listing his charitable donations between 1845 and 1875 was found among his effects after his death. The personal gifts, always itemized by recipients,

as "John Brown . . . a poor Italian . . . Mrs. Garnaut
. . . poor . . . refugee," came to over $65,000.

During the troubled years following the murder of
Lovejoy, Phillips went on dozens of "abolitionizing"
trips through neighboring towns in Massachusetts or beyond the borders of the state. He would return each
time to report to his wife, a nervous invalid seldom able
to leave her couch, whose famous injunction: "Wendell,
don't shilly-shally!" rang in the memories of their friends.
And Phillips did not shilly-shally. He followed Garrison
through his most intransigent phases, cursed the Constitution, and defied mobs by calling for the dissolution of
this "Union with Slaveholders." He stood for a multitude of causes, demanding equal rights for women,
temperance, freedom for Ireland, justice for the American Indian, abolition of capital punishment, kinder
treatment of the mentally ill.

The life of agitation had its dangers. Mobs followed
him about, and Phillips, who had once been welcome at
the elegant doors of the most exclusive homes in Boston,
learned to slip out of the rear exits of churches and lecture halls and make his way to safety through side
streets and narrow alleyways. He became the favorite
target of the brokers' clerks and cotton traders' minions
who often packed his meetings for sport. In the winter
of 1860–1 he was mobbed three times within a month
and might have been killed but for a bodyguard of
husky young Turnvereiners who formed a cordon
around him. At one of these meetings, as his guards
stood impassive below, Phillips remained on the platform for an hour waiting to be heard while a hostile
crowd bellowed and stamped in the galleries. Then he
spoke quietly to the reporters sitting directly beneath
him in the pit until the hecklers demanded that he raise
his voice for them to hear. He made of agitation an art

and a science. "Wendell Phillips," complained a Virginia newspaper, "is an infernal machine set to music."

II

The abolitionist movement was based upon a moral frenzy, not an economic discontent. After about 1830 almost all abolitionists were resident in the North. For the most part they were middle-class people who had no material stake in the conservation or destruction of the slave system, which was in the most literal sense none of their business. Since slavery was a moral offense rather than an economic injury to them, they came to look upon it not as an economic institution but as a breach of the ordinations of God. Abolitionism was a religious movement, emerging from the ferment of evangelical Protestantism, psychologically akin to other reforms—women's rights, temperance, and pacifism—which agitated the spirits of the Northern middle classes during the three decades before the Civil War. Its philosophy was essentially a theology, its technique similar to the techniques of revivalism, its agencies the church congregations of the towns. "Our enterprise," declared Phillips, "is eminently a religious one, dependent for success entirely on the religious sentiment of the people." Again: "The conviction that SLAVERY IS A SIN is the Gibraltar of our cause." Theodore Weld, one of the most effective leaders of the Western wing of the movement, once wrote:

> In discussing the subject of slavery, I have always presented it as pre-eminently a moral question, arresting the conscience of the nation. . . . As a question of politics

and national economy, I have passed it with scarce a look
or a word, believing that the business of the abolitionists
is with the heart of the nation, rather than with its purse
strings.

The rarefied moral atmosphere in which the abolitionists treated slavery was heightened by the fact that,
unable to agitate or discuss the subject in the South,
they were closed off from direct observation of the
institution and from contact with those who were defending it. All they could do, in effect, was to go among
the people of the North who were not slaveowners and
persuade them that slavery was an evil thing from
which they should divorce themselves. They had, to be
sure, originally planned to make their campaign an appeal to the conscience of the slaveowners themselves,
but sober observation of the Southern mind soon
showed the hopelessness of such an effort. The minds
of the masters were closed, and the abolitionists had
precious little access to the minds of the slaves—nor did
they want to incite insurrection. As a result they were
driven inward intellectually, and their thinking on
slavery assumed an increasingly theological and mil-
lennial cast. They dealt of necessity in wholesale con-
demnations and categorical imperatives, which offended
many who sympathized with their purposes. James Russell Lowell thought that the abolition leaders "treat ideas
as ignorant persons do cherries. They think them un-
wholesome unless they are swallowed stones and all."
It was understandable, then, that the abolitionists
should not have had too clear a conception of how the
slave was to be freed nor how an illiterate, landless, and
habitually dependent people were to become free and
self-sufficient citizens in the hostile environment of the
white South. The Garrisonian abolitionists were also

misled by the heartening case of abolitionism in England. In the British Empire slavery had been abolished by law in 1833; the system of postponed emancipation provided in the law had proved inferior to immediate liberation, which was adopted with considerable success in Antigua. Taking inspiration from the English precedent, the Americans concluded that the only possible strategy for them was to demand "immediate" abolition. This conclusion, of course, took additional strength from their theological prepossession: slavery was a sin, and one does not seek to purge oneself of sinfulness by slow degrees—one casts it out. Abolition was a question of right, not expediency, said Garrison, "and if slaves have a right to their freedom, it ought to be given them, regardless of the consequences."

Other abolitionists, feeling that it would be impossible to make a quick jump from slavery into freedom, and realizing that slavery in the United States was not legally a national but a state institution, which might be dropped in one place while it was flourishing in another, played with the metaphysics of "immediatism" by calling for "immediate emancipation which is gradually accomplished." Gradual methods, in short, should be immediately begun. Thus James Thome receded from the high ground of the Garrisonians: "We did not wish [the slaves] turned loose, nor even to be governed by the same Code of Laws which are adapted to intelligent citizens." To Garrison's followers this sounded like a proposal to leave the Negroes in some kind of subject condition, like a plan for forced labor—"the substitution of one type of slavery for another." Further, there were few people of any liberal cast of mind who would not agree that somehow, some time, in the distant future, the slaves ought surely to be free—Lincoln, for example, became one of these—and it was important to the militants to dissociate themselves from such Fabian abolitionism. They felt, therefore, that they must cling to the dogma of immediatism even though they could not translate it into a plan of action. Their solution of this propagandistic and doctrinal dilemma took a theological form: slavery was a sin, and one needs no plan to stop sinning. "Duty is ours and events are God's," blared Garrison. ". . . All you have to do is to set your slaves at liberty!" "To be without a plan," cried his followers, "is the true genius and glory of the Anti-Slavery enterprise!"

The abolitionists were even less clear on how the Negro was to become an independent human being after he was freed. Southern proslavery apologists were quick to seize upon this weakness of the abolition case; they grasped all too well the anticipated difficulties of emancipation, and expounded them with the tenacity of the obsessed. Lincoln, who struggled conscientiously to imagine what could be done about slavery, confessed sadly that even if he had full power to dispose of it he would not know how. The abolitionists likewise did not know, but they did not know that they did not know. The result was that when formal freedom finally came to the Negro, many abolitionists failed entirely to realize how much more help he would need or what form it should take. Phillips, however, had learned to transcend Garrisonian thought. In the critical hour of Reconstruction he dropped the veil of dogma and turned to the realities.

His long acceptance of William Lloyd Garrison's leadership was the greatest handicap that Phillips carried into his abolition activities. Recent historical research, especially that of Gilbert Hobbs Barnes, has shown that Garrison does not deserve his historical repu-

tation as the towering figure of American abolitionism.
Abolitionism was not a centrally organized movement.
Its largest effective units were the state societies, not
the national ones. Garrison was not only not the leader
of the movement at large, but he was not even accepted
as its leader in New England. The American Anti-
Slavery Society, which he captured in 1840 and controlled thereafter, existed chiefly in name.[2] The question
has been raised whether he did not do the movement
more harm than good, especially in the period after
1840. A harsh and quarrelsome fanatic with an unnecessarily large number of irrelevant peripheral enthusiasms
—among them anti-Sabbatarianism, women's rights,
and nonresistance—which he insisted on intruding into
his abolition activities in the most damaging way, Garrison estranged many potential friends. The influential
Western abolitionists who held Phillips in considerable esteem found Garrison intolerable. ("I wonder,"
wrote James G. Birney to Elizur Wright in 1844, "how
such a man as Phillips can quietly stomach all the
wretched stuff he has to receive from his associates.")[3]

The secular philosophy of the abolitionists, insofar
as they had one, was taken from the Declaration of Independence. They wanted natural rights for the colored
man. This philosophy had a particularly strong voice

---

2. "Probably not one in a hundred of even the New England
abolitionists ever accepted the special views which the Garrisonian organization adopted after 1843," concludes Jesse Macy
in *The Antislavery Crusade*. After Garrison captured the American
Anti-Slavery Society in 1840, its annual income fell from $47,000
to $7,000, and did not rise above $12,000 until 1856.

3. Cf. Thoreau on Phillips in a letter, March 12, 1845: "He
stands so firmly and so effectively alone, and one honest man
is so much more than a host that we cannot but feel that he does
himself an injustice when he reminds us of the American [Anti-
Slavery] Society, which he represents. . . . Here is one who is
at the same time an eloquent speaker and a righteous man."

in Phillips. James Otis, John Hancock, Sam Adams, and Colonel Warren were all but contemporaries of his, and he enlisted them in his campaigns as naturally as he did his audiences in the lyceums. But the natural-rights philosophy, as well as his Christian training, led logically to the higher law doctrine. When Garrison, during the 1840's, turned upon the Constitution and urged abolitionists to call for the dissolution of the Union—"No Union with Slaveholders"—Phillips followed his lead, closed his law office because he could not be an attorney without swearing an oath of allegiance, and in 1845 wrote a pamphlet for the American Anti-Slavery Society entitled *Can Abolitionists Vote or Take Office Under the United States Constitution?* The answer, of course, was in the negative. Every compromise with evil, reasoned Phillips, is fatal. Any man who votes thereby supports the Constitution, since he consents to appoint as his political agent an officeholder who must swear to uphold the Constitution of the United States. That Constitution is a proslavery instrument; in its very apportionment of representation for Congress it sanctions Southern slaveholding. The common military forces of the Union can be called upon to suppress a revolt of slaves. To support such an instrument of government would be to participate in the moral guilt of slavery. Although Phillips did not suggest that the abolitionists support no human government at all (the position preferred by Garrison), he insisted that they must not support "*this* Government based upon and acting for slavery." Every man is a free moral agent who must bear responsibility for his political acts. It is the bounden duty of the individual not to give even indirect sanction to slavery. "Immoral laws are doubtless void, and should not be obeyed."

Following this creed, the Garrisonians called upon

the Northern states to separate from the South. This
demand was characteristic of their religious psychology:
it was doubtful how much disunion through Northern
secession would have accomplished for the slaves, but
by dissolving the Union the abolitionists could wash
away *their* personal sin of participating in a slaveholding commonwealth. Garrison's flamboyant and in-
flammatory device of tearing up or burning the Constitution in public probably did the cause considerable
harm. But the most damaging aspect of the Garrisonians' attitude toward the Union was that it cut them off
from the possibilities of propagandizing through political action. Other abolitionists made excellent propagandistic use of the right of petition by demanding that
Congress abolish slavery in the District of Columbia.

After 1840 the non-Garrisonian abolition movement
became increasingly political, and although it never
gathered much numerical strength as an independent
political force, it had an appreciable effect on the major
parties. When James G. Birney, running on the Liberty
Party ticket in 1844, took enough votes from the New
York State Whigs to cost Henry Clay the state's electoral votes, and with them the presidency, the lesson was
obvious: abolition sentiment was strategically important.
It became increasingly so as the years went on. Thus it
was men like Birney who helped to convince men like
Lincoln that the moral revulsion from slavery could not
be "safely disregarded." Moreover, the abolitionists
themselves learned much from participation in politics,
not the least of which was the lesson that a strategy
dictated by absolute moral intransigence, however defensible in logic, was not so effective in reality as a
strategy qualified by opportunism. They learned that
the abolition of slavery must be linked with other, more

material issues to reach its full political strength.[4] Political abolitionism, as it became more and more dilute in principle, somehow became stronger and stronger as an actual menace to slavery. The Liberty Party disappeared after two campaigns, but was superseded by the Free-Soil Party, which, in 1848, again held the critical balance in New York State and again determined the outcome of a national election. At length the Free-Soil principle became the central issue of the Republican Party. Misled by Garrison's anti-political point of view, Phillips failed until the last moment to appreciate the contribution of political friction to the growth of antislavery sentiment. He saw only the fact that the antislavery emphasis of the political parties grew weaker with time and less defensible in abstract principle. "The Liberty party," he declared in 1858, "was on the defensive, the Free Soil party was on the defensive, the Republican party is on the defensive, and each one of them has been driven back, back, back, until now the Republican party has nothing to defend." Only after Lincoln's election did he begin to perceive the possibilities of the major political party as an abolition vehicle. "The Republican party," he then correctly predicted, "have undertaken a problem the solution of which will force them to our position."

At one point Phillips parted company with Garrison.

---

4. One of his colleagues, Theodore Foster, wrote to Birney, December 7, 1845: "I am more and more convinced by reflection that the antislavery feeling alone will never bring over to the Liberty party a majority of all the voters of the United States. We must have some other motives to present to people, which will appeal directly to their own interests. Unless we secure support from other considerations, we shall never, as a party, become a majority, and our *principles* will find some other channel of operation than the Liberty Party."

There was an inconsistency between the Garrisonian philosophy of nonresistance and the natural-rights doctrine of the Declaration of Independence. Natural rights meant the right to resist, the right to rebel. If the Fathers could revolt, so could the Negro. The Fugitive Slave Law should be resisted by force, Phillips believed, and he would defend the murder of a slave-catcher by a slave. As to slave insurrection:

> I do not believe that . . . we shall see the total abolition of slavery, unless it comes in some critical conjuncture of national affairs, when the slave, taking advantage of a crisis in the fate of his masters, shall dictate his own terms. . . . The hour will come—God hasten it!—when the American people shall so stand on the deck of their Union, "built i' the eclipse, and rigged with curses dark." If I ever live to see that hour, I shall say to every slave, Strike now for Freedom! . . . I know what anarchy is. I know what civil war is. I can imagine the scenes of blood through which a rebellious slave-population must march to their rights. They are dreadful. And yet, I do not know that to an enlightened mind, a scene of civil war is any more sickening than the thought of a hundred and fifty years of slavery. . . . No, I confess I am not a non-resistant. The reason why I advise the slave to be guided by a policy of peace is because he has no chance.

Even after the execution of John Brown, however, Phillips asserted his belief that slavery would "not go down in blood": "I believe in moral suasion. The age of bullets is over." Even during the secession crisis he still vested his hopes in the general sweep of progress, which he pointed out had a firm material basis.

> You see exactly what my hopes rest upon. Growth! . . . You perceive my hope of freedom rests upon these

rocks: 1st, mechanical progress. First man walked, dug
the earth with his hands, ate what he could pick up . . .
then sewing machines lift woman out of torture, steam
marries the continents, and the telegraph flashes news
like sunlight over the globe. Every step made hands worth
less, and brains worth more; and that is the death of
slavery. . . . I am sure you cannot make a nation with
one-half steam-boats, sewing-machines and Bibles, and
the other half slaves. Then another rock of my hope is
these Presidential canvasses,—the saturnalia of American
life,—when slaves like Seward . . . fling all manner of
insult on their masters. Then the ghost of John Brown
makes Virginia quick to calculate the profit and loss of
slavery. Beside this, honest men, few, but the salt of the
times. . . .

Phillips joyously welcomed the crisis caused by Lincoln's election:

If the telegraph speaks truth, for the first time in our
history the *slave* has chosen a President of the United
States. . . . Not an abolitionist, hardly an anti-slavery
man, Mr. Lincoln consents to represent an antislavery
idea. . . . He seems to govern; he only reigns. . . .
Lincoln is in *place*, Garrison in power.

Precisely how Lincoln's victory would further the cause
he did not know. It was enough that the country now
had a major political party which "dares to say that
slavery is a sin—in *some* places!"

With other abolitionists, Phillips persisted in saying
that the South should be allowed to secede in peace.
For almost twenty years he had been advocating disunion; it made little difference whether the North or the
South should be first to bow out. The Union had been a
moral failure; only the money interests wanted to save
it. In fact, however, the North would be materially bet-

ter off by itself. We might have a right to prevent secession, but why exert ourselves to save an artificial and unprofitable Union? The rest of the slave states would follow South Carolina out of the Union, he foresaw, but the Gulf states in the new Confederacy would open the slave trade and bring ruin upon the slave-breeding states and North Carolina, which then would "gravitate to us free." The standing army, maintained at Northern as well as Southern expense, helped to secure the Southern states from insurrection; let them go free and insurrection would break out. In the end, economic progress would undermine slavery—a strong new note in Phillips's propaganda:

What is the contest in Virginia now? Between the men who want to make their slaves mechanics for the increased wages it will secure, and the men who oppose, for fear of the influence it will have on the general security of slave property and white throats. Just that dispute will go on, wherever the Union is dissolved. Slavery comes to an end by the laws of trade. . . .

Indeed, the Gulf States are essentially in a feudal condition, an aristocracy resting on slaves,—no middle class. To sustain government on the costly model of our age necessitates a middle class of trading, manufacturing energy. The merchant of the nineteenth century spurns to be subordinate. The introduction of such a class will create in the Gulf States that very irrepressible conflict which they leave us to avoid,—which alive now in the Border States makes these unwilling to secede,—which once created will soon undermine the aristocracy of the Gulf States and bring them back to us free.

Phillips was confident that the Confederacy would be too weak to attack the North "for the only annoyance we can give her—the sight and influence of our nobler civilization." But less than a month later, when the Confederacy did strike at Sumter, he saw the situation in a new light. This was a defensive war, therefore justified; and out of it emancipation might come. The abolitionists, he confessed in his first post-Sumter address, had imagined that everything could be settled by freedom of thought and discussion.

> Our mistake, if any, has been that we counted too much on the intelligence of the masses, on the honesty and wisdom of statesmen as a class. Perhaps we did not give weight enough to the fact we saw, that this nation is made up of different ages; not homogeneous, but a mixed mass of different centuries. The North *thinks,*—can appreciate argument,—is the nineteenth century,—hardly any struggle left in it but that between the working class and the money kings. The South dreams,—it is the thirteenth and fourteenth century,—baron and serf,—noble and slave. . . . Our struggle is therefore between barbarism and civilization. Such can only be settled by arms.

For Phillips the great goal of the war was not to save the Union but to free the slave. Lincoln's delay stirred Phillips to those tirades which have done so much to cloud his reputation. Like the Radicals in Congress, he saw the futility of waging a conservative war. The South was fighting to save slavery; the North was fighting "not to have it hurt." Lincoln doubtless meant well, but he was no leader—"he is a first-rate second-rate man . . . a mere convenience waiting like any other broomstick to be used." But if the agitator was hard on the President, he was sound in his estimation of Lincoln's strategy. "The President never professed to be a leader. The President is the agent of public opinion. He wants to know what you will allow and what you demand that he shall do." Lincoln was waiting to see if public opinion would sustain emancipation. Very well, then, Wendell Phillips would see to it that public opinion would sustain nothing else.[5] In July 1861 he said:

> I put my faith in the honesty of Abraham Lincoln as an individual, in the pledge which a long life has given of Chase's love for the antislavery cause; but I do not believe either of them, nor all their comrades, have the boldness to declare an emancipation policy, until, by a pressure which we are to create, the country forces them to do it. . . .

Phillips was impatient with the idea that the war could be waged in a static, defensive political mood. Every drop of blood was shed without purpose until the slaves were declared free. Was the government determined to conduct the war in such a way as to preserve slavery? How could the social basis of the Southern oligarchy, which waged the war, be cut away without freeing its labor? "No social state is really annihilated except when it is replaced by another."

The abolitionist saw the complex relationship between emancipation and diplomacy. England and France stood for the South, he said in 1861. England wants to divide the United States, to "undermine the manufacturing and commercial supremacy of the North." The English middle classes lack the virtue to resist the call of imperial ambition. Ultimately the

5. This was how Phillips saw his own function: "I must educate, arouse, and mature a public opinion which shall compel the administration to adopt and support it in pursuing the policy I can aid. This I do by frankly and candidly criticising its present policy, civil and military. . . . My criticism is not, like that of the traitor presses, meant to paralyze the administration, but to goad it to more activity and vigor."

European governments and the silent masses of slaves will take an active hand in the war, and it is a matter of great moment which moves first.[6] Lincoln must hurry before Europe intervenes; Cameron must arm the Negroes; McClellan must go.

In his desperate eagerness to force a more vigorous conduct of the war Phillips dropped the old emphasis on the formality of sin and turned his attention to economic issues. To the horror of many old comrades, he supported Lincoln's practical proposal to abolish slavery among loyal slaveholders through compensated emancipation. No longer did he disdain the economic appeal for the Union—its disruption would "defraud us of mutual advantages relating to peace, trade, national security." In March and April 1862 he went on a six-week lecture tour, which took him to the capital and through New York, Pennsylvania, Ohio, Illinois, and Michigan, where he spoke in several cities. At Washington he lectured twice and visited Congress. Vice President Hamlin left the presiding seat in the Senate to greet him; he dined with the Speaker of the House, and had an interview with Lincoln. At a time when emancipation was the order of the day he had become the outstanding abolitionist in the country, the field agent of the Radicals in Congress. Greeley's *Tribune* estimated that 50,000 people heard his lectures and speeches dur-

6. Later Phillips stressed the role of American wheat in staving off intervention on behalf of the Confederacy. "Today," he said in July 1863, "the logic of events is that we may save the nation from English and French interference because Illinois is full of wheat, and English harvests are very barren; because France starves, and the valley of the Mississippi is loaded with grain, and she dares not interfere." He once suggested that if Napoleon III tried to plant thrones in the Western Hemisphere, the United States should subsidize European republicans like Garibaldi to overturn the European system.

ing the winter of 1861–2, and that almost 5,000,000 read them. Returning from his trip, Phillips was convinced that the West was stronger than the East for emancipation. The President, he reported, was honest, and desirous of seeing an end to slavery. In good time he was to say of the President he had pilloried: "Lincoln was slow, but he got there. Thank God for him."

Phillips had few illusions about the completeness of emancipation under Lincoln's Proclamation, much as he rejoiced in it. "That proclamation," he said, "frees the slave but ignores the negro." To declare the Negro free was one thing, to arm and employ him another. The Republicans were not thorough enough. They had been educated as Whigs, and the Whig Party "had no trust in the masses." When the South began to feel exhausted, Phillips predicted, she would free the Negro and try to use him. He proposed that 10,000 Negro troops be sent east from Louisiana, then occupied by Union troops, not primarily to fight, but to carry word of emancipation. They would soon draw around them a menacing force of 200,000, and the South would be unable to keep her white men at the front. Where lands were captured, the government should confiscate them,

> break them up into farms of one hundred acres, and sell those farms to the sons of Vermont and New York, with a deed from the Union guaranteeing the title, and guaranteeing compensation if the owner be evicted, and you have commenced a State. . . .

Presumably these white Northerners would employ free Negro labor. But by 1864, when he started to criticize Lincoln's plan of Reconstruction, Phillips began to look upon the land as the key to the Negroes'

welfare and to advocate, with Congressional Radicals
like Sumner and Stevens, that the land be turned over
to the freedmen themselves. Now that tendency to look
to the economic basis of politics which had become
marked in him at the beginning of the crisis ripened
into fruition. Lincoln's plan, which would allow slaveholders to return to their estates, would not sufficiently
change the structure of political power in the South, he
argued.

> What does that mean? Every man knows that land dic-
> tates government. If you hold land, every man his own
> farm, it is a democracy; you need not curiously ask of the
> statute book. If a few men own the territory it is an
> oligarchy; you need not carefully scan its laws. . . .
> Daniel Webster said, in 1820, the revolution in France
> has crumbled up the nobles' estates into small farms; the
> throne must either kill them or they will kill out the
> throne. . . . Now while these large estates remain in the
> hands of the just defeated oligarchy, its power is not
> destroyed. But let me confiscate the land of the South, and
> put in into the hands of the negroes and white men who
> have fought for it, and you may go to sleep with your
> parchments.

It was Phillips's idea that the country owed the Negro
"real freedom—not merely technical freedom." For this
he must have land, citizenship, education, and the vote.
"The moment a man becomes valuable or terrible to the
politician, his rights will be respected. Give the negro a
vote in his hand, and there is not a politician from
Abraham Lincoln down to the laziest loafer in the lowest ward of this city who would not do him honor." The
Negro must be free to bargain for a wage contract. To
those who argued that gradual progress would be made

in the future toward Negro equality Phillips prophetically replied that there would soon be a loosening of
tension, a conservative reaction, and that if a good
bargain was to be made for the Negro, it must be struck
now.

> When the war closes the South it is to be made like a
> garden. . . . Welcome labor there from the North, the
> East, and the West, and you keep wages high throughout
> the nation. . . . Disgrace labor down there, make the
> negro, worth $100 a month, work for $8, and no white
> man will go there to compete with him. You dam up the
> labor of the North; you leave the South aristocratic, labor
> depressed and discredited, and an aristocratic class thrown
> upward into being above it inevitably.[7]

In June 1865 Garrison and Phillips broke decisively at
a meeting of the National Anti-Slavery Society. Garrison
proposed that since the purpose of the society had been
fulfilled in the thirteenth amendment, it should dissolve.
Phillips insisted that the society must continue to work
for suffrage for the freedman. Garrison held that it was
not reasonable to expect that Southern states give suffrage to the Negro before they should be readmitted to
the Union; on the same principle, many Northern states,

---

7. Cf. Thaddeus Stevens in his Lancaster speech of September 7, 1865: "The whole fabric of southern society *must* be
changed, and never can it be done if this opportunity is lost. . . .
How can republican institutions, free schools, free churches, free
social intercourse exist in a mingled community of nabobs and
serfs; of the owners of twenty-thousand acre manors with lordly
palaces, and the occupants of narrow huts inhabited by 'low
white trash'? If the south is ever to be made a safe republic let
her lands be cultivated by the toil of the owners or the free
labor of intelligent citizens. This must be done even though it
drive her nobility into exile."

like Illinois, would have to be put out of the Union.[8]
Phillips carried the day, and the society voted to remain in being and elected him president. Keenly aware
of the limitations of what had been done, he continued
to demand a thoroughgoing Reconstruction policy. In
October 1865 he delivered a speech in Boston entitled
"The South Victorious," in which he asserted that the
Negro still endured every characteristic of slavery except the legal fact of permanent bondage. Race subordination, "the great principle of the South," still survived.
In 1868, summarizing the progress of Reconstruction, he
pointed out that of the three great aims he had set down
for the black and white masses of the South, land, education, and the ballot, the Negro had only the ballot,
and this insecurely. He fought on for ratification of the
fifteenth amendment, which was meant to provide the
Negro with the ballot; but he sensed the ebb of the
radical tide. "Immediate" emancipation had come, and
the more closely it was examined, the more "gradual" it
seemed. In the kernel of victory he had found the bitter
nut of defeat.

III

The abolitionists had received little aid from the
fledgling American labor movement in the years before
the war. Labor leaders, approached by the middle-class

---

8. This was typical of Garrison's formal style of reasoning. It
made no difference to him either that Illinois was firmly in the
Union and the Southern states were firmly out, or that there were
a few thousand Negroes in Illinois and hundreds of thousands in
the Southern states.

folk or wealthy philanthropists of the cause, tended to reply that they would do well to bestow as much sympathy on the wage slave as the chattel slave, and turned abruptly to their own problems.[9] Abolitionists, in turn, were wont to reply that there was a world of difference between the situation of the free and the slave laborer; that the peculiar sinfulness of the subjection of the Negro more than justified giving him special concern. Phillips agreed. In 1847, challenged by a Utopian socialist in the *Harbinger* on the subject of "wage slavery," he declared:

> There are two prominent points which distinguish the workers in this country from the slaves. First, the laborers, as a class, are neither wronged nor oppressed: and secondly, if they were, they possess ample power to defend themselves by the exercise of their own acknowledged rights. Does legislation bear hard upon them? Their votes can alter it. Does capital wrong them? Economy will make them capitalists. . . . To economy, self-denial, temperance, education, and moral and religious character, the laboring class and every other class in this country must owe its elevation and improvement.

Twenty-four years later Phillips was calling for "the overthrow of the whole profit-making system."

When the Civil War ended, most of the abolitionists returned to their workaday pursuits, content to rest upon

---

9. Ely Moore, the first president of the National Trades Union, told the House of Representatives in 1839 that emancipation would bring the Negro slave into the labor market in competition with the Northern white worker. Should that happen, "the moral and political character, the pride, power and independence of the latter are gone forever."

their formal success and to luxuriate in their new roles as respected citizens who had once been the prophets of a great moral reform. But Phillips, who had been an agitator by profession, had no other occupation. He was only fifty-four in 1865, and it was natural for him to look for another cause in which to expend his talents.

The success of the Republican Party in 1860 and the few preceding years had begun a change in Phillips's style of thought, which became complete during the Civil War. The moral and religious agitation of the abolitionist movement had awakened men's minds, but of itself had not been sufficient to shape a practical movement to free the slave. In spite of Garrisonian theories, slavery had become a major issue in the American consciousness only as a subject of political action, the theme of a major political party, which drew strength from other issues like free land and protective tariffs. In several speeches delivered before the attack on Sumter, Phillips expressed hope that economic progress, not war, would end slavery—"Slavery comes to an end by the laws of trade"—and began to interpret American history as a series of class struggles. He reached back into the eighteenth century to point out that the American Revolution was fought because American merchants wanted direct trade with the West Indies and planters "wanted to cheat their creditors." The American Revolution gave the people independence and nationality. But the North remained conservative, was "bound in the aristocracy of classes." Then

Virginia slaveholders, making theoretical democracy their passion, conquered the Federal Government, and emancipated the working classes of New England. Bitter was the cup to honest Federalism and the Essex Junto. Today,

Massachusetts only holds to the lips of Carolina a beaker of the same beverage.[10]

Phillips soon came to look upon the Civil War as a Second American Revolution, a contest between bourgeois and feudal civilization. Once a moralist pure and simple, he was becoming a moralist with a philosophy of history.

During Reconstruction, Phillips's attention was focused upon the land. He saw that if the Negro was to win political and personal freedom he must have possession of the means of production. He was forced to think of slavery not merely as a sin to be purged but as a labor system that must be replaced by some new economic order. The demand for confiscation of the aristocracy's land fixed his attention on property and the relation of its distribution to human rights and political democracy, while the emergence of the ex-slave as a potential agricultural wage worker brought the problems of wage labor into the center of his consciousness.

On November 2, 1865, when he made his first important speech on behalf of labor in Faneuil Hall at a demonstration in favor of the eight-hour day, Phillips declared:

The labor of these twenty-nine years has been in behalf of a race bought and sold. The South did not rest their system wholly on this claim to own their laborers; but according to Chancellor Harper, Alexander H. Stephens, Governor Pickens, and John C. Calhoun, asserted that the laborer must necessarily be owned by capitalists or

10. This interpretation Phillips borrowed, with some of his language, from Richard Hildreth, the Yankee historian, whose work he acknowledged. Cf. the passage in Hildreth's interesting little volume, *Despotism in America* (Boston, 1854), pp. 16–26, 32–3.

individuals. The struggle for the ownership of labor is now somewhat near its end; and we fitly commence a struggle to define and to arrange the true relations of capital and labor.

Karl Marx, looking upon slavery as a socialist, had said that white labor could never be free while black labor was in bondage. Phillips, approaching socialism as an abolitionist, was arriving at the conclusion that black labor could never be truly free until all labor was released from wage slavery. "We protected the *black* laborer, and now we are going to protect the Laborer, North and South, labor everywhere."

Long in revolt against the values of Massachusetts capitalism, Phillips now saw in the money power a menace to republican government. "I confess," he said, "that the only fear I have in regard to Republican institutions is whether, in our day, any adequate remedy will be found for this incoming flood of the power of incorporated wealth." New Jersey was no more than "a railroad station," the laws of New York were being made "in Vanderbilt's counting house," Tom Scott owned the legislature of Pennsylvania, and in his own state it was impossible to get a railroad-dominated legislature to pass laws for the safety of train passengers or to vote a trivial sum for a factual inquiry into the condition of the workers. This was not his conception of democracy. He had always maintained that each separate interest in society must have its own representation in the councils of state. No man can properly vote in behalf of a woman, no white for a Negro, no lawyer or capitalist for a manual laborer. The principle of the Founding Fathers was that "no class is safe unless government is so arranged that each class has in its own hands the means of protecting itself. That is the idea of republics." If corporations can buy legislatures, equality of suffrage is useless and the republican principle is dead. The only force sufficiently numerous, and capable of uniting against the threat of corporate capital, is united labor. "The labor movement," said Phillips, ". . . is my only hope for democracy."

Phillips now became as stoutly devoted to political action as he had been to political inaction during his career as an abolitionist. In 1865 he even attributed the success of the abolitionists to their force at the ballot-box. He was sure that the ballot was the only alternative to a violent outcome of the class struggle. One could not simply wait and discuss while people were hungry; it was just this sort of thing that would lead to an explosion. "We rush into politics because politics is the safety valve." "Avoid all violence," he advised the workers. "Appeal to discussion and the ballot. You outnumber the capitalists at any rate. The ballot was given for just such crises as these." The strike was useful as a tactic—"Never let a man say a word against strikes" —but, for the time being, labor's motto should be: "NEVER FORGIVE AT THE BALLOT BOX!"

In politics, however, there was no place to go. Phillips rapidly became disillusioned with the Republican Party, which he finally described in 1878 as no more than a tool of the capitalist class. He encouraged labor to form its own party and joined the Massachusetts workingmen in their political experimentation from 1869 to 1871. He was the labor party's candidate for governor in 1870 and narrowly missed being nominated by the National Labor Union for the presidency in 1872. But these experiments were all doomed to failure. Phillips's association with the unsavory Benjamin F. Butler in his campaign for the governorship of Massachusetts in 1871 cost him many friends. At last, it was believed, Phillips had soiled himself, and Emerson, who had admired him for thirty years, made it clear that he did not wish to see him in Concord.

V. L. Parrington, in his sympathetic account of Phillips, found "pretty much all of Marxianism" in the philosophy of his later period; but except for his reliance upon the working class and his general economic interpretation of politics, there was little of the Marxist in the American labor reformer. Phillips's socialism was a homespun Yankee product, woven out of several strains of native reform ideology, not the least of which was that of the co-operative movement. "Inaugurate cooperative industry," he urged in 1868:

> Let the passengers and the employees own the railway. Let the operatives own the mill. Let the traders own the banks. Make the interests of Capital and the Community identical. In no other way shall we have free, self-government in this country.

The most militant and most famous expression of his views came in resolutions presented at the Labor-Reform Convention at Worcester in 1871:

> We affirm, as a fundamental principle, that labor, the creator of wealth, is entitled to all it creates.
>
> Affirming this, we avow ourselves willing to accept the final results of the operation of a principle so radical,— such as the overthrow of the whole profit-making system, the extinction of all monopolies, the abolition of privileged classes, universal education and fraternity, perfect freedom of exchange, and best and grandest of all, the final obliteration of that foul stigma upon our so-called Christian civilization,—the poverty of the masses. . . . We are still aware that our goal cannot be reached at a single leap. We take into account the ignorance, selfishness,

prejudice, corruption, and demoralization of the leaders of the people, and to a large extent, of the people themselves; but still we demand that some steps be taken in this direction: therefore,—

Resolved,—That we declare war with the wages system . . . war with the present system of finance, which robs labor and gorges capital, makes the rich richer and the poor poorer, and turns a republic into an aristocracy of capital. . . .

The author of these resolutions had no economic theory. His realism was incomplete because it was not supplemented by any conception of economic evolution, and the few ventures that Phillips made into explaining his economic point of view were lamentable. Although he was a city man, he had been born at a time when Boston was hardly more than an overgrown village and the Common was still used as a pasture. He never accepted urban life or industry, and never squared his socialist sympathies with the facts of the Industrial Revolution.

What we need is an equalization of property,—nothing else. My ideal of a civilization is a very high one; but the approach to it is a New-England town of some two thousand inhabitants, with no rich man and no poor man in it, all mingling in the same society, every child at the same school, no poorhouse, no beggar, opportunities equal, nobody too proud to stand aloof, nobody too humble to be shut out. That's New England as it was fifty years ago. . . .

The activities of the First International were sympathetically reported in Phillips's paper, the *National Standard*. When the test of the Paris Commune came, Phillips refused to join the general condemnation in

America and hailed the Communard movement. He held Thiers responsible for the bloodshed in France, declared: *"There is no hope for France but in the Reds,"* and described the Communards as "the foremost, the purest and the noblest patriots of France."

Such sentiments forced him into a deeper and deeper isolation. As an exponent of socialism in the Gilded Age, Phillips was deprived even of the consolation that the abolitionists had had of the company of churchmen, poets, millionaires, and the marginal allegiance of some distinguished men and women of good-will. In 1881, however, he was invited to give the Phi Beta Kappa address at Harvard. This at least was an opportunity for the aging orator to heal the old breach with the scholarship of Cambridge, which had spurned him and his causes for forty years. Instead he flung his last challenge at respectability. He chose as his topic "The Scholar in a Republic." His theme was an arraignment of American learning for its lack of social leadership and its moral cowardice.

The duty of the scholar, he began, "is to help those less favored in life," and to educate the mass of the people. And yet very few of the great truths about society had grown out of scholarly inquiry, "but have been first heard in the solemn protest of martyred patriotism and the loud cries of crushed and starving labor." The world makes history in anguish, and scholars write it in half-truths, blurring and distorting it with their prejudices. The people learn deeply from the agitations of life, and timid scholars shrink from these agitations or denounce them. "A chronic distrust of the people pervades the book-educated class of the North." They do not even scruple to defend the principle of free speech. American scholarship, in truth, had not given its hand to aid in the solution of a single great social question of the age. It had denounced the slavery crusade, spurned the reform of penal legislation, ignored intemperance, and laughed at women's rights. It had never shown sympathy for the victims of oppression abroad—for the Irish or (here Phillips grew particularly shocking) for the Nihilists of Russia, whom it was then condemning so strongly. Seizing upon the Nihilists as an extreme symbol of resistance and rebellion, Phillips launched into an impassioned defense of them and lashed out at "that nauseous hypocrisy which, stung by a threepenny tea tax, piles Bunker Hill with granites and statues, prating all the time of patriotism and broadswords, while, like another Pecksniff, it recommends a century of dumb submission and entire non-resistance to the Russians, who for a hundred years have seen their sons by thousands dragged to death or exile . . . and their maidens flogged to death in the marketplace." It was time, he concluded, that scholarship fulfill its duties, time at last that it take the side of the wage worker and the woman in their coming campaigns for justice. "Sit not, like the figure on our silver coin, ever looking backward."

"It was a delightful discourse," remarked one of his hearers, "but preposterous from beginning to end." Conventional history has been less charitable than Phillips's contemporaries, finding him always preposterous and never delightful. But the agitator who had given no quarter expected none, and perhaps sensed that the scholarship of the future would treat him in the same spirit as had the scholarship of his time. He returned from Cambridge to Boston, exhilarated and grimly satisfied, we may imagine, at the thought that as long as anyone in the old town could remember, he had been a thorn in the side of complacency.

CHAPTER VII

THE SPOILSMEN:
AN AGE OF CYNICISM

❧

PARTIES *are not built by deportment, or by ladies' magazines, or gush.* ROSCOE CONKLING

NOTHING *is lost save honor!* JIM FISK

IN THE years from Appomattox to the end of the nineteenth century the American people settled half their continental domain, laid down a vast railroad system, and grew mighty in the world on their great resources in coal, metals, oil, and land. There is no other period in the nation's history when politics seems so completely dwarfed by economic changes, none in which the life of the country rests so completely in the hands of the industrial entrepreneur.

The industrialists of the Gilded Age were such as one might expect to arise where great waste is permitted for great accomplishment, where many temptations are offered and few restraints imposed. For the most part they were parvenus, and they behaved with becoming vulgarity; but they were also men of heroic audacity and magnificent exploitative talents—shrewd, energetic, aggressive, rapacious, domineering, insatiable. They directed the proliferation of the country's wealth, they seized its opportunities, they managed its corruption, and from them the era took its tone and color.

In business and politics the captains of industry did their work boldly, blandly, and cynically. Exploiting workers and milking farmers, bribing Congressmen, buying legislatures, spying upon competitors, hiring armed guards, dynamiting property, using threats and intrigue and force, they made a mockery of the ideals of the simple gentry who imagined that the nation's development could take place with dignity and restraint under the regime of laissez-faire. Their exploits created the moral atmosphere that caused such an honorable conservative of the old school as E. L. Godkin to say:

> I came here fifty years ago with high and fond ideals about America. . . . They are now all shattered, and I have apparently to look elsewhere to keep even moderate hopes about the human race alive.

Yet it would be a mistake to assume that conscience had died among the business barons. What made it possible for them to operate in the proximate spheres of politics and industry with such cheerful and unstinted rapacity was the fact that they had, in terms of those ultimate rationalizations upon which conscience rests, the most plausible, the profoundest reasons to believe that what they were doing would work to a final good. If they could buy Congressmen without making an apology, even to themselves, it was because they operated—or so they thought—in behalf of a benign transformation of tremendous magnitude. Because the abiding significance of their deeds would be so great and so good, they did not need to fret about their day-by-day knaveries. Far from humble and apologetic, they were confident and arrogant. When Collis P. Huntington wrote to a political agent concerning some of his bribery for the Southern Pacific:

> If you have to pay money to have the right thing done, it is only just and fair to do it. . . . If a man has the power to do great evil and won't do right unless he is bribed to do it, I think the time spent will be gained when it is a man's duty to go up and bribe the judge. A man that will cry out against them himself will also do these things himself. If there was none for it, I would not hesitate—

he was not being a sanctimonious hypocrite; he was merely expressing his passionate American conviction that he had every honest right to come into his own, and it is doubtful that many tycoons of his time would have differed in principle. To imagine that such men did not sleep the sleep of the just would be romantic sentimentalism. In the Gilded Age even the angels sang for them.

The honest rationalization of the captains of industry were manifold. Perhaps their primary defense was that they were building a great industrial empire; it was wasteful building, but their America thought it could afford waste. A few of their number—the name of Jay Gould stands out—were speculators, exploiters, and wreckers, pure and simple, but the majority could think of themselves as titans, not merely of speculation and combination, but of industrial creativity on an epic scale.

Further, they stood squarely upon the American mythology of opportunity for the common man. The great industrial leaders had started life in the lower or lower-middle classes; most of them could point to early careers of privation, hard work, and frugality. When Andrew Carnegie declared at the close of the period that "the millionaires who are in active control started as poor boys and were trained in the sternest but most efficient of all schools—poverty," he could cite, besides his own case, over a dozen other eminent industrialists. Many biographies substantiate his opinion.[1] Of course there were men like William Vanderbilt, whose fortune and properties had been left him by his father, the Commodore. There were others who had begun in comfortable circumstances, like Edward Harriman and Henry Villard, or had excellent family connections, like Henry Clay Frick, who was related on his mother's side to the Overholts of distillery fame. But Carnegie was the son of a painfully poor Scottish weaver; Philip Armour, Gustavus Swift, Daniel Drew, and Jay Gould had been children of humble farmers; Jim Fisk's father had been the proprietor of a little "travelling emporium," and John D. Rockefeller's an itinerant salesman of patent medicines. Jay Cooke and James J. Hill had begun their business careers as clerks on the frontier. Leland Stanford, although a product of the upper-middle class and the beneficiary of a fair education, had arrived in California almost penniless. Collis Huntington had been self-supporting at fourteen. Such men could tell themselves and the world that their riches and power were the results of hard work and special

1. The cases of the few outstanding industrialists are in fact somewhat misleading. C. Wright Mills, in his study of "The American Business Elite: a Collective Portrait," based upon businessmen included in the *Dictionary of American Biography,* has shown that for the generation in question (born 1820–49), 43.0 per cent of the business elite came from the "lower" or "lower middle" classes. This is a smaller percentage than would be found among the top score of industrialists for the same period. However, Mills's study does show that opportunity was more prevalent for ascent from the lower classes in this generation than for any other in American history. The previous generation (born 1790–1819) showed only 37.2 per cent of the business elite derived from the "lower" or "lower middle" classes; the subsequent generation (born 1850–79) shows only 29.3 per cent.

talents, could hold themselves up to the ambitious American middle class as exemplars of an economy of magnificent opportunities. And, being successful only in the way everyone aspired to be, they enjoyed more freedom from moral condemnation than one can appreciate in the sickly retrospect of the twentieth century. They felt they had a good title to everything they could get. It was genuine indignation that could make a man like Hill say at the time of the Northern Securities antitrust prosecution: "It really seems hard when we look back upon what we have done . . . that we should be compelled to fight for our lives against political adventurers who have never done anything but pose and draw a salary." Joseph Wharton, the Philadelphia nickel monopolist, resented an insinuation that his enterprises were "dependent" upon tariff favors:

> I have supported and aided the Government more than it has supported and aided me. I am not a pauper nor a lawyer. . . . I am one of the men who create and maintain the prosperity of the nation and who enable it to survive even the affliction of wrong-headed and cranky legislators.

Even Jay Gould, whose hand spoiled everything it touched, lashed back at Senators who presumed to inquire into his affairs: "*We* have made the country rich, *we* have developed the country." John D. Rockefeller said simply that "The good Lord gave me my money." Carnegie, when he observed of George Pullman that he "monopolized everything," added: "It was well that it should be so. The man had arisen who could manage and the tools belonged to him."

The ideas of the age were tailored to fit the rich barons. Economists, journalists, educators, and writers who rushed to do them honor found a strikingly plausible rationale in Darwinian biology and Spencerian philosophy, which were growing every year more popular. Since the publication of Darwin's *Origin of Species* in 1859, educated Americans had been learning eagerly of the new biological theory and constructing new cosmologies for themselves. From Darwin and his popularizers they learned that life is a fierce and constant struggle which only the fittest survive. Confusing evolution with progress, as was natural to optimistic spokesmen of a rising class and a rising nation, they concluded that the bitter strife of competitive industry, which seemed to mirror so perfectly Darwin's natural world, was producing a slow but inevitable upward movement of civilization. Those who emerged at the top were manifestly the fittest to survive and carry on. Herbert Spencer, whose evolutionary philosophy glorified automatic progress, who threw all his authority into support of the thesis that natural economic processes must be allowed to go on without hindrance from reformers, was idolized in the United States as has been no other philosopher before or since. His visit in 1882 was practically an occasion of state; the intellectual and social leadership of the East turned out to do him honor, and reporters eagerly recounted how he hailed his great patron, Andrew Carnegie, as one of his closest friends.

It was natural, then, for a Rockefeller to say that "the growth of a large business is merely a survival of the fittest," and that the splendor of the American Beauty rose could be produced only by sacrificing the early buds that grow up around it. Or for James J. Hill to assert that "the fortunes of railroad companies are determined by the law of the survival of the fittest." Or for George Hearst, entering a Senate so filled with business magnates that it was popularly called "the Millionaire's Club," to declare:

I do not know much about books; I have not read very much; but I have travelled a good deal and observed men and things and I have made up my mind after all my experience that the members of the Senate are the survivors of the fittest.

For the most part the millionaires of the Gilded Age felt no immediate need of vindicating themselves by large-scale philanthropies. Although fortunes made between 1865 and 1900 are the source of many great philanthropic foundations, in almost every case the foundations were created after 1910, when their originators were very old or had passed off the scene. Andrew Carnegie, who believed that "Amassing wealth is one of the worst species of idolatry," and that "Few millionaires are clear of the sin of having made beggars," was almost unique in feeling a sense of guilt during the earlier period. Assured by intellectuals of the progressive and civilizing value of their work, encouraged by their status as exemplars of the order of opportunity, and exhilarated by the thought that their energies were making the country rich, industrial millionaires felt secure in their exploitation and justified in their dominion.

From the business of industry the business of politics took its style. Accumulating wealth and living richly, the industrialists set the model of behavior for the less scrupulous politicians. The wealth they acquired and enjoyed set standards of consumption and emulation; overflowing into politics, it multiplied among politicians opportunities for pecuniary enrichment. Standards of success in politics changed. It was not merely self-expression or public service or glory that the typical politician sought—it was money. Lord Bryce found that the cohesive force in American politics was "the desire

for office and for office *as a means of gain.*" The spoilsmen looked upon political power as a means of participating in the general riches, of becoming wealthy in
their smaller ways and by their lesser standards, as did
the captains of industry. Never before had the motive
been so strong; never before had temptations been so
abundant.

II

The parties of the period after the post-Civil War
were based on patronage, not principle; they divided
over spoils, not issues. Although American political parties are never celebrated for having sharp differences
in principle, the great age of the spoilsmen was notable
for elevating crass hunger for office to the level of a
common credo. "The American parties now continue
to exist, because they have existed," wrote Lord Bryce
in *The American Commonwealth.* An eminent journal-
ist observed to him as late as 1908 "that the two parties
were like two bottles. Each bore a label denoting the
kind of liquor it contained, but each was empty." In
1879 young Woodrow Wilson expressed in eight words
his disgust with the degradation of American politics:
"No leaders, no principles; no principles, no parties."

The Republicans were distinguished from the Democrats chiefly by being successful. From the war and
Reconstruction onwards, when it sought actively to
strengthen its social base by espousing the policies of
American industrialists, the Republican Party existed
in an unholy and often mutually hostile conjunction
with the capitalistic interests. Capitalists, seeking land
grants, tariffs, bounties, favorable currency policies,

freedom from regulatory legislation and economic reform, supplied campaign funds, fees, and bribes and
plied politicians with investment opportunities. Seward
had said that "a party is in one sense a joint stock company in which those who contribute the most, direct
the action and management of the concern." The interests owned important shares in both parties, but they
occasionally grew restive under what they considered
the excessive demands of the politicians. Until the
1880's, in fact, the machines depended very heavily
upon the contributions of their officeholders to party
treasuries, and it was not until businessmen, feeling
their power, began to go into politics themselves on a
more considerable scale that the parties came more
fully under their sway. Before business learned to buy
statesmen at wholesale, it had to buy privileges at
retail. Fabulous sums were spent. A disgruntled Congressman from Ohio declared in 1873 that "the House
of Representatives was like an auction room where
more valuable considerations were disposed of under
the speaker's hammer than in any other place on earth."
Between 1866 and 1872, for example, the Union Pacific spent $400,000 on bribes; between 1875 and 1885
graft cost the Central Pacific as much as $500,000 an-
nually. Little wonder that an honest Republican of the
old school like Walter Q. Gresham could describe his
party as "an infernally corrupt concern," or that Senator Grimes of Iowa, once an important leader, could
say in 1870: "I believe it is to-day the most corrupt and
debauched political party that ever existed." "One
might search the whole list of Congress, Judiciary, and
Executive during the twenty-five years 1870 to 1895,"
concluded Henry Adams, "and find little but damaged
reputation."

The case of the Crédit Mobilier is a classic source in

the ethical perspectives of the Gilded Age. The Crédit Mobilier was a construction company organized by the directors of the Union Pacific. As stockholders of the railroad they allowed to themselves, in their capacity as stockholders of Crédit Mobilier, exorbitant prices for the work of construction. Since the Union Pacific was the beneficiary of almost ten million acres of public land, there was a danger that Congress might inquire too closely into the transaction. To forestall this, Oakes Ames, Congressman from Massachusetts and Union Pacific stockholder, distributed a block of shares in Crédit Mobilier among influential Congressmen. When the case was investigated by Congress in the campaign year 1872, Ames's conduct was "absolutely condemned" by a House resolution, passed 182 to 36. Significant, however, was the attitude of the Congressmen who immediately afterward surrounded Ames's desk to assure him that they had acted with reluctance, and that they had every confidence in the rectitude of his intentions. In the press there was widespread sympathy for Ames and the beneficiaries of his bribes, who, incidentally, were not similarly disciplined. Ames himself, without denying the facts, refused to acknowledge the slightest culpability. His distributing stock among Congressmen, he said, was "the same thing as going into a business community and interesting the leading business men by giving them shares." "I think," he wrote to a colleague, "a member of Congress has a right to own property in anything he chooses to invest in," and on another occasion he observed that "there is no difficulty in inducing men to look after their own property." The implication is unmistakable: it was to be expected that Congressmen would use their political power to look after their own investments, and there was nothing untoward about the whole proceeding.

A defense like this was made in confidence that a large segment of public opinion would sustain such conceptions of political morality. Such was the contemporary estimate of Benjamin F. Butler. During his service as Military Governor of New Orleans he had requisitioned from a bank of the city $8,000 which he never accounted for. Later, when a lawyer hired by the bank to sue Butler for the money—the suit was successful—reproached him with the remark that his neighbors in Lowell would think little of him for living on stolen funds, Butler replied: "The people would think I was a fool for not having taken twice as much." Mary Abigail Dodge reported that when John Bingham was taunted about possessing free shares in the Crédit Mobilier, he replied that he "only wished he had ten times more." Henry Adams concluded that the public did not care about reform: "The moral law had expired—like the Constitution."

There were, of course, untainted politicians, and they were esteemed. Grant was happy to have Hamilton Fish in his Cabinet, a man of conspicuous rectitude who adorned the group like a jewel in the head of a toad. The impeccable Carl Schurz became Secretary of the Interior under President Hayes.[2] Hayes and Harrison, two of the five Republican Presidents of the period, had tolerable reputations; but these two were as innocent of distinction as they were of corruption and have become famous in American annals chiefly for their obscurity. Their relation to underlying political realities is expressed in the retort of Boss Matt Quay to Harrison's remark upon his election in the close cam-

---

2. Garfield writes of the appointment of this notorious reformer as though it were a bold experiment: "The appointment of Schurz is unfortunate and unwise, but still ought to be confirmed to give the President a chance to test his policy."

paign of 1888. "Providence," breathed the aristocratic Harrison solemnly, "has given us the victory." "Think of the man," snorted Quay. "He ought to know that Providence hadn't a damn thing to do with it." Harrison would never know, he added, "how close a number of men were compelled to approach the gates of the penitentiary to make him President." Harrison found out soon enough what his role was expected to be. "When I came into power," he once lamented in Theodore Roosevelt's presence, "I found that the party managers had taken it all to themselves. I could not name my own Cabinet. They had sold out every place to pay election expenses."

Of the remaining three Presidents not much need be said. Grant's administrations are notorious for their corruption.[3] Hayes's successor, the sanctimonious Garfield, although essentially an honest and worthy soul, was tainted by a few minor scandals. Garfield's successor by virtue of assassination, Chester A. Arthur, had been before his vice-presidential nomination the major domo of Conkling's notorious New York Customhouse machine, a spoilsman's spoilsman. ("My God! Chet Arthur in the White House!" a friend was reported to have exclaimed.) Nevertheless Arthur, trying to rise to his office, sought conscientiously but ineffectually to promote a few reforms; ironically, his signature made the Pendleton Civil Service Act a law.

---

3. No one admired the great capitalists more than Grant, who saw nothing incongruous about a President's accepting the most lavish gifts from the rich. As fully as Carnegie or Rockefeller he accepted the idea that Providence planned to turn over to these men the control of as much of the world as they could grasp. In what other era could a President say so complacently and so candidly, by way of advocating the acquisition of Santo Domingo, that if his policy had only been adopted, "the soil would soon have fallen into the hands of the United States capitalists"?

It was not the Presidents who gave the machine its dynamic force, but the factional leaders and bosses of the Republican Party, men like Roscoe Conkling and James G. Blaine. In spite of their violent mutual animosity, these two seem now to have had much in common. Above all, both looked upon life as an amusing and rather profitable game of wits.

Conkling was incredible. Tall, elegant, showy—he wore white flannel trousers and florid waistcoats—he was voluptuously abandoned to his own egotism, which, as Henry Adams remarked, was so grotesquely comic that it rose above ridicule. An observer watching him perform in the Senate might have had difficulty deciding whether this was an actor burlesquing a senator or a senator burlesquing an actor. "A great fighter, inspired more by his hates than his loves," Garfield called him; he is best remembered for his malevolent interchanges with Blaine and his pitiless assault on George William Curtis and other reformers, whom he branded "the man-milliners, the dilettanti and carpet knights of politics." The *New York Times* once described him quite seriously as "a typical American statesman—a man by whose career and character the future will judge of the political standards of the present."

Conkling had come from a well-to-do New York family; it was characteristic that as a lawyer he tried and won his first case before his father, a judge who sat in the United States District Court. Well-born and well married, he could indulge his fancies without resorting to personal corruption; he is not known to have accepted graft, but graft was the milieu in which he lived. One of Grant's most powerful supporters, master of the rich patronage of the New York Customhouse, he was a machine product par excellence, flagrantly contemptuous of reformers who tried to challenge orthodox politics. Of course a party was a machine run by machine methods, and how else did the proprietors of ladies' magazines propose to manage them?

> We are told the Republican party is a machine. Yes. A government is a machine; a church is a machine; an army is a machine . . . the common school system of the State of New York is a machine; a political party is a machine.

Conkling was so steeped in the villainous practices of orthodox politics that he could conceive of reformers themselves as nothing but rival operators. "Their real object," he once proclaimed, "is office and plunder"— he could imagine no other intelligible end for political life. Therefore: "When Dr. Johnson defined patriotism as the last refuge of a scoundrel, he was unconscious of the then undeveloped capabilities of the word reform."

The magnetic Blaine was the most popular Republican of his time. Only once, in 1884, was he nominated by his party for the presidency, but in all other conventions from 1876 to 1892 he was a formidable possibility. His popularity persisted long after his spotty financial record became an open story to those who cared to read it; and while his little sins were a handicap that may have cost him the presidency, they never ruled him out of consideration.

Blaine's actual transgression was not especially gross by the standards of his fellows. As Speaker of the House he had been instrumental in killing a bill that would have blocked a land grant by the state of Arkansas to the Little Rock and Fort Smith Railroad. This he had done of his own volition and without any solicitations or inducements, so that he was technically clear of accepting an outright bribe. But he subsequently presumed upon this favor to secure a very liberal commission for selling the railroad's bonds to friends in Maine. The transaction turned out to be of no profit to him, because his friends lost on their investment, and Blaine, whose sense of private obligation was as healthy as his sense of public duty was frail, recompensed them for their losses. The incident, however, represented only one of a number of Blaine's railroad transactions; obviously the Republican leader, who had a sizable family and several homes and a taste for gracious living, spent more than the salaries of his offices.

It is not so much Blaine's relations with the railroads that are here significant, but the series of flagrant and well-dramatized lies to which they led. In 1876, not long before the party convention which was expected to nominate Blaine for the presidency, his various transactions with the railroads came under Congressional scrutiny. With heroic audacity Blaine made off with the private letters that held the most damaging evidence against him, selected innocent sequences from them to read on the floor of the House, and brilliantly turned upon his investigators with a false but plausible charge of scheming to suppress evidence that exonerated him. Although this bit of play-acting convinced Republican admirers of his innocence, anxiety took its toll from the protagonist, then at the height of his ambition. His friend and official biographer, Gail Hamilton, has left a memorable picture of him, lying ill on the sofa in his home, raising his clenched fist, and declaiming histrionically: "When I think, when I think, that there lives in this broad land one single human being who doubts my integrity, I would rather have stayed—" and finishing the sentence only with a flourishing gesture. Not long thereafter on a Sunday morning he fell in a faint all too conveniently at the door of the Congregational church that he attended.

All this, one is inclined to think, is too much. The New York *Evening Post* published during the campaign of 1884 a pamphlet documenting without difficulty ten separate lies Blaine had told about his private financial transactions. Blaine had even gone so far as to compose a letter to be sent to himself over the signature of Warren Fisher, an official of the Little Rock and Fort Smith Railroad. Fisher was to say in part—as Blaine wrote it:

> . . . your action was as open and fair as the day. When the original enterprise failed, I knew with what severity the pecuniary loss fell upon you and with what integrity and nerve you met it . . . your conduct was in the highest degree honorable and straightforward.

This testimony of James G. Blaine on behalf of James G. Blaine makes edifying reading. Here was the "Plumed Knight" of the Republican Party! A reputation built upon eulogies of the high protective tariff, which he believed to be the real source of American prosperity, on waving the bloody shirt over the conquered South, on twisting the British lion's tail for the benefit of his Irish and Anglophobic following, and on dubious and unsuccessful schemes for promoting imperialism in South America had to be protected, as though it were the most precious thing in the world, at the cost of the most desperate lies, desperately advertised.

Blaine has been accounted by both contemporaries and historians as a man of unusual intellectual faculties for a politician. His major intellectual effort, a massive two-volume history, *Twenty Years of Congress*, is still of some use; but its governing conception is simply that the Republic was safe only in the hands of the Republican Party, and it can be judged as well by what it omits as by what it includes. Blaine saw fit, for example, to say nothing at all of the corruptions and scandals of the Grant administrations. And this was characteristic: so much of his life was spent in obscuring the truth that falsehood and evasion blanket even his historical prose. By common testimony he was a man of intense personal charm, warm and tender in his private relationships, facile, clever, and winning in his public role. Yet he left behind him not a single constructive achievement, hardly even a constructive suggestion; his chief contribution to American politics was to lower its tone. Roscoe Conkling, when asked to campaign for him in 1884, snarled, out of his morbid hatred: "No thank you, I don't engage in criminal practice"; and for once Conkling was right: harmless as a private citizen, Blaine was an antisocial being in his public capacity. "When I want a thing," the Plumed Knight once said to his wife, "I want it dreadfully." It might have been the motto of a whole generation of Americans who wanted things dreadfully, and took them.

III

The isolation of the reformers was as characteristic as the cynicism and corruption of the regulars. Party warhorses, who tended to identify rapacity with manliness, looked upon "good" men in politics as dudes, freaks, immune to the spirit of their time not out of virtue but perversity—"man-milliners," as Conkling said in his famous diatribe. Blaine referred to them in a letter to Garfield as "upstarts, conceited, foolish, vain . . . noisy but not numerous, pharisaical but not practical, ambitious but not wise, pretentious but not powerful."

The tart Senator John J. Ingalls of Kansas, who believed that purity in politics is "an iridescent dream," described them as

> effeminate without being either masculine or feminine; unable to beget or to bear; possessing neither fecundity nor virility; endowed with the contempt of men and the derision of women, and doomed to sterility, isolation, and extinction.

This was savage, but it had some truth: in politics the reformers were both isolated and sterile. Intellectuals, obsessed with the abstract ideal of public service, businessmen tired of the cost of graft, patricians worried about the need of honesty in government, they did not know the people, and the people with good reason did not know them. While reformers were concerned with public uplift, farmers and workers were trying to stave off private downfall. The steady deflationary movement of prices was ruinous to farmers, whose history in this period was one of economic tragedies and largely futile struggles against money and monopoly. Industrialism brought down upon the working class that pall of oppression and misery which is found in every chronicle of the Industrial Revolution, and it was unrelieved by fitful and brutal labor struggles. Violent business fluctuations, the great depressions of the seventies and nineties, and the sharp crisis of the mideighties spread poverty and insecurity.

It is not surprising, therefore, that reformers who concentrated upon a Civil Service Act, the tariff, or exposing the peccadilloes of politicians did not excite mass enthusiasm. Single-minded concern for honesty in public service is a luxury of the middle and upper classes. The masses do not care deeply about the honesty of public servants unless it promises to lead to some human fruition, some measurable easing of the difficulties of life. If a choice is necessary, the populace of an American city will choose kindness over honesty, as the nation's enduring Tammanys attest. The rural masses look for statesmen of the cheap dollar.

Twice during the heyday of the spoilsmen organized reform movements arose within the Republican Party —in the liberal Republican movement that ran Horace Greeley for the presidency in 1872, and the Mugwump bolt of 1884, which helped to defeat Blaine. The chief purposes of the first were expressed by Godkin in 1870 when he called for a party "having for its object Tariff Reform, Civil Service Reform, and Minority Representation." Since the most flagrant corruption of the Grant administrations took place after 1872, and general discontent did not grow keen until after the panic of 1873, the movement was premature. In any case, it was not attractive to workers and farmers, and was hardly meant to be. Its candidate, the eccentric Greeley, was unable to throw even the vulnerable Grant on the defensive; when the campaign was over, finding himself the worst-beaten man in the history of the presidency, he grieved: "I was assailed so bitterly that I hardly knew whether I was running for the Presidency or the Penitentiary."

In 1884 some dissident Republicans, who were strong in the strategic state of New York, where the electoral vote was perilously close, refused to swallow Blaine's candidacy and helped elect Cleveland. But whatever these Mugwumps contributed to Cleveland's victory, economic radicalism was no part of it; indeed, a good part of Cleveland's appeal for them consisted in the fact that he yielded nothing to the Republican leadership in conservatism.

The fate of political reform was paralleled by the failure of economic reform. During the first Cleveland administration the Cullom committee, which had been investigating railroads, concluded that "upon no public question are the people nearly so unanimous" as that Congress should regulate interstate commerce. Congress accordingly gave "the people" the Interstate Commerce Act. But as Senator Nelson W. Aldrich, already the watchdog of the corporations, said, the act was "a delusion and a sham . . . an empty menace to the great interests, made to answer the clamor of the ignorant and the unreasoning"; Senator Cullom, the act's sponsor, described it as "conservative legislation" passed in the guise of a reform measure. Railroads were soon circumventing regulation by the Interstate Commerce Commission with ease. Six years after the law was passed, Richard Olney, Cleveland's Attorney General, advised the president of the Chicago, Burlington, & Quincy that to ask for its repeal would be unwise:

> The Commission, as its functions have now been limited by the courts, is, or can be made, of great use to the railroads. It satisfies the popular clamor for government supervision of the railroads at the same time that that supervision is almost entirely nominal. Further, the older such a commission gets to be, the more inclined it will be found to take the business and railroad view of things. It thus becomes a sort of barrier between the railroads and the people and a sort of protection against hasty and crude legislation hostile to railroad interests.

The second economic reform, the Sherman Anti-Trust Act, passed during the election year of 1890, likewise in response to public clamor against monopolists, was equally cynical in design. Republican Senator Orville

Platt of Connecticut charged during the Sherman bill debate:

> The conduct of the Senate . . . has not been in the line of the honest preparation of a bill to prohibit and punish trusts. It has been in the line of getting some bill with that title that we might go to the country with. The questions of whether the bill would be operative, or how it would operate . . . have been whistled down the wind in this Senate as idle talk, and the whole effort has been to get some bill headed: "A Bill to Punish Trusts" with which to go to the country.

IV

The best defense of the two-party system is the argument that while it permits the majority party to govern, as it should, it also centralizes the opposition in a single minority group, thus preventing the dissipation of minority energy in sectarian disputes and checking any tyrannical tendencies on the part of the "ins." This argument has seldom fitted the facts of American life, where party differences have rarely been profound and party structure has been so rigid that minorities, instead of being focused in either major party when it was out, have rather had to sunder their traditional party ties and—in most cases—drown alone in the political seas. The first post-Civil War victory of the Democrats, in 1884 (when they had the estimable assistance of the Mugwump Republicans), is one of the few exceptions to this American story of party loyalty; but the subsequent Democratic administration only confirmed the profound uniformity between Republican and Democratic principles. In Grover Cleveland, however, the

Democrats at least had a man who stood out, if only for honesty and independence, as the sole reasonable facsimile of a major President between Lincoln and Theodore Roosevelt.

Grover Cleveland's father, Richard Falley Cleveland, was a poor, studious Presbyterian parson of modest abilities who raised a family of nine children on the niggardly salaries of his village pastorates, never taxed himself to rise in the ministry, and died at forty-nine, when Grover was sixteen. The son took on his father's moral imperatives and accepted his lack of ambition as normal. In him the balance between the call of duty, as he saw it, and the call of ambition was heavily weighted in favor of duty. Simple, sentimental, and unimaginative, he worked for security and comfort and expected little more. On the night of his election to the governorship of New York, at the age of forty-five, he wrote to his brother: "Do you know that if Mother were alive I should feel so much safer? I have always thought her prayers had much to do with my success."

The hardship of being thrown on his own resources at an early age made Cleveland neither bitter nor rebellious. A tinge of what psychologists call moral masochism may have made it easier for him to carry his early burdens and, in his later years, to bear the odium that fell upon him. Writing reminiscently about his first years in Buffalo as an underpaid law student and clerk, he declared that he "had adversity in abundance . . . actually enjoyed his adversities." His working habits were irregular: spurts of incredible energy and self-punishing conscientiousness were followed by spells of the easygoing laxity of bachelorhood. Corpulent, rugged, and amiable, falling quickly into the social tone of Buffalo, a thriving city with a large, *gemütlich* German population, Cleveland joined what

Professor Allan Nevins aptly calls "the hotel lobby and bar-room set."

Cleveland's rise to power was rapid and freakish. In the spring of 1881 he was a well-established Buffalo lawyer with a comfortable livelihood and a brief history of conscientious and unaspiring tenure in two minor political offices. In the spring of 1885 he was in Washington, taking the oath of office as President of the United States. A series of chance events catapulted him upward. In 1881 a particularly flagrant Republican boodler was nominated for the mayoralty of Buffalo; the Democrats, searching for an aggressively honest opponent and remembering Cleveland's past services as sheriff, offered him a nomination, which he accepted without enthusiasm. The new mayor dealt roughly with local grafters, winning himself a good reputation throughout New York Democracy just on the eve of a gubernatorial contest. Circumstances in the state happened to be favorable: New York County delegates who were revolting against Tammany and seeking a suitable candidate threw the nomination to Cleveland after a brief deadlock between two more prominent men. An equally fortuitous split in the New York State Republican Party between the followers of Governor Cornell and those of Conkling made Cleveland's election a certainty. The physical decline of Tilden and the impoverished state of Democratic leadership made Cleveland a logical choice for his party in 1884. His campaign opponent, Blaine, damaged by old sins, the defection of the Mugwumps, and the incredible "Rum, Romanism, and Rebellion" speech of the Rev. Samuel Burchard, lost to Cleveland by the slimmest margin: a change of some 600 votes in New York State could have swung the election the other way. It was through a series of improbabilities that a man of

Cleveland's caliber became President in the Gilded Age.

The legacy of Samuel J. Tilden went to Cleveland. His chief advisers were Tilden protégés and lieutenants like Daniel Manning, the newspaper-owner who became his first Secretary of the Treasury, and the millionaire corporation lawyer William C. Whitney, recently mated with Standard Oil wealth. Such friends only confirmed Cleveland's views, which were conservative from the beginning; but they may also have insulated the politician from the broadening effect of contact with public opinion, which was so notable in changing the outlook of the two Roosevelts and Woodrow Wilson. It is disarming to find Whitney writing to President Cleveland in 1892:

> . . . the impression of you got by the people is that you do not appreciate their suffering and poverty . . . and have your ideas formed by Eastern money power, etc.— *the usual twaddle.* . . . As you said to me, it is unaccountable what ideas they get and where they get them.

Yet it was hardly a mistake for conservatives of the East to regard Cleveland as their own man or for many normally Republican businessmen to support him even as early as 1884. One of his most notable acts as governor had been to veto a bill reducing elevated-railway fares in New York City from ten to five cents, in spite of the obvious popularity of the bill among the people of the city. Such acts had given Andrew D. White cause to exult that Cleveland had overcome his "sympathies for the working people" and to praise him for having "not the slightest germs of demagogism." After his first election Cleveland received from Jay

Gould the telegraphic message: "I feel . . . that the vast business interests of the country will be entirely safe in your hands." When Cleveland turned back the tide of free silver, Respectability was rewarded for its confidence. The Republican Senator Allison told Horace White in 1894 that it was "God's mercy" that Cleveland had won over Harrison in 1892 because no Republican President could have secured repeal of the Sherman Silver Purchase Act. Many years later Woodrow Wilson, converted from Cleveland Democracy to progressivism, denied that Cleveland's administration had been Democratic at all—"Cleveland was a conservative Republican." "Too conservative," says Professor Nevins, "to be a great constructive statesman."

Cleveland regarded the duties of public office in the most serious light. "It seems to me," he wrote to an old friend in June 1885, "that I am as much consecrated to a service as the religionist who secludes himself from all that is joyous in life and devotes himself to a sacred mission." Vetoes had made him famous as mayor and governor, and from the very first he conceived of his presidential task as a negative one: he was the righteous executive; his assignment was to *police* other politicians, to prevent them from giving favors or taking graft. The key to his mind was his dislike of "paternalism" in government. The people, he believed, were entitled to economy, purity, and justice in their government, and should expect no more. "A fair field and no favor." Industry must not expect to be coddled by tariffs; veterans and their dependents must not expect overindulgence in pensions; railroad corporations must give strict account of their use of land grants. Cleveland's experience with the tariff was evidence of both the earnestness and the futility of his philosophy.

Carl Schurz recalled how Cleveland had asked him shortly after his election in 1884 what issues he should take up. When Schurz replied that he should strike at the tariff, the President-elect, visibly moved, replied candidly: "I am ashamed to say it, but the truth is I know nothing about the tariff. . . . Will you tell me how to go about it to learn?" He devoted the greater part of his annual message of 1887 to an attack upon high rates. Warned by the politicians that his aggressiveness on the tariff question would cost him re-election, he replied in characteristic tones: "What is the use of being elected or reelected unless you stand for something?" His fight for reform, however, was ineffectual; the Wilson-Gorman tariff was at one with the Interstate Commerce Act and the Sherman Anti-Trust Act.

Cleveland's philosophy of laissez-faire, like the classic theory, was dependent upon one grand assumption: things must work out smoothly without government action, or the whole system, coherent enough in theory, would fall from the weakness of its premises. That these were unrealistic Cleveland had to recognize by the time of his fourth annual message to Congress, written in December 1888, after his defeat by Harrison. This message rumbled with protests that might have been written by a Populist:

. . . we find the wealth and luxury of our cities mingled with poverty and wretchedness and unremunerative toil. A crowded and constantly increasing urban population suggests the impoverishment of rural sections, and discontent with agricultural pursuits. . . .

We discover that the fortunes realized by our manufacturers are no longer solely the reward of sturdy industry and enlightened foresight, but that they result from the discriminating favor of the government, and are largely built upon undue exactions from the masses of our people. The gulf between employers and the employed is constantly widening, and classes are rapidly forming, one comprising the very rich and powerful, while in another are found the toiling poor.

. . . We discover the existence of trusts, combinations, and monopolies, while the citizen is struggling far in the rear, or is trampled to death beneath an iron heel. Corporations, which should be carefully restrained creatures of the law and the servants of the people, are fast becoming the people's masters.

Nevertheless, Cleveland held to the view that the government could do little to check the forces that brought such results. His only recourse was to appeal to businessmen to improve their morals and become trustees of the public. "Must we always," he asked pathetically of the Philadelphia Commercial Exchange in 1887, "must we always look for the political opinions of our business men precisely where they suppose their immediate pecuniary advantage to be found?" Businessmen should be "guided by better motives than purely selfish and exclusive benefit."

Lacking a more positive conception of social action, Cleveland fell quietly and naturally into an implicit partnership with the interests during the crisis of the nineties. The man who thought that tariffs and bounties were an unwarranted boon to business and a gross violation of justice and equity thought nothing of sending federal troops to break the Pullman strike in 1894, or of putting them substantially under the charge of a railroad attorney. Years later he asserted that he and others of responsibility in the strike were to be "congratulated" for the part they played. He was equally resolute in rebuffing the farmers over the silver question. One did not have to be a plutocrat, of course, to be a rigid adherent of the gold standard; but an equally rigid adherence to laissez-faire required Cleveland to deny the responsibility of the government to produce any alternative to free silver as a remedy for agrarian distress. Few men would have the blunt solidity to do what Cleveland did—or rather to fail to do what he failed to do. It demanded his far from nimble mind to display all the imbecile impartiality of a philosophy that lumped together both the tariff racketeers and the poor bedeviled farmers as illegitimate petitioners of the government. It has been said to Cleveland's credit that he was strong enough to resist popular pressures that no other man could have withstood; it can also be said that he turned his back on distress more acute than any other President would have had the *sang-froid* to ignore.

Cleveland, in short, had made a defect of his merits. He was not a cruel man, but he was dogmatic, obtuse, and insensitive. Making whatever allowance one will, there is something odd about a President's writing during a year of popular agony like 1895 to the man who acted as his broker: "You know rich investors like me have to keep an account of income in these days." The intended note of jocularity rings false. "I find," he writes soon again, "I am developing quite a strong desire to make money"—and curiously, "and I think this is a good time to indulge in that propensity." One is reminded of Carnegie's thoughtful words: "The man who has money during a panic is the wise and valuable citizen."

Certainly this is the spirit of the faithful bourgeois. And Cleveland, this product of good conscience and self-help, with his stern ideas of purity, efficiency, and service, was a taxpayer's dream, the ideal bourgeois statesman for his time: out of heartfelt conviction he gave to the interests what many a lesser politician might have sold them for a price. He was the flower of American political culture in the Gilded Age.

CHAPTER VIII

WILLIAM JENNINGS BRYAN:
THE DEMOCRAT AS REVIVALIST

❁

A MAN *can be born again; the springs of life can be cleansed instantly. . . . If this is true of one, it can be true of any number. Thus, a nation can be born in a day if the ideals of the people can be changed.* WILLIAM JENNINGS BRYAN

THOSE who know American revivalism are familiar with the story of the skeptic who comes to the camp meeting to scoff and stays to be converted. Bryan's great "Cross of Gold" speech at the Democratic convention of 1896 had the same galvanic effect. One of his followers who was sitting in the gallery reported the behavior of a nearby gold Democrat who had been sneering at every friendly reference to the silver cause. When Bryan finished his appeal the gold Democrat "lost control of himself and literally grabbed hold of me and pulled me up from a sitting to a standing position on my chair. He yelled at me, 'Yell for God's sake, yell,' as Bryan closed his speech."

The Great Commoner was a circuit-riding evangelist in politics; the "Cross of Gold" speech, with its religious imagery, its revivalist fervor, its electric reaction upon the audience, was a miniature of his career. Many who laughed at the gospel of his first years in politics came in time to accept much of it as commonplace. Bryan himself, emerging suddenly from obscurity at an hour when the people were in an angry mood, framing his message for a simple constituency nursed in evangelical Protestantism and knowing little literature but the Bible, helped to lead a Great Awakening which swept away much of the cynicism and apathy that had been characteristic of American politics for thirty years.

Bryan was equally at home in religion and politics. In his lecture "The Prince of Peace," which he gave many times and in almost every corner of the world, he declared:

> I am interested in the science of government, but I am more interested in religion. . . . I enjoy making a political speech . . . but I would rather speak on religion than on politics. I commenced speaking on the stump when I was only twenty, but I commenced speaking in the church six years earlier—and I shall be in the church even after I am out of politics.

Unfortunately Bryan's political leadership and social philosophy were as crude as the theology of his evangelical brethren.

Charles Willis Thompson once remarked that "Bryan's hold on the West lay in the fact that he was himself the average man of a large part of that country; he did not merely resemble that average man, he was that average man." In this Bryan was different from the other great leaders of the Progressive era. Theodore Roosevelt, with his leisure-class background and tastes, Wilson with his professional reserve, La Follette with his lonely stubbornness and his craftsmanlike interest in the technical details of reform, were singular men. They sensed popular feelings; Bryan embodied them.

Byran's typical constituent was the long-suffering staple farmer of the West and South. This farmer had broken the prairie or survived the rigors of Reconstruction. His wheat or cotton had fed and clothed the growing industrial population of the cities; exported to Europe, his produce had bought the foreign capital that financed American industrial expansion. For thirty years, since 1865, he had kept his eyes on the general price level, watching it sink downward almost without interruption until at last the dollar had trebled in value. This meant slow agony for the farmer; he was a debtor, and his long-term debts were appreciating intolerably. A debt that he could have paid in 1865 with 1,000 bushels of wheat now cost him 3,000 bushels. To one who owes money and finds it hard to come by, economic hardship appears in its simplest guise as a shortage of money. If money was scarce, the farmer concluded, then the logical thing was to increase the money supply. The silver campaign of 1896 was a struggle between those who wanted money cheap and those who wanted it dear.

But in 1896 free silver ranked among the heresies with free love. Except in the farm country, wherever men of education and substance gathered together it was held beneath serious discussion. Economists in the universities were against it; preachers were against it; writers of editorials were against it. For almost forty years after the campaign was over, the single gold standard remained a fixed star in the firmament of economic orthodoxy, to doubt which was not merely wrong but dishonest. (As late as 1933, when Franklin D. Roosevelt took the United States off the gold standard, Lewis W. Douglas was heard to moan: "Well, this is the end of Western civilization.")

In fact, however, the logic of the silver inflationists

was not so wrongheaded as Bryan's orthodox contemporaries believed. Some eminent authorities look back upon the single gold standard as a vicious *idée fixe*,[1] and few will deny that there was a profound need for currency reform in 1896. The farmers were indeed being milked by the interests, in part through contraction of the currency. Accused during the election campaign of fighting for a dishonest dollar, Bryan had by far the better of the argument when he replied that "A dollar approaches honesty as its purchasing power approaches stability."

But free-silverites went on to the disastrous conclusion that currency was the great cause of their miseries, and that currency reform would end them. The many ways in which farmers were victimized by tariffs, railroads, middlemen, speculators, warehousers, and monopolistic producers of farm equipment were all but forgotten; yet these things had been subjects of much sound agitation in the Bryan country not long before; to revive them would have been neither novel nor strange. In 1892, before the depression brought popular discontents to fever pitch, General James B. Weaver, campaigning on a well-rounded platform of reform issues, had polled over a million votes for President on the Populist ticket. The time seemed ripe for a many-sided attack on abuses that had flourished since the Civil War. Instead, the growing demand for free silver so completely overshadowed other things in the minds of

1. John Maynard Keynes found in the gold standard one of the major causes of the modern world tragedy. In *The General Theory of Employment, Interest, and Money* he stated: "Under the system of domestic *laissez faire* and an international gold standard such as was orthodox in the latter half of the nineteenth century, there was no means open to a government whereby to mitigate economic distress at home except through the competitive struggle for markets."

the people as to fix them on a single issue that was at best superficial. This neglect of other facets of reform caused Henry Demarest Lloyd, one of the most intelligent and principled reform spokesmen, to complain:

> Free silver is the cow-bird of the reform movement. It waited until the nest had been built by the sacrifices and labour of others, and then it laid its eggs in it, pushing out the others which lie smashed on the ground.

In defense of the free-silver politicians it must be said that they only stressed the issue that the farmers themselves greeted most responsively. "During the campaign of 1892," writes John D. Hicks in *The Populist Revolt*, "the Populists had learned that of all the planks in their platform the silver plank had the widest appeal." And not only to the farmers—it was the only fund-raising issue the Bryan-Altgeld Democrats had; it attracted the Western silver-mineowners who, eager to enlarge their market, gave liberally to the cause, distributed 125,000 copies of W. H. Harvey's plausible free-silver pamphlet, *Coin's Financial School*, and supplied Bryan with most of his meager campaign resources.

Byran was content to stress free silver to the exclusion of everything else, and thus to freeze the popular cause at its lowest level of understanding. No one can read his campaign speeches in *The First Battle* without being struck by the way the free-silver obsession elbowed all other questions out of the way. It was the only time in the history of the Republic when a candidate ran for the presidency on the strength of a monomania. At Hartford Bryan asserted warmly: "Of all the instrumentalities which have been conceived by the mind of man for transferring the bread which one man earns to another man who does not earn it, I believe the gold standard is the greatest." In the "Cross of Gold" speech he claimed that "when we have restored the money of the Constitution all other necessary reforms will be possible; but . . . until this is done there is no other reform that can be accomplished."

There seems to have been an element of expediency in Bryan's original acceptance of free silver. "I don't know anything about free silver," he told an audience during his campaign for Congress in 1892. "The people of Nebraska are for free silver and I am for free silver. I will look up the arguments later." Many other politicians have gone through just such an intellectual process, but Bryan's simplicity was unique: he saw nothing to be ashamed of in such a confession. The cause of the people was just; therefore their remedies must be sound; his duty was simply to look up the arguments. That he came to believe earnestly in free silver can hardly be questioned, for his capacity to convince himself, probably the only exceptional thing about his mind, was boundless. "It is a poor head," he once declared, "that cannot find plausible reason for doing what the heart wants to do."

"Of all the men I have seen at close range in thirty-one years of newspaper service," Oswald Garrison Villard has written, "Mr. Bryan seemed to me the most ignorant." The Commoner's heart was filled with simple emotions, but his mind was stocked with equally simple ideas. Presumably he would have lost his political effectiveness if he had learned to look at his supporters with a critical eye, but his capacity for identifying himself with them was costly, for it gave them not so much leadership as expression. He spoke for them so perfectly that he never spoke to them. In his lifelong stream of impassioned rhetoric he communicated only what they already believed.

If Bryan failed to advance a well-rounded program for his farm followers in 1896, he did still less for labor. Aside from one uninspiring address in which he assailed government by injunction—a nod to the Pullman strikers—he did not go far out of his way to capitalize the bitter working-class discontent of the campaign year. Subsequently he was friendly toward labor, but he never sponsored a positive program of labor legislation, and it is doubtful that he had any clear conception of the trials of working-class existence. When he first ran for Congress, he told an audience of farmers that he was "tired of hearing about laws made for the benefit of men who work in shops." In 1896 he won the support of the A.F. of L., then a struggling organization of some 270,000 members, although such labor leaders as Gompers were well aware that "the cause of our ills lies far deeper than the question of gold or silver." In Mark Hanna's estimation Bryan's appeal was too narrow: "He's talking Silver all the time, and that's where we've got him." Bryan ran stronger in the industrial cities of the East than he did in the East generally, but his labor support was too weak to win him any of the heavily populated states.

Bryan's social philosophy, which can be reconstructed from speeches made from 1892 to 1896, was not a grave departure from the historic ideology of the Democratic Party. Protesting against the drift of government from the popular will, he set down his faith in Jeffersonian principles in the most forthright terms:

> I assert that the people of the United States . . . have sufficient patriotism and sufficient intelligence to sit in

judgment on every question which has arisen or which will arise, no matter how long our government will endure. The great political questions are in their final analysis great moral questions, and it requires no extended experience in the handling of money to enable a man to tell right from wrong.

The premise from which Bryan argued was that social problems are essentially moral—that is to say, religious. It was inconceivable that the hardworking, Bible-reading citizenry should be inferior in moral insight to the cynical financiers of the Eastern cities. Because they were, as Bryan saw it, better people, they were better moralists, and hence better economists. In after years when he bustled to the support of the anti-evolution laws with the argument that he was defending the democracy of Tennessee, he was simply carrying this variety of political primitivism to its logical end.

The second principle of Bryan's philosophy was summarized in the old Jacksonian motto that he often quoted: "Equal rights to all and special privileges to none." Like the men of 1828, Bryan felt that he represented a cause that was capable of standing on its own feet without special assistance from the government. The majority of the people, he declaimed, who produced the nation's wealth in peace and rallied to its flag in war, asked for nothing from the government but "even-handed justice." "It is the duty of government to protect all from injustice and to do so without showing partiality for any one or any class."

Several writers have argued that Bryanism marked the beginning of the end of laissez-faire in the United States, but this is true only in the most indirect and attenuated sense. The Democratic platform of 1896 called for no sweeping restrictions of private enterprise;

none of its planks required serious modification of the economic structure through government action.[2] Most of its demands, on the contrary, can be summed up in the expression: "Hands off." The call for a return to bimetallism was a call for the removal of a restriction on silver coinage imposed as late as 1873, not for some thoroughly novel policy. The labor planks asked only that the federal government keep its hands off labor disputes and leave them to state authority—a victory for John P. Altgeld over Grover Cleveland. The income-tax plank was not accounted a means of redistributing wealth on any considerable scale, but merely of forcing the plutocracy to pay for its own services. It was the great merchant, not the farmer, who needed a navy, cried Bryan, echoing the Jeffersonians of old; it was the capitalist, not the poor man, who wanted a standing army "to supplement the local government in protecting his property when he enters into a contest with his employees." Then let the merchant and the capitalist pay their share in maintaining the army and navy. The spirit of the agrarians, throughout defensive rather than aggressive, was aptly expressed by Mary E. Lease when she said that the people were "at bay," and by Bryan himself when he proclaimed: "We do not come as aggressors. . . . We are fighting in defense of our homes, our families and our posterity."

In Bryan's mind the purpose of "the first battle" was to preserve classic American individualism. In one of the most frequently quoted passages of the "Cross of Gold" speech he tried to assimilate the cause of the

---

2. The Populist platform, which included proposals for unemployment relief, public works, and government ownership, was more positive in its demands. Bryan deftly dissociated himself, without being too specific, by stating that there were some planks in the Populist platform of which he did not approve.

people to American traditions of enterprise—to restore it, in effect, to respectability by underlining its bourgeois aspirations:

> When you come before us and tell us that we are to disturb your business interests, we reply that you have disturbed our business interests by your course. We say to you that you have made the definition of a business man too limited in its application. The man who is employed for wages is as much a business man as his employer. The attorney in a country bank is as much a business man as the corporation counsel in a great metropolis; a merchant at the crossroads store is as much a business man as the merchant of New York; the farmer who goes forth in the morning and toils all day—who begins in the spring and toils all summer—and who by the application of brawn and muscle to the natural resources of the country, creates wealth, is as much a business man as the man who goes upon the Board of Trade and bets upon the price of grain.

When he came to New York to deliver his acceptance address he declared in words strikingly similar to Jackson's bank message:

> Our campaign has not for its object the reconstruction of society. We cannot insure to the vicious the fruits of a virtuous life; we would not invade the home of the provident in order to supply the wants of the spendthrift; we do not propose to transfer the rewards of industry to the lap of indolence. Property is and will remain the stimulus to endeavor and the compensation for toil. We believe, as asserted in the Declaration of Independence, that all men are created equal; but that does not mean that all men are or can be equal in possessions, in ability, or in merit; it simply means that all shall stand equal before the law. . . .

After one hundred years of change in society the Jeffersonian-Jacksonian philosophy was intact. To those who accept that philosophy, this will appear as steadfastness of faith; to those who reject it, as inflexibility of mind.

II

Ridiculed and condemned by all Eastern Respectability in 1896, denounced as an anarchist, a socialist, a subverter of religion and morals, the victim of every device that wealth and talents could bring to bear, Bryan has gained a place among the celebrated American rebels. But in an important psychological sense he was never a rebel at all—and this is a clue to the torpor of his mind. What was lacking in him was a sense of alienation. He never felt the excitement of intellectual discovery that comes with rejection of one's intimate environment. The revolt of the youth against paternal authority, of the village agnostic against the faith of his tribe, of the artist against the stereotypes of philistine life, of the socialist against the whole bourgeois community—such experiences were not within his ken. Near the end of his life his own party laughed him off the stage, but that came too late to be instructive.

Politicians cannot be expected to have the traits of detached intellectuals, but few men in any phase of life have been so desolately lacking as Bryan in detachment or intellectuality. While he was eager to grapple with his opponents in the political arena, he was incapable of confronting them in the arena of his own mind. His characteristic mental state was not that of a man who has abandoned the assumptions of his society or his class after a searching examination, but rather of one who has been so thoroughly nurtured in a provincial heresy that it has become for him merely another orthodoxy. Colonel House relates that Bryan often told him "that a man who did not believe in the free and unlimited coinage of silver at 16 to 1 was either a fool or a knave." Bryan was rooted in a section of the country where his panaceas were widely taken as gospel; even the substantial citizenry of the West gave him a following. As he complacently observed in *The First Battle* concerning the men who helped him launch the Nebraska Democratic free-silver movement in 1894, "They were all men of standing in the State and most of them men of considerable property." He referred to the East as "the enemy's country." When he went to battle for the Western farmer, therefore, it was not in the spirit of a domestic quarrel in which one's object is to persuade, but of a war against a foreign power in which an exchange of views is impossible. He could no more analyze the issues of his day than the Confederates could realize the obsolescence of slavery.

Intellectually, Bryan was a boy who never left home. His father, Silas Bryan, was a Baptist and a Democrat of Southern origin, who carved out a successful career in the "Egypt" section of Illinois, became a judge in the state courts, owned a large house, and provided his family with the stale culture and niggardly comfort that usually result when ample means are used to achieve Puritan ends. In 1872, when Bryan was twelve, Silas Bryan ran for Congress with the endorsement of the Greenback Party. The father believed in the supremacy of the Anglo-Saxon race, the value of education as an instrument of success, democratic opportunity, the God of the Old Testament, and an expanded currency. The son never found reason to question these convictions: there was no ideological tension in the

Bryan household. William Jennings did break with his father's church to join the Presbyterians, abandoning his ambition to become a Baptist minister because he was frightened by the strenuous dunking of the baptismal ceremony, but he learned that his conversion had hurt Silas Bryan's feelings only long after his father was dead.

From his father's home Bryan was sent to Whipple Academy and Illinois College at Jacksonville, Illinois. His six years there did nothing to awaken his mind. The faculty of Illinois College consisted of eight men, and its curriculum carried no subject except mathematics and classics beyond an introductory course. During his years of attendance Bryan withdrew eighteen books from the college library (which was closed to students all but a few hours of the day), and they were chiefly fiction. (Bryan especially liked the novels of Charles Dickens.) The president of the college, Julian Monson Sturtevant, was the author of a textbook, *Economics*, which defended free trade and bimetallism. "The President of the College," Bryan declaimed happily, "is for free trade, our ex-President is for free trade, and *I myself* am for free trade." After what Bryan had heard in his father's home and absorbed from Sturtevant, the protective tariff and monometallism seemed outlandish.

For two years after leaving college Bryan read law at the Union College of Law in Chicago and in the office of Lyman Trumbull, after which he returned to Jacksonville, married the daughter of a prosperous storekeeper, and for five years practiced law without distinction. Smarting with realization of his mediocrity as a lawyer, Bryan fled westward and settled in Lincoln, Nebraska, where he soon edged into politics under the protective wing of J. Sterling Morton, the Democratic political agent of the railroads. He was fond of saying that he had entered politics by accident, but in a franker mood he once confessed: "Certainly from the time I was fifteen years old, I had but one ambition in life, and that was to come to Congress. I studied for it. I worked for it, and everything I did had that object in view."

In 1890, with the backing of the business and liquor interests of Omaha, he won a seat in Congress. Two years later, after many months of arduous study, he made an impressive anti-tariff speech in the House, which focused national attention upon him. Then, quickly perceiving the decline of the tariff as a political issue, and observing the rapid rise of Populism, which was especially strong in his own state, he took up free silver. Nebraska districts had been rearranged; Omaha was no longer in his bailiwick; Bryan now "looked up the arguments" on silver as he had on the tariff, negotiated financial backing from the Utah and Colorado silver-mine operators, and won re-election from a more rural constituency. In 1893 he made another spectacular speech in Congress against repeal of the Sherman Silver Purchase Act, of which almost a million copies were distributed by silver-mineowners. The following year he tried for election to the Senate, but the legislature spurned him, and he turned to an ill-paid position as editor of the Omaha *World-Herald*, which had been procured by his patrons among the silver interests. With cool nerve and considerable skill, he set to work to make the *World-Herald* an instrument of his presidential ambitions, which then seemed fabulously premature to everyone but himself.

Bryan's political career after 1896 was a long, persistent search for an issue comparable in effect to free silver, and an equally persistent campaign to keep himself in the public eye. In 1899 anti-imperialism seemed a likely issue. Democratic and Populist opponents of expansion were planning to block annexation of the Philippines by rejecting the peace treaty with Spain in the Senate. To Bryan, fighting in this way as an organized minority seemed wrong; the people themselves must decide—and the issue must be exploited in a campaign. Assuming that an anti-imperialist platform in 1900 would appeal to the idealism of the American people, as the cause of Cuba had before the war, he managed to persuade just enough Democratic Senators to permit the treaty to pass. He proposed to win a mandate for Philippine independence in the election. This was the most grotesque miscalculation of his life. Anti-imperialism would have been a much more live issue if the treaty had been rejected and the question of annexing the Philippines was still hanging fire. Once the treaty was ratified, the people were quite content to let the matter rest. Bryan found anti-imperialism such a sterile issue during his 1900 campaign that he turned increasingly to others—anti-trust and free silver—but prosperity had returned and he was unable to excite the electorate as before.

Bryan's attempt to revive the stale free-silver issue during the campaign also backfired. The world production of gold, stimulated by the new cyanide extraction process and the discovery of fresh deposits, had risen markedly, and the price level had also gone up, but when followers like the sociologist E. A. Ross pointed out to Bryan that the new gold supplies had relieved the money shortage and undermined the cause of silver, the Commoner was unimpressed. Considerations of practical economics, Ross recalls, meant little to him. "He . . . merely suggested how to parry arguments based upon them brought out by our opponents. . . . I saw that Mr. Bryan was no realist." From a strategic standpoint, Bryan was worse than wrong, he was impractical. By insisting on the free-silver plank in the 1900 platform he may have lost whatever chance he had of winning some of the Eastern states, while he did not need the issue to win the West or the South. "Bryan," quipped Thomas B. Reed, "had rather be wrong than president."

In 1902 Bryan took a trip abroad and observed state ownership of utilities as it was practiced in European countries. Thrown aside by his party in 1904 in favor of the conservative Alton B. Parker, he continued to press for a more radical program, including government ownership and operation of the railways. And yet, after Theodore Roosevelt's overwhelming victory, he visited the Rough Rider at the White House, greeting him with the words: "Some people think I'm a terrible radical, but really I'm not so very dangerous after all." To the New York *Tribune* he wrote: "It is time to call a halt on Socialism in the United States. The movement is going too far." Then in the summer of 1906, returning from a grand tour of the world, he went back to government ownership of railroads. He had now achieved a synthesis: government ownership would be a way of avoiding socialism.

The man who argues that there is an economic advantage in private monopoly is aiding socialism. The socialist, asserting the economic superiority of the monopoly, insists that its benefits shall accrue to the whole people, and his conclusion cannot be denied if his assertion is admitted. The Democratic party, if I understand its position, denies the economic as well as the political advantage of private monopoly and promises to oppose it wherever it manifests itself. It offers as an alternative competition where competition is possible, and public monopoly wherever circumstances are such as to prevent competition.

Like free silver in 1900, government ownership of railways did not take with the voters. Preparing for his third presidential nomination in 1908, Bryan scurried to haul down his flag, promised that he would not "force government ownership upon the country against the will of the people," and testified in a letter to the *Wall Street Journal* that he was in "no hurry about government ownership." Instead he campaigned on the trust question, proposing a rule-of-thumb system of curbing big business that must have caused apoplexy in hundreds of clubrooms.[3] The campaign was rather listless, and the mammoth Taft beat the Commoner more soundly than McKinley had in 1896 or 1900.

And yet, while Bryan had the smallest percentage of the total vote received by any Democrat candidate except Parker for the past sixty years, his ideas were about to reach the peak of their influence. Theodore Roosevelt, during both his terms, had been appropriating one after another of Bryan's smaller issues. Progressive Democrats, held in cohesion by the Bryan influence, were to harass Taft in collaboration with the Progressive Republicans. Finally, in 1912 Bryan was to help swing the Democratic nomination to Woodrow Wilson. The Commoner, always defeated, had, in the course of a sixteen-year quest for issues, effectively turned public attention upon one reform after another;

---

3. According to Bryan's formula, when a corporation engaged in interstate commerce came to control as much as 25 per cent of the business in its field of enterprise it must obtain a federal license; the provisions of this license would guarantee the public against watered stock and prevent the corporation from controlling more than 50 per cent of the traffic in its product or products.

and many of his proposals had had a core of value. Mary Bryan, completing her husband's *Memoirs* in 1925, listed with understandable pride the Bryan projects that had become law: the federal income tax, popular election of United States Senators, publicity in campaign contributions, women's suffrage, a Department of Labor, more stringent railroad regulation, currency reform, and, in the states, the initiative and referendum.

Bryan accepted his perennial defeats with a good humor that seems extraordinary, in the light of the earnestness of his campaigns and the vituperation that was heaped upon him. There is good reason, however, to doubt that at heart he ever really expected to win. He had risen overnight from comparative obscurity to become a major presidential candidate—a thrilling and profoundly gratifying experience. He was grateful that he could run at all, that he could run again, and yet again, that he could earn a good and easy living at the Chautauquas, that he could constantly command national attention, thrill millions with his fine voice, throw a Democratic convention into an uproar with a barbed phrase. For Silas Bryan's son who had once seemed on the verge of failure in the law, this was ample achievement. As prices turned upward and the temper of his following eased, Bryan grew fat and genial, and on occasion passed jests about the futility of his campaigns. It was never success that he demanded, but an audience, and not until audiences began to laugh at him did he become the bitter and malignant old man of the Scopes trial.

III

When Woodrow Wilson reluctantly appointed him Secretary of State, Bryan held a leading office for the only time in his career and the State Department at last had a head who was committed to oppose imperialism and dollar diplomacy. But those who remembered his earlier career wondered what this might mean in practice. Bryan had been a most eloquent Christian pacifist, and yet when the Spanish War came he had fulfilled his idea of "service" by enlisting in the First Nebraska Volunteers, rising to a colonelcy, and camping with his troops in a sinkhole near Jacksonville, Florida, until the war was over. The inconsistency between his participation in the war and his discipleship of the Prince of Peace seemed not to trouble him. (Paxton Hibben remarked that the Commoner "appeared unable to grasp that the sole business of a soldier is to kill. To Bryan the function of a soldier was to be killed—he saw war a game to be won by sacrifice hits.")

Bryan in power was like Bryan out of power: he made the same well-meant gestures, showed the same willingness under stress or confusion to drop ideas he had once been committed to, the same inability to see things through. His most original enterprise was to promote a series of international arbitration treaties, a task that he undertook with moral earnestness such as had not be seen in his Department for many years. These treaties provided that when disputes arose between contracting parties, there should be a "cooling-off" period to permit animosities to wane, followed by arbitration. He had great hopes for the treaties; they would help materially to dissipate the danger of war. "I believe there will be no war while I am Secretary of State," he declared fervently in 1913, "and I believe there will be no war so long as I live."

Bryan's inability to hold steadily to a line of principle was nowhere so well illustrated as in his imperialist policies in the Caribbean, where, as Selig Adler has shown, he was "chiefly responsible for a distinct acceleration of American penetration." Wilson, harassed by the Mexican question and the problems of neutrality, gave Bryan a substantially free hand in Caribbean policy, and the former anti-imperialist, in dealing with Nicaragua, Haiti, and Santo Domingo, was fully as aggressive as his Republican predecessors. Root, Knox, or Hay could have been no more nationalistic or jealous of the prerogatives of American capital in the face of foreign penetration. Apropos of the Haitian situation, Bryan wrote to Wilson, April 2, 1915:

As long as the [Haitian] Government is under French or German influence American interests are going to be discriminated against there as they are discriminated against now. . . . The American interests are willing to remain there with a view of purchasing a controlling interest and making the Bank a branch of the American bank . . . providing their Government takes the steps necessary to protect them. . . . I have been reluctant to favor anything that would require an exercise of force there, but there are some things that lead me to believe that it may be necessary to use as much force as may be necessary [*sic*] to compel a supervision which will be effective.

Bryan also wanted to father a sweeping policy of financial intervention in Latin America, which he outlined in two memoranda to Wilson in 1913. He proposed to counteract the influence of European creditors of Latin-American nations by having the United States government go to their "rescue." The United States would make available the funds necessary for the education, sanitation, and internal development of these nations, and relieve them of the necessity of applying to private financiers in other countries, thus making "absolutely sure our domination of the situation." This would so increase the nation's influence in Latin America "that we could prevent revolutions, promote education, and advance stable and just government." In proposing to wave aside private interests and make economic penetration a state function, Bryan, in the words of Samuel Flagg Bemis, anticipated "the formula of the newer dollar diplomacy of our day." Wilson, however, was not impressed by Bryan's plans.

With the advent of the World War Bryan was the one major figure in the Wilson administration who represented a genuinely neutral point of view. A Midwesterner and an old opponent of the international gold power, Bryan did not look at Britain with the soft eyes of the middle- and upper-class East. His great aim was not to further the Allied cause, but to maintain such relations with both sides as would make possible American arbitration. For his persistent criticism of administration policies Wilson's biographer, Ray Stannard Baker, has found him "the statesman of largest calibre" among Wilson's advisers. Urging mediation upon the President in September 1914, Bryan wrote prophetically:

It is not likely that either side will win so complete a victory as to be able to dictate terms, and if either side does win such a victory it will probably mean preparation for another war. It would seem better to look for a more rational basis for peace.

When American bankers brought pressure upon the administration to allow them to make large loans to the Allies, Bryan was primarily responsible for choking off the project. Money, he pointed out, was the worst of all contrabands because it could command all other goods; such economic commitments to the Allies would be inconsistent with the spirit of neutrality and would ultimately lead to war. Events proved him right, but he characteristically refused to hold to his position and quietly gave his consent when it was proposed to jettison his original ban on loans. Just as he had gone back on anti-imperialism, pacifism, and government ownership of railways, so he backed down on the loans question.

It was neither courage nor sincerity but simply steadfast and self-confident intelligence that Bryan lacked. The steady drift of the United States away from neutrality caused him untold anguish. When Wilson began a long train of controversy with Germany by permitting American citizens to travel on British vessels that were likely to be sunk by U-boats, Bryan alone perceived the folly of the stand. The question, as he put it, was "whether an American citizen can, by putting his business above his regard for his country, assume for his own advantage unnecessary risks and thus involve his country in international complications." He also urged acceptance of the German proposal that relaxation of submarine warfare be exchanged for relaxation of the British food blockade against Germany, but the idea received no sympathy in Britain. "Why be shocked," he then asked Wilson, "at the drowning of a few people, if there is to be no objection to starving a nation?" Troubled by Wilson's protests to Germany over the sinking of the *Lusitania*, he resigned, June 8, 1915.

Bryan decayed rapidly during his closing years. The postwar era found him identified with some of the worst tendencies in American life—prohibition, the crusade against evolution, real-estate speculation, and the Klan. For the sake of his wife's health he moved to Florida, where he became a publicity agent for the real-estate interests, in which capacity his incurable vulgarity stood him in good stead—"What is our vision of what Magic Miami should be?" He collected such magnificent fees for his real-estate promotion and his prohibition lectures that he was able to bequeath a small fortune. His last political appearance took place at the Democratic convention of 1924 in New York City, when the party was racked with conflict over the famous resolution denouncing the Ku Klux Klan by name, and the delegations from the Bryan country were filled with Klan supporters. It was a magnificent opportunity for a man who had read Jefferson on tolerance to give a great lecture on bigotry. Instead, fearing more than anything else a further decline in his influence, Bryan delivered a weak appeal not to rend the "Christian Church" nor destroy party unity. Of the Klan he said: "We can exterminate Ku Kluxism better by recognizing their honesty and teaching them that they are wrong." Fat, balding, in wrinkled clothes, taxed by the heat, bereft of the splendid voice that had made him famous, he was unequal to the merciless heckling from the galleries, and when he descended from the platform after a ludicrous effort to promote compromise candidates, he told Senator Heflin with tears in his eyes that he had never in his life been so humiliated.

When the convention, in a stalemate between Al Smith and William Gibbs McAdoo, nominated John W. Davis, a lawyer for Morgan and Standard Oil, Bryan, who had once scourged the Morgan forces in a party conclave, lent his brother Charles to the Davis ticket as vice-presidential nominee and supported Davis in the campaign. Bryan's old principles were represented that year by Robert M. La Follette on an independent progressive ticket, but La Follette got no support from the man whose followers had so often united with him in Congressional fights. The Commoner could no more think of leaving the Democratic Party than of being converted to Buddhism. He had never failed to support a Democratic nominee. The party, he confessed to the 1924 convention, was a great passion of his life; he owed it an unpayable debt, for it had taken him out of obscurity, a young, penniless man, and had lifted him to exalted heights, three times honoring him with nominations.

But even in the Democratic Party, Bryan knew, his influence was on the wane. He was an agrarian leader, whose strength lay in his appeal to a certain type of Protestant mind in the hinterland; the growing urbanism of the country was submerging him. He was not forgotten by his old followers, but as he wrote an acquaintance in 1923, "the wets are against me and they have the organization and the papers in all the big cities of the north. I cannot get before the public."

As his political power slipped away, Bryan welcomed an opportunity to divert himself with a new crusade and turned with devotion to his first interest. To one correspondent he wrote:

While my power in politics has waned, I think it has increased in religious matters and I have invitations from preachers in all the churches. An evidence of the change is found in the fact that my correspondence in religious subjects is much larger than my correspondence in political subjects. My interest is deeper in religious subjects because I believe that the brute theory has paralyzed the influence of many of our preachers and undermined the faith of many of our young people in college.

He once explained that he thought himself fit to be a leader in the fight against evolution because he had had a measure of success in his life that would dispel all doubts as to his "mental ability." He began to give lectures to the college youth of the nation bearing the message: "No teacher should be allowed on the faculty of any American university unless he is a Christian."

Bryan's presence for the prosecution at the trial of John Thomas Scopes for teaching evolution in Tennessee surprised no one who had been following his talks. The Scopes trial, which published to the world Bryan's childish conception of religion, also reduced to the absurd his inchoate notions of democracy. His defense of the anti-evolution laws showed that years of political experience had not taught him anything about the limitations of public opinion. The voice of the people was still the voice of God. The ability of the common man to settle every question extended, he thought, to matters of science as well as politics and applied equally well to the conduct of schools as it did to the regulation of railroads or the recall of judges or the gold standard. In prosecuting Scopes the people were merely asserting their right "to have what they want in government, including the kind of education they want." Academic freedom? That right "cannot be stretched as far as Professor Scopes is trying to stretch it. A man cannot demand a salary for saying what his employers do not want said. . . ."

So spoke the aging Bryan, the knight-errant of the oppressed. He closed his career in much the same role as he had begun it in 1896: a provincial politician following a provincial populace in provincial prejudices. From all corners of the country, but especially from the old Bryan territory, came messages of encouragement. "MY DEAR BROTHER BRYAN," wired an admirer from Smackover, Arkansas, "FIGHT THEM EVOLUTIONS UNTIL HELL FREEZES OVER AND THEN GIVE THEM A ROUND ON THE ICE." When a few weeks after the trial's close Bryan's heart gave out, there was profound grief among those who had followed him faithfully from the fight against gold to the fight against the ape. Fiery crosses were burned in his memory, and one of his constituents celebrated him as "the greatest Klansman of our time." A cruel and inaccurate characterization, it underscored the fatal weakness of a man who at sixty-five had long outlived his time.

CHAPTER IX

THEODORE ROOSEVELT:
THE CONSERVATIVE AS PROGRESSIVE

❦

How I wish I wasn't a reformer, oh, Senator! But I suppose I must live up to my part, like the Negro minstrel who blacked himself all over!

THEODORE ROOSEVELT TO CHAUNCEY DEPEW

THE coarse, materialistic civilization that emerged in the United States during the years after the Civil War produced among cultivated middle-class young men a generation of alienated and homeless intellectuals. Generally well-to-do, often of eminent family backgrounds, clubmen, gentlemen, writers, the first cluster of a native intellectual aristocracy to appear since the great days of Boston and Concord, the men of this class found themselves unable to participate with any heart in the greedy turmoil of business or to accept without protest boss-ridden politics. Money-making was sordid; politics was dirty; and the most sensitive among them made their careers in other ways. Those who were less interested in public affairs usually managed to fit themselves into the interstices of American existence. Some, like Henry James, escaped abroad or, like his brother William, immersed themselves in academic life. One, Oliver Wendell Holmes, Jr., found sanctuary on the Massachusetts bench and at length rose to the Supreme Court; another, Henry Adams, made a sort of career of bitter detachment. Some who were strong enough to overcome their distaste for business entered it without finding much personal fulfillment and left without regret. Charles Francis Adams, Jr., upon retiring from an unhappy career as a railroad executive, observed that among all the tycoons he had met, "not one . . . would I care to meet again in this world or the next; nor is one associated in my mind with the idea of humor, thought, or refinement."

Conventional politics, on the other hand, offered a choice between merely serving the business class or living off it in a sort of parasitic blackmail.[1] For the more scrupulous this was impossible; in the case of the fastidious Adamses, Brooks and Henry, even the weight of a great family tradition and an absorbing concern with political affairs was not enough to counter-balance distaste. They were, as Henry put it, "unfashionable by some law of Anglo-Saxon custom—some innate atrophy of mind." The era impelled the frustrated politician into scholarship and forced his interest in politics to find wistful expression in the writing of history. Among hardier and somewhat younger souls, however, there appeared the scholar-in-politics, a type represented by Albert J. Beveridge, John Hay, Henry Cabot Lodge, Theodore Roosevelt, and Woodrow Wilson. Such men, though hardly typical politicians, held their noses, made the necessary compromises, worked their way into politics, and bided their time until the social milieu gave them a chance to ride into power. These were the practical men of the breed, men of steady nerves, strong ambition, tenacity, and flexible scruples.

---

1. "No one wanted him," wrote Henry Adams of his own dilemma. "No one wanted any of his friends in reform; the blackmailer alone was the normal product of politics as of business."

The most striking among them was Theodore Roosevelt.

In his *Autobiography* Roosevelt tells how horrified his friends were when he first broached to them his determination to enter politics. "The men I knew best," he recalled, "were the men in the clubs of social pretension and the men of cultivated taste and easy life." Politics, they told him, is a cheap affair run by saloon-keepers and horse-car conductors and shunned by gentlemen. "I answered that if this were so it merely meant that the people I knew did not belong to the governing class, and that the other people did—and that I intended to be one of the governing class." And so Roosevelt began at the bottom by joining an organization that met in a spittoon-furnished hall over a barroom, the Jake Hess Republican Club of New York's 21st Assembly District.

The ends for which Roosevelt and his peers entered politics were not mere boodling or personal advancement. Searching for goals that they considered more lofty, ideals above section or class or material gain, they were bent on some genuinely national service, sought a larger theater in which to exercise their statecraft, and looked down with the disdain of aristocrats upon those who, as Roosevelt said, had never felt the thrill of a generous emotion. Adventurers in a sense they undoubtedly were, tired of "that kind of money-maker whose soul has grown hard while his body has grown soft." In an article written for the *Century* when he was only twenty-eight, Roosevelt aired his disgust at rich Americans as a political type:

The wealthier, or, as they would prefer to style themselves, the "upper" classes, tend distinctly towards the bourgeois type, and an individual in the bourgeois stage of development, while honest, industrious, and virtuous, is also not unapt to be a miracle of timid and short-sighted selfishness. The commercial classes are only too likely to regard everything merely from the standpoint of "Does it pay?" and many a merchant does not take any part in politics because he is short-sighted enough to think that it will pay him better to attend purely to making money, and too selfish to be willing to undergo any trouble for the sake of abstract duty; while the younger men of this type are too much engrossed in their various social pleasures to be willing to give up their time to anything else. It is also unfortunately true . . . that the general tendency among people of culture and high education has been to neglect and even to look down upon the rougher and manlier virtues, so that an advanced state of intellectual development is too often associated with a certain effeminacy of character.

But if Roosevelt was in revolt against the pecuniary values of "the glorified huckster or glorified pawnbroker type," it was not from the standpoint of social democracy, not as an advocate of the downtrodden. He despised the rich, but he feared the mob. Any sign of organized power among the people frightened him; and for many years he showed toward the labor movement an attitude as bitter as that expressed in John Hay's anonymously published novel, *The Breadwinners*. The most aggressive middle-class reformers also annoyed him. Until his post-presidential years, when he underwent his tardy but opportune conversion to radicalism, there was hardly a reform movement that did not at some time win his scorn. His writings are dotted with tart characterizations of "extremists," "radical fanatics," "muckrakers," and "the lunatic fringe." "Sentimental humanitarians," he asserted in his life of Benton, "always form a most pernicious body, with an influence for bad hardly surpassed by that of the professional criminal class."

What Roosevelt stood for, as a counterpoise to the fat materialism of the wealthy and the lurking menace of the masses, were the aggressive, masterful, fighting virtues of the soldier. "No amount of commercial prosperity," he once said, "can supply the lack of the heroic virtues," and it was the heroic virtues that he wished to make central again in American life. His admiration went out most spontaneously to the hunter, the cowboy, the frontiersman, the soldier, and the naval hero. Herbert Spencer, whose ideas were supreme in American thinking during Roosevelt's formative years, taught that Western society was passing from a militant phase, dominated by organization for warfare, to an industrial phase, marked by peaceful economic progress. Roosevelt, whom Spencer would have called atavistic, was determined to reverse this process and restore to the American spirit what he fondly called "the fighting edge." Despite his sincere loyalty to the democratic game, this herald of modern American militarism and imperialism displayed in his political character many qualities of recent authoritarianism—romantic nationalism, disdain for materialistic ends, worship of strength and the cult of personal leadership, the appeal to the intermediate elements of society, the ideal of standing above classes and class interests, a grandiose sense of destiny, even a touch of racism.

It is customary to explain Theodore Roosevelt's personality as the result of compensation for physical inferiority.[2] His sight was always poor, and at length he

---

2. "One can state as a fundamental law that children who come into the world with organ inferiorities become involved at an early age in a bitter struggle for existence which results only

lost the use of his left eye. As a child he was tormented by asthma and shamed by a puny body of which he grew increasingly conscious. An encounter at the age of fourteen left an inexpungeable mark on his memory. He was riding on a stagecoach to Moosehead Lake when he met two other boys of his own age who teased him beyond endurance; and when he tried to fight back, "I discovered that either one singly could not only handle me with easy contempt, but handle me so as not to hurt me much and yet to prevent my doing any damage whatever in return." Upon coming back to New York he began taking boxing lessons, and his life thereafter was cluttered with the paraphernalia of physical culture—boxing gloves, dumbbells, horizontal bars, and the like. From his Harvard days there survives a picture of him in boxing costume; his muscular arms are folded histrionically across his chest, and on his face there is a fierce paranoid scowl. He was still boxing in the White House at forty-three.

Possibly there is no such thing as a saturation point in such psychological compensations; but if there is, Roosevelt, above all men, should have been able to find salve for his ego. He sparred with professional prize-fighters; he rode with cowboys; he led a famous cavalry charge; he hunted Spaniards and big game; he once had the exquisite pleasure of knocking out a tough in a Western barroom; he terrorized an entire police force;

---

too often in a strangulation of their social feelings. Instead of interesting themselves in an adjustment to their fellows, they are continually occupied with themselves and with the impression which they make on others. . . . As soon as the striving for recognition assumes the upper hand . . . the goal of power and superiority becomes increasingly obvious to the individual, and he pursues it with movements of great intensity and violence, and his life becomes the expectation of a great triumph." Alfred Adler: *Understanding Human Nature*, pp. 69, 191.

he defied a Pope; he became President of the United States and waved his fist under J. P. Morgan's nose. If all this was supposed to induce a sense of security, it seems to have failed badly. At the age of sixty he was still waving the flag and screaming for a regiment. One can only suspect that he was fleeing from some more persistent sense of deficiency than that induced by the obvious traumatic experiences of his childhood. He fled from repose and introspection with a desperate urgency that is sometimes pitiable. In 1886, two years after the simultaneous death of his first wife and his mother, he wrote his biography of Thomas Hart Benton in four months, during most of which he was on fourteen- or sixteen-hour ranching schedules and "pretty sleepy, all the time." In this period he poured out seven volumes of history and essays within five years, while active both in politics and on his ranch. "Get action, do things; be sane," he once raved, "don't fritter away your time; create, act, take a place wherever you are and be somebody: get action." A profound and ineluctable tendency to anxiety plagued him. His friends noticed with wonder that Roosevelt, at the time of his engagement to Alice Lee, who became his first wife, lived in a stew of fear lest someone run off with her, threatened acquaintances with duels, and actually smuggled a set of French dueling pistols through the customhouse in preparation for the event. "There were all kinds of things of which I was afraid at first," he confessed in his memoirs, ". . . but by acting as if I was not afraid I gradually ceased to be afraid." [3]

---

3. Roosevelt was writing in particular about his reaction to hunting dangerous game, but the remark may illuminate a larger pattern of behavior. In many cases what the hunter hunts is nothing so much as his own fear; trophies are esteemed because they are evidence of risks undergone and fears surmounted.

"Manly" and "masterful," two of the most common words in Roosevelt's prose, reflect a persistent desire to impose himself upon others. Such a personal motive, projected into public affairs, easily became transformed into the imperial impulse. It was no mere accident that the Rough Rider's popularity grew most rapidly as a result of his Spanish War service. The depression of the nineties found the American middle classes in an uneasy and fearful mood as they watched the trusts growing on one side and the labor and Populist movements massing on the other. For them, as for him, a fight served as a distraction; national self-assertion in the world theater gave them the sense that the nation had not lost its capacity for growth and change. The same emotions that made the people so receptive to the unnecessary Spanish War made them receptive to a man of Roosevelt's temperament. Stuart Sherman has suggested also that his popularity was due in large part to the fact that Americans, in the search for money and power that had grown so intense in the Gilded Age, had lost much of their capacity for enjoyment, and that Roosevelt, with his variety and exuberance and his perpetual air of expectation, restored the consciousness of other ends that made life worth living.[4] "On the whole," the colonel proclaimed in 1899, "we think that the greatest victories are yet to be won, the greatest deeds yet to be done, and that there are yet in store for our peoples and for the causes that we uphold, grander triumphs than have yet been scored."

Roosevelt himself loved the company of rough and aggressive men. Some of the most disarming writing in his *Autobiography* deals with the cowboys and hard

---

4. It should be remembered also that his talents as a comedian were by no means slight.

characters he knew in the Bad Lands. "Every man," he declared in one of his essays,

> who has in him any real power of joy in battle knows that he feels it when the wolf begins to rise in his heart; he does not then shrink from blood or sweat or deem that they mar the fight; he revels in them, in the toil, the pain, and the danger, as but setting off the triumph.

The joy of battle could be found in warfare against primitive and inferior peoples. This feeling was first aroused in Roosevelt by the Indians, whom he saw with the eyes of a cowboy. He took the Western view, he confessed in 1886.

> I don't go so far as to think that the only good Indians are the dead Indians, but I believe nine out of every ten are, and I shouldn't like to inquire too closely into the case of the tenth. The most vicious cowboy has more moral principle than the average Indian.

Roosevelt's major historical work, *The Winning of the West*, which was written during his thirties, was an epic of racial conflict in which he described "the spread of the English-speaking peoples over the world's waste space" as "the most striking feature of the world's history." Only "a warped, perverse, and silly morality" would condemn the American conquest of the West. "Most fortunately, the hard, energetic, practical men who do the rough pioneer work of civilization in barbarous lands, are not prone to false sentimentality."

Roosevelt lauded the expansionist efforts of all the nations of western Europe. In September 1899 he declared at Akron:

> In every instance the expansion has taken place because the race was a great race. It was a sign and proof of

greatness in the expanding nation, and moreover bear in mind that in each instance it was of incalculable benefit to mankind. . . . When great nations fear to expand, shrink from expansion, it is because their greatness is coming to an end. Are we still in the prime of our lusty youth, still at the beginning of our glorious manhood, to sit down among the outworn people, to take our place with the weak and craven? A thousand times no!

The Rough Rider was always ready for a foreign war, and did not lack the courage of his convictions; as his most discerning biographer, Henry Pringle, points out, he was a perennial volunteer. In 1886, braced at the encouraging prospect of a set-to with Mexico, he proposed to Cabot Lodge that he organize the "harum-scarum" riders of his ranch into a cavalry battalion. Nine years later, when Cleveland's quarrel with the British over the Venezuela boundary seemed likely to bring war, he was all jingo enthusiasm. Let American cities be bombarded and razed, he somewhat irrelevantly told a reporter for the New York *Sun*, rather than pay a dollar to any foe for their safety. War with England would certainly be followed by the conquest and annexation of Canada—a delightful prospect. "This country needs a war," he wrote to Lodge in December 1895, and when he was denounced by President Eliot of Harvard as a jingoist, he struck back at "the futile sentimentalists of the international arbitration type" who would bring about "a flabby, timid type of character which eats away at the great fighting qualities of our race." A few years later he was pumping hard for the annexation of Hawaii, even at the risk of war with Japan. In June 1897, as Assistant Secretary of the Navy, he made a classic militaristic speech before the Naval War College in which he dwelt again on his pet theme of the authority of military to pecuniary values. The most dangerous mood for the nation would be an over-pacific, not a warlike mood, he insisted. A wealthy nation "is an easy prey for any people which still retains the most valuable of all qualities, the soldierly virtues." All the "great masterful races have been fighting races."

> No triumph of peace is quite so great as the supreme triumphs of war. . . . We of the United States have passed most of our few years of national life in peace. We honor the architects of our wonderful material prosperity. . . . But we feel, after all, that the men who have dared greatly in war, or the work which is akin to war, are those who deserve best of the country.

A war with Spain, he assured a naval officer as the crisis over Cuba grew more acute, would be justified from two standpoints. First, both humanity and self-interest required interfering on behalf of the Cubans and taking another step in freeing America from "European domination." Second, there would be "the benefit done to our people by giving them something to think of which isn't material gain, and especially the benefit done our military force by trying both the Army and Navy in actual practice." The hesitancy of big business to launch upon a martial adventure at a time when prosperity was returning won Roosevelt's scorn. "We will have this war for the freedom of Cuba, in spite of the timidity of the commercial interests," he warned Mark Hanna.[5] Not long afterward the war began.

---

5. "The big financiers and the men generally who were susceptible to touch on the money nerve, and who cared nothing for national honor if it conflicted even temporarily with business prosperity, were against the war," he recalled in his *Autobiography*.

The Spanish War, Roosevelt believed, should be waged as aggressively as possible, and he urged that a flying squadron should be sent through Gibraltar at night to strike against Barcelona and Cádiz. Such counsels were ignored. But it was at Roosevelt's instance and without authorization from his superior, Secretary J. D. Long, that Admiral Dewey launched his attack upon the Spanish fleet in the Philippines. The extraordinary initiative Roosevelt took on this occasion has drawn sharp comment from historians; but to the chief actor himself there seemed nothing exceptionable in it. He never suffered from an over-developed sense of responsibility. Some years later he complained to Cecil Spring-Rice that "our generals . . . had to grapple with a public sentiment which screamed with anguish over the loss of a couple of thousand men . . . a sentiment of preposterous and unreasoning mawkishness."

Once the fighting began, a desk job was too dull. To the despair of his friends and family—even John Hay, who thought this a "splendid little war," called him a *"wilder werwegener"* for leaving the Navy Department —Roosevelt went off to form a volunteer cavalry regiment, the famous Rough Riders. He chafed under training, fearing that the fighting would be over before the War Department delivered him to the front; but at last the great hour came; the Rough Riders reached Cuba and participated in several actions, including the so-called San Juan charge. Roosevelt was magnificent. "Are you afraid to stand up when I am on horseback?" he asked some laggards; and many years later he remembered how "I waved my hat and we went up the hill with a rush." ". . . I killed a Spaniard with my own hand," he reported to Lodge with pride—"like a Jack-rabbit," was the expression he used to another. At the end came the supreme human profanity of his moment of triumph: the exhortation to "look at those damned Spanish dead"! Less than three years later he became President of the United States.[6]

II

It was a tortuous path that took Roosevelt to the executive chair. After serving three highly moral terms as a New York State "reform" assemblyman, he deserted the reform element during the presidential race of 1884 under Lodge's guidance, and threw his support to Blaine. Two years later he carried the Republican standard in a hopeless contest, the three-cornered New York City mayoralty campaign, in which he ran a weak third to Abram S. Hewitt and Henry George. President Harrison appointed him to the Civil Service Commis-

---

6. During his presidency Roosevelt showed greater restraint in the conduct of foreign policy than might have been expected. Although foreign policy remained a primary interest to him, he did not seek war. His three most significant acts—intervention in the Morocco crisis of 1905, mediation in the Russo-Japanese War, and the intrigue that led to acquisition of the Panama Canal Zone—were marked by considerable noise and a fine show of activity, but no long-range accomplishments from the standpoint of "national interest." His contribution to the settlement of the Morocco crisis, probably the most successful of his ventures, gained nothing for the United States and involved a serious risk of inciting animosity. Of his mediation in the Russo-Japanese War, Professor Samuel Flagg Bemis concludes that it "did some harm and no good to the United States." The intrigue with the Panamanian revolutionists, which brought the United States the Canal Zone on Roosevelt's terms—a source of great pride to him—has been condemned by most American historians who deal with it, on grounds of national expediency and international morality. At best it is conceded that he gained some months' time in constructing the canal, at the cost of adding tremendously to the United States' burden of ill will in Latin America.

sion in 1889, where his zealous activity on behalf of the merit principle won him a nonpartisan reappointment from Cleveland. In 1895 he returned to New York to become president of the city's Board of Police Commissioners. At length Lodge's influence procured him the Assistant Secretaryship of the Navy under McKinley. He became a popular hero after his derring-do in the Spanish War, and was elected Governor of New York in 1898. There he proved troublesome to the Platt machine; the bosses welcomed a chance to kick him upstairs, and a combination of friends and enemies gave him the vice-presidential place on the McKinley ticket in 1900. Reluctant though he was to run for an office that seemed to promise only obscurity, Roosevelt campaigned effectively. His ultimate reward was the presidency.

Coming into the world under the best stand-pat auspices, Roosevelt had been indoctrinated with a conservatism that could be tempered only by considerable experience. His father, whom he described as "the best man I ever knew . . . a big powerful man with a leonine face, and his heart filled with gentleness for those who needed help or protection," was engaged in the glass-importing business and in banking. He held the conventional views of the big-business Republicans and had no truck with political reforms, although he engaged actively in philanthropies.

At Harvard, where J. Laurence Laughlin was preaching an extreme version of laissez-faire, Roosevelt recalled that he was exposed to orthodox canons. Beyond this he seems to have had few concrete ideas about economic policy; he admits freely that after twenty years of public life he came to the White House with only a slight background in economics. Given a college assignment on the character of the Gracchi, which could have led him to review one of the great social struggles of antiquity, he displayed, as he puts it, "a dull and totally idea-proof resistance." But the frigate and sloop actions between American and British ships during the War of 1812 fascinated him; his first historical work, begun during his senior year in college, was a loving and highly competent technical account of *The Naval War of 1812*.

Roosevelt's determination to enter politics and become a member of "the governing class" was not inspired by a program of positive aims, but rather by a vague sense of dedication. Beyond a conviction that the pure in heart should participate more actively in politics, a disdain for purely material ends, and a devotion to the national State, one can find little deliberate ideology in the early Roosevelt. He summed up the greater part of his positive faith in a letter to his brother-in-law, Admiral William Cowles, April 5, 1896:

> Although I feel very strongly indeed on such questions as municipal reform and civil service reform, I feel even more strongly on the question of our attitude towards the outside world, with all that it implies, from seacoast defense and a first-class navy to a properly vigorous foreign policy. . . . I believe it would be well were we sufficiently foresighted steadily to shape our policy with the view to the ultimate removal of all European powers from the colonies they hold in the western hemisphere.

On of the best indices of Roosevelt's place in the political spectrum was his attitude toward labor. The mid-eighties and the nineties were punctuated by hard-fought strikes. Since his own city and state were centers of the growing labor movement, he was in constant contact with organized labor pressure.

Early in his tenure in the New York Assembly Roosevelt was appointed to a commission to investigate tenement sweatshops in the New York City cigar industry. Shocked by the filthy conditions he found on his tour of inspection, he supported a bill, then considered dangerous and demagogic by his friends, designed to abolish tenement cigar-manufacturing—although he acknowledged the measure to be "in a certain sense . . . socialistic." Subsequently he voted for bills to limit the working hours of women and children in factories and for legislation dealing with industrial safety. Beyond this he would not go. His attitude toward other labor legislation won him a bad reputation in labor circles. His views at this time were well to the right of such liberal capitalists as Abram S. Hewitt and Mark Hanna. Not long after his first year in the legislature he wrote that it had been a bad year "because demagogic measures were continually brought forward in the interests of the laboring classes." Among these "demagogic" measures was one that Roosevelt was instrumental in blocking, requiring the cities of New York, Brooklyn, and Buffalo to pay their employees not less than two dollars a day or twenty-five cents an hour. Objecting to the cost it would impose on New York City, he characterized it as "one of the several score of preposterous measures that annually make their appearance purely for the purposes of buncombe." He also opposed bills to abolish contract convict labor, to raise the salaries of New York City police and firemen, and to improve enforcement of the state's eight-hour law; he indignantly fought a bill to set a twelve-hour limit on the workday of horse-car drivers in street-railway systems.

His next important contact with labor was as New York City's police commissioner. In this capacity he won applause from the labor and reform movements for getting many tenement houses condemned; he made a practice of touring the slums in the enlightening company of Jacob Riis; he began to read in the literature of housing and showed an interest in social work. But he clashed with labor time and again over his method of policing strikes. In 1895 he was quoted in the *Evening Post* as saying:

We shall guard as zealously the rights of the striker as those of the employer. But when riot is menaced it is different. The mob takes its own chance. Order will be kept at whatever cost. If it comes to shooting we shall shoot to hit. No blank cartridges or firing over the head of anybody.

The industrial unrest stirred by the depression of the nineties was a constant torment to Roosevelt. When the notorious Bradley-Martin ball was planned in the midst of the pall of hunger and unemployment that hung over the city, the police commissioner, deeply irritated by the needless provocation the affair would give to the poor, remarked with felicitous irony: "I shall have to protect it by as many police as if it were a strike."

By 1899 Roosevelt had learned that he could assimilate some of the political strength of the labor movement (or other popular movements) by yielding to it in many practical details. As governor he showed increasing flexibility in dealing with labor. He worked hard to get the legislature to pass a law against sweatshops; he was the first governor ever to make a tour of the sweatshop districts; he consulted labor leaders regularly on matters affecting labor's interests; and, as though to measure the change in his philosophy, put his signature to just such a bill as he had fought most bitterly while in the Assembly, an eight-hour law for workers on government contracts. Although he identified himself closely with the authority of the State and the defense of property, he saw the justice and necessity of making authority benevolent and improving the condition of the people through social legislation. But any display of independent power by the masses, especially in the form of a strike, set off a violent reflex. He epitomized his philosophy during his governorship when he remarked of a current dispute: "If there should be a disaster at the Croton Dam strike, I'd order out the militia in a minute. But I'd sign an employer's liability law, too." He still displayed, as Howard L. Hurwitz describes it, "a trigger-like willingness to use troops. . . . His mind was a single track when it came to strikes, and that track always carried troops to the scene of the dispute."

Roosevelt followed events on the national scene with a similar impatience and showed the same penchant for sudden violence that appears again and again in this period of his life. At the time of the Haymarket affair he had written proudly from his ranch that his cowboys would like "a chance with rifles at one of the mobs. . . . I wish I had them with me and a fair show at ten times our number of rioters; my men shoot well and fear very little." The discontent of the nineties brought a new attack of hysteria. During the Pullman strike (when Mark Hanna was proclaiming before the outraged gentry of the Cleveland Union Club that "A man who won't meet his men half-way is a Goddamn fool") Roosevelt wrote Brander Matthews: "I know the Populists and the laboring men well and their faults. . . . I like to see a mob handled by the regulars, or by good State-Guards, not over-scrupulous about bloodshed." He was among those who saw in the events of 1896 a threatened repetition of the French Revolution.

"This is no mere fight over financial standards," he informed his sister in July.

> It is a semi-socialistic agrarian movement, with free silver as a mere incident, supported mainly because it is hoped thereby to damage the well to do and thrifty. "Organized labor" is the chief support of Bryan in the big cities; and his utterances are as criminal as they are wildly silly. All the ugly forces that seethe beneath the social crust are behind him.

He had not forgiven John P. Altgeld for pardoning three of the Chicago anarchists or for protesting when Cleveland sent federal troops to Illinois to break the Pullman strike. He now refused to meet Altgeld personally, because he said, he might yet have to face him "sword to sword upon the field of battle." While Hanna was snorting at his Union Club friends: "There won't be any revolution. You're just a lot of damn fools," Roosevelt was reported as saying:[7]

> The sentiment now animating a large proportion of our people can only be suppressed as the Commune in Paris was suppressed, by taking ten or a dozen of their leaders out, standing . . . them against a wall, and shooting them dead. I believe it will come to that. These leaders are plotting a social revolution and the subversion of the American Republic.

The passing of the silver crisis, the diversion of the Spanish War, and the return of prosperity did not entirely dissipate Roosevelt's worried mood. In 1899 he was still writing Lodge from Albany that the workers and small tradesmen in his state were in a mood of "sul-

---

7. Roosevelt heatedly denied having uttered these words, which were reported by Willis J. Abbot, an editor of the Democratic New York *Journal*.

len discontent." Brooks Adams came to visit him during the summer, and the two talked of the danger to the nation of the trade-union eight-hour movement and the possibility that the country would be "enslaved" by the organizers of the trusts. They were intrigued by the idea that Roosevelt might lead "some great outburst of the emotional classes which should at least temporarily crush the Economic Man." [8]

Roosevelt was none too happy over McKinley's victory in 1896. Anything, of course, to beat Bryan and Altgeld; but he looked on McKinley as a weakling who could not be relied on in a "serious crisis, whether it took the form of a soft-money craze, a gigantic labor riot, or danger of a foreign conflict." The triumph of 1896 represented, after all, the victory of the type of moneybags he had always condemned, and he wrote sadly to his sister after attending the Republican celebration dinner that he was "personally realizing all of Brooks Adams' gloomiest anticipations of our gold-ridden, capitalist-bestridden, usurer-mastered future."

Because he feared the great corporations as well as the organized workers and farmers, Roosevelt came to think of himself as representing a golden mean. After he had sponsored, as governor, a tax on public-service franchises, which alarmed the corporate interests, he was accused by the incredible Boss Platt of being too "altruistic" on labor and the trusts. Roosevelt replied that he merely wanted to show that "we Republicans hold the just balance and set our faces as resolutely against the improper corporate influence on the one

---

8. This was probably in reference to the distinction Adams had drawn two years earlier in *The Law of Civilization and Decay* between the imaginative, emotional, and artistic types of men and the economic man. Roosevelt wrote a significant review of this book for the *Forum*, January 1897.

hand as against demagogy and mob rule on the other."
This was the conception that he brought to the presidency. He stood above the contending classes, an impartial arbiter devoted to the national good, and a custodian of the stern virtues without which the United States could not play its destined role of mastery in the world theater.

III

"Wall Street has desperate need of men like you,"
Brooks Adams had taunted in 1896, as he urged Theodore Roosevelt to hire himself out to the commercial interests. The thought of being such an outright mercenary was revolting to the Rough Rider, and he was doubtless uneasy in the presence of Adams's cynicism.
But the more independent and statesmanlike role of stabilizer of the *status quo*, of a conservative wiser than the conservatives, appealed to him. It became his obsession to "save" the masters of capital from their own stupid obstinacy, a theme that runs consistently through his public and private writings from the time of his accession to the presidency. During his first term he was keenly aware, as Matthew Josephson remarks, that he was a "captive president" for whom it would be unwise to break the chains that bound him to the interests.
"Go slow," Hanna advised him. "I shall go slow," the new President replied.[9]

The advisers to whom Roosevelt listened were al-

---

9. The relationship between these two became increasingly cordial. In 1909 Philander C. Knox, asked whether he had ever witnessed an argument between them, answered that he had—just once. Roosevelt had been maintaining that the Grangers, the agrarian reformers of the seventies, were maniacs, Hanna that they were useful citizens.

most exclusively representatives of industrial and finance capital—men like Hanna, Robert Bacon and George W. Perkins of the House of Morgan, Elihu Root, Senator Nelson W. Aldrich, A. J. Cassatt of the Pennsylvania Railroad, Philander C. Knox, and James Stillman of the Rockefeller interests. When his brother-in-law, Douglas Robinson, wrote from Wall Street to urge that he do nothing to destroy business confidence, Roosevelt answered:

> I intend to be most conservative, but in the interests of the corporations themselves and above all in the interests of the country, I intend to pursue cautiously, but steadily, the course to which I have been publicly committed . . . and which I am certain is the right course.

Toward the close of his first term Roosevelt suffered attacks of anxiety for fear that some of his policies had offended the interests, and late in 1903 he did his best to assure them that his intentions were honorable.[10] Although the Democrats named a gilt-edged conservative candidate, Judge Alton B. Parker, Roosevelt held his own in business circles. Handsome donations poured into the treasure chest of the Republican National Committee from Morgan and Rockefeller corporations, from Harriman, Frick, Chauncey Depew, and George J. Gould. Roosevelt's opponent falsely accused him of

---

10. "The opposition to you among the capitalists is confined to a group of Wall Street and Chicago people," Lodge reassured him, June 2, 1903, "but even in Wall Street there is a large body of men who are with you, and I do not find here on State Street any manifest hostility on account of your merger [Northern Securities] case, rather the contrary."

Senator Orville Platt of Connecticut found late in the same year that the opposition to Roosevelt came "from both ends of the party—from the moneyed influences in Wall Street and the agitators in the labor movement—one as much as the other."

having "blackmailed" the corporations and promising them immunity in return for their donations.[11] But Parker was overwhelmed at the polls. Roosevelt had convinced the people that he was a reformer and businessmen that he was sound.

A qualification is necessary: some business elements did fear and hate Theodore Roosevelt. And yet, by displaying their opposition, they and the conservative newspaper editors unwittingly gave him the same kind of assistance that the du Ponts later gave to Franklin D. Roosevelt: they provided the dramatic foil that enabled him to stay on the stage plausibly as a reformer. His attitudes toward many public questions were actually identical with those of the shrewder capitalists. This was particularly true where labor was concerned, and it was illustrated by Roosevelt's compromise of the formidable anthracite strike of 1902. The frame of mind of old-fashioned capitalists was expressed during that dispute by George F. Baer when he said that "the Christian men whom God in his infinite wisdom has given the control of the property interests of this country" were alone qualified to look after the welfare of the workingman. The attitude of the more statesman-like business interests was represented by Morgan and Hanna, both of whom pressed the mine operators to accept the method of arbitration proposed by Roosevelt and Root.[12] Throughout the controversy the Presi-

---

11. According to Oswald Garrison Villard's report in *Fighting Years*, Henry Clay Frick suffered from the delusion that Roosevelt had made positive commitments in return for the financial support he solicited. "He got down on his knees before us," Frick remembered angrily. "We bought the son of a bitch and then he did not stay bought!"

12. "If it had not been for your going in the matter," Roosevelt said in thanking Morgan, "I do not see how the strike could have been settled at this time."

dent fumed at the obstinacy of the mineowners. ". . . From every consideration of public policy and of good morals they should make some slight concession," he wrote to Hanna. And "The attitude of the operators will beyond a doubt double the burden on us while standing between them and socialistic action." "I was anxious," he recalled years afterward, "to save the great coal operators and all of the class of big propertied men, of which they were members, from the dreadful punishment which their own folly would have brought on them if I had not acted. . . ."

Roosevelt worried much about the rise of radicalism during his two administrations. The prominence of the muckraking literature (which was "building up a revolutionary feeling"), the growing popularity of the socialist movement ("far more ominous than any populist or similar movements in times past"), the emergence of militant local reformers like La Follette, the persistent influence of Bryan—such things haunted him. "I do not like the social conditions at present," he complained to Taft in March 1906:

> The dull, purblind folly of the very rich men; their greed and arrogance . . . and the corruption in business and politics, have tended to produce a very unhealthy condition of excitement and irritation in the popular mind, which shows itself in the great increase in the socialistic propaganda.

His dislike of "the very rich men" caused Roosevelt to exaggerate their folly and forget how much support they had given him, but his understanding of the popular excitement and irritation was keen, and his technique for draining it into the channels of moderate action was superb. (His boxing instructors had taught him not to charge into his opponents' punches but to roll with them.) In 1900 Bryan had puffed about the trusts, and Roosevelt responded in 1902 with an extremely spectacular anti-trust prosecution—the Northern Securities case. Between 1904 and 1906 Bryan agitated for government ownership of railroads, and Roosevelt answered by supporting the Hepburn bill, which made possible the beginnings of railroad rate-control by the Interstate Commerce Commission. During the fight over the bill he wrote to Lodge to deplore the activities of the railroad lobbyists: "I think they are very short-sighted not to understand that to beat it means to increase the danger of the movement for government ownership of railroads." Taking several leaves from Bryan's book, Roosevelt urged upon Congress workmen's compensation and child-labor laws, a railway hour act, income and inheritance taxes, and a law prohibiting corporations from contributing to political parties; he turned upon the federal courts and denounced the abuse of injunctions in labor disputes; he blasted dishonesty in business with some of the showiest language that had ever been used in the White House. Only a small part of his recommendations received serious Congressional attention, and in some instances—especially that of the Hepburn bill—his own part in the making of legislation was far more noteworthy for readiness to compromise than to fight against the conservative bosses of his party. But his strong language had value in itself, not only because it shaped the public image of him as a fighting radical, but because it did contribute real weight to the sentiment for reform. His baiting of "malefactors of great wealth" and the "criminal rich" also gave his admirers the satisfaction of emotional catharsis at a time when few other satisfactions were possible.

*　　*　　*

In retrospect, however, it is hard to understand how Roosevelt managed to keep his reputation as a strenuous reformer. Unlike Bryan, he had no passionate interest in the humane goals of reform; unlike La Follette, no mastery of its practical details. "In internal affairs," he confessed in his *Autobiography*, "I cannot say that I entered the presidency with any deliberately planned and far-reaching scheme of social betterment." Reform in his mind did not mean a thoroughgoing purgation; it was meant to heal only the most conspicuous sores on the body politic. And yet many people were willing and eager to accept his reform role at its face value. Perhaps the best proof that the Progressive mind was easy to please is his reputation as a trust-buster. Let it serve as an illustration:

Roosevelt became President without any clearly defined ideas or strong principles on the question of big business. As early as August 7, 1899 he had written H. H. Kohlsaat that the popular unrest over trusts was "largely aimless and baseless" and admitted frankly that he did not know what, if anything, should be done about them. But, as we have seen, he distrusted and despised the ignoble "bourgeois" spirit in politics. While bigness in business frightened the typical middle-class citizen for economic reasons, it frightened Roosevelt for political reasons. He was not a small entrepreneur, worrying about being squeezed out, nor an ordinary consumer concerned about rising prices, but a big politician facing a strong rival in the business of achieving power. He did not look forward to breaking up bigness by restoring competitive conditions. He did not have, in short, the devotion of the small man to small property that won the sympathy of such contemporaries as Brandeis, La Follette, and Wilson. Bigness in business filled him with foreboding because it presaged a day when the United States might be held in thrall by those materialistic interests he had always held in contempt, a "vulgar tyranny of mere wealth." Anti-trust action seems to have been to him partly a means of satisfying the popular demand to see the government flail big business, but chiefly a threat to hold over business to compel it to accept regulation. And regulation, not destruction, was his solution for the trust problem. Psychologically he identified himself with the authority of the State, and jealously projected his own pressing desire for "mastery" into the trust problem. The trusts must never be allowed to grow stronger than the State; they must yield to its superior moral force.

From the beginning Roosevelt expressed his philosophy quite candidly—and it is this that makes his reputation as a trust-buster such a remarkable thing. On December 2, 1902 he informed Congress:

> Our aim is not to do away with corporations; on the contrary, these big aggregations are an inevitable development of modern industrialism, and the effort to destroy them would be futile unless accomplished in ways that would work the utmost mischief to the entire body politic. . . . We draw the line against misconduct, not against wealth.

He repeated this theme again and again. At the beginning of his second term he declared: "This is an age of combination, and any effort to prevent all combination will be not only useless, but in the end vicious, because of the contempt for law which the failure to enforce law inevitably produces."

In his *Autobiography* Roosevelt argued with brilliant historical insight for his thesis that regulation rather than dissolution was the answer:

One of the main troubles was the fact that the men who saw the evils and who tried to remedy them attempted to work in two wholly different ways, and the great majority of them in a way that offered little promise of real betterment. They tried (by the Sherman-law method) to bolster up an individualism already proved to be both futile and mischievous; *to remedy by more individualism the concentration that was the inevitable result of the already existing individualism.* They saw the evil done by the big combinations, and sought to remedy it by destroying them and restoring the country to the economic conditions of the middle of the nineteenth century. This was a hopeless effort, and those who went into it, although they regarded themselves as radical progressives, really represented a form of sincere rural toryism. . . .

On the other hand, a few men recognized that corporations and combinations had become indispensable in the business world, that it was folly to try to prohibit them, but that it was also folly to leave them without thoroughgoing control. . . . They realized that the government must now interfere to protect labor, to subordinate the big corporation to the public welfare, and to shackle cunning and fraud exactly as centuries before it had interfered to shackle the physical force which does wrong by violence. . . .

Roosevelt did, of course, engage in a few cleverly chosen prosecutions which gave substance to his talk about improving the moral code of the corporations. The prosecution of the Northern Securities Company in 1902, near the beginning of his first term, was his most spectacular effort.

The Northern Securities holding company, organized by James J. Hill, J. P. Morgan, and others, had established a gigantic railroad monopoly in the Northwest, embracing the Northern Pacific, the Great Northern, and the Chicago, Burlington, & Quincy railroads. The roads involved had been very much in the public eye because of an extremely bitter and well-publicized rivalry between Hill and E. H. Harriman. And yet the monopoly was anything but a vital concern in the life of the business community or the affairs of the House of Morgan. To prosecute it was a brilliant stroke of publicity that could hardly have been resisted even by a more conservative politician.[13]

Nevertheless, the announcement of the Northern Securities case caused a real shock in the ranks of big business and brought Morgan himself bustling down to Washington with Senators Depew and Hanna to find out if the President was planning to "attack my other interests." He was told that this would happen only if "they have done something that we regard as wrong."

Roosevelt was never keen to find wrongdoing among the trusts. "As a matter of fact," he admitted privately toward the close of his presidential career, "I have let up in every case where I have had any possible excuse for so doing." A few outstanding cases were tried during his second term—after he had weathered the trial

13. It is possible that McKinley might have undertaken such a prosecution had he lived. Hanna, who was as usual calm about the whole affair, refused to intercede: "I warned Hill that McKinley might have to act against his damn company last year. Mr. Roosevelt's done it. I'm sorry for Hill, but just what do you gentlemen think I can do?"

The prosecution, technically successful, did not restore competition. It is illuminating that Roosevelt, when he heard the news of the Supreme Court's decision in the Northern Securities case, proclaimed it "one of the great achievements of my administration. . . . The most powerful men in this country were held to accountability before the law." As Mr. Justice Holmes maliciously pointed out in his dissenting opinion, this was precisely what had not happened, for the Sherman Act logically required criminal prosecution of Messrs. Morgan, Harriman, Hill, and others involved in the company. Roosevelt never forgave Holmes.

of re-election with the help of large donations from business—but even such obvious subjects of anti-trust action as Standard Oil and the American Tobacco Company were left untouched. There was a hundred times more noise than accomplishment. Historians have often remarked that Taft's administration brought ninety anti-trust proceedings in four years, while Roosevelt brought only fifty-four in seven years. The most intense and rapid growth of trusts in American business history took place during Roosevelt's administrations.

The ambiguity that can be seen in his trust policies came naturally and honestly to Theodore Roosevelt. In his early days it had always been his instinct to fight, to shoot things out with someone or something—imaginary lovers of his fiancée, Western Indians, Mexicans, the British navy, Spanish soldiers, American workers, Populists. But before he became President he had learned that an ambitious politician must be self-controlled and calculating. His penchant for violence, therefore, had to be discharged on a purely verbal level, appeased by exploding in every direction at once. The straddle was built like functional furniture into his thinking. He was honestly against the abuses of big business, but he was also sincerely against indiscriminate trust-busting; he was in favor of reform, but disliked the militant reformers. He wanted clean government and honest business, but he shamed as "muckrakers" those who exposed corrupt government and dishonest business. (Of course, he was all in favor of the muckrakers' revelations—but only if they were "absolutely true.") "We are neither for the rich man nor the poor man as such," he resounded in one of his typical sentences, "but for the upright man, rich or poor." Such equivocations are the life of practical politics, but while they often sound weak and halting in the mouths of the ordinary politician, Roosevelt had a way of giving them a fine aggressive surge.

Roosevelt had a certain breadth and cultivation that are rare among politicians. He read widely and enthusiastically, if not intensely, remembered much, wrote sharply at times and with a vivid flair for the concrete. He had generous enthusiasms. He invited Booker T. Washington to the White House, elevated Holmes to the Supreme Court, and gave Edwin Arlington Robinson a political sinecure. Thoughtful and cultivated men found him charming, and it is hard to believe that this was merely because, as John Morley said, he was second in interest only to Niagara Falls among American natural phenomena. Yet those who knew him, from shrewd political associates like Root to men like Henry Adams, and John Hay and Cecil Spring-Rice, refused to take him altogether seriously as a person. And rightly so, for anyone who today has the patience to plow through his collected writings will find there, despite an occasional insight and some ingratiating flashes of self-revelation, a tissue of philistine conventionalities, the intellectual fiber of a muscular and combative Polonius. There was something about him that was repelled by thoughtful skepticism, detachment, by any uncommon delicacy; probably it was this that caused him to brand Henry James and Henry Adams as "charming men but exceedingly undesirable companions for any man not of strong nature," and to balk at "the tone of satirical cynicism which they admired." His literary opinions, which he fancied to have weight and importance and which actually had some influence, were not only intolerably biased by his political sentiments but, for all his proclaimed robustiousness, extremely traditional and genteel. Zola, for example, disgusted him with his "conscientious descriptions of the unspeakable"; Tolstoy he disliked because he preached against both marriage and war, and *The Kreutzer Sonata* he considered a "filthy and repulsive book"; Dickens, who did not like America, was no gentleman; Gorki, who came to the United States with a woman who was not his legal wife, was personally immoral, like so many Continentals, and in politics a "fool academic revolutionist."

The role in which Roosevelt fancied himself was that of the moralist, and the real need in American public life, he told Lincoln Steffens, was "the *fundamental fight for morality*." Not long before leaving Washington he predicted to Ray Stannard Baker that economic questions—the tariff, currency, banks—would become increasingly important, but remarked that he was not interested in them. "My problems are moral problems, and my teaching has been plain morality." This was accurate enough; Roosevelt's chief contribution to the Progressive movement had been his homilies, but nothing was farther from his mind than to translate his moral judgments into social realities; and for the best of reasons; the fundamentally conservative nationalist goals of his politics were at cross-purposes with the things he found it expedient to say, and as long as his activity was limited to the verbal sphere the inconsistency was less apparent.

His mind, in a word, did not usually cut very deep. But he represented something that a great many Americans wanted. "Theodore Roosevelt," said La Follette caustically, "is the ablest living interpreter of what I would call the superficial public sentiment of a given time, and he is spontaneous in his reactions to it." What made him great, commented Medill McCormick, was that he understood the "psychology of the mutt." While Bryan had been able to do this only on a sectional basis, Roosevelt spoke the views of the middle classes of all parts of the country, and commanded the enthusiastic affection of people who had never walked behind a plow or raised a callus. He had a special sense for the realities they wished to avoid; with his uncanny instinct for impalpable falsehoods he articulated their fears in a string of plausible superficialities. The period of his ascendancy was a prosperous one, in which popular discontent lacked the sharp edge that it had had when Bryan rose to prominence. Although the middle classes, which contributed so much to the strength of progressivism, were troubled about the concentration of power in political and economic life and the persistence of corruption in government, it is doubtful that many middle-class men would have been more willing than Roosevelt to face the full implications of an attempt to unravel the structure of business power, with the attendant risk of upsetting a going concern. The general feeling was, as Roosevelt wrote Sir George Trevelyan in 1905, that "somehow or other we shall have to work out methods of controlling the big corporations *without* paralyzing the energies of the business community."

This sentence is characteristic of the essentially negative impulses behind Roosevelt's political beliefs. It was always: We shall have to do this in order to prevent that. Did he favor control of railroad rates more because he was moved to correct inequities in the existing tolls or because he was afraid of public ownership? Did he force the mine operators to make a small concession to their employees because he bled for the men who worked the mines or because he feared "socialistic action"? Did he advocate workmen's compensation laws because he had a vivid sense of the plight of the crippled wage earner or because he was afraid that Bryan would get some votes? "There were all kinds of things of which I was afraid at first," he had said of his boyhood, ". . . but by acting as if I was not afraid I gradually ceased to be afraid." But did he lose his fears, or merely succeed in suppressing them? Did he become a man who was not afraid, or merely a man who could act as though he was not afraid? His biographer Henry Pringle has pointed out how often he actually underwent attacks of anxiety. In his anxieties, in fact, and in the very negative and defensive quality of his progressivism, may be found one of the sources of his political strength. The frantic growth and rapid industrial expansion that filled America in his lifetime had heightened social tensions and left a legacy of bewilderment, anger, and fright, which had been suddenly precipitated by the depression of the nineties. His psychological function was to relieve these anxieties with a burst of hectic action and to discharge these fears by scolding authoritatively the demons that aroused them. Hardened and trained by a long fight with his own insecurity, he was the master therapist of the middle classes.

IV

Of Taft, whom he chose as his successor, Roosevelt said revealingly to Gilson Gardner: "It is true he has never originated anything that would savor of progressiveness, but he has been close enough to this Administration to know what it stands for." Taft, however, could not mold public opinion, nor run with the hare and hunt with the hounds in the Roosevelt manner. When the ex-President returned in 1910 from his self-imposed exile to Africa, he found the Republican insurgents, who had never broken so far out of line, growing bold enough to challenge Taft for control of the party. "The Administration," he complained to Nicholas Longworth, July 11, 1910, "has certainly wholly failed in keeping the party in substantial unity, and what I mind most is that the revolt is not merely among the party leaders, but among the masses of the people." [14]

Roosevelt was too young to cease to care about his reputation or to abandon political ambitions. With his customary quickness he perceived that the Progressive impulse had not yet reached its high-water mark. Starting with his famous "New Nationalism" speech of August 1910, he began to present himself as a "new" political personality. The "New Nationalism" was a transparent amalgam of the old Roosevelt doctrines with some of the more challenging Progressive ideas. Democratic ends, Roosevelt proclaimed, must now be sought through Hamiltonian means. A strong, centralized State, extended governmental interference in economic life, freedom of politics from concern for special interests—these were to be the main lines of development. Specifically Roosevelt endorsed the initiative, referendum, and recall, popular election of Senators, and direct primaries. He shocked conservatives by assailing the federal judiciary for obstructing the popular will, and advocated that decisions of state courts nullifying social legislation should be subject to popular recall. He supported compensation laws, limitation

---

14. La Follette remarked in his *Autobiography* that the Progressive movement in the Republican Party made greater headway in Taft's first two years than in Roosevelt's two terms. "This," he concluded, "was largely due to the fact that Taft's course was more direct, Roosevelt's devious."

of the hours of labor, a graduated income tax, inheritance taxes, physical evaluation of railroad properties to enforce "honest" capitalization, and government supervision of capitalization of all types of corporations in interstate commerce.

Democracy, Roosevelt proclaimed, must be economic, not merely political. And labor? He echoed Lincoln: "Labor is the superior of capital and deserves much the higher consideration." "I wish to see labor organizations powerful," he added. But in the language of the old Roosevelt he made it clear that as they became powerful they must, like the big corporations, accept regulation by the State.

Among these proposals there were only a few things that Roosevelt had not endorsed before, and nothing for which others had not worked for at least ten years, but an appearance of newness was provided by shearing off some of the familiar Roosevelt equivocations and intensifying his paternalistic nationalism. Elihu Root found the new Roosevelt suspect: "I have no doubt he thinks he believes what he says, but he doesn't. He has merely picked up certain ideas which were at hand as one might pick up a poker or chair with which to strike." In a moment of candor Roosevelt himself declared that he was still working along familiar strategic lines. "What I have advocated," he said in 1910, ". . . is not wild radicalism. It is the highest and wisest kind of conservatism." [15]

Roosevelt's practical aims were probably centered at first on the election of 1916. Professor George Mowry

---

15. On Roosevelt's Confession of Faith before the 1912 Progressive convention Frank Munsey made the charming comment: "While splendidly progressive it is, at the same time, amply conservative and sound."

suggests that he anticipated Republican defeat in 1912 and would have been happy to see Taft bear the brunt of it, leaving himself to come back to the White House at the head of a rejuvenated and reunited party in 1916, when he would be only fifty-eight. If these were his plans, he altered them as the Progressive movement came to the boiling-point.

Robert M. La Follette, by virtue of his accomplishments in Wisconsin and in the Senate, seemed the natural leader of the Progressives as they rallied for the 1912 convention. Roosevelt himself, who had written privately in 1908 of "the La Follette type of fool radicalism," praised him in 1910 for having made of his home state "an experimental laboratory of wise governmental action in aid of social and economic justice." La Follette seemed to have an excellent chance of capturing the nomination if he could get Roosevelt's backing. He subsequently charged that he had had a definite promise from Roosevelt. Although proof has never been offered, this much is certain: Roosevelt did at first give the Progressive leader informal encouragement, but withheld positive public endorsement and at length sapped the vitality of the La Follette movement by refusing to disavow his own candidacy. La Follette's friends grew indignant. "You would laugh if you were in this country now," wrote Brand Whitlock to a friend abroad, December 5, 1911, "and were to see how the standpatters are trying to bring [Roosevelt] out as a candidate for President again, in order to head off La Follette, who is a very dangerous antagonist to Taft." "The Colonel," Lincoln Steffens reported a few weeks later, "is mussing up the whole Progressive movement with his 'To be or not to be.'"

Roosevelt's seeming indecision helped to strangle the

La Follette boom. By January 1912, outstanding Progressives like the Pinchots and Medill McCormick had switched to Roosevelt. In February, Fighting Bob, ill, harassed, and worried, suffered a momentary breakdown. Soon afterward, in response to a carefully prearranged "solicitation" by seven Progressive governors, the ex-President threw his hat in the ring and the La Follette boom collapsed entirely. One of the most interesting comments on the mentality of the Progressives is the fact that most of them turned to Roosevelt not only without resentment but enthusiastically, and when he bolted the Republican convention to form a third party, followed him with a feeling of fervor and dedication that had not been seen since 1896. As William Allen White later recalled, "Roosevelt bit me and I went mad." [16]

Having aroused the hopes of the Progressives and having sidetracked their most effective leader, Roosevelt went on to use their movement for the purposes of finance capital. One of several practical advantages that Roosevelt had over La Follette was his ability to command the support of men of great wealth. Most important among these was George W. Perkins, ex-partner in the House of Morgan, director of International Harvester, and organizer of trusts. Perkins belonged to that wing of business which was aroused by Taft's more vigorous anti-trust policy, especially by the prosecution of so vital a Morgan concern as the United

16. It is interesting that as late as October 27, 1911 Roosevelt could have written to Hiram Johnson: "I have no cause to think at the moment that there is any real or widely extended liking for or trust in me among the masses of the people." Events proved him wrong, but it may be that this projection of dislike and distrust upon the people represented the way he imagined they might be expected to feel about him.

States Steel Corporation.[17] He was among those who therefore preferred Roosevelt to Taft or La Follette; this preference was shared by Frank A. Munsey, the influential publisher, a large stockholder in United States Steel. Perkins and Munsey pressed Roosevelt to run, later supplied, according to the revelations of the Clapp committee, over $500,000 to his campaign, and spent even larger sums in indirect support. When Roosevelt failed to win the Republican nomination, they spurred him on to form a new party, Munsey with the grand promise: "My fortune, my magazines, my newspapers are with you." To the bitter disappointment of Progressives like Amos Pinchot, Perkins forced upon the Progressive platform a plank stating the Perkins-Roosevelt approach to the trust problem.[18]

The strong showing of the Progressives in the election—Roosevelt ran second to Wilson and almost 700,000 votes ahead of Taft—promised much for the future. But Roosevelt soon abandoned the movement. It would be impossible, he asserted, to hold the party together; there were "no loaves and fishes." Four years later when a forlorn group of Progressives again tendered him a nomination, he spurned it and tossed them a final insult by suggesting that they name his friend

---

17. In an address on "The Sherman Law," delivered to the Economic Club of Philadelphia in 1915, Perkins scourged Taft bitterly for having betrayed the moderate plank on trusts prepared by Roosevelt for Taft's 1908 campaign and expounded the Roosevelt-Perkins approach to the trust question.

18. When Pinchot complained to Roosevelt about Perkins's influence in the party, Roosevelt assured him that the matter of the trust plank was "utterly unimportant" and attributed the Progressive Party's defeat to its being "too radical." At last Pinchot aired in public the rift in the party over Perkins and blamed Roosevelt for the collapse of the movement. "When I spoke of the Progressive party," replied Roosevelt to Pinchot, "as having a lunatic fringe, I specifically had you in mind."

Henry Cabot Lodge, whose principles, if any, were
thoroughly reactionary.

Roosevelt's attempt to promote Lodge was prompted
by the fact that he had lost interest in the domestic
aspects of the Progressive movement. War was now
raging in Europe, and the colonel had little regard for
the notions of foreign policy that prevailed among the
more sentimental adherents of the third party. As he
wrote to Lodge in the spring of 1917, the typical American Progressive was like his liberal brother in England
—"an utterly hopeless nuisance because of his incredible silliness in foreign affairs."

Although in nominal retirement at the outbreak of
the World War, Roosevelt was still in search of excitement. At first he seems to have been torn between the
impulses of the hardened realist who could look upon
the affairs of nations with detachment, and those of the
strategist and man of action who would welcome an
opportunity to engage the nation's power and see some
fighting. His initial remarks on the war, although calm
and impartial, were more friendly to Germany than
prevailing opinion in the United States. Concerning
the invasion of Belgium, which shocked so many Americans, he patiently explained that "When giants are
engaged in a death wrestle, as they reel to and fro they
are certain to trample on whomever gets in the way
of either of the huge straining combatants." Disaster
would have befallen Germany if she had not acted so
resolutely in Belgium. The Germans had proved themselves "a stern, virile, and masterful people." The sole
policy of the United States should be to protect her
own interests and "remain entirely neutral."

As late as October 11, 1914 Roosevelt voiced a "thrill
of admiration for the stern courage and lofty disinter-

estedness which this great crisis laid bare" in the souls of the German people, and hoped that the American public would show similar qualities should the need arise. To cripple Germany or reduce her to impotence, he warned, would be "a disaster to mankind."

Yet the preceding August Roosevelt had written to Steward Edward White that if Germany should win, "it would be only a matter of a very few years before we should have to fight her," adding that he would consider it "quite on the cards to see Germany and Japan cynically forget the past and join together against the United States and any other power that stood in their way." By early 1915 this point of view had made its way into his public statements as he fulminated against Wilson for "supine inaction"—and for failing to help the Belgians! Thenceforth he devoted himself to baiting pacifists and scolding at Wilson's neutrality policies. The American people themselves, he once complained to Lodge, "are cold; they have been educated by this infernal peace propaganda of the last ten years into an attitude of sluggishness and timidity."

Long before the United States entered the war, Roosevelt was thinking of participating. An army officer visiting him at Oyster Bay in January 1915 found him pacing the floor, protesting American inaction, asserting his eagerness to fight. The boyish demand for excitement—"You must always remember," Spring-Rice had written a decade earlier, "that the President is about six"—was as strong in him as ever. He applied to the War Department for permission to let him raise a division, and, anticipating rejection, told Ambassador Jusserand that he would lead an American division to France if the French would pay for it. Wilson's refusal to commission him brought on a new fit of rage. Wilson was "purely a demagogue," "a doctrinaire," "an utterly selfish and cold-blooded politician always."

But the last exploit was denied him. Ravaged by the strenuous life, saddened by the loss of his son Quentin at the front, he grew suddenly old and became ill. Lodge journeyed to his bedside and the two schemed to spike Wilson's League of Nations. On January 6, 1919, Roosevelt died of a coronary embolism.

CHAPTER X

WOODROW WILSON:
THE CONSERVATIVE AS LIBERAL

❦

THE *truth is, we are all caught in a great economic system which is heartless.*   WOODROW WILSON

WOODROW WILSON's father was a Presbyterian minister, his mother a Presbyterian minister's daughter, and the Calvinist spirit burned in them with a bright and imperishable flame. Their son learned to look upon life as the progressive fulfillment of God's will and to see man as "a distinct moral agent" in a universe of moral imperatives. When young Tommy Wilson sat in the pew and heard his father bring the Word to the people, he was watching the model upon which his career was to be fashioned. He never aspired to be a clergyman, but he made politics his means of spreading spiritual enlightenment, of expressing the powerful Protestant urge for "service" upon which he had been reared. At an early age he was afflicted with an almost impersonal ambition to become great in order that he might serve greatly. Deadly in earnest, rigid, self-exacting, Wilson suffered acutely from his Presbyterian training. "I am too intense!" he cried in one of his early letters to Ellen Axson; and on two occasions in his youthful career he broke under pressure from the compulsions that worked obscurely in him. Capable himself

308

of intense feelings of guilt, he projected his demand for unmitigated righteousness into public affairs, draining his intellectual capacity for tolerance. In an early essay on Burke he commented feelingly that "we should not expect a man to be easy and affable when he deems himself fighting in a death-grapple with the enemies of his country." "Tolerance," he declared in an article written during the same period,

> is an admirable intellectual gift; but it is of little worth in politics. Politics is a war of *causes;* a joust of principles. Government is too serious a matter to admit of meaningless courtesies.

Too much in earnest to be an easy companion or an easy combatant, Wilson nevertheless had a powerful need for affection. A deep sense of isolation, a cramped capacity for personal communication, tortured and stunted his emotional life. "When I am with anyone in whom I am specially and sincerely interested," he once wrote, "the hardest subject for me to broach is just that which is nearest my heart." "It isn't pleasant or convenient to have strong passions," he confided. ". . . I have the uncomfortable feeling that I am carrying a volcano about with me. My salvation is in being loved. . . . There surely never lived a man with whom love was a more critical matter than it is with me!" Wilson was aloof; he concealed himself with a habitually drawn curtain of reserve; but he was not, as many have concluded, a cold man. "I have to . . . guard my emotions from painful overflow," he told his first wife. And again:

> Sometimes I am a bit ashamed of myself when I think how few friends I have amidst a host of acquaintances.

Plenty of people offer me their friendship; but, partly, because I am reserved and shy, and partly because I am fastidious and have a narrow, uncatholic taste in friends, I reject the offer in almost every case; and then am dismayed to look about and see how few persons in the world stand near me and know me as I am,—in such wise that they can give me sympathy and close support of heart. Perhaps it is because when I give at all I want to give my whole heart, and I feel that so few want it all, or would return measure for measure. Am I wrong, do you think, in that feeling? And can one as deeply covetous of friendship and close affection as I am afford to act upon such a feeling?

A strange personality for a politician, it may seem. And yet not so strange: for with masses of men Wilson was beautifully articulate, and in public he often got the sense of communion, if not affection, that he so missed in private.

I have a sense of power in dealing with men collectively [he wrote in 1884] which I do not feel always in dealing with them singly. In the former case the pride of reserve does not stand so much in my way as it does in the latter. One feels no sacrifice of pride necessary in courting the favour of an assembly of men such as he would have to make in seeking to please one man.

When he finally went into politics, signs of public affection pleased him deeply. "At last I feel that I have arrived in politics," he told newspapermen in 1912, after making a speech in a small town from the rear platform of his train. Pressed for explanation, he replied: "Somebody out there in that crowd waved his arms and yelled 'Hello, Woody' at me!" His personal friends were not given to calling him "Woody." Even in public relations, however, he failed to get the full measure of affection he craved. As he wistfully confessed to Tumulty one night in the White House, "I want the people to love me, but I suppose they never will." He could command respect; from some, because they felt in him the embodiment of a cause, he had devotion. But love he could not win, and there was something insubstantial about his relationship with the people, something forced; the fact that he strove so consciously to be a democrat is the best evidence that by instinct he was not. All his life he carried with him a burning intensity that found no object other than ideas on which to expend itself, and ideas did not satisfy him. He said that his salvation was in "being loved," but failed to add "in loving." How he sought to avoid that "sacrifice of pride"! He devoted himself to principles, to humanity in the abstract, not to men in the flesh—and he left behind him a trail of broken friendships and a singularly impersonal public reputation. Although he achieved an extraordinary measure of success before the war broke him, the course of his ascent was parallel to rather than identical with the main course of American development. He was a serious educator in philistine university circles, a British liberal in progressive America, a would-be dispenser of sanity and justice to a world maddened by wartime hatreds, and finally the preacher of a mission of world service to the most insular and provincial people among all the great powers. In success or in failure, the essential isolation of Woodrow Wilson was always preserved.

During Woodrow Wilson's youth the Wilsons, although both were Northerners, lived at various places in the South—in Virginia, Georgia, South Carolina, North Carolina. The boy's earliest memory was of hearing that Mr. Lincoln had been elected and now there would be a war; his family lived in Augusta at the time when Sherman was ravishing Georgia. "The only place in the country, the only place in the world," said Wilson many years later, "where nothing has to be explained to me is the South." When, as a young lawyer, he appeared to testify against the protective tariff before the Tariff Commission in Atlanta and declared: "The people of the South will insist on having the fruits of peace, and not being kept down under the burdens of war," the faded voices of Calhoun and McDuffie might have been speaking.

In Wilson's case it was not odd that one whose family roots in the South were so recent should assimilate himself so completely. At heart he was a sentimental traditionalist. One of the most striking things about his spirit was his urgent need to achieve a sense of belonging by affixing himself to a tradition, to a culture, to a historic body of institutions. One of his keenest limitations as an intellectual was his incapacity for detachment—not from himself, for he often held himself at arm's length, but from the political values of the society in which he lived. Neither an aggressive critic nor an intellectual innovator, he was essentially a spokesman of the past. Even as a reformer, he held up for approval not so much the novel aspects of his work as its value in sustaining the organic continuity of tradition. It was natural, then, that he should adopt wholeheartedly the traditional party of the militant South, that his first political cause should be the timeless issue of the cotton-growers—free trade.

As Wilson's political roots were Southern, his intellectual traditions were English. He liked the self-conscious traditionalism of the British thinkers. His heroes among statesmen were conservatives and Manchester-

ians: Burke, Gladstone, Cobden, Bright; among thinkers, Walter Bagehot, and that transplanted Englishman
E. L. Godkin of the *Nation*. His model of political action was a somewhat romantic version of British statecraft: a system in which great and magnanimous constitutional statesmen, who cherished a driving zeal for
the public interest, debated important questions in
well-fashioned rhetoric. Believing heartily in outstanding personal leadership, he disliked the American Congressional system because it no longer gave play to the
powers of great debaters like Webster, Hayne, and Calhoun, but favored the off-stage machinations of petty
and venal personalities and conducted its most important business in the insidious privacy of the committee
room. His first book, *Congressional Government*, was a
critique comparing the American system unfavorably
with cabinet government.

Bagehot, above all, won Wilson's admiration. This
Lombard Street intellectual had his faults, Wilson
granted, for he lacked "sympathy with the voiceless
body of the people . . . the stout fibre and the unques-
tioning faith in the right and capacity of inorganic majorities which makes the democrat." But in philosophic
insight, in perception, in understanding, wit, expression, Bagehot was supreme. A Darwinian conservative
who believed implicitly in the necessity of growth, he
knew that growth in politics, as in organisms, is slow,
that it has a natural, unhurried pace. "He would much
rather . . . see [society] grow than undertake to reconstruct it." In his own study of *The State*, which
appeared in 1889, Wilson elaborated the gradualist
Darwinian view of social change. "In politics nothing
radically novel may safely be attempted," he wrote.
"No result of value can ever be reached . . . except

through slow and gradual development, the careful adaptations and nice modifications of growth."

What Wilson liked best about America's democratic traditions was their broad resemblance to England's. Political growth in both countries was founded on the same deliberate and unhurried marshaling of thought, the same accretion of habits and practices. Aware that their national history had begun with a provincial revolution, Americans had unfortunately contracted some wrong ideas about themselves. "We deemed ourselves rank democrats, whereas we were in fact only progressive Englishmen." Democracy in America has no communion of spirit with the turbulent thing that passes for democracy in Continental Europe.

> There is almost nothing in common between popular outbreaks such as took place in France at her great Revolution and the establishment of a government like our own. Our memories of the year 1789 are as far as possible removed from the memories which Europe retains of that pregnant year. We manifested one hundred years ago what Europe lost, namely, self-command, self-possession. Democracy in Europe, outside of closeted Switzerland, has acted always in rebellion, as a destructive force; it can scarcely be said to have had, even yet, any period of organic development. . . . Democracy in America, on the other hand, and in the English colonies has had, almost from the first, a truly organic growth. There was nothing revolutionary in its movements; it had not to overthrow other polities; it had only to organize itself. It had not to create, but only to expand, self-government. It did not need to spread propaganda: it needed nothing but to methodize its ways of living.

Accordingly, Wilson stood far closer to Edmund Burke than to Thomas Jefferson. He admired even the Burke of *Reflections on the French Revolution*. Burke, he found, "hated the French revolutionary philosophy and deemed it unfit for free men. And that philosophy is in fact radically evil and corrupting. No state can ever be conducted on its principles." The "French philosophy," which assumes that governments can be made over at will, emphasizes contractual and rational reorganization of society instead of habit; it holds that the object of government is liberty, instead of justice for all classes. Burke was a true Englishman; "the history of England is a continuous thesis against revolutions." Jefferson's failure to understand these things, Wilson believed, was his chief defect. A natural democrat, with a fine devotion to the cause of the common people, Jefferson was nevertheless weakened by French speculative philosophy, "which runs like a false and artificial note through all his thought." For this reason, "we must pronounce him, though a great man, not a great American." [1] During his days as a law student at the University of Virginia Wilson did not even trouble himself to make the short pilgrimage up the mountain to Jefferson's house at Monticello, and it was not until 1906, when he was first beginning to take notice of the progressive ferment, that he found good words to say of Jefferson in a public address. Among the leading historic figures of his own party, the man who most attracted Wilson was Grover Cleveland, the leader of the Eastern financial wing.

In his political and historical writing Wilson often expressed the same general prejudices that young Theodore Roosevelt showed.[2] His treatment of crises in

---

1. It is amusing that later on, in the first stirrings of his progressive phase, Wilson pronounced the same judgment on Hamilton, though for different reasons.
2. "Ever since I have had independent judgments of my own," Wilson told A. B. Hart, "I have been a Federalist."

American History from Shays' Rebellion to the Pullman strike and the Haymarket affair was in the conventional ruling-class vein. Although he had written to John Bates Clark in 1887 that economic life should be Christianized and that "a sane well-balanced sympathizer with organized labor is very dear to my esteem," his attitude toward organized labor was generally hostile. As late as 1909 he described himself as "a fierce partizan of the Open Shop and of everything that makes for individual liberty." He had as little use for agrarian radicalism, for he was revolted by the "crude and ignorant minds" of the Populists.

As one might expect of a Manchesterian who believed that a temperate and honest pursuit of private good was a public blessing, Wilson was not nearly so critical of the business community as of Populists and trade unions. As William Diamond points out in his excellent study of Wilson's economic thought, the professor felt that trade was still the carrier of ideas, progress, and broad, catholic views. "Every great man of business," he told the Chicago Commercial Club in 1902, "has got somewhere . . . a touch of the idealist in him . . . this love of integrity for its own sake . . . this feeling of the subtle linking of all men together . . . and all the dear ideals which we are ready to leave our business for and give our lives to vindicate."

However, Wilson was far from complacent about the development of trusts. The trusts, he asserted in his *History of the American People,* gave "to a few men a control over the economic life of the country which they might abuse to the undoing of millions of men, it might even be to the permanent demoralization of society itself and of the government. . . ." But strong as his language was he seldom pursued this theme before 1912.

The broad parallel between the brand of conservatism shown by Wilson before 1910 and by Theodore Roosevelt before 1902 is compelling. Both men were of socially secure background, although Wilson went through a long spell of poverty and frustration. Both, within the limits of their respective party traditions, accepted conventional laissez-faire. Both were convinced that they stood for the general welfare rather than any special interest—a notion common to the middle class and its political spokesmen. Both looked with disdain upon the labor and Populist movements; both were suspicious of the trusts, chiefly as a political menace, although neither had any clear ideas of what should be done about business combination. Both became late converts to the main body of progressive views.

The difference between them, in their conservative and progressive phases alike, is the difference between fervor and hysteria. Wilson's early conservatism was based upon a deliberate and reasoned philosophy of politics and social change. By comparison Roosevelt's brand of politics, with its shrill impatience and its suppressed tendency toward violence, seems like a nervous tic. The early Wilson made room in his philosophy for change, for reform, as an organic principle, and his ultimate conversion is no more drastic than a change of emphasis. Roosevelt, despite his oft-expressed desire for political purification, had no principle of change rooted in his philosophy, and his switch to progressivism seems not so much a change of views as a violent change in language prompted by the call of ambition. In Roosevelt there appears to be no real movement of the mind because the mind has hardly ever come into focus. In Wilson one feels a genuine and pleasurable groping toward the new, and a coherent articulation of new and old. Both men, probably without full consciousness, seem to have been converted to the rising progressive philosophy in part because that philosophy was more opportune for their political careers. Although each, in his way, was sincere, in sincerity there are depths and depths. The quality of Wilson's sincerity is illuminated in one of his attacks upon hypocrisy in education, where a striking sentence voices the moral compulsion upon which his relation with the public was based: "We must believe the things we tell the children."

II

"Southerners," Wilson once observed, "seem born with an interest in public affairs." Seized by the Southern passion for rhetoric, he practiced speechmaking in his youth with a cold, persistent deliberation. While still a Princeton undergraduate, he wrote out a number of cards with the legend: THOMAS WOODROW WILSON, SENATOR FROM VIRGINIA. When he turned from Princeton to the University of Virginia law school, it was with the expectation that law would serve him as a means to another end:

> The profession I chose was politics; the profession I entered was law. I entered the one because I thought it would lead to the other. It was once the sure road; and Congress is still full of lawyers.

He was "most terribly bored by the noble study of Law sometimes," but completed his course and began law practice in Atlanta in 1882. Unsuccessful and unhappy in "the scheming and haggling practice" of his profession, he stayed only one year and then entered the graduate school of Johns Hopkins University. His object, he told his future wife, was to get the training to further "my ambition to become an invigorating and enlightening power in the world of political thought and a master in some of the less serious branches of literary art." Even then he felt he was predestined to great things:

> . . . those indistinct plans of which we used to talk grow on me daily, until a sort of calm confidence of great things to be accomplished has come over me which I am puzzled to analyze the nature of. I can't tell whether it is a mere figment of my own inordinate vanity, or a deep-rooted determination which it will be in my power to act up to.

In some ways Wilson found himself as discontented at Hopkins as he had been in law school. The university, of course, was flourishing. Herbert Baxter Adams was offering his famous seminars in history, and young Richard T. Ely, newly returned from his graduate studies in Germany, was teaching political economy. Frederick Jackson Turner was a fellow student. Among the famous visitors in Wilson's time were Edmund Gosse, James Bryce, and Josiah Royce, the last described by Wilson as "one of the rarest spirits I have met." But the sort of historical and constitutional interest fostered in Adams's seminars did not suit Wilson. The Hopkins professors were working on institutional history, tracing the evolution of town meetings, local organizations, and land systems, all of which Wilson found tiresome "in comparison with the grand excursions amongst imperial policies which I had planned for myself." In economics he seems to have been only slightly influenced by the German historical school of which he learned through Ely, and his fundamental loyalty to laissez-faire traditions was not seriously impaired.

Wilson took his Ph.D. in 1886 and set out upon his academic career, which for some years was the familiar story of the talented young professor: meager salaries, marriage, children, overwork, writing for money to supplement his income, gradual upward progress. He moved from Bryn Mawr to Wesleyan, and at thirty-four became Professor of Jurisprudence and Politics at Princeton.

As a teacher Wilson suffered from a deepening sense of frustration. He had aimed to be a statesman, but, like Henry Adams before him, found himself no more than an intellectual wet-nurse to undergraduates, while men of inferior talents and inferior motives ran the country. Frederick C. Howe, who often heard Wilson lecture during Wilson's periodic visits to Johns Hopkins between 1887 and 1897, recalled the "note of moral passion in his speech." Great men, Wilson would say, had departed from Capitol Hill. Public life in America had degenerated into a struggle of vulgar interests; Americans were abandoned, in politics as in personal relations, to moneymaking; democracy must be reclaimed from the spoilsmen. To a friend Wilson poured out his heart:

> I do feel a very real regret that I have been shut out from my heart's *first*—primary—ambition and purpose, which was to take an active, if possible, a leading, part in public life, and strike out for myself, if I had the ability, a statesman's career. . . . I have a strong instinct of leadership, and unmistakably oratorical temperament, and the keenest possible delight in affairs; and it has required

very constant and stringent schooling to content me with the sober methods of the scholar and the man of letters. I have no patience with the tedious world of what is known as "research"; I have a passion for interpreting great thoughts to the world; I should be complete if I could inspire a great movement of opinion, if I could read the experiences of the past into the practical life of the men of today and so communicate the thought to the minds of the great mass of the people as to impel them to great political achievements. . . . My feeling has been that such literary talents as I have are *secondary* to my equipment for other things: that my power to write was meant to be a handmaiden to my power to speak and to organize action. . . .

Wilson nevertheless rose rapidly at Princeton. He published six books. He lectured widely and met influential men. Trustees were impressed with his gravity, his solidity, his high sentiments, doubtless with his very appearance, and in June 1902, upon the retirement of President Francis L. Patton, they unanimously elected Wilson his successor.

The new president had broad, ambitious plans for improving instruction. He wrung large sums from alumni, added fifty young preceptors to the staff, and worked out a series of eleven systematic curricula, all with unqualified success. Professor E. E. Slosson, in his *Great American Universities*, described Princeton as "the most interesting of American universities to study just now." When Wilson made the daring suggestion that the sacred Princeton eating clubs be abolished in favor of a more democratic system of undergraduate life, he went down in defeat, but the publicity aroused by the dispute helped to popularize him as a democrat at a moment when the progressive impulse was on the upswing.

While he was fighting his educational battles, Wilson was preaching in public addresses and essays political ideas that brought him to the attention of influential Democrats. On rare occasions he had critical things to say of entrenched wealth, particularly of bankers and speculators. Along with the Progressives, he recognized that the power of accumulated capital was "in the hands of a comparatively small number of persons" who "have been able in recent years as never before to control the national development in their own interest." In 1908, voicing the discontents of the middle classes, he declared:

> The contest is sometimes said to be between capital and labor, but that is too narrow and special a conception of it. It is, rather, between capital in all its larger accumulations and all other less concentrated, more dispersed, smaller, and more individual economic forces; and every new policy proposed has as its immediate or ultimate object the restraint of the power of accumulated capital for the protection and benefit of those who cannot command its use.

But the president of Princeton also made it clear again and again that he had not abandoned the conservatism of his formal political writings. He had no sympathy for Populistic democracy. Privately he proposed to knock Bryan "into a cocked hat," and publicly he remarked that the Boy Orator, though "the most charming and lovable of men personally," was "foolish and dangerous in his theoretical beliefs." He also criticized organized labor, which he called "as formidable an enemy to equality and freedom of opportunity" as the "so-called capitalistic class." Later, when he ran for the governorship of New Jersey, he was opposed by the state Federation of Labor, which could not be placated by several warm assurances that he had always criticized labor as a friend rather than an enemy.

Somehow, Wilson believed, the nation must steer a middle course between the plutocracy and the masses. The government must be an impartial agency, mediating between extremes and representing the common interest. The solution of economic problems, however, did not lie in an extreme of governmental interference or regulation. Socialism represented "a danger of the very sort we seek to escape, a danger of centralized and corruptible control." Further, it would be undesirable, even impossible, to attack all big-business combinations; those which had developed as a result of "natural forces" rather than tariff protection or unfair competitive methods were legitimate: "It is necessary to have them if modern society is to be conducted with success." To try to regulate their affairs in detail would require a series of expert commissions, and such commissions tend to go beyond regulation to the point of actually conducting business. In 1907 Wilson stated that the United States was already "on the high road to government ownership of many sorts, or to some other method of control which will in practice be as complete as actual ownership." The proper way to control business, where control was necessary, was to put good laws on the books and enforce them through the courts instead of leaving dangerously broad discretionary powers to committees. As a conservative Democrat, he said, he believed in firm and effective regulation, but repudiated "the prevailing principles of regulation, the principles which the Republican party has introduced and carried to such radical lengths. . . ." In short, he would not go so far as Theodore Roosevelt. The solution? It must be found in a movement of moral regeneration, which would find its source in the hearts of the people and its arbiter in the government. Punishment must fall upon evil individuals—must be personal, not corporate. The corporation, he explained in one of his most frequently used metaphors, was an automobile; the maleficent corporation official was the irresponsible driver. It would be pointless to administer punishment to the machine; only innocent stockholders were penalized by fining corporations. The joyrider himself must be held responsible, and if he could not be exhorted into morality, then he must be bludgeoned. "One really responsible man in jail, one real originator of the schemes and transactions which are contrary to public interest legally lodged in the penitentiary, would be worth more than one thousand corporations mulcted in fines, if reform is to be genuine and permanent." Society could be saved only by "the insurgence of individuals . . . who will say, 'I am indeed a part of this organization; but I will not allow my moral consciousness to be crushed by it.'"

To sophisticated conservatives this approach to economic problems seemed a harmless way of draining popular discontents out of the arena of serious action. The Democratic conservatives of the North and East became interested in the political potentialities of a man who could preach such sound doctrine with so much force. "They were perhaps all the more interested," writes Wilson's authorized biographer, "because they did not at all believe that 'personal guilt' could ever really be established, or 'rich malefactors' be put in jail." (The Northern Securities case showed they were right.) Although Wilson's preachments were broadly the same as Roosevelt's, he seemed safer and more sober than the unpredictable Rough Rider; that, among Democrats, he was safer than Bryan was beyond question.

It was, then, the Eastern capitalistic wing of the Democratic Party, out of the Seymour-Tilden-Cleveland tradition, within whose orbit the Wilsonian comet was first seen. Wilson was originally taken up by Colonel George B. M. Harvey, editor of *Harper's Weekly*, president of the publishing house of Harper & Brothers, and minor associate of J. P. Morgan. Harvey brought Wilson to the attention of Thomas Fortune Ryan, master of a great fortune in traction, speculation, and mining interests, August Belmont, the banker, William Laffan, editor of the ultra-conservative New York *Sun*, Adolph Ochs, owner of the *New York Times*, and other influential Eastern Democrats. The "steady-going bankers" who felt that "the country is sick of too much government," Harvey wrote to Wilson, December 17, 1906, were eager to nominate such a man as Wilson and felt that they could elect him. Submitting himself to a personal examination by Ryan and Laffan in 1907, Wilson prepared a statement of faith in which he reiterated the more acceptable doctrines he had been preaching in his public appearances.

Wilson, however, did not fail to maintain the feeling and the aspect of independence. In January 1910 he came to New York City to give a widely publicized lecture to a meeting of bankers. With J. P. Morgan sitting at his side, he declared:

> The trouble today is that you bankers are too narrow-minded. You don't know the country or what is going on in it and the country doesn't trust you. . . . You take no interest in the small borrower and the small enterprise which affect the future of the country, but you give every attention to the big borrower and the rich enterprise which has already arrived. . . . You bankers . . . see

nothing beyond your own interests. . . . You should be broader minded and see what is best for the country in the long run.

When Boss Jim Smith's well-knit New Jersey Democratic machine approached him about the governorship, Wilson was puzzled. He thought the bosses knew him as "an absolutely independent person," but when he asked them why they wanted him to run, he got no satisfactory answer, "so I had to work one out for myself. I concluded that these gentlemen had been driven to recognize that a new day had come in American politics, and that they would have to conduct themselves henceforth after a new fashion." He thus persuaded himself that he could co-operate with them on righteous terms. But no sooner had he launched his campaign than a subtle change came over him. Forced upon the Democratic Party by the machine steamroller, his candidacy had been greeted with sharp cries of complaint by Progressives. "Dr. Wilson," complained the Hoboken *Observer*, "was induced to enter the race by a combination of the very elements which the Progressives are fighting . . . and these elements have assumed charge of his candidacy." Wilson began to feel this criticism personally, and he had enough regard for the Progressives to respond to it. In a letter written toward the close of the campaign he expressed his concern "that so much credence has been given to the statement that I was out of sympathy with the point of view of the plain people, that I put conventional property rights above human rights, as it were, and held a sort of stiff academic view of things." Hitherto, in order to get a foothold in politics, it had been necessary for him to please the capitalists and the bosses; now, if he was to keep this foothold—and his own self-esteem—he must please the people. The young Progressives began to rub their eyes at Wilson's forthright replies to their challenges; they thrilled with approval when he declared that he would enter the governorship, if elected, "with absolutely no pledges of any kind."

Thus, after a quarter of a century in the comparative quiet of academic life, Wilson won his first public office. A projected magnum opus, which was to have been called *The Philosophy of Politics,* was put away in his files. When Jim Smith and some of his henchmen visited Princeton and were ushered into Wilson's serene and comfortable study, luxuriously lined with books, they found their strange new associate's aspirations hard to understand. "Can you imagine anyone," asked Boss Smith, "being damn fool enough to give this up for the heartaches of politics?"

III

When Wilson told the electorate that he had made "absolutely no pledges of any kind," the bosses doubtless wrote off his words as good campaign talk. Accustomed to the corrupt geniality of politics, they had yet to learn of the ruthlessness of the pure in heart, but the professor did not wait long to give them a schooling. Boss Smith had been in the Senate and wished to return. Although the people had expressed preference for another man, Thomas E. Martine, in the primaries, it was the legislature that would actually make the choice, and nothing could stop Smith except the opposition of the governor. But the "Presbyterian priest," as Smith called him, refused to co-operate. He had endorsed the principle of popular election of Senators during the campaign, and he would not turn on it. He appealed to the legislature to elect Martine, and Martine was elected. The bosses, said Wilson, were "warts upon the body politic"; the people would destroy them.

"An ingrate in politics," commented Boss Richard Croker of Tammany, "is no good." But Wilson was not simply an ingrate. For him public obligations were much greater than private, principles larger than personalities. His relationship with the man Smith was unimportant, but if he could not believe that he was acting in the service of a high ideal his personality would have withered and his powers would have lapsed. He habitually drew upon his spiritual reserve to key himself up as other men will go to alcohol for relaxation. "Sometimes," he confided during this period, ". . . my whole life seems to me rooted in dreams —and I do not want the roots of it to dry up." "I shall make mistakes," he wrote in another letter, "but I do not think I shall sin against my knowledge of duty."

As governor, Wilson was successful beyond his hopes. During the first legislative session of his term he won everything he had aimed at and more—a primary and elections law, a corrupt practices act, workmen's compensation, utilities regulation, school reforms, and an enabling act giving cities the right to adopt the commission form of government. The young Progressives who had begun by suspecting him—men like Devlin, Record, Kerney, and Tumulty—became his ardent supporters. Presidential talk was rife, and Wilson rose to it with his usual gravity. "There are serious times ahead," he wrote, April 23, 1911.

It daunts me to think of the possibility of my playing an influential part in them. There is no telling what deep waters may be ahead of me. The forces of greed and the forces of justice and humanity are about to grapple for a bout in which men will spend all the life that is in them. God grant I may have strength enough to count, to tip the balance in the unequal and tremendous struggle!

Into his speeches there crept a new and more aggressive note, a ringing demand for change, and yet for change that would preserve "established purposes and conceptions." In this idea—that we must have a forward-looking return to the past—was the link between the old and the new Wilson. In a series of speeches delivered between the spring of 1911 and the 1912 presidential campaign Wilson propounded his new faith:

. . . The *machinery of political control must be put in the hands of the people* . . . for the purpose of recovering what seems to have been lost—their right to exercise a free and constant choice in the management of their own affairs. . . .

The service rendered the people by the *national government must be of a more extended sort* and of a kind not only to protect it against monopoly, but also to facilitate its life. . . .

We *do not mean to strike at any essential economic arrangement;* but we do mean to drive all beneficiaries of governmental policy into the open and demand of them by what principle of national advantage, as contrasted with selfish privilege, they enjoy the extraordinary assistance extended to them. . . .

The great monopoly in this country is *the money monopoly.* So long as that exists our old variety and freedom and individual energy of development are out of the question. . . . The growth of the nation, therefore, and all our activities are in the hands of a few men . . . who necessarily, by very reason of their own limitations, chill and check and destroy genuine economic freedom. This is the greatest question of all. . . .

What do we stand for here tonight and what shall we stand for as long as we live? We stand for setting the Government of this country free and the business of this country free. . . .

Now, the real difficulty in the United States . . . is not the existence of great individual combinations—that is dangerous enough in all countries—but the real danger is the combination of the combinations, the real danger is that the same groups of men control chains of banks, systems of railways, whole manufacturing enterprises, great mining projects, great enterprises for the developing of the natural water power of this country, and that threaded together in the personnel of a series of boards of directors is a community of interest more formidable than any conceivable combination in the United States. . . .

What we have got to do . . . is to disentangle this colossal community of interest . . . to pull apart, and gently, but firmly and persistently dissect.

When I think over what we are engaged in doing in the field of politics, I conceive it this way, men who are behind any interest always unite in organization, and the danger in every country is that these special interests will be the only things organized, and that the common interest will be unorganized against them. *The business of government is to organize the common interest against the special interests.*

Wilson's endorsement of the progressive creed was followed by a break with his original sponsor and a complete change in the social base of his support. Told by his public-relations advisers that Colonel Harvey's support was arousing criticism in the West, he let Harvey know that it was doing him serious damage, and a growing coolness set in between the two. The breach with Harvey was balanced by a rapprochement with Bryan. Fortunately for Wilson, Bryan had an uncommonly generous spirit, and the Governor was able to make satisfactory amends for the Joline letter of 1907, in which he had aired that desire to knock Bryan "into a cocked hat." Harvey's support may have proved a liability; Bryan's was invaluable both in the Democratic convention of 1912 and in the national campaign. And, as Bryan expressed it in the *Commoner* early in the year, Wilson's "political strength today is in exact proportion to the confidence that [the masses] have in the completeness of the change he has undergone."

In the campaign of 1912 Wilson emerged as the middle-of-the-road candidate, flanked on the right by Taft and on the left by Roosevelt in his new pose. The bulk of left-wing reform sentiment went with the Progressive Party, and many moderate Republicans seem to have deserted Taft for Wilson. Since Taft was obviously out of the running, Wilson centered his fire on Theodore Roosevelt and stressed the one issue that chiefly distinguished their points of view—the trusts. Wilson's program, the result of his first serious thinking on the trust problem, was taken from the preachings of Louis D. Brandeis and formulated with the lawyer's guidance. Wilson's speeches, the best parts of which are printed in *The New Freedom,* sound like the collective wail of the American middle class.

What has happened in America, Wilson told the voters, is that industry has ceased to be free because the laws do not prevent the strong from crushing the weak. The best, the most gifted part of the nation, the rising workingman and the thrifty ambitious bourgeois, are being cramped and confined. "The middle class is being more and more squeezed out by the processes which we have been taught to call processes of prosperity." The established interests make a concerted effort to squeeze out the beginner; they cripple his credit; they undersell him in his local market until his business withers on the vine; they discriminate against the retailer who buys from their rival; they withhold raw materials from the small man. In short, they compete unfairly.

Those who criticize the competitive order assert that free competition itself has made it possible for the big to crush the little. This Wilson denied. "I reply, it is not free competition that has done that; it is illicit competition." A big business that survives competition through intelligence, efficiency, and economies deserves to survive. But the trust is "an arrangement to get rid of competition"; it "buys efficiency out of business." "I am for big business," said Wilson, succumbing to the equivocation that invariably creeps into politicians' discussions of the trust problem, "and I am against the trusts." [3]

The interests that have squeezed out the middle class are the same that control politics, Wilson went on. "The government of the United States at present is a foster-child of the special interests." But the people will regain control and return to their old competitive, democratic principles. "America will insist upon recovering in practice those ideals which she has always professed." The new order will be woven into the texture of the old: "If I did not believe that to be progressive was to preserve the essentials of our institutions, I for one could not be a progressive."

---

3. A position much like that of Albert J. Beveridge at the Progressive Party convention: "We mean to make little business big, and all business honest, instead of striving to make Big Business little, and yet letting it remain dishonest."

The New Freedom would address itself to the fundamental problem of the present age. "What this country needs above everything else is a body of laws which will look after the men who are on the make rather than the men who are already made." "The man who is on the make is the judge of what is happening in America, not the man who has made good . . . that is the man by whose judgment I, for one, wish to be guided." The hope of the nation, its real creative energies, had always been in the men "out of unknown homes" who rise to be masters of industry and politics.

Wilson conceded that there were many handsome and magnanimous reform proposals in the Progressive platform that stirred all the sympathies of a man of goodwill; but the Progressives were not even proposing to do the fundamental thing, which was to wrestle with the trusts. They proposed instead to work *through* the trusts, to guarantee, as it were, that the trusts would be merciful: "We will make these monopolies kind to you." "But," answered Wilson, "I do not want the sympathy of the trusts for the human race . . . their condescending assistance." The procedure Roosevelt stood for led up a blind alley.[4] "You can't find your way to social reform through the forces that have made social reform necessary." The Progressive program was "perfectly agreeable to the monopolies," and for that reason "not a progressive program at all." Its method of pretended trust-control was the method proposed ev-

---

4. Roosevelt in turn pointed out that New Jersey was one of the most notorious corporation states in the country. After the election Wilson secured the passage of the "Seven Sisters" laws, which placed serious restrictions on corporations within the state. The companies transferred their seat of incorporation to the complaisant neighbor state of Delaware, and New Jersey lost the revenue from fees. Later New Jersey again became a notorious home of corporations.

erywhere by "the very men who are interested in the maintenance of the present economic system of the United States."

Shrewdly Wilson exposed the interlocking structure of business and governmental power that would exist under what he called "the Roosevelt plan."

> I find, then, the proposition to be this: That there shall be two masters, the great corporation, and over it the government of the United States; and I ask who is going to be master of the government of the United States? It has a master now,—those who in combination control these monopolies. And if the government controlled by the monopolies in its turn controls the monopolies, the partnership is finally consummated.

The conceptions set forth in Wilson's speeches of 1912 were translated into legislation with remarkable success and fidelity during his first four years of office. The first Wilson administration, in fact, produced more positive legislative achievements than any administration since the days of Alexander Hamilton. Professor Lindsay Rogers has observed that the ex-professor "more than any of his predecessors has exerted an almost absolute authority over Congress." Wilson's administration was the first to secure a material downward tariff revision since the Civil War. In the Federal Reserve Act it revamped the nation's banking and credit system and placed it under public control. For the benefit of the farmers it passed the Federal Farm Loan Act, putting the government in the business of supplying agricultural credits, and the Warehousing Act, a measure that embodied several provisions of the old Populist independent treasury scheme. Its middle-class program for the control of big business was embodied in the Clayton Act, which was meant to implement the Sherman Anti-Trust Act, and in the creation of the Federal Trade Commission, which was to enjoin what Wilson had called "illicit competition." Labor also won gains, primarily in the clause of the Clayton Act exempting unions from harassment by anti-trust suits, and also in the La Follette Seamen's Act, the Adamson Act (passed under threat of a major railroad strike), setting an eight-hour day for railroad workers in interstate commerce, a child-labor act (soon, however, to be declared unconstitutional in one of the Supreme Court's most curious decisions), and a compensation law for Civil Service workers.[5]

Under a system of finance capitalism the government of the United States can hardly carry on without at least the passive co-operation of the financial community. Within the limits of the possibilities Wilson carried out the work of his first administration in a spirit of independence, a course maintained under the pressure of Bryan's wing of the party and such advisers as Louis D. Brandeis, whose opinions won Wilson's respect.[6] Not warfare, in fact, but simply a rather uneasy

---

5. The one important Wilson recommendation that was not enacted into law was the proposal that the Interstate Commerce Commission be empowered to regulate the issuance of securities by railroad companies.

6. A sharp struggle occurred when bankers tried to get control of the proposed Federal Reserve Board. They came to Washington in force, confronted Wilson across his desk, and with a great show of knowledge presented their arguments to the comparative financial innocent in the executive chair. When they had finished, Wilson asked the leaders: "Will one of you gentlemen tell me in what civilized country of the earth there are important government boards of control on which private interests are represented?" After a long silence he inquired: "Which of you gentlemen thinks the railroads should select members of the Interstate Commerce Commission?" These unanswered questions closed discussion of banker control of the Federal Reserve System. Resentment of Wilson among bankers became intense. Oswald

peace was the condition that prevailed between the administration and business up to 1917. Wilson proposed no fundamental alteration in the economic order. He still aimed to preserve competition, individualism, enterprise, opportunity—things that he regarded as vital in the American heritage. He had changed his mind, however, about regulation; his espousal of regulatory legislation by the federal government signified the abandonment of his earlier laissez-faire views. Brandeis had said during the 1912 campaign that the issue was regulated competition versus regulated monopoly, and all but the die-hards had abandoned the view that the State must keep its hands clear of the economic system. Wilson proposed that the force of the State be used to *restore* pristine American ideals, not to strike out sharply in a new direction. (*"If I did not believe that to be progressive was to preserve the essentials of our institutions, I for one could not be a progressive."*)

After the passage of the Clayton Act and the crea-

Garrison Villard in his memoirs recalls a luncheon with Thomas W. Lamont of the House of Morgan at which Lamont told him that Wilson had recently refused categorically to receive any member of that firm. Lamont's comment reflects on the curious position of an "independent" administration. What puzzled him, he said, was why the State Department was calling upon the House of Morgan to advance its Central American policies by floating loans. "We are either one thing or the other," he complained. "We are either respectable business men with whom the government can do business or we are not fit to associate with: we can't be both at the same time."

Actually the connection of government and finance continued, although at some remove. As Matthew Josephson emphasizes, the bankers had indirect access to Wilson's mind through his trusted adviser Colonel E. M. House, whom they saw on frequent occasions and who served as a conveyer belt for their views. This process saved Wilson's feeling of independence and integrity, a matter of vital importance to him.

tion of the Federal Trade Commission, Wilson felt that his basic program had been fulfilled. In his message to Congress, December 8, 1914, he declared:

> Our program of legislation with regard to the regulation of business is now complete. It has been put forth, as we intended as a whole, and leaves no conjecture as to what is to follow. The road at last lies clear and firm before business . . . the road to ungrudged, unclouded success.

Essentially the New Freedom was an attempt of the middle class, with agrarian and labor support, to arrest the exploitation of the community, the concentration of wealth, and the growing control of politics by insiders, and to restore, as far as possible, competitive opportunities in business. Walter Lippmann, then in his socialist phase, characterized the New Freedom as "the effort of small business men and farmers to use the government against the larger collective organization of industry." It had no sympathy, he complained, in harsh but essentially accurate language, "for the larger collective life upon which the world is entering." It was "a freedom for the little profiteer, but no freedom from the narrowness, the poor incentives, the limited vision of small competitors . . . from the chaos, the welter, the strategy of industrial war."

But the New Freedom was forgotten during American participation in the World War, and its gains largely wiped out by the reaction that followed. Wilson's classic philosophy of competition and enterprise underwent its climactic test not in "normalcy" but in waging war and making peace.

IV

Wilson grew up when the South was slowly recovering from the ravages of the Civil War; there he had imbibed a horror of violence, which was confirmed by his training in the pacific liberalism of nineteenth-century British thinkers. Professor Charles Callan Tansill in his extremely critical study of Wilson's wartime diplomacy observes that "In the long list of American Chief Executives there is no one who was a more sincere pacifist than the one who led us into war in April, 1917." Yet, as the nation's chief executive, Wilson felt the pull of every major force that drew the United States toward the conflict.

When Wilson told the people that America must be the example of peace "because peace is the healing and elevating influence of the world and strife is not," he was expressing a deeply ingrained moral bias. "The more I read about the conflict across the seas," he wrote to Charles R. Crane in the opening weeks of war, "the more open it seems to me to utter condemnation." Speaking before Congress, he called it "a war with which we have nothing to do." He told Stockton Axson that it would not lead to the permanent settlement of a single problem, and to Colonel House he predicted that it would "throw the world back three or four centuries." His conception of the proper role of America, as outlined in his speeches, was high-minded. The United States was the only great Western power not involved; it was her duty, her mission, to do something that no other nation had ever done in such a crisis— maintain "absolute self-mastery." Standing aloof from the issues of the conflict, without a single selfish interest, she should make herself ready to serve, to be an impartial mediator, to help bring the war to as early an end as possible, to assist in healing the world's wounds and in preparing for a lasting peace. "It would be a calamity to the world at large," he wrote in an early wartime letter, "if we should be drawn actively into the conflict, and so deprived of all disinterested influence over the settlement."

At the outset Wilson urged that the people be "impartial in thought as well as in action," but he and his most important advisers were utterly incapable of obeying the injunction themselves. One of the signal facts in the train of events leading to American participation was the overwhelming sympathy with the Allies that prevailed in administration circles, and the disposition of Wilson and his counselors to work for an outcome in Europe that would favor the Entente. Wilson's Allied sympathies were as vital as his love of peace. He was a thorough Anglophile. He had learned his greatest lessons from English thinkers; he had taken English statesmen as his models of aspiration and the British Constitution as his model of government; his work as president of Princeton had been, in large measure, an effort to introduce the English idea of a university; even his favorite recreation was to bicycle about the villages of the Lake Country with the *Oxford Book of English Verse* in his pocket. He was surrounded by pro-Ally advisers, especially Robert Lansing, Counselor of the State Department and later Secretary of State, and Colonel House (whom he called "my second personality . . . my independent self"). His Ambassador to England, Walter Hines Page, took it upon himself to represent Britain's cause to America.

These men were concerned with the prospect of a

German victory, which, they felt, would force the United States off the course of its peaceful, progressive development. House wrote to Wilson, August 22, 1914:

> Germany's success will ultimately mean trouble for us. We will have to abandon the path which you are blazing as a standard for future generations, with permanent peace as its goal and a new international ethical code as its guiding star, and build up a military machine of vast proportions.

A week later House recorded in his diary that Wilson had concurred with this analysis, and had gone "even further than I" in his condemnation of Germany's part in the war, including the German people themselves in his indictment. German philosophy, Wilson told him, "was essentially selfish and lacking in spirituality." [7] "England is fighting our fight," Wilson stated in the presence of Tumulty. ". . . I will not take any action to embarrass England when she is fighting for her life and the life of the world." His Attorney General recalled that when some Cabinet members urged him to embargo exports to England early in 1915, he replied:

> Gentlemen, the Allies are standing with their backs to the wall fighting wild beasts. I will permit nothing to be done by our country to hinder or embarrass them in the prosecution of the war unless admitted rights are grossly violated.

---

7. Wilson's "second personality" kept him vividly in mind of this conception of the balance of power. On June 16, 1915 House wrote to him: "I need not tell you that if the Allies fail to win, it must necessarily mean a reversal of our entire policy." A month later, urging preparedness on Wilson, he warned: "I feel that we are taking a terrible gamble ourselves in permitting our safety to rest almost wholly upon the success of the Allies. . . ."

When Brand Whitlock, visting him in December 1915, declared: "I am heart and soul for the Allies," Wilson replied: "So am I. No decent man, knowing the situation and Germany could be anything else." If the Germans succeeded, the President predicted to Sir Cecil Spring-Rice, "we shall be forced to take such measures of defence here as would be fatal to our form of Government and American ideals." In September 1915 he admitted to House that "he had never been sure that we ought not to take part in the conflict and, if it seemed evident that Germany and her militaristic ideas were to win, the obligation upon us was greater than ever."

This feeling, this desire to throw the United States in the scales if necessary to tip the balance of power against Germany, made real neutrality impossible; it caused Wilson to make legalistic discriminations on behalf of the Allies and intensify American economic involvement with them; and in the end he became a prisoner of his own policies. England as well as Germany violated American interests on the high seas and overrode those concepts of international law which the Wilson administration chose to invoke. Both nations were confronted with American protests from time to time, but the protests to Britain were inconclusive, while those to Germany were backed with serious threats. England adopted an extraordinarily sweeping definition of contraband, took astounding liberties with the traditional right of visit and search on the seas at much cost to American shippers, violated traditional concepts of a "legal" blockade, mined the North Sea in a manner intensely obstructive and costly to neutrals, stole American trade with other neutral nations, confiscated valuable American commercial information, and blacklisted American firms that she accused of trading with Germany. But the British diplomats knew that they had administration sympathies (had not Wilson himself told Spring-Rice that "a dispute between our two nations would be the crowning calamity"?); Page was present in London to soften the impact of every American protest; and serious action by the United States to enforce its rights against British practices seemed unlikely. As House wrote to Page in October 1914, "I cannot see how there can be any serious trouble between England and America, with all of us feeling as we do." [8]

A critical factor in turning sympathy into open alliance was the growing American economic commitment to the Allies. During 1914 a serious recession had begun in the United States, which showed signs of developing into the first major depression since 1893. However, by 1915 the stimulus of Allied war orders began to be strongly felt; by April 1917 over two billion dollars' worth of goods had been sold to the Allies. America became bound with the Allies in a fateful union of war and prosperity. The Allies' dependence on American supplies gave Wilson an enormous bargaining leverage, which he could have employed to moderate their blockade, but just as Sir Edward Gray chose not to quarrel with his munitions depot, Wilson chose not to quarrel with his country's best customer.[9]

In fact, Wilson was made acutely aware of American

8. At times, however, Wilson almost lost patience. "I am, I must admit, about at the end of my patience with Great Britain and the Allies . . ." he wrote House, July 23, 1916. "I am seriously considering asking Congress to authorize me to prohibit loans and restrict exportations to the Allies. . . ."

9. "The United States," comments Professor Charles Seymour, "possessed no means of bringing effective pressure to bear upon the Allies without injuring so deeply its own commercial interests that the price seemed too high to pay."

dependence on Allied war orders. Original Allied purchases drew upon Allied credit balances in the United States, but these were soon exhausted. When the problem arose whether to permit American bankers to make loans to the Allied governments, the administration, acting on Bryan's thesis that "money is the worst of all contrabands because it commands everything else," refused to encourage the bankers to proceed, and the bankers decided not to act without governmental sanction. However, the urgent Allied need of loans to support continued purchases caused representatives of the National City Bank to reopen the question with Lansing. Both Lansing and Secretary of the Treasury McAdoo impressed upon the President that the Bryan ban on loans stood in the way of continued prosperity. "Great prosperity is coming," wrote McAdoo, August 21, 1915. "It will be tremendously increased if we can extend reasonable credits to our customers. . . . To maintain our prosperity we must finance it. Otherwise it may stop and that would be disastrous." Two weeks later Counselor Lansing added his voice:

> If European countries cannot find means to pay . . . they will have to stop buying, and our present export trade will shrink proportionately. The result would be restriction of outputs, industrial depression, idle capital and idle labor, numerous failures, financial demoralization and general unrest and suffering among the laboring classes. . . . Can we afford to let a declaration as to our conception of "the true spirit of neutrality" stand in the way of our national interests, which seem to be seriously threatened?

The ban on loans was accordingly lifted, and the purchases and the prosperity went on. It is easy to conjecture how Wilson could have justified his action to himself. Let Allied purchases stop, let a crash come, let unemployment and discontent stalk the land, let the people turn his administration out in 1916 and restore to power a party that had such men as Roosevelt and Lodge high in its counsels—and what chance then would there be for peace or world leadership on a disinterested and elevated plane? No, the best course of action would be to keep the American people busy and prosperous at their peaceful wartime pursuit, the manufacture of munitions.

After American supplies had been flowing to England and France for six months, the German government announced, February 4, 1915, that it would attempt to destroy all enemy ships within a stated war zone around the British Isles. The submarine was the effective German weapon on the high seas, and Wilson's quixotic position toward this novel means of warfare led to a long train of controversy. A frail craft, extremely vulnerable to the deck guns of armed merchant vessels, the submarine could not be used for the sanctioned practice of visit and search. Since many British merchantmen were armed, the U-boats, to be effective at all, had to remain submerged and rely on hit-and-run warfare, which meant that there would be no way of providing for the safety of those aboard enemy vessels. This was the German answer to the British blockade, which was intended to starve out the German civilian population. The U-boat retaliation, although less inhumane, was more spectacular. The sinking of the *Lusitania* in the spring of 1915 confirmed the growing impression in America that the Germans were monsters. Neither the administration nor the public was much impressed by the Germans' standing offer to relax their methods of submarine warfare if the British would end their blockade on food.

In the face of this situation Wilson continued to allow armed Allied merchant vessels to clear American ports.[10] He further insisted, in spite of strong opposition in Congress, on asserting the right of Americans to travel on belligerent merchant ships in the war zone. When this stand was challenged in the Senate, he declared in a letter to Senator Stone:

> I cannot consent to any abridgement of the rights of American citizens in any respect. . . . Once accept a single abatement of right, and many other humiliations would certainly follow, and the whole fine fabric of international law might crumble under our hands piece by piece. What we are contending for in this matter is of the very essence of the things that have made America a sovereign nation.

This was rationalization of the flimsiest sort, for Wilson continued to accept a great deal more than "a single abatement of right" at the hands of the British without the same concern for the effect upon "the whole fine fabric of international law." In dealing with the Allies he made expediency the dominant consideration; in dealing with the Germans, an extremely forward defense of technical rights—a discrimination for which he and Lansing offered the excuse that British misdeeds involved only property rights whereas German actions involved human rights and took human lives. But Representative Claude Kitchin was among those who pointed out that if Americans would sacrifice their

---

10. This decision was made with some misgivings. "It is a question of many sides," Wilson naïvely wrote, "and is giving Lansing and me some perplexed moments."

"right" to go on belligerent ships in the submarine zone as readily as they had sacrificed their equal "right" to try to force Britain's "illegal" North Sea mine zone, Germany would not have been guilty of taking American lives. If Wilson's legal dialectics appeared singularly weak, it was because he was forced to find legal reasons for policies that were based not upon law but upon the balance of power and economic necessities.

Under the stress of a series of irritations, Wilson seems to have veered toward war with Germany in the spring of 1916; during the winter and spring he delivered a number of emphatic speeches calling for a preparedness program. But in reply to a virtual ultimatum threatening severance of diplomatic relations, the German government at last, on May 4, 1916, gave a satisfactory pledge: henceforth submarine warfare would be conducted in accordance with American demands.[11] For nine months the submarine controversy subsided. At the Democratic national convention a Wilson orator brought rousing cheers with the boast that Wilson, without shedding one drop of blood, had "wrung from the most militant spirit that ever brooded over a battlefield the concession of American demands and American rights." But this concession had been won by a virtual threat of war, and Wilson had placed himself in a position that would require a declaration of war if the pledge should be withdrawn.

After the summer of 1914, when his first wife died, Wilson found his office a source of misery. "The place has brought me no personal blessing," he wrote in the

---

11. The pledge was qualified with the warning that unless the United States could force Britain to relax her food blockade, Germany reserved the right to resume submarine warfare. Wilson wisely ignored the reservation.

fall of that year, "but only irreparable loss and desperate suffering." He felt an increasing sense of alienation from his position, and often mused over his inability to think of himself as *being* the President instead of merely acting for a time in the presidential office—which suggests that he hoped, by keeping alive in his mind the distinction between Woodrow Wilson and the President of the United States, to relieve Woodrow Wilson of some of the burden of responsibility.

> Everything is persistently impersonal [he wrote]. I am administering a great office . . . but I do not seem to be identified with it: it is not me and I am not it. I am only a commissioner, in charge of its apparatus, living in its offices, and taking upon myself its functions. This impersonality of my life is a very odd thing, and perhaps robs it of intensity, as it certainly does of pride and self-consciousness (and, maybe, of enjoyment) but it at least prevents me from becoming a fool and thinking myself *It!*

As time went on he began to feel that the functions of the office were invading and crowding out his private personality. "I never knew before that it was possible, when necessary, for a man to lose his own personal existence, even seem to himself to have no individual life apart from his official duties."

But, like every President before him, Wilson hoped and worked for re-election. The 1916 campaign slogan: "He kept us out of war," was not of his devising; in fact, it frightened him. He seemed to have developed a rather exaggerated sense of his powerlessness to live up to such a commitment.[12] "I can't keep the country out of

---

12. In his Milwaukee speech, January 21, 1916, Wilson declared: "There may at any moment come a time when I cannot preserve both the honor and the peace of the United States. Do not exact of me an impossible and contradictory thing."

war," he complained to Josephus Daniels. "They talk of me as though I were a god. Any little German lieutenant can put us into the war at any time by some calculated outrage." Since the Republican Party was no longer split, the election was extremely close, but Wilson ran well ahead of the rest of the Democratic ticket. Now secure in office for another four years, with the submarine controversy in temporary abeyance, and the conflict with Britain at a relatively high pitch, he turned increasingly toward neutrality. War seems never to have been farther from his mind than in the winter of 1916–17. Although he had not definitively ruled out the possibility of entering the war, it seems—so far as it is possible to understand him—that he had not reconciled himself to going in if he could see any other recourse consistent with his main objectives.

Just before Christmas 1916 Wilson sent a note to both belligerents calling upon them to state their peace terms, with the impartial observation that "the objects which the statesmen of the belligerents on both sides have in mind in this war are virtually the same, as stated in general terms to their own people and to the world." On January 22, 1917 he made an address before the Senate in which he analyzed the consequences of a crushing defeat of either side and declared that a lasting peace must be a "peace without victory."

Victory would mean peace forced upon the loser, a victor's terms imposed upon the vanquished. It would be accepted in humiliation, under duress, at an intolerable sacrifice, and would leave a sting, a resentment, a bitter memory upon which terms of peace would rest, not permanently, but only as upon quicksand. Only a peace between equals can last.

The appeal for terms and the call for "peace without victory" were bitterly resented by the Allies, who had been led to feel that the United States was thoroughly committed to them.[13] Colonel House complained in his diary that the President had lost his "punch," that things were drifting aimlessly, that Wilson now stood for "peace at any price." When he once again brought up the matter of preparedness for war, Wilson said flatly: "There will be no war."

At this juncture notice was received from the German government that submarine warfare would be resumed —and in an unrestricted form, directed against neutral as well as belligerent shipping. In one instant Wilson reaped the whirlwind of unneutrality that he had sown in the first two years of the war. For the Germans, realizing that the United States was already heavily engaged against them with its productive capacity, and assuming that she could not otherwise intervene effectively before a fatal blow could be struck against the Allies, were calculating on American entrance into the war.[14]

---

13. The inhibitions felt by Wilson's advisers about issuing a call to belligerents for peace terms was revealingly put by Secretary Lansing: "But suppose that the unacceptable answer comes from the belligerents whom we could least afford to see defeated on account of our national interest and on account of the future domination of the principles of liberty and democracy in the world—what then?"

14. Paul Birdsall has emphasized, in his article "Neutrality and Economic Pressures 1914–1917," that the renewal of submarine warfare was an economic as well as a military fact. The Germans reasoned that the chief assistance the United States could render the Allies in the event of her entering the war was economic— but this assistance the Allies were already getting. As Holtzendorff put it, "The United States can scarcely engage in more hostile activities than she has already done up to this time." The Germans gambled on knocking Britain out by starvation before

When Tumulty brought to Wilson the Associated Press bulletin bearing the news of Germany's decision, the President turned gray and said in quiet tones: "This means war. The break that we have tried to prevent now seems inevitable." Still Wilson waited, as though hoping for some miraculous turn in events that would relieve him of any further decision.[15] In the meantime the plight of the Allies was pressed upon him. Both belligerents were badly strained, in fact, but it was the case of the Allies that he knew. Russia had undergone the March revolution, and her future effectiveness as an ally was extremely doubtful. Morale in the French army was desperately low. ("If France should cave in before Germany," House warned, "it would be a calamity beyond reckoning.") The submarine war would soon constitute a dire threat to England's supply line and bring her to the brink of starvation. Not least, the Allies, their credit facilities exhausted, were facing an economic collapse from which it seemed that nothing short of American participation could save them. This situation Page outlined in his famous cablegram to Wilson of March 5: "Perhaps our going to war is the only way in which our preeminent trade position can be maintained and a

the United States could bring her force to bear; this gamble almost succeeded in the summer of 1917.

15. Almost two years earlier, during the excitement after the *Lusitania* sinking, when he was the victim of a flood of abuse for for his "too proud to fight" speech, he had warned Tumulty against precipitate action. If he went to Congress, he explained, he could get an immediate declaration of war. But when the casualties began to roll in, the people would ask: "Why did Wilson move so fast in this matter? . . . Why could he not have waited a little longer?" As the only great nation free to represent peace and sanity, the United States must hold off until the last possible moment. "When we move against Germany we must be certain that the whole country not only moves with us but is willing to go forward to the end with enthusiasm."

panic averted. The submarine has added the last item to the danger of a financial world crash." Should Germany win, it appeared, the United States would have the hatred of both victors and vanquished, its influence on the future of Europe and on world peace would be at a minimum, and all the gains of recent years would be lost in an armaments race. Finally, public opinion at home, newly aroused by the revelation of the Zimmermann note, proposing an alliance of Germany, Mexico, and Japan and the annexation of Texas, New Mexico, and Arizona to Mexico, was well prepared for participation. Wilson could not face the consequences, as he saw them, of *not* going to war.

Still he delayed. Even after German attacks on American ships had begun, Lansing came away from him feeling "that he was resisting the irresistible logic of events." At the end of March, House came to Washington and found him repeating desperately: "What else can I do? Is there anything else I can do?" He told his friend that he did not consider himself fit to be President under wartime conditions. Frank Cobb, of the New York *World*, one of his best friends among the journalists, visiting the sleepless President on the night of April 1, the eve of his war message to Congress, found him still unresolved. Again he asked: "What else can I do? Is there anything else I can do?" Should Germany be defeated, he feared, there would be a dictated peace. There would be no bystanders left with enough power to moderate the terms. "There won't be any peace standards left to work with." As Cobb remembered it:

W. W. was uncanny that night. He had the whole panorama in his mind. . . .

He began to talk about the consequences to the United

States. He had no illusions about the fashion in which we were likely to fight the war.

He said when a war got going it was just war and there weren't two kinds of it. It required illiberalism at home to reinforce the men at the front. We couldn't fight Germany and maintain the ideals of Government that all thinking men shared. He said we would try it but it would be too much for us.

"Once lead this people into war," he said, "and they'll forget there ever was such a thing as tolerance. To fight you must be brutal and ruthless, and the spirit of ruthless brutality will enter into the very fibre of our national life, infecting Congress, the courts, the policeman on the beat, the man in the street." . . .

He thought the Constitution would not survive it; that free speech and the right of assembly would go. He said a nation couldn't put its strength into a war and keep its head level; it had never been done.

"If there is any alternative, for God's sake, let's take it," he exclaimed.

But Wilson's war message lay on his desk as he spoke to Cobb, and on the following day he read it to Congress. "It is a fearful thing," he confessed, "to lead this great, peaceful people into war, into the most terrible and disastrous of all wars. . . ." But "the right is more precious than peace." Without rancor, without a single selfish interest, the United States would fight for the principles she had always cherished—"for democracy, for the right of those who submit to authority to have a voice in their own Governments, for the rights and liberties of small nations, for a universal dominion of right by such a concert of free peoples as shall bring peace to all nations and make the world itself at last free."

Woodrow Wilson had changed his means before, but

in accepting war he was forced for the first time to turn his back upon his deepest values. The man who had said that peace is the healing and elevating influence of the world was now pledged to use "Force, Force to the utmost, Force without stint or limit." Having given the nation into the hands of a power in which he did not believe, he was now driven more desperately than ever in his life to justify himself, and the rest of his public career became a quest for self-vindication. Nothing less than the final victory of the forces of democracy and peace could wash away his sense of defeat—and Wilson was conscious of defeat in the very hour in which he delivered his ringing war message in tones of such confident righteousness. Returning from the Capitol with the applause of Congress and the people still echoing in his ears, he turned to Tumulty and said: "My message today was a message of death for our young men. How strange it seems to applaud that."

V

Wilson's uncertain course during the neutrality period revealed two inconsistent strategic ideas. The first was that the United States must remain the Great Neutral, the conservator of sane and just peacetime values, the exponent of "peace without victory." The second was that the Allies must not be allowed to lose the war, that the "military masters of Germany" must be crushed.

This same contradiction pursued him to the Peace Conference. What he really wanted was not simply a "peace without victory," but a victory to be followed by an unvictorious peace. He wanted the Allies and Germany to come to the conference table as victors and vanquished and sit down as negotiators. Events soon impressed upon him the impossibility of any such thing. He told one of the American experts who accompanied him to Paris that "we would be the only disinterested people at the Peace Conference, and that the men whom we were about to deal with did not represent their own people." The second statement was in some ways an unhappy delusion, but the first was true: the United States, thanks in part to Wilson's restraining influence, was the only nation among the victors that came without a set of strictly national aims, without a single claim for territory, indemnities, or spoils, with the sole demand that the Allies restrain themselves in the interest of a just and more durable peace. The Conference was an affair of three sides—the victors, the vanquished, and Wilson.

In the absence of American claims, which might have been used for trading purposes, Wilson had two cards to play: the threat of a separate peace with Germany, and the financial supremacy of the United States. The mere hint of a separate peace by Colonel House in November 1918 threw the Allied representatives into consternation and precipitated their acceptance of the Fourteen Points as the basis of the Armistice; but this threat was pushed no further. Wilson, just as he had failed to use his country's economic position to bargain with England over blockade practices, failed to use this advantage at the Peace Conference. Although he wrote to House, July 21, 1917:

> England and France have not the same views with regard to peace that we have by any means. When the war is over we can force them to our way of thinking, because by that time they will among other things, be financially in our hands,

this strategy also was neglected. A very large proportion of American governmental loans to the Allies was contracted *after* the close of hostilities, but their bargaining potentialities were not exploited.

Wilson's conception of a just peace demanded that the United States play an independent and leading role. But his conception that a durable peace also depended upon an Allied victory bound him to the Allied powers with economic and moral sinews. It was inconceivable to go to the Peace Conference only to risk a breach with one's former allies by taking the part of the defeated powers. A statesman who looks forward to a peaceful world based upon international co-operation will not drive a hard bargain with the very nations upon whose collaboration he feels most dependent. Wilson might force Clemenceau and Lloyd George to accept the Fourteen Points as the theoretical basis of the peace, but once the talks began, the dynamics of the situation delivered him into their hands, for his very hopes and ideals tended to paralyze him as a negotiator. At Paris he realized the prophetic truth of his own words to Frank Cobb: the war *had* overthrown peacetime standards and values, and not even Woodrow Wilson was left to uphold them.[16] "Only a peace between equals can last," he had said, but the peace that ensued was a peace between masters and slaves, and the President of the United States found himself holding a whip with the others. "It is a very severe settlement with Germany," he affirmed in September 1919, "but there is not anything in it that she did not earn."

---

16. "Why deceive ourselves," asked Peace Commissioner General Tasker Bliss. "We are making no Peace here in Paris. What is there to make it out of?"

The program Wilson took to Paris envisioned a world order based upon national self-determination, free trade, and a League of Nations to keep the peace. "What we seek," he explained, "is the reign of law, based upon the consent of the governed and sustained by the organized opinion of mankind." National self-determination, the international equivalent of democracy in domestic politics, would embody the principle of consent of the governed. Free trade would soften national rivalries and broaden prosperity. The League was to give security to the whole system through mutual guarantees of territorial integrity and common action against an aggressor.

Conspicuously absent from the Fourteen Points was any meaningful demand for a substantial change in international economic relations. Eight of the Fourteen Points applied the doctrine of self-determination to specific parts of Europe. The remaining six points were of general application, and of these only three dealt with economic matters: freedom of the seas in peace and in war, the removal of all economic barriers between nations, and an impartial adjustment of colonial claims. Not one of these three points represented anything more than a pious hope, and not one was even remotely realized in fact. The structure of colonial claims was hardly touched by the mandate system of the League. Freedom of the seas had to be waived at the outset upon the insistence of the British, who would not even indulge in the hypocrisy of endorsing it on principle.[17] The removal of economic barriers was an idle suggestion if one could not remove the economic and social structures, the profit motives and systems of domestic business power that made trade barriers inevitable; Wilson dared not even

---

17. Clemenceau's comment on the matter is illuminating: "I do not understand this principle of the Freedom of the Seas. War would not be war if there was freedom of the seas."

try to commit his own country to further removal of trade barriers—and it was the United States that actually began international tariff warfare in the postwar era. Finally, the idea of multiplying national sovereignties and expecting a reduction of international trade barriers to follow was certainly tempting the wrath of the gods.

The peace that was signed at Versailles was a political peace in which the fundamental economic arrangements of nineteenth-century Europe were taken for granted. Wilson himself told his commission of American experts that he was "not much interested in the economic subjects" that might be discussed at Paris; and John Maynard Keynes has remarked that "the fundamental economic problems of a Europe starving and disintegrating before their eyes was the one question in which it was impossible to arouse the interest of the Four." Thorstein Veblen wrote in 1919 that the Covenant of the League

> is a political document, an instrument of realpolitik, created in the image of nineteeth century imperialism. It has been set up by political statesmen, on political grounds, for political ends, and with political apparatus to be used with political effects. . . . True to the political tradition, the Covenant provides for enforcing the peace by recourse to arms and commercial hostilities, but it contemplates no measures for avoiding war by avoiding the status quo out of which the great war arose.

Wilson, in short, failed again to grapple with economics, as he had failed to grapple with it in the political theory of his academic years. During his career in practical politics he had learned to mold his appeal along the lines of group and class interests and to resolve political conflicts into economic issues, but somehow when he stepped into the world theater he lapsed once again into the intellectual primness and gentility of the old-fashioned professor who had been enthralled with what he thought was the disinterestedness of the great British statesmen, and who had said of the American Senate in the Gilded Age that it was "divorced from class interests." The end of his career was full of contradictions, in which the Wilson of *Congressional Government* struggled with the Wilson who had acquired a more mature and realistic education in American party battles. What he said about the causes of the war had little relation to the manner in which he made the peace.

In an address on September 27, 1918 he had declared:

> Special alliances and economic rivalries and hostilities have been the prolific source in the modern world of the plans and passions that produce war. It would be an insincere as well as insecure peace that did not exclude them in definite and binding terms.

Having made just such an insecure peace, he returned to the United States to defend it, and in the course of his defense said again at St. Louis, September 5, 1919:

> Why, my fellow citizens, is there any man here or any woman, let me say is there any child here, who does not know that the seed of war in the modern world is industrial and commercial rivalry? The real reason that the war that we have just finished took place was that Germany was afraid her commercial rivals were going to get the better of her, and the reason why some nations went into the war against Germany was that they thought Germany would get the commercial advantage of them. . . . This war, in its inception was a commercial and industrial war. It was not a political war.

No wonder, then, that Wilson's League, which was not intended or designed to change the system of commercial and industrial rivalries, was inadequate to prevent war. Europe, desperately in need of economic unity under large-scale industrial technology, was partitioned into an increased number of economically unstable and strategically indefensible small states. Germany, the economic hub of the Continent, was crippled insofar as Britain and France found it in their power to do. This disorganized and broken world of competing nationalist enterprises the League was expected to preserve and make secure. The League itself did not represent a vital change, but simply an attempt to give organization to the old chaos.

No matter how historians may dramatize Wilson's struggle with Clemenceau and Lloyd George, it was not a struggle between an Old Order and a New Order, but merely a quarrel as to how the Old Order should settle its affairs. In this attempt to organize and regulate a failing system of competitive forces the theme of Wilson's domestic leadership was repeated on a world scale. Just as the New Freedom had been, under the idealistic form of a crusade for the rights and opportunities of the small man, an effort to restore the archaic conditions of nineteenth-century competition, so the treaty and the League Covenant were an attempt, in the language of democracy, peace, and self-determination, to retain the competitive national state system of the nineteenth century without removing the admitted source of its rivalries and animosities. It had always been Wilson's aim to preserve the essentials of the *status quo* by reforming it; but failing essentially to reform, he was unable in the end to preserve.

In March 1919 Wilson's old friend of the New Jersey period, George L. Record, who had played a large part in converting him to progressivism, sent him a remarkable letter, analyzing the inadequacy of Wilson's conceptions to the present era. Wilson, Record wrote frankly, had

> ignored the great issue which is slowly coming to the front, the question of economic democracy, abolition of privilege, and securing to men the full fruits of their labor or service.
>
> There is no glory . . . in standing for the principles of political democracy . . . [which] is like standing for the Ten Commandments. . . .
>
> The issue of political democracy has passed. The issue is now one of industrial or economic democracy.
>
> The League of Nations idea will not help your position, either now or in history, because, like all your other policies, it does not go to the root of the problem. Wars are caused by privilege. Every modern state is governed by the privileged, that is, by those who control industry by owning railroads, lands, mines, banks, and credit. These men thus obtain enormous and unearned capital, for which there is no use in the country where it is produced, because the poverty of the workers limits the home market. Those who control this surplus capital must seek new countries and new people to exploit, and this clash of selfish interests leads to war. The cure for war is the reign of justice, i.e., the abolition of privilege in each of the great nations. I do not believe that you can set up machinery which will maintain justice in international relations among governments which deny justice to their own people. If the League works, it will be when and to the extent that justice is established within the countries which are parties to the League. Indeed, it is entirely possible, if not probable, that such a league established by the present governments of the Allies, if it has any real power, is very likely to be used as an international bulwark of privilege. That danger looms large after you pass off the scene. . . .

Record urged Wilson to supplement his international program with a social-democratic program at home, including a demand for public-utility ownership and limitation of great fortunes. It might be impossible to realize this program, he admitted, but Wilson's failure would be only temporary. Future generations would recognize his wisdom and acclaim him "a truly great man."

Wilson acknowledged Record's letter cordially. Almost a year before receiving it he had expressed somewhat similar sentiments to Professor Axson. The two were talking about the qualifications of the next President, and Wilson remarked that he must be a philosophical man, capable of thinking in world terms. At present, "the only really internationally minded people are the labor people."

> The world is going to change radically, and I am satisfied that governments will have to do many things which are now left to individuals and corporations. I am satisfied for instance that the government will have to take over all the great natural resources . . . all the water power, all the coal mines, all the oil fields, etc. They will have to be government-owned.
>
> If I should say that outside, people would call me a socialist, but I am not a socialist. And it is because I am not a socialist that I believe these things. I think the only way we can prevent communism is by some such action as that. . . .

But if Wilson's private convictions were really evolving from American progressivism to an international social-democratic point of view, the fact is not registered in his public policies. The last part of his career seems like the work of a somnambulist who repeats unerringly his appointed workday rounds while his mind moves in an insulated shadow world. If he believed his fine statements with the depth and emphasis with which he made them, he may well have accounted his career as a world statesman a series of failures. He appealed for neutrality in thought and deed, and launched upon a diplomatic policy that is classic for its partisanship. He said that American entrance into the war would be a world calamity, and led the nation in. He said that only a peace between equals would last, and participated in the *Diktat* of Versailles. He said that the future security of the world depended on removing the economic causes of war, and did not attempt even to discuss these causes at the Peace Conference. He declared his belief in the future of government ownership, and allowed his administration to close in a riot of reaction. He wanted desperately to bring the United States into the League, and launched on a course of action that made American participation impossible. No wonder that in one of his moments of apprehension he should have confessed to George Creel: "What I seem to see—with all my heart I hope that I am wrong—is a tragedy of disappointment."

And yet it is his hopes and promises that make Wilson's record seem so bleak. Set against the dark realities, it is defensible. In the Fourteen Points he produced a more sane and liberal, if not enduring, basis for peace than anyone else among the belligerents. By appealing to the hopes of Germany he helped to bring an earlier armistice. Harsh as the treaty was, it would have been materially worse without his influence. He went to Europe handicapped by his apparent repudiation in the Congressional elections of 1918, limited by the national claims and secret treaties of his allies, tied to the technique of compromise by his hopes for the League, committed by his belief in capitalism and nationalism to accept the major consequences of the disaster they had wrought. Confronted time and time again at Paris with a series of insoluble dilemmas, faced with too many battles on too many fronts, he became, in Charles Seymour's words, "the plaything of events." Granting the severe limitations imposed upon his work by the logic of the situation, Paul Birdsall, in his *Versailles Twenty Years After*, finds "an extraordinary consistency in Wilson's fight for his program under overwhelming difficulties, as well as a high degree of political intelligence in translating the abstract principles of his program into concrete details of application."

Clemenceau habitually dozed off when matters unrelated to French security were under consideration at the Conference. Lloyd George on more than one occasion admitted lightheartedly his ignorance of some of the most elementary facts of European economics and geography. ("Please refresh my memory," he once asked an aide. "Is it Upper or Lower Silesia that we are giving away?") Wilson begged his experts: "Tell me what is right and I will fight for it. Give me a guaranteed position," and went down on hands and knees in his suite until the small hours of the mornings, poring over maps and charts, trying to master the complicated maze of fact involved in the negotiations. Although he felt obliged to defend the peace in the United States, sometimes in incredible language—"a people's treaty," "the great humane document of all time"—he well knew how vulnerable it was. His remark that the much-criticized Shantung settlement was the best that could be salvaged from "a dirty past" might well have been his verdict on the treaty as a whole.

One thing, he believed, might save the whole structure—the Covenant of the League. The effort to save the

League became a matter of the most desperate psychological urgency for him.[18] His plans had been hamstrung, his hopes abandoned one after another, until nothing but the League was left. The New Freedom, as he had predicted, had disappeared in the war, and a liberal democratic peace had gone by the board at Paris. The League was now a question of moral salvation or annihilation, for everything he stood for hung in the balance. If a lasting peace were not realized, what justification could he find for having led his country into war? His sense of guilt hung over him like a cloud. In the American cemetery at Suresnes he broke out fervently: "I sent these lads over here to die. Shall I—can I—ever speak a word of counsel which is inconsistent with the assurances I gave them when I came over?" In the long speech delivered at Pueblo on the day he suffered his stroke, he made a striking confession:

Again and again . . . mothers who lost their sons in France have come to me and, taking my hand, have shed tears upon it not only, but they have added, "God bless you, Mr. President!" Why . . . should they pray God to bless me? I advised the Congress of the United States to create the situation that led to the death of their sons. I ordered their sons overseas. I consented to their sons being put in the most difficult parts of the battle line, where death was certain, as in the impenetrable dif-

18. That the United States, or the world, had as much at stake is difficult to believe. The idea cultivated by liberal internationalists that the course of history would have been completely changed and the second World War averted if only the United States had joined the League is too arbitrary and flimsy an assumption to warrant serious discussion here. This argument served its purpose in persuading Americans to join the United Nations. Now that the ineffectuality of the UN as an agency of peace is beginning to be evident, the simplicity of the argument grows painfully clear.

ficulties of the forest of Argonne. Why should they weep upon my hand and call down the blessings of God upon me? Because they believe that their boys died for something that vastly transcends any of the immediate and palpable objects of the war. They believe, and rightly believe, that their sons saved the liberty of the world.

Stung by conscience, goaded by a series of frustrations, worn by fatigue and illness, Wilson lost his political judgment. Having already made a ream of compromises to frame the Covenant, he refused to budge an inch to get it accepted in the United States. Yet compromise was an absolute necessity if the United States was to join the League. To get ratification of the Versailles Treaty containing the League Covenant Wilson had to win a two-thirds vote from a Senate in which the opposition party had a majority of two members. By refusing to accept the mildest reservations upon American membership, even those which merely reaffirmed provisions of the United States Constitution, he did as much to keep the United States out of the League as isolationists like Borah or partisans like Lodge. When the possibility of rejection by the Senate was broached to him, he snapped: "Anyone who opposes me in that, I'll crush!" When Ambassador Jusserand brought him the news that the Allies would be glad to accept American membership with a set of reservations that would satisfy an influential group of Republican Senators, he said curtly: "Mr. Ambassador, I shall consent to nothing. The Senate must take its medicine." During the fight over the treaty a sort of perverse co-operation underlay the hatred between Wilson and Lodge, which Borah recognized when he said that he and his irreconcilables were standing with Wilson—to have the treaty rejected. "There is just as much of an understanding," he commented sardonically, "between the President of the United States and myself as there is between the Senator from Massachusetts [Lodge] and myself."

Having failed in Washington, Wilson carried his case to the country in one of the most futile stumping tours in history. Since he could not expect to get a two-thirds majority for his party, even if his efforts should defeat every Republican Senator up for re-election in 1920, the objective reason for the tour is hard to understand. But its personal function is clear: Wilson was in search of martyrdom. Although warned by his physician that after the strain of the war years and the Paris meetings he might not survive the rigors of his proposed campaign, he told Tumulty: "Even though, in my condition, it might mean the giving up of my life, I will gladly make the sacrifice to save the Treaty." In his Spokane speech he declared: "I am ready to fight from now until all the fight has been taken out of me by death to redeem the faith and promises of the United States."

Was Wilson simply going through a ritual of self-purification? Or did he, consciously or unconsciously, hope that through martyrdom he might win enough popular sympathy to save his case in the Senate? Whatever his intentions, everything went against him. Had he killed himself with his exertions, he might have stirred a wave of sympathy; instead he suffered a stroke, which for a long time incapacitated him for his duties and prompted malicious talk about a complete loss of mind. The drift away from Wilsonian idealism went on. He hoped that the campaign of 1920 would be a "solemn referendum" on the League issue, but it turned out a dull and hopeless farce. His party tried to steer clear of him by nominating James M. Cox, who had never been closely associated with the Wilson administration and whose choice Wilson himself had said would be "a joke."

When Cox, moved by Wilson's gallantry, decided after all to make his campaign on the League issue, he was overwhelmed at the polls as no other candidate has ever been—defeated, as Franklin K. Lane remarked, "not by those who dislike him but by those who dislike Wilson and his group."

On March 4, 1921 Wilson attended the inauguration of Warren G. Harding, a man who was his very antithesis—a thoroughly native type, handsome, genial, kindly, ignorant, complacent, and weak, a model of normal mediocrity. Wilson, who had practiced speechmaking as a child before the empty pews of his father's church so that he might learn to interpret great thoughts to the world, could see now by a glance at the man who rode beside him, chosen President by an unprecedented majority, that there was nothing more he could say that the people would be in a mood to hear. In the final moment of his office the retiring President delivered to a hated representative of Congress a last symbolic message which set the seal upon his public life: "Senator Lodge, I have no further communication to make."

CHAPTER XI

HERBERT HOOVER AND THE CRISIS OF AMERICAN INDIVIDUALISM

❦

THE *test of the rightfulness of our decisions must be whether we have sustained and advanced . . . prosperity.*

HERBERT HOOVER

IN THE autumn of 1919 John Maynard Keynes, out of his disgust and bitterness with the terms of the Versailles Treaty, wrote a devastating book, *The Economic Consequences of the Peace*. Keynes's judgments of the peacemakers were severe, but concerning one, Herbert Hoover, he wrote:

> Mr. Hoover was the only man who emerged from the ordeal of Paris with an enhanced reputation. This complex personality, with his habitual air of weary Titan (or, as others might put it, of exhausted prizefighter), his eyes steadily fixed on the true and essential facts of the European situation, imported into the Councils of Paris, when he took part in them, precisely that atmosphere of reality, knowledge, magnanimity, and disinterestedness which, if they had been found in other quarters also, would have given us the Good Peace.

Of the work that had been carried out during the first six months of that year by the American Relief Administration under Hoover's direction, Keynes said:

Never was a nobler work of disinterested goodwill carried through with more tenacity and sincerity and skill, and with less thanks either asked or given. The ungrateful Governments of Europe owe much more to the statesmanship and insight of Mr. Hoover and his band of American workers than they have yet appreciated or will ever acknowledge. The American Relief Commission, and they only, saw the European position during those months in its true perspective and felt towards it as men should. It was their efforts, their energy, and the American resources placed by the President at their disposal, often acting in the teeth of European obstruction, which not only saved an immense amount of human suffering, but averted a widespread breakdown of the European system.

These words did not seem extravagant in 1919; nor did they sound unfamiliar in either Europe or America. Hoover appeared a gigantic figure—"the biggest man," said the London *Nation*, "who has emerged on the Allied side during the war." He had risen to this international acclaim—second only to Wilson's and considerably more lasting—from a background as dramatic as it was obscure. The outbreak of the war had found Hoover living quietly in London, unknown to the general public of any nation, an international businessman and mining engineer of modest repute. At the age of forty he had accumulated a considerable fortune; this was not remarkable, but the global scope of his career was.

Between 1899 and 1911, in addition to a few engineering tasks undertaken in his native country, Hoover had dug mines, supervised a variety of enterprises, and acquired interests on four continents. Starting in Australia in 1897–8, he had spent part of 1899 in China, 1901 in Japan, 1902 in New Zealand, 1903 in India, 1904 in Rhodesia and the Transvaal, 1905 in Egypt, 1907 in Burma, the Malay States, and Ceylon, 1908 in Italy,

1909 in Russia, Korea, and Germany, 1910 in France, and 1911 again in Russia. He had offices in San Francisco, New York, London, Melbourne, Shanghai, and for periods in St. Petersburg and Mandalay. He had lived a large part of his mature life on ocean liners. He was associated with over a score of business concerns. In Russia he had managed various interests on an estate containing about seventy-five thousand tenants and laborers. In China he had witnessed the Boxer Rebellion and superivsed the construction of barricades to defend Tientsin against siege. At Tomsk in Siberia he had felt reverberations of the 1905 Revolution. In Burma he had been down with tropical malaria. He had found time to publish two books: a textbook on *Principles of Mining*, and a translation with his wife's aid of Georgius Agricola's sixteenth-century metallurgical treatise, *De Re Metallica*.

Hoover's first war job had been to remove thousands of American tourists who were stranded in Europe when the war broke out. Then he accepted the chairmanship of the Commission for Relief in Belgium. For four years, in spite of terrible obstruction by both Germany and the Allies, Hoover's commission fed ten million people. The task was accomplished with astonishing efficiency, and when the commission's accounts were tallied at the close of operations its overhead was found to be only three eighths of one per cent of total expenditures, and a surplus was bequeathed for the peacetime reconstruction of Belgium. In 1917, assuming the position of Food Administrator for the United States, Hoover conducted, with spectacular success and without power to employ rationing, a program of food supply and conservation that made his name a household word. As head of the economic restoration of Europe at the close of the war, he distributed twenty million tons of food to three hundred million people, ran a fleet of ships, directed the railroads and coal mines of central Europe, and restored crippled communications.

In a time of havoc and hatred the name Hoover came to mean food for the starving and medicine for the sick. From the ranks of his co-workers a fanatic body of admirers had gathered about him. In several European countries streets were named for him. After five years of war service without salary and without attention to his private affairs, his fortune had been somewhat scaled down, but he was rich in popularity.

Within little more than a decade the story of Hoover's wartime career was all but forgotten. The man who had fed Europe had become a symbol of hunger, the brilliant administrator a symbol of disaster. The *Hoover-strassen* of the Armistice period had given way to the dismal Hoovervilles of the depression. And the great engineer left the White House under as dark a cloud of public disfavor as any President since John Quincy Adams, over a century before.

II

There was nothing mythical about Hoover's vaunted ability. The bare outlines of his career show that the admirers of the Relief Commissioner, the Food Administrator, and the Cabinet Secretary were not mistaken in thinking they had found a man of extraordinary energy, initiative, and efficiency. What ruined Hoover's public career was not a sudden failure of personal capacity but the collapse of the world that had produced him and shaped his philosophy.

The things Hoover believed in—efficiency, enterprise,

opportunity, individualism, substantial laissez-faire, personal success, material welfare—were all in the dominant American tradition. The ideas he represented—ideas that to so many people made him seem hateful or ridiculous after 1929—were precisely the same ideas that in the remoter past of the nineteenth century and the more immediate past of the New Era had had an almost irresistible lure for the majority of Americans. In the language of Jefferson, Jackson, and Lincoln these ideas had been fresh and invigorating; in the language of Herbert Hoover they seemed stale and oppressive. It is a significant fact that in the crisis of the thirties the man who represented these conceptions found himself unable even to communicate himself and what he stood for. Almost overnight his essential beliefs had become outlandish and unintelligible. The victim of his faith in the power of capitalism to survive and prosper without gigantic governmental props, Hoover was the last presidential spokesman of the hallowed doctrines of laissez-faire liberalism, and his departure from Washington marked the decline of a great tradition.

Most striking about Hoover's social philosophy is the doggedness with which he holds to it and his willingness to endure opprobrium by acting upon it. Hoover's administration after the crash of 1929 is one protracted rite of hara-kiri. No President, not even Grover Cleveland, has ever been seduced by his convictions into blunter defiance of majority opinion. On this score Hoover can always be acquitted of the charge of revising his ideas to cater to mass sentiment.

Hoover's confidence in what he calls the American system owes a good deal to the circumstances of his early career. He is a self-made man out of ancient American mythology, whose early life story would have delighted Abraham Lincoln. Since Andrew Johnson, whose father was a porter and who began life as an illiterate tailor's apprentice, no occupant of the White House has arisen from circumstances more modest. Hoover's father was a blacksmith who ran a sales agency for agricultural machinery as a sideline; he was the descendant of perennially obscure pioneering stock dating from colonial times. During the nineteenth century the Hoover family had moved from North Carolina to Ohio and from Ohio to Iowa, where Hoover was born in 1874. Both parents were practicing Quakers.

Hoover's father died when the boy was six, his mother when he was not yet ten, leaving their savings of fifteen hundred dollars to three children. Young Hoover went west to Willamette, Oregon, in the care of his maternal uncle, Dr. John Minthorn, who soon made rich profits in the Northwestern land boom; Hoover entered his uncle's business as an office boy.

On the suggestion of a visiting engineer, the boy took qualifying examinations in 1891 for the newly opened Stanford University. Although his preparation was inadequate, the institution relaxed its standards to swell the freshman class. When a shrewd university examiner saw in Hoover a redeeming flair for mathematics, he was admitted under the modest handicap of being "conditioned" in English. For the rest of his life he struggled with his prose, which has always been suggestive of a light fog moving over a bleak landscape.

At Stanford Hoover studied under Professor John Branner, an eminent geologist. To support himself he not only took on a number of odd jobs, but, more important, worked during summers as Branner's assistant on geological surveys and during school terms as Branner's secretary. He also plunged into campus politics on the side of the anti-fraternity or "democratic" faction, organizing the poorest element of the student body, boys

who lived in abandoned workmen's shacks on the edge
of the campus. In such relatively extroverted roles Hoover partially overcame his shyness and quickly won
respect. Will Irwin, a fellow undergraduate, recalls:
"'Popularity' is not exactly the word for his reaction and
influence on his fellows. A better word probably would
be 'standing.'" In 1893 Hoover was elected treasurer of
the student body, his sole experience in running for
office until the presidential campaign of 1928. At Stanford he also met the daughter of a Monterey banker,
Lou Henry, whom he married in 1899.

Stanford did a great deal for Hoover, and he later became a patron, a trustee, and the founder of its Hoover
War Library. But when he took his engineering diploma
in 1895 a depression was approaching its depths, and his
prospects were not immediately promising. Unable to
get a post as engineer, young Hoover took a common
laborer's job in a mine near Nevada City, and the summer after his graduation found him working deep in the
Sierras, pushing a hand-car and shoveling ore at two
dollars and a half a day.

Hoover did not stay buried in the mines. In a few
months he became office assistant to Louis Janin, a well-
known San Francisco engineer, and graduated rapidly
to more responsible positions. Then a call came to Janin
from a large British mining firm for an American engineer who could direct new gold mines at Coolgardie in
Australia. Not yet twenty-four, Hoover found himself on
a steamer bound for a job in the Antipodes at a salary
of $7,500, standing at the threshold of the fabulous busi-
ness career that was to make him a millionaire before he
was forty.

For one who was to advise at the Peace Conference,
Hoover's background was in some ways propitious. He

came to the war with a Quaker heritage. Unlike the elder statesmen who were running the show, he had no political outlook and no worries over a constituency. He was more immune to the terrible passions the war had stirred, he had seen with his own eyes the falsity of Allied atrocity stories, and he knew that cruelty was not the exclusive quality of the Germans. His point of view was much like a nonbelligerent's, and, so far as possible, it was free of other than practical economic considerations. As he put it many years later in speaking of the Peace Conference: "I dealt with the gaunt realities which prowled about outside."

But Hoover's program for peace was not confined to the relief of hunger. With Wilson he shared the belief that Europe should be reconstructed on the principles of liberal capitalism. He was in favor of withdrawing from Europe "lock, stock, and barrel" unless the Allies would accept the Fourteen Points, and he was relentlessly determined that the United States should keep a free hand in all economic matters. Wherever food relief was concerned, Hoover kept one eye on the market for American agricultural surpluses, which gave him a practical as well as a humanitarian reason for criticizing the blockade maintained against Germany between the Armistice and March 1919. When Allied economic collaboration was proposed in November 1918, Hoover cabled one of his Paris representatives to veto

anything that even looks like inter-allied control of our economic resources after peace. . . . After peace over one half of the whole export food supplies of the world will come from the United States, and for the buyers of these supplies to sit in dictation to us as to prices and distribution is wholly inconceivable. The same applies to raw materials.

This businesslike reply settled all possibility of inter-Allied economic action.

On the whole, Hoover's letters and memoranda to Wilson were perspicacious. Because he was sure that it would be a hundred times more difficult to maintain capitalism and democracy in Europe if Germany were economically destroyed, he argued for a settlement without vengeance and opposed many of the worst features of the final treaty. It might be necessary to plunder Germany for the satisfaction of the Allies, but he knew there was a political and economic limit to it. Germany might even be stripped of her surplus for a generation, he wrote Wilson on June 5, 1919, but more than this was utterly impossible, for it would kill the chances of democracy in Germany and "she will turn either to Communism or Reaction, and will thereby become either militarily or politically on the offensive." The treaty would go far to destroy the seeds of democracy in Germany and would hamper the course of world recovery. As for the post-Armistice blockade, it was "absolutely immoral. . . . We do not kick a man in the stomach after we have licked him."

An important part of his work, which had the ardent support of the Allied Supreme Council, was Hoover's anti-Bolshevik policy. In addition to the "transcendent purpose" of American relief, which was to feed the starving, he later explained:

> my job was to nurture the frail plants of democracy in Europe against . . . anarchy or Communism. And Communism was the pit into which all governments were in danger of falling when frantic peoples were driven by the Horsemen of Famine and Pestilence.

"The whole of American policies during the liquidation of the Armistice was to contribute everything it could to prevent Europe from going Bolshevik or being over-run by their armies," he stated in 1921. To Wilson he suggested that during the postwar period food be distributed in Russia only on condition that the Soviets cease military operations.

When Hoover returned from Europe late in 1919 it was as a major political figure whom both parties were eager to claim, but whose politics were unknown. In March 1920 he described himself in a public statement as "an independent progressive" who objected "as much to the reactionary group in the Republican Party as I do to the radical group in the Democratic Party." First he denied that he was seeking public office. Then he announced that he would accept the Republican nomination if the party would adopt "a forward-looking, liberal, constructive platform on the treaty and on our economic issues." (He was for the League with reservations.)

By thus announcing his affiliation, without receiving any party commitments in return, Hoover lost one of his trump cards. Assured that his towering popularity would not be available to the Democrats, the Republican Party professionals, who had no use for the engineer, felt free to nominate a party regular. Hoover had popular following and plenty of funds and publicity; he was far better known than Harding, far more appealing than Lowden or Wood. But the bosses won and Harding became President. In any case it is unlikely that Hoover could have captured the Republican nomination, but Wendell Willkie's feat in 1940 suggests that it was within the bounds of possibility. Had Hoover become President in 1920, it is easy to believe that the country would have been spared the ghastly farce of the Harding administration and that Hoover himself could have left office in 1929 after two terms, one of the most admired chief executives in all American history! Instead Hoover qualified as one of Harding's "Best Minds" and entered the Cabinet as Secretary of Commerce.

It was ironic, in view of his later attitudes, that when Hoover took over the Department of Commerce he became a great bureaucrat. Once considered the least of the Cabinet posts, the Secretaryship of Commerce rose under Hoover to equal Mellon's Treasury Department in its importance to the big-business government that settled upon Washington in the twenties. Its functions grew rapidly: several subdivisions sprang up, others were taken from the Interior Department, plans were made for a huge new building, and activities were accelerated to a remarkable pitch. Many years later Hoover observed: "No one with a day's experience in government fails to realize that in all bureaucracies there are three implacable spirits—self-perpetuation, expansion, and an incessant demand for more power."

One common criticism of the bureaucrat—inefficiency —has never been made of Hoover's regime in the Commerce Department, for its results were far out of proportion to its increase in expenditures and personnel. Business trends were studied and reported as never before. One relatively minor division, the Office of Simplified Practice, rendered annual savings to business and the public which alone more than repaid the nation for the Department's budget, and Simplified Practice was only a small part of a grand, well-publicized campaign waged by the ex-engineer against economic waste.

The Secretaryship of Commerce was a strategic spot from which to advance Hoover's presidential ambitions, and he launched a course of activity which brought him press attention that rivaled Coolidge's. During the honeymoon of the twenties it was not difficult to woo the public and big business at the same time. Hoover particularly ingratiated himself with public-utility interests by making several strong speeches opposing federal regulation of power and favoring state regulation, the effectuality of which had been sharply reduced by court decisions. These speeches were distributed in pamphlet lots of 25,000 to 500,000 by the National Electric Light Association, the propaganda agency of the utility companies.

Hoover also tried to promote business by encouraging foreign investments and fighting for optimum markets for American buyers. His championship of American trade warranted the boast of Assistant Secretary of State William R. Castle to an exporters' convention that "Mr. Hoover is your advance agent and Mr. Kellogg is your attorney." The expansion of foreign investments, however, proved to be an inflationary boomerang. Every dollar invested abroad called for returns. When the total overseas investment became so huge that the annual interest payments and other returns in a given period exceeded the new investment flowing out, the balance of international payments on these invisible items would swing back to the United States and some of our foreign markets would eventually be lost. It was impossible to sell to the world, lend to the world, and refuse to buy from the world without eventually courting disaster.

But few people worried over such things in the heyday of Republican prosperity, and Hoover's Cabinet service maintained his popularity. His work in Mississippi flood relief in 1927 reminded the electorate of his earlier humanitarian career. In the public mind he was the fit and proper successor to Coolidge. Yet he was still distrusted by the professional politicians, and, curious as it may seem, Wall Street politicos were afraid of him, longing for the renomination of the reliable Coolidge or, failing that, the nomination of Andrew Mellon. William

Allen White in his biography of Coolidge records Chief Justice Taft's wonderment and disgust as he watched the Wall Streeters line up against Hoover because they knew he had "grumbled at the market."

Hoover was generally reputed the "most liberal" of the Harding-Coolidge Cabinet. He had sat quietly through the scandals of the Harding era. He had done nothing wrong, even though he had done nothing to stop those who did.[1] There were murmurings of suspicion about him in some quarters, particularly among farmers who doubted that he had any solution for the ills of agriculture, but none of his failings loomed very large in 1928. Although he had given no support to the liberal proposals of the twenties, other than a child-labor amendment and unemployment insurance, he was looked upon with an indulgent suspension of judgment. Perhaps his progressivism was only in hiding; perhaps he would be a more liberal man when he was no longer in political fetters under Harding and Coolidge. "It may be fair to say," wrote a liberal economist, "that he has done as well in that *milieu* as anyone could be expected to do." Such was the state of opinion when he captured the Republican nomination.

---

1. Along with other respectables of the Harding regime, Hoover has been criticized for failing to expose or halt the corruption in the Interior Department, of which it is said "he must have known." When Albert B. Fall resigned shortly before the exposure of his part in the Teapot Dome affair, Hoover wrote him: "In my recollection that department [Interior] has never had so constructive and legal a headship as you gave it." (Quoted in Samuel Hopkins Adams: *The Incredible Era*, p. 304.)

III

Hoover had worked hard for the presidency and he wanted to make the office his crowning triumph. He must have dreamed of the image he would leave for historians—a success in business, a fabulous success in humanitarian undertakings, a magnificent success in presidential leadership. Hoover the engineer would be the symbol of the coming age of material fulfillment, as Jefferson had been of democracy and Lincoln of emancipation.

But as a politician Hoover proved a failure, in dealing both with other politicians and with the public. He was unaccustomed to running for office and changing in response to popular will. His background in business, where he was supremely persuasive in working with his peers, had not trained him in give-and-take with masses of men. A good part of his life had been spent giving orders to Orientals and what he confidently called the "lower races." [2] A rough and speculative occupation like mining and mine promotion demands a considerable sacrifice in human values, and it failed to develop in Hoover such compensating graces as diplomacy or social flexibility. There is evidence that he had developed a vein of arrogance beneath his matter-of-fact exterior. Once in a communication to an English mining journal he had waved aside the misappropriation of investors' funds by corporation officials with the remark that capital is "often invested" by such insiders "to more reproductive purpose than if it had remained in the hands of

---

2. In *Principles of Mining* (1909).

the idiots who parted with it." [3] Accustomed as he was to successes and popular esteem, to managing men and machines with remarkable effects, it is unlikely that he had ever felt helpless before the bigness and difficulty of the world. Hoover was one of those bright and energetic businessmen who, precisely because of the ease with which success has been attained in their immediate experience, refuse to learn deeply from anything outside of it.

Psychologically, Hoover was ill-adapted to the peculiar requirements of political life. Still shy, still far from articulate, he was anything but a dynamic public figure; he detested politics and its countless silly indignities, he was addicted to worry, and he was sensitive to criticism. Little gifted with the arts that make for facile human relationships, he would have found his position uncomfortable even in prosperous times. Small wonder that near the end of his term he should have groaned: "This office is a compound hell."

Hoover's greatest handicap, however, lay not in his personal limitations but in his philosophy. He devoutly believed in the comparatively unregulated profit system under which he had grown up. He would not say that the system was invulnerable—it could, of course, be thrown out of gear by wrong thinking and unwise practices; he knew also that it was subject to cyclical fluctuations, which he felt could be diminished. But its basic principles were thoroughly "sound." If it were allowed to proceed with no more than a smack and a dab of government regulation here and there to prevent "abuses," it could not fail to minister more and more effectively to human welfare. From the end of the 1893

---

3. *Mining Magazine*, May 1912, p. 371.

depression, in fact, to the crash of 1929—a stretch of about thirty-two years covering Hoover's entire maturity —this system had suffered no major setback. To be sure, there had been a "banker's panic" in 1907—very short-lived and easily ascribed, as its name suggests, to unsound practices. There had been a downward turn in business just before the World War—but that was inconclusive. There had been a brief depression in the early twenties—but that was an outcome of wartime dislocation, not a natural ingredient of the "normal" economic situation. Plainly the system worked, and it worked well.

But this was not all. Since his childhood Hoover had seen a marked rise in American wages and standards of living. The productivity of American workmanship and technology had been steadily growing. Telephones, radios, automobiles, electric lights, refrigerators—all these inventions had come into broad popular use. American ingenuity and enterprise, Hoover believed, would continue to manufacture the goods of life more efficiently and cheaply. Prices would fall. Increased productivity and lower costs would enable industry to pay higher wages, and higher wages would provide an expanding sales outlet. Through skillful promotion of foreign markets, surpluses could be sold abroad. Thus the whole economy would spiral upward in a never ending cycle: more telephones, more radios, more automobiles, more schools, more opportunities for everybody. It was the dawn of a golden age. In his triumphant Acceptance Address of 1928 Hoover declared: "We in America today are nearer to the final triumph over poverty than ever before in the history of any land. . . . We shall soon with the help of God be in sight of the day when poverty will be banished from this nation." He had become a wild-eyed Utopian capitalist.

Hoover has always described his brand of economics as "true liberalism," which he contrasts with the false liberalism of his critics on the left, and in the sense that his liberalism is more akin to historic nineteenth-century economic doctrines he is correct. He had come out of an Iowa farm environment that was intensely Republican in politics and had migrated into the open economic atmosphere of the far West. His international experiences in business and long residence abroad had done no more to modify the native cast of his thinking than to change his typical mid-American accent. Just as Jefferson's travels in Europe had confirmed his political prejudices, so Hoover's acquaintance with European economic life had intensified his opposition to statism and his confidence in the superiority of "American" ways of doing things. With Jefferson and the economic individualists he agreed, on the whole, that that government is best which governs least, a conviction that was confirmed by his successes with local and voluntary forms of action. Even as a bureaucrat in Washington he had made it his concern to prime the pump of private business initiative rather than play a paternalistic role. Although his government experience and his allegiance to progressivism —he had been a mild Bull Mooser in 1912—qualified somewhat his allegiance to the abstract principle of laissez-faire, he was determined to keep centralized government activity at what he considered a reasonable minimum.[4]

---

4. In his *Principles of Mining* (1909) Hoover, in the course of a passage expressing his approval of business unionism, added: "The time when the employer could ride roughshod over his labor is disappearing with the doctrine of 'laissez faire' on which it was

Hoover, moreover, was trained as an engineer, and his social philosophy was infected with a professional bias. Economy and efficiency became ends in themselves. To him it mattered dearly not only what goals were adopted but exactly *how* a job was done. This craftsmanlike concern for technique, a legitimate thing in itself, stood him in bad stead politically during the depression, when the people grew impatient for results regardless of method.

Hoover's postwar function as the defender of Western capitalism from the Bolsheviks also seems to have made its mark on his style of thought. One of his most persistent themes has been the unworkability of socialism, another his tendency to see Bolshevism in every measure of public ownership. In 1922 he declared that the failure of socialism in Russia, for all the misery that accompanied it, was not an unmitigated misfortune to humanity, because it was "necessary for the world to have this demonstration." Not only did he refuse to recognize the Soviet government; he also refused to recognize Soviet economics.[5] Trade with Russia was impossible, he declared during the twenties, because the Soviets, under their economic system, could never "return to produc-

---

founded. The sooner the fact is recognized, the better for the employer." Hoover always endorsed such invasions of pure laissez-faire as the state social-welfare laws of the Progressive period. But the principle of regulation by the states, initially a measure of progress from the old days of unbridled exploitation, tended increasingly to become a plausible conservative alternate to more effective federal regulation. By the time Hoover became nationally prominent, the defense of state welfare laws as opposed to federal laws had become a stock argument of those who represented the business point of view.

5. "We cannot even remotely recognize this murderous Bolshevist tyranny without stimulating actionist radicalism in every country in Europe and without transgressing every national ideal of our own," he wrote to Wilson, March 28, 1919.

tion," would never be able to export, and hence never able to buy.[6]

Even the platform of the Raskob-financed Democrats in 1928 represented "state socialism" because it had liberal planks on power and agricultural relief. As Hoover later explained in *The Challenge to Liberty*, public ownership "of no matter how small a segment of an industry will be followed rapidly by other steps." Indignantly he vetoed Senator Norris's bill to establish a government plant at Muscle Shoals with authority to sell power and nitrates:

> I am firmly opposed to the Government entering into any business the major purpose of which is competition with our citizens. . . . The remedy for abuses in the conduct of that industry [power] lies in regulation. . . . I hesitate to contemplate the future of our institutions, of our Government, and of our country if the preoccupation of its officials is no longer the promotion of justice and equal opportunity but is to be devoted to barter in the markets. That is not liberalism; it is degeneration. . . .
>
> The real development of the resources and the industries of the Tennessee Valley can only be accomplished by the people in that valley themselves . . . solely for the benefit of their communities and not for purposes of pursuit of social theories or national politics. Any other course deprives them of liberty.

In 1922, disturbed by world-wide ferment, Hoover expounded his social philosophy in a little book entitled *American Individualism*. He admitted that individualism, untempered, would produce many injustices, but

6. The theoretical incapacity of the Soviets to produce did not prevent Hoover from listing Russian dumping in the world market as one of the important causes of the depression.

asserted that in the United States it had fortunately been qualified by the great principle of equality of opportunity:

> Our individualism differs from all others because it embraces these great ideals: *that while we build our society upon the attainment of the individual, we shall safeguard to every individual an equality of opportunity to take that position in the community to which his intelligence, character, ability, and ambition entitle him; that we keep the social solution free from frozen strata of classes; that we shall stimulate effort of each individual to achievement; that through an enlarging sense of responsibility and understanding we shall assist him to this attainment; while he in turn must stand up to the emery wheel of competition.*

Americans have learned, Hoover went on, that the strong are not necessarily the most fit, that society runs more smoothly when they are restrained. But we also know that "the one source of human progress" is the opportunity of the individual to use his personal equipment as best he can. The idea that men are really equal "was part of the claptrap of the French revolution." The most the individual can expect from the government is "liberty, justice, intellectual welfare, equality of opportunity, and stimulation." As evidence that substantial equality of opportunity still existed in the United States, Hoover observed: "Of the twelve men comprising the President, Vice-President, and Cabinet, nine have earned their own way in life without economic inheritance, and eight of them started with manual labor." For a man who presided over one of the greatest statistical agencies in the world, Hoover's idea of an adequate statistical sample was pretty meager; but his choice of the Harding Cabinet to illustrate the opportunities that awaited the self-made man showed a magnificently perverse intuition.

While campaigning against Smith, Hoover again stated that American individualism is no free-for-all, that it calls for "economic justice as well as political and social justice. It is no system of laissez faire."

> It is as if we set a race. We, through free and universal education provide the training of the runners; we give to them an equal start; we provide in the government the umpire of fairness in the race. The winner is he who shows the most conscientious training, the greatest ability, and the greatest character.

The conception that the banker's son and the sharecropper's son have equal chances in life because there is a free public-school system, and that the government provided by Harding, Coolidge, and Mellon was simply "the umpire of fairness" in the race, may seem an eccentric one, but it was not peculiar to Hoover. The entire generation of businessmen of which he was a part was under singular disadvantages in understanding the twentieth century. They had been brought up by the masterful post-Civil War generation of business magnates and had inherited their ideas. The success of the earlier generation had been impressive, and the prestige of its ideas, despite their inherent weaknesses, ran correspondingly high wherever the old promises of American individualism still warmed the spirits of men. That life is a race which goes to the swift was still plausible to many people in 1891 when Hoover entered Stanford, and classic spokesmen of the *staus quo* like William Graham Sumner at Yale were still thundering at undergraduates the truth that millionaires are the bloom of a competitive civilization. Although the heated criticisms of the Progressive era slightly tarnished these notions, they were refurbished and repolished in the New Era of the twenties. The terrible and sudden collapse of 1929 left the inheritors of the old tradition without a matured and intelligible body of ideas to draw upon and without the flexibility or morale to conceive new ones. Driven to reiterate with growing futility the outworn creed upon which they had been suckled, the very men who had made such a fetish of being up to date, pragmatic, and hardheaded in their business activities now displayed in politics the sort of archaic, impractical, and flighty minds that made the Liberty League possible.

Hoover, had he been challenged with the overpowering implausibility of his notion that economic life is a race that is won by the ablest runner, would have had a ready answer from his own biography: had he not started in life as a poor orphan and worked in the mines for a pittance, and had he not become first a millionaire and then President of the United States? There are times when nothing is more misleading than personal experience, and the man whose experience has embraced only success is likely to be a forlorn and alien figure when his whole world begins to fail.

IV

In October 1929 Hoover ceased to be the philosopher of prosperity and turned to the unexpected and melancholy task of rationalizing failure. His interpretation of the depression was simply that the "American system," though fundamentally healthy, had been brought to grief temporarily by incidental and accidental influences, chiefly from abroad.

"The origins of this depression lie to some extent

within our own borders through a speculative period,"
the President admitted in his December 1930 message
to Congress; but, he continued, if overspeculation had
been its only cause, the depression would have been
easily conquered. It was a world depression, and its
roots were in the World War. "The major forces of depression," Hoover concluded, "now lie outside of the
United States."

During the 1932 campaign he amplified his thesis. He
reminded his Democratic opponents of the enormous
cost of the war in lives and money, of huge government
debts, of political instability that had "paralyzed confidence," of the growth of standing armies, of revolutions
and agitations in China, India, and Russia, of overproduction of key products in the Indies, Cuba, Brazil,
Ecuador, the Congo, Burma, Australia, and other parts
of the world. Overproduction had "crashed into the
immutable laws of supply and demand" and had
"brought inevitable collapse in prices and . . . a train
of bankruptcies and destruction of buying power for
American goods." Panic-stricken countries had dumped
their holdings of securities into the American market;
gold had thus been withdrawn from the United States,
and "the consequent fear that swept over our people"
caused them to draw huge sums from the banks. How
mistaken, then, to believe that the most serious causes
of the depression could be located in the United States.
"We," concluded Hoover reproachfully, "did not inaugurate the Great War or the panics in Europe." The final
article in Hoover's version of the depression was that it
had been beaten at last by his policies,[7] only to be re-

---

7. An upturn in business activity during the summer of 1932
gave some color to this belief, although it is simply an act of
faith to assume that it would have continued to full recovery
under Hoover's program.

vived by the uncertainties of the 1932 election and Roosevelt's failure to reassure business.

If the American system (which, as Hoover said, "its enemies call capitalism") was basically sound, such psychological factors as loss of confidence might be playing an important part in deterring recovery. So earnestly did Hoover believe in the importance of confidence that he journeyed from Washington to Philadelphia in the gloomy fall of 1931 in part because he felt that his attendance at a World Series game would be a public demonstration of his own serenity. This desire to stimulate confidence was the cause of the absurdly optimistic statements by Hoover and others that flooded the press in the months following the crash. Shortly after the market break he made one of his most famous remarks: "The fundamental business of the country, that is, the production and distribution of commodities, is on a sound and prosperous basis." Other hopeful statements followed. On March 8, 1930 he assured the country that the crisis would be over in sixty days.

It has been widely assumed, because of this series of sanguine announcements from the White House, that Hoover had no conception how serious the situation was. A close study of his actions behind the scenes shows that this was not true. Privately he had a dark view of the nature and probable duration of the crisis. He had been warned almost at the outset by Federal Reserve officials that "the situation . . . is honeycombed with weak spots. . . . It will take perhaps months before readjustment is accomplished." The psychology of "confidence" economics, however, demanded that the public be given sweeping reassurances, and the President took the risk of sacrificing what was left of his reputation as a prophet. Unfortunately, he was saddled for the rest of his life with the "prosperity-is-around-the-corner" theme.

It was, in fact, not Hoover's initial estimate of the crisis, but his subsequent estimate of his own remedies that was really at fault. On November 21, 1929 he called a grand conference of business moguls and told them confidentially, according to Myers's and Newton's summary of his prepared notes:

> that he viewed the crisis more seriously than a mere stock market crash; that no one could measure the problem before us or the depth of the disaster; that the depression must last for some time; and that there were two or three millions unemployed by the sudden suspension of activities.

He continued that steps must be taken to prevent distress and "maintain social order and industrial peace." The burden must not be thrown immediately upon labor. Such a course would cut purchasing power and bring about "industrial strife, bitterness, disorder, and fear." Instead, wages should be "temporarily maintained" until intensified competition and the shrinkage in demand forced the price level down.[8] Then later, when wages were reduced, they should not fall faster or farther than the cost of living. Values could thus be "stepped down" gradually and without undue hardship.[9] Both industry and labor promised to support this program, the former by maintaining production and wage rates, the latter by withdrawing some wage demands already made. Faithful adherence to his plan,

---

8. This was, for a crucial part of industry, a false assumption. The price structure was very inelastic in the monopolized heavy industries. Many economists attribute the severity of the depression and the difficulty of recovery to this stickiness in prices.

9. The quotations in the preceding passage are not direct from Hoover's notes, but from Myers's and Newton's paraphrase of them. The program of the November 21 conference was ratified and adopted by a subsequent meeting on December 5.

Hoover believed, might reduce price levels sufficiently to lower costs of production to a point at which profits could again be made; inflated capital values would be reduced until they approached realities. Then the normal upward and onward course could be resumed. As Hoover told the people, "We have come out of each previous depression into a period of prosperity greater than ever before. We shall do so this time."

Hoover was asking the businessmen to forswear all their natural inclinations. The first impulse of industrialists was to reduce production and employment, cut wages, and so far as possible maintain prices. The most businesslike reaction in administration councils came from Andrew W. Mellon, who said in the fall of 1930: "Curtailment of output, without question, will correct the present condition within a short time," and who, in his own vast system of enterprises, was curtailing output with admirable zeal. But under Hoover's plan the industrialists were to continue to produce and pay prevailing wage rates, even though there was no market for their goods in sight. It is surprising, perhaps, that they agreed to follow his plan, and even more surprising that, so far as wage rates were concerned, they generally made an effort to comply. Not until the summer of 1931 did manufacturers generally reduce wage scales. Production, however, was another matter. They would not produce for a nonexistent market; the volume of output and the total wage bill shrank drastically; the depression deepened.

Had the fundamental business of the country actually been sound, one might perhaps have expected Hoover's program to work.[10] In the teeth of the evidence he seems

---

10. Very likely Hoover hoped for a repetition of the brief 1921–2 depression, when prices fell so rapidly that the real wages of the employed workers actually rose quite sharply.

indeed to have believed that it was taking effect, and there soon began in his curiously stubborn mind a series of flights from reality which took him farther and farther into a private world in which things behaved as he expected. Because, on his postulates, his program should have been successful, he went on talking as though it were, and the less his ideas worked, the more defiantly he advocated them. A half-year after his November conference, when a group of manufacturers, bankers, and bishops came to urge more positive action against unemployment, he said: "Gentlemen, you have come six weeks too late." In the bitter summer of 1931, ignoring the shrinkage in employment and the fact that business was on the verge of a panic of wage-cutting, he boasted that his administration had "steadily urged the maintenance of wages and salaries."

Carried to its logical conclusions, a deflationary solution of the depression would have required, as it always had in the past, a considerable number of bankruptcies in foundering enterprises. In a time of falling prices this was the most important way in which a large part of the great debt burden could be liquidated and inflated capital claims reduced. But as the depression deepened, it became evident that such a procedure now involved the gigantic risk of toppling the entire social-economic structure. A large part of the debt was held by saving banks and mortgage and life-insurance companies, in which the savings of millions were invested, and it would have been fatal to let them fail. To shore up the financial structures of such institutions with government credits, Hoover at last in December 1931 asked Congress to create the Reconstruction Finance Corporation. In this respect the hands-off policy had to be abandoned.

If Hoover's economics did not call for strong governmental action, it did require a great deal more initiative than any President had ever brought to bear to meet a depression. The historic policy in all previous major depressions had been almost complete laissez-faire, and Hoover was the first President in American history to bring any federal leadership to such an emergency. But like a timid beast he shied away from any federal compulsion over business, when compulsion was necessary even to his own modest program. Without legal power he could not ensure that business leaders would maintain production and wage rates, to say nothing of employment. And yet to one with his political philosophy such compulsion was unthinkable. The entrepreneur's right *not* to produce, his right to let factories remain idle, is, after all, one of those great traditional rights of private ownership that Hoover was so eager to defend. To destroy it would revolutionize inherited law and morals.

However, it was not merely his political scruples but his economic doctrines that held Hoover back. A refusal to look for domestic causes of the depression, and hence for positive domestic remedies, grew logically out of his theory that the depression was a foreign product. From the premise, which few cared to deny, that this was a world depression which had aggravated the internal depression of the United States, Hoover reasoned to the conclusion, which was thoroughly questionable, that there was no major flaw in America's domestic economy. One can search in vain among his public statements, with their dolorous allusions to revolutions in China and overproduction of cocoa in Ecuador, for an appreciation of the fact that there were vital domestic causes for depression that might have made themselves felt even if the Creditanstalt had never failed. More than ever in history the business boom of the twenties had been based upon expansion in consumers' goods, and more than any other it was dependent upon sustained consumption. The level of consumption in the United States was high, but it did not continue to grow in proportion to the vast productive capacity of American industry. There had been a persistent agricultural depression under the prosperous surface of the twenties. In industry unemployment had slightly increased, and the growth in real wages was small. Important factors upon which the boom had been built slackened before the stock-market crash of 1929. Investment in housing, for example, one of the vital sources of the boom, fell off after 1925, declined drastically between 1928 and 1929; and in the last year of prosperity the decline spread from residential to industrial and commercial building. The rate of expansion in automobile-manufacturing and road-building flattened out before the crash came. Such things were reflected in the rate of investment in capital goods, which went into decline a year before the market crash. The country was overstocked with savings to be invested and goods to be sold, and the inability of savings to find good investment outlets in industries that were rapidly saturating their markets drove capital into speculative channels. This unhealthy speculation Hoover saw and disapproved, but he preferred to look abroad rather than to see what lay behind it.

During his career as Secretary of Commerce Hoover had answered the problem of America's tremendous productive capacity with the injunction: sell abroad; and the problem of its accumulated savings he had likewise answered: invest abroad. His thesis that the depression began in the rest of the world and spread to America, if true, was a boomerang. No one had been more active than he in increasing the equity of the United States in this floundering world economy. But the conception that America's economic salvation lay in overseas markets and investments, once again, rested upon a misconception of the domestic economy.

Never did Hoover acknowledge how feeble was the purchasing power of the American people in comparison with the forces of production they had created. It was quite in character when, in *The Challenge to Liberty* (1934), he airily denied that there was any serious maldistribution of wealth in the United States. Propagating this insidious idea, he declared, was a device "of those who are anxious to destroy liberty. A competent study will show that over 90 per cent of the national income goes to persons receiving less than $10,000 per annum income and over 97 per cent to persons receiving less than $50,000 annually." The income classes chosen for this illustration were so broad as to conceal the relevant facts about income distribution and purchasing power. The Brookings Institution study, *America's Capacity to Consume*, which appeared in the same year as *The Challenge to Liberty,* showed that the nation's 631,000 richest families had a total income considerably larger than the total income of 16,000,000 families at the bottom of the economic scale. From the standpoint of purchasing power, these 16,000,000 families, the Brookings economists concluded, had incomes too small even to purchase "basic necessities." Such was the potential market at home during the years when Secretary Hoover had been working so hard to expand American markets abroad.

The inflexible state of mind that underlay Hoover's approach to the depression can be seen in two vital policies: his prescription for the ills of agriculture and his attitude toward relief. In the first of these he was trapped by an optimistic miscalculation; in the second by his loyalty to the American folklore of self-help.

The President's farm policy was embodied in the Agricultural Marketing Act of 1929, which established the Federal Farm Board. During periods of glut the Farm Board was to enter the market and buy the surpluses of "overproduced" crops, thus sustaining prices until the market returned to "normal." It was taken for granted—and this was typical of Hoover—that any overproduction that might occur would be occasional, not chronic; in short, that the fundamental position of American agriculture was sound. This supposition had no foundation in reality. American agriculture since the World War had completely outgrown the sum total of its domestic and foreign markets; partly, as Hoover was sometimes aware, because new competing areas had opened elsewhere in the world, partly because of the changed position of the United States from a debtor to a creditor nation, which made it difficult for other countries to buy our exports, partly because of changing consumer habits, and partly because of those same high tariffs which Hoover had insistently defended.[11] The result of the Hoover policies was that the government became burdened with enormous and growing stores of unmarketable wheat and cotton. Each year's unsold surplus in government warehouses hung heavily over the next year's market,[12] and prices plummeted downward to disastrous new lows. Finally in 1932 the Cotton

---

11. During the 1928 campaign Hoover stoutly denied that high tariffs had hurt the farmer. He conceded that some change would be warranted and suggested that higher tariffs be levied on agricultural imports! Two years later he signed the Smoot-Hawley Tariff Act, which was a virtual declaration of economic war on the rest of the world.

12. The comment of Wilbur and Hyde on this conventional criticism is charming: "The partial answer is that it [Hoover's policy] succeeded for two years, that the depression lasted too long. It was made worse by a sequence of bumper crops. Under other circumstances it would have got by better."

Corporation began to beg farmers to plow up every third row in their fields. This coordinated scarcity, which Hoover's administration sought in vain through voluntary action, was achieved by the Roosevelt administration through heavy inducements and at times compulsion.

More than anything else it was his attitude toward relief that shaped the image of Hoover which still prevails in the popular mind. After successfully distributing relief on various occasions to over 150,000,000 people throughout the Western world, the President understandably thought himself an authority on the subject; here, as in other fields, his views could not be changed. When he discussed relief in public, it was generally as a question of political and moral theory, not of economics or human need. He earnestly believed that relief was a job for "the voluntary agencies of the country together with the local and state governments." His reasons for keeping relief a local concern he made clear in February 1931:

> The moment responsibilities of any community, particularly in economic and social questions, are shifted from any part of the nation to Washington, then that community has subjected itself to a remote bureaucracy. . . . It has lost a large part of its voice in the control of its own destiny.

No need to debate the merits of this as a statement of political theory. The depleted treasuries of local governments were simply inadequate to the relief burdens of the crisis. Hoover did pledge that if the time came—as he was sure it would not—when local agencies failed, he would "ask the aid of every resource of the Federal Government because I would no more see starvation amongst our countrymen than would any senator or congressman." But no direct federal relief was undertaken. "I am opposed," said the President firmly, "to any direct or indirect government dole. The breakdown and increased unemployment in Europe is due in part to such practices." Huge relief appropriations would also make impossible the balanced budget that he considered "indispensable to the restoration of confidence."

The peculiar economic theology that underlay Hoover's attitude toward relief was highlighted by the political aftermath of the 1930 drought. In December Hoover approved a Congressional appropriation of $45,-000,000 to save the livestock of stricken Arkansas farmers, but opposed an additional $25,000,000 to feed the farmers and their families, insisting that the Red Cross could take care of them. Finally, when Congress did vote an additional twenty million to feed the farmers, it was stipulated, to satisfy presidential scruples, that the money should go as a loan rather than a gift. Endorsing the loan, Hoover remarked that for the federal government to *give* money for relief "would have injured the spiritual responses of the American people. . . . We are dealing with the intangibles of life and ideals," he added. ". . . A voluntary deed is infinitely more precious to our national ideals and spirit than a thousandfold poured from the Treasury."

Even for a people brought up in the same folklore, it was becoming hard to understand the Hoover *mystique*. Hoover had never been so solicitous about the "spiritual responses" of the businessmen who had been beneficiaries of federal subsidies or of Secretary Mellon's handsome tax refunds. And the idea that money given by the federal government would demoralize reliefers, while money given by their neighbors or the Red Cross or local governments would not, seemed too fanciful to command respect. Resentment was aggravated by Hoover's political gaucheries. During these black, hungry days he allowed newsreel men to photograph him feeding his dog on the White House lawn. A final touch was added by his reception of the bonus marchers at Washington.

V

No longer a Utopian, Hoover assumed in his post-presidential career the role of a hopeful Jeremiah. Now that affairs had fallen into the hands of reckless men, he seized every possible occasion to give warning. In his earnest book *The Challenge to Liberty* and in a series of speeches before Republican conventions he predicted that the managed economy foreshadowed in the New Deal would of necessity destroy economic freedom, the basis of all other freedoms, and that tampering with "Socialist methods" would only bring a middle-class reaction toward fascism.

When foreign affairs took the spotlight from the domestic transgressions of the New Dealers, Hoover at first threw himself on the side of isolationism, but after the outbreak of the war he retreated to a more equivocal position and after Pearl Harbor became a qualified internationalist.[13]

---

13. The first of the Japanese, Italian, and German aggressions had taken place during Hoover's presidency when the Japanese invaded Manchuria. At that time, speaking to his Cabinet, Hoover said: "The whole transaction is immoral . . . outrageous." But he pared down his indignation by adding, first, that this was "primarily a controversy between China and Japan," second, that the Japanese could not subdue China anyway, and third, that "there is something on the side of Japan." Under the last head-

In 1938 the ex-President went on a tour of ten European countries. Hitler gave him the rare privilege of a forty-minute interview, after which Hoover issued a press statement reaffirming his belief in freedom and popular government. Upon his return to the United States Hoover promptly launched a campaign against American intervention in Europe. The idea of collective security, whether through economic or military action, he asserted, was "dead." Besides, the aggressions of the Axis would be vented upon others than the United States: "The face of Germany is turned more east than toward Western Europe. The face of Japan is turned west into Asia." Even if the democracies should be aligned against the totalitarian states, the United States must stay out of a European war; otherwise ours would become "practically a fascist government."

"If the world is to keep the peace," Hoover advised, "then we must keep peace with dictatorships as well as with popular governments." Totalitarianism, he ar-

---

ing he said that China was unable to stem Bolshevism and anarchy, and that this was vital to Japan's economy. He concluded that we ought to co-operate with the League of Nations in every effort of negotiation or conciliation. "But that is the limit. We will not go along on war or any of the roads to war."

In the spring of 1932 some members of the State Department, including Secretary of State Stimson, favored American participation in some sort of economic sanctions. Hoover firmly opposed it. Then as an alternative he proposed what Messrs. Wilbur and Hyde call "a great moral sanction": namely, that all nations should agree to refuse recognition to territory obtained in violation of the Kellogg Pact. The principal nations of the world so agreed and—Wilbur and Hyde add helplessly—"so far as the expressed reprobation of the nations can have effect, there it lies." The historical reputation of any statesman caught between domestic crisis and foreign aggression is bound to suffer. If Hoover had taken a belligerent stand against Japanese aggression, critics would have been quick to insinuate that he was trying to use friction abroad to distract attention from a crisis at home.

gued, is nothing new; it is very much like the personal autocracies of earlier times—and we have always "had to live with such bedfellows." The people of the democracies "must reconcile themselves to the fact that nations of that sort are going to continue to exist." Even the people of dictator nations, after all, have a right to pursue their destinies under whatever form of government they please, however repugnant to Americans. Confident that fascism, like that other heresy, Marxian socialism, would "fail some time," he urged Americans to hold fast to their traditional liberties and "revitalize" democracy at home. Shortly after the Munich Conference he reaffirmed his belief that "there is more realistic hope of military peace for the next few years than there has been for some time."

Less than a year later Europe was at war. But Hoover was not discouraged. To publisher Roy Howard he predicted: "The Allies can defend their empire. I do not see any possibility of their defeat. They will control the seas and sit there until their enemies are exhausted." In one of his first wartime statements he suggested that the United States sell only defensive weapons to the Allies, excluding such things as heavy bombers, which by involving us in offensive warfare against civilians would incur lasting ill will.

Three days after the French surrender to Hitler, Hoover made his quadrennial address to the Republican national convention. Perhaps to spike a current rumor that he wanted to lead a Hoover-Lindbergh isolation ticket, he acknowledged that we could no longer be insulated against great world wars. "There is no such thing as economic isolation. . . . There is no such thing as moral isolation." But he repeated his warnings against entering a democratic world crusade. "Whatever the outcome of this world cataclysm, whatever the solution of our domestic crisis," he advised gloomily, "the pattern of the world will not again be the same. Dictatorships, totalitarian economics, and militarism will long continue over a large part of the earth." America's proper task in this crisis was to arm itself for defense of the Western Hemisphere. In the meantime we might give cautious help to nations that were "fighting for their freedom."

Less than two months before Pearl Harbor, Hoover urged the nation to pursue neither an outright isolationist nor an interventionist foreign policy. We should simply concentrate on war production, send tools to Britain, and "await developments." With the help of our weapons England would be able to withstand a German invasion; we need not send men. By remaining at peace we could preserve our strength and "give real aid to reconstruction and stabilizing of peace when Hitler collapses of his own overreaching." Hoover made it clear that he expected a German collapse even if the Nazis should suffer no military defeat. In another statement he warned that if the United States joined Britain in the war and undertook an invasion of Europe, the preparations alone would take five years or more.

In 1942 Hoover collaborated with Hugh Gibson, a veteran American diplomat, in a book entitled *The Problems of Lasting Peace,* which set forth no less than fifty conclusions on how to make a lasting settlement. The Hoover-Gibson program was based upon a compromise between the extremes of isolation and American world dominion, and it accepted "the American idea of 1919 that peace should be built on fostering representative government." In general tone the proposals were strongly reminiscent of the position Hoover had taken at the close of the First World War. They called for a settlement that would nurture, and not strangle, the chances of representative government in the enemy nations, for a peace without plunder and revenge, for disarmament, and an international organization that would enforce peace by means of an international air force.

The key to the problem of peace, however, was in economics, and the postwar economic world envisioned by Hoover and Gibson was the same will-o'-the-wisp that Hoover had sought on the domestic front. A few of the fifty conclusions came strangely from one who had signed the Smoot-Hawley Tariff Act, particularly the suggestion that tariffs be no higher than will "preserve fair competition of imports with domestic production." The authors also favored international monetary stabilization, easy access to raw materials through equal prices and open markets, the disruption of monopolies and cartels, and the abolition of trade quotas and privileges.

> Lasting peace [they declared] must include economic freedom regulated to prevent abuse. . . . The long view should be to *restore international trade to free enterprise.* . . .
> International economic freedom cannot function if there is to be a degree of domestic managed economy which stifles free enterprise, for then there would be no substantial force behind private trading, and government must take over.

One cannot escape the feeling that the authors were prescribing a peace for the wrong war. Were they not proposing again that an essentially Wilsonian settlement be made, but without Wilson's mistakes? Hoover had always had criticisms of Wilson, but they concerned means, not ends. (Wilson, he declared in 1942, "made a magnificent fight" for "the best ideals of America.") A few things that were vital to Wilson were of small concern to Hoover—for example, the independence of the smaller nations.[14] But on the whole it was the similarities, not the differences, that stood out. Freedom of the seas, removal (in some measure) of economic barriers among nations, the creation of some sort of League, open diplomacy, a "fair" adjustment of colonial claims, disarmament, a sanely merciful settlement, no annexations or indemnities—all these principles are shared by the historic Fourteen Points of 1918 and the fifty proposals of 1942.

Thus in world as in domestic affairs the keynote of Hoover's public career remained the same—a return to the conditions, real or imagined, of the past. Free trade, free enterprise, competition, open markets, open opportunities—this was the logic of *American Individualism* and *The Challenge to Liberty* projected on a larger scale. The future would be just like the past, but more so; we would go back, back to the rosier world of 1913 —and even beyond that, for the men of 1913 themselves turned to the mid-nineteenth century for their governing principles.

Speaking to his party in 1940, Hoover explained his 1938 trip to Europe by saying that he had gone abroad to find out what causes dictatorships. There were many complex factors involved, he admitted, but he had had no difficulty in spotting the main source: it was *economic planning*. "In every single case before the rise of the totalitarian governments there had been a period dominated by economic planners."

---

14. It was the hostile attitude of Hoover and Gibson toward the small nations that caused Rebecca West to remark: "We have been bitten by the hand that fed us."

Here in all its rigidity was revealed Hoover's religious faith in the planless world of the free market. For a generation managed economies had been developing in all the industrialized nations of the world. This trend had been enormously spurred by the war. Hoover himself had said two years earlier that managed economies would "long continue over a large part of the earth." Could he have seriously believed that free enterprise might be restored to the postwar world? In all history no more heroic setting-back of the clock had ever been proposed. Since economic planning had become such a universal phenomenon, it might have been natural to ask: "If planning caused dictatorships, what caused planning? Was it, perhaps, the universal decline of the planless economy under the stewardship of the Hoovers?" That the New Deal might presage an American fascism, as Hoover insisted, was at least a possibility— one that conventional liberals generally refused to admit; but that Hooverism had brought a reaction toward the New Deal was a historical certainty. That there was anything natural, not to say inevitable, about this trend toward managed economies was a conclusion Hoover could never acknowledge without abandoning the premise upon which his public life had been built —that unmanaged capitalism was an economic system without a major flaw.[15] No, it must be a series of un-

---

15. At Madison Square Garden Hoover had said, October 31, 1932: "This thirty years of incomparable improvement in the scale of living . . . did not arise without right principles animating the American system which produced them. Shall that system be discarded because vote-seeking men appeal to distress and say that the machinery is all wrong and that it must be abandoned or tampered with? Is it not more sensible to realize the simple fact that some extraordinary force has been thrown into the mechanism, temporarily deranging its operation?" As Karl Mannheim observes in *Ideology and Utopia*, "Nothing is more removed

wise choices based on novel and fallacious thinking; things could easily have happened otherwise; *it was simply a strange coincidence, a curious universal mistake*. Perhaps, then, if we should gird ourselves for a new try, perhaps if we were Spartan enough and wise enough, if we would think a little straighter and work a little harder, we might leap out of the fading world of the twentieth century and land in the one that flourished so brightly in Hoover's mind.

But at times, it appears, even Hoover became tired of his own unheeded warnings, and at the Republican national convention of 1944 he dropped a hint of his weariness. Recalling his speeches at the two previous conventions, he said:

> Each time I knew even before I spoke that our people would not believe that the impairment of freedom could happen here. Yet each subsequent four years has shown those warnings to have been too reserved, too cautious.

How frustrating it was to find one's predictions so startlingly confirmed and yet discover again and again that one really had no audience! This very confession was made before a convention whose platform substantially capitulated to the Roosevelt domestic programs. Could it be true that the great American tradition was nearing its end because the people had no ear for spokesmen of the old faith? Could it be true that a salvation so plainly in sight, so near to our grasp, would be blindly refused? If this should come to pass, Herbert Hoover at least had earned his absolution. He had

---

from actual events than the closed rational system. Under certain circumstances, nothing contains more irrational drive than a fully self-contained, intellectualistic world-view."

tried to lead the nation out of the wilderness and back to the comforts and splendors of the old regime. He had given his warnings and they had been spurned. Perhaps, after all, it was the spirit of the people that was not fundamentally sound.

CHAPTER XII

FRANKLIN D. ROOSEVELT:
THE PATRICIAN AS OPPORTUNIST

❦

THE country needs and, unless I mistake its temper, the country demands bold, persistent experimentation. It is common sense to take a method and try it. If it fails, admit it frankly and try another. But above all, try something.

FRANKLIN D. ROOSEVELT

ONCE during the early years of the Wilson administration Eleanor Roosevelt and her husband, then Assistant Secretary of the Navy, were lunching with Henry Adams. Roosevelt was speaking earnestly about some governmental matter that concerned him, when his aged host turned on him fiercely: "Young man, I have lived in this house many years and seen the occupants of that White House across the square come and go, and nothing that you minor officials or the occupants of that house can do will affect the history of the world for long."

It was not often that Adams's superlative ironies were unintentional. Although the influence of great men is usually exaggerated, Roosevelt must be granted at least a marginal influence upon the course of history. No personality has ever expressed the American popular temper so articulately or with such exclusiveness. In the Progressive era national reform leadership was divided among Theodore Roosevelt, Wilson, Bryan, and La Follette. In the age of the New Deal it was monopolized by one man, whose passing left American liberalism demoralized and all but helpless.

At the heart of the New Deal there was not a philosophy but a temperament. The essence of this temperament was Roosevelt's confidence that even when he was operating in unfamiliar territory he could do no wrong, commit no serious mistakes. From the standpoint of an economic technician this assurance seemed almost mad at times, for example when he tossed back his head, laughed, and said to a group of silver Senators: "I experimented with gold and that was a flop. Why shouldn't I experiment a little with silver?" And yet there was a kind of intuitive wisdom under the harum-scarum surface of his methods. When he came to power, the people had seen stagnation go dangerously far. They wanted experiment, activity, trial and error, anything that would convey a sense of movement and novelty. At the very beginning of his candidacy Roosevelt, without heed for tradition or formality, flew to the 1932 nominating convention and addressed it in person instead of waiting for weeks in the customary pose of ceremonious ignorance. A trivial act in itself, the device gave the public an impression of vigor and originality that was never permitted to die. Although, as we shall see, Roosevelt had been reared on a social and economic philosophy rather similar to Hoover's, he succeeded at once in communicating the fact that his temperament was antithetical. When Hoover bumbled that it was necessary only to restore confidence, the nation laughed bitterly. When Roosevelt said: "The only thing we have to fear is fear itself," essentially the same threadbare half-true idea, the nation was thrilled. Hoover had lacked motion;

Roosevelt lacked direction. But his capacity for growth, or at least for change, was enormous. Flexibility was both his strength and his weakness. Where Hoover had been remote and abstract, a doctrinaire who thought in fixed principles and moved cautiously in the rarefied atmosphere of the managerial classes, Roosevelt was warm, personal, concrete, and impulsive. Hoover was often reserved with valued associates. Roosevelt could say "my old friend" in eleven languages. He had little regard for abstract people but a sharp intuitive knowledge of popular feeling. Because he was content in large measure to follow public opinion, he was able to give it that necessary additional impulse of leadership which can translate desires into policies. Hoover had never been able to convey to the masses a clear picture of what he was trying to do; Roosevelt was often able to suggest a clear and forceful line of policy when none in fact existed.

Raymond Moley tells an instructive story of Roosevelt's relations with Hoover in the interim between Roosevelt's election and inauguration. A conference had been arranged between the two men to discuss continuity of policy on the vexing question of foreign debts. Roosevelt, ill-informed on the facts, brought Moley with him as ballast and also carried a set of little cards in his hand as reminders of the questions he wanted to put to Hoover. Hoover talked for some time, revealing a mastery of all facets of the question which profoundly impressed Professor Moley. In contrast with the state of their information was the manner of the two men. Hoover, plainly disconcerted at this meeting with the man who had beaten him in the campaign, was shy and ill at ease and kept his eyes on the pattern of the carpet in the Red Room. Roosevelt was relaxed, informal, and cordial. That he was operating in *terra incognita* did not seem to trouble him in the least.

Roosevelt's admirers, their minds fixed on the image of a wise, benevolent, provident father, have portrayed him as an ardent social reformer and sometimes as a master planner. His critics, coldly examining the step-by-step emergence of his measures, studying the supremely haphazard way in which they were so often administered, finding how little he actually had to do with so many of his "achievements," have come to the opposite conclusion that his successes were purely accidental, just as a certain portion of a number of random shots is likely to hit a target. It is true, it is bound to be true, that there is a vast disproportion between Roosevelt's personal stature and the Roosevelt legend, but not everything that comes in haphazard fashion is necessarily an accident. During his presidential period the nation was confronted with a completely novel situation for which the traditional, commonly accepted philosophies afforded no guide. An era of fumbling and muddling-through was inevitable. Only a leader with an experimental temper could have made the New Deal possible.

Roosevelt was, moreover, a public instrument of the most delicate receptivity. Although he lacked depth, he had great breadth. A warmhearted, informal patrician, he hated to disappoint, liked to play the bountiful friend. He felt that if a large number of people wanted something very badly, it was important that they be given some measure of satisfaction—and he allowed neither economic dogmas nor political precedents to inhibit him. The story of the WPA cultural projects illustrates his intensely personal methods and the results they yielded. When relief was being organ-

ized in the early stages of the New Deal, someone
pointed out to him that a great many competent painters were poverty-stricken and desperate. Now, Roosevelt had no taste for painting, very little interest in
artists and writers as a group, and no preconceived
theories about the responsibility of the State for cultural welfare; but his decision to help the artists came
immediately and spontaneously. "Why not?" he said.
"They are human beings. They have to live. I guess the
only thing they can do is paint and surely there must
be some public place where paintings are wanted."
And so painters were included in the benefits of CWA.
Ultimately, under the WPA, relief was extended to mu-
sicians, dancers, actors, writers, historians, even to students trying to finance themselves through college. A
generation of artists and intellectuals was nursed
through a trying period and became welded to the
New Deal and devoted to Roosevelt liberalism.

II

James and Sara Delano Roosevelt, Franklin's parents, are reminiscent of secondary characters in Edith
Wharton's novels who provide the climate of respectable and unfriendly opinion in which her unfortunate
heroines live. James Roosevelt, vice-president of several corporations, was a handsome country gentleman
who dabbled in Democratic politics, enjoyed a stable
of trotting-horses, and lived in leisure on his Hyde
Park estate. Sara Delano, James's second wife, was also
from an upper-class family with deep roots in American history; her father had owned copper lands, iron
and coal mines, acreage on New York harbor, and a

fleet of clipper ships. When they were married Sara was twenty-six and James was fifty-two. Two years later, on January 30, 1882, an entry in James Roosevelt's diary noted the birth of "a splendid large baby boy."

The only child of a fond mother, treated like a grandson by his father, Franklin was brought up with unusual indulgence. He had governesses and tutors; his playmates were from his own class; he owned a pony and a twenty-one-foot sailboat. Eight times before his adolescence he was taken on jaunts to Europe. At fourteen he entered the Reverend Endicott Peabody's Groton School, a little Greek democracy of the elite, which, as its headmaster said, stood for "everything that is true, beautiful, and of good report." The Groton boys, about ninety per cent from social-register families, lived in an atmosphere of paternal kindness and solicitude and swallowed huge gulps of inspiration at Peabody's weekly chapel performances.

From Groton Roosevelt followed a well-beaten path to Harvard. Although he was privileged to hear James, Royce, Norton, Shaler, and other illuminati, his life flowered chiefly outside the classroom. He became a prodigious doer and joiner, with memberships in more than a half-dozen campus clubs and a position on the *Crimson* that won him a good deal of college renown. A large part of his work on the *Crimson* was devoted to petty crusades for campus reforms. At an age when many boys are kicking over the traces, flirting with heresies, defying authority, and incidentally deepening their intellectual perspectives, young Roosevelt was writing exhortations about "school spirit" and football morale. On one occasion he urged in patriarchal fashion that "the memories and traditions of our ancestors and of our University be maintained during our lives and be faithfully handed down to our children in the years to come." His most serious public interest and possibly his first manifestation of sympathy for an underdog was in a college drive for the Boers. He left Harvard in 1904; his youth is summed up in his mother's words: "After all he had many advantages that other boys did not have."

Since it had been decided that Franklin should become a lawyer, he entered Columbia Law School. The following year he married his distant cousin Eleanor, to whom he had secretly been engaged, and moved into a home in New York City under the managerial eye of his mother. He was not happy in law school. "I am . . . trying to understand a little of the work," he wrote plaintively to Rector Peabody. Bored by the tenuous subtleties of the law, he failed some of his courses and left school without taking a degree, although he had absorbed enough to pass bar examinations. He joined the well-known New York firm of Carter, Ledyard, & Milburn as managing clerk. In Hyde Park he assumed the public-spirited role that his position required, became a member of the local volunteer fire department, a director of the First National Bank of Poughkeepsie, and a delegate to the 1910 New York Democratic convention.

Peopled by rich gentry and their hangers-on, the Hudson Valley counties were overwhelmingly Republican. Democratic nominations were conventionally given to prominent men of means who could pay the expenses of their campaigns. In 1910 the Democratic Mayor of Poughkeepsie, who had come to like his agreeable young neighbor from up the river, got him the party nomination for state senator in a district that had elected only one Democrat since 1856. But 1910 was a bad year for Republicans, and Roosevelt, who bore the name of his wife's uncle, the popular twenty-sixth President, conducted a vigorous, unconventional campaign by automobile, ran well ahead of his ticket, and was elected on the crest of a Democratic wave.

In the legislature Roosevelt promptly became a leader among Democratic insurgents who blocked the nomination of Tammany Boss Murphy's choice for United States Senator. He appeared a typical progressive in his voting record, stood for the civil service, conservation, direct primaries, popular election of Senators, women's suffrage, and social legislation. "From the ruins of the political machines," he predicted hopefully, "we will reconstruct something more nearly conforming to a democratic government." In 1911 he visited Wilson at Trenton and returned an enthusiastic supporter. He served well in the 1912 campaign and was rewarded with the Assistant Secretaryship of the Navy. Just turned thirty-one, he had had only three years of experience in politics.

From his childhood when he sailed his own knockabout, Roosevelt had been in love with ships and the sea. He collected ship models and prints, he read avidly in naval history, particularly Mahan, and had thought of entering Annapolis. During the Spanish War he had run away from Groton to enlist in the navy—an escapade cut short by a siege of scarlet fever. After his appointment Roosevelt began to campaign for naval expansion in magazine articles and speeches, revealing a somewhat nationalistic and bellicose spirit. The United States, he said, could not afford to lose control of the seas unless it was content to be "a nation unimportant in the great affairs of the world, without influence in commerce, or in the extension of peaceful civilization." Although the American people could look forward to ultimate international limitations of arms, they must in the present "keep the principles of a possible navy conflict always in mind." At the time Wilson delivered his war message to Congress, *Scribner's Magazine* was featuring a monitory article by Roosevelt entitled "On Your Own Heads," which called for quintupling the navy's personnel. No one could say, argued Roosevelt, that we were free from the danger of war. "We know that every boy who goes to school is bound sooner or later, no matter how peaceful his nature, to come to blows with some schoolmate. A great people, a hundred million strong, has gone to school." Later he demanded a system of national conscription for women as well as men. He believed that service in the navy smooths out sectionalism and class feeling and teaches equality. As an administrator Roosevelt was aggressive and efficient, cutting through red tape with genial disregard for regulations. Against the advice of most of the admirals he took an important part in promoting the unprecedented Allied mine barrage in the North Sea.

In 1920 his party, needing a good name and an effective campaigner, nominated Roosevelt as James M. Cox's running-mate. He made a grand tour of the country, delivering about a thousand speeches. On the primary issue, the League of Nations, he argued effectively, but his enthusiasm was not comparable to his energy. "The League may not end wars," he conceded, "but the nations demand the experiment." During the campaign he made one slip which indicates that his mood was one of imperialistic *Realpolitik* rather than idealistic internationalism. At Butte, answering the argument that the United States would be outvoted by the combined British Commonwealth in the League's Assembly, he said: "It is just the other way . . . the

United States has about twelve votes in the Assembly."
He went on to explain that Latin-American countries
in the projected Assembly looked to his country as "a
guardian and big brother," and that it would control
their votes.

> Until last week I had two [votes] myself, and now
> Secretary Daniels has them. You know I had something
> to do with the running of a couple of little republics. The
> facts are that I wrote Haiti's Constitution myself, and,
> if I do say it, I think it a pretty good Constitution.

Immediately the opposition kicked. Roosevelt was
simply voicing some of the realities of politics, but the
cynicism of his remarks, which smacked so strongly of
the bad neighbor, was too open. He covered himself as
best he could by saying that he had only meant that
the Latin-American countries had the same interests
as the United States and would normally vote the same
way. For the boast that an alien official had written the
Constitution of a neighbor republic there could be no
satisfactory explanation.[1]

But it was a campaign in which mistakes did not
matter. After Harding's victory Roosevelt, now thirty-
eight, became a private citizen for the first time in ten
years. He resumed his slight law practice, served as an
overseer of Harvard, and took up his old life. A yacht-
ing companion, Van Lear Black, gave him a position
in the New York office of the Fidelity and Deposit
Company of Maryland which carried a salary of $25,-
000. But in August 1921 it appeared that both Roosevelt's public and professional careers were over. After

---

1. The boast was untrue as well as unwise. Roosevelt did not
write the Haitian Constitution but merely approved a draft submitted to the Navy Department by the State Department.

an exhausting spell in the heat of New York City he left for a vacation at his summer home on Campobello Island and soon found himself in the grip of severe pain, unable to move his muscles from the hips down.

III

To be sick and helpless is a humiliating experience. Prolonged illness also carries the hazard of narcissistic self-absorption. It would have been easy for Roosevelt to give up his political aspirations and retire to the comfortable privacy of Hyde Park. That he refused to relinquish his normal life was testimony to his courage and determination, and also to the strength of his ambition. From his bed he resumed as many of his affairs as possible. By the spring of 1922 he was walking on crutches, sometimes venturing to his office, and after 1924, when he found the pool at Warm Springs, he made good progress in recovering his strength. Above his enfeebled legs he developed a powerful torso.

In the long run this siege of infantile paralysis added much to Roosevelt's political appeal. As a member of the overprivileged classes with a classic Groton-Harvard career he had been too much the child of fortune. Now a heroic struggle against the cruelest kind of adversity made a more poignant success story than the usual rags-to-riches theme; it was also far better adapted to democratic leadership in a period when people were tired of self-made men and their management of affairs.

There has been much speculation about the effect of Roosevelt's illness upon his sympathies. Frances Perkins, who writes of him with intelligence and detachment and who knew him before his illness as a pleasant but somewhat supercilious young man, feels that he underwent a "spiritual transformation," in which he was purged of "the slightly arrogant attitude" he had occasionally shown before. She now found him "completely warmhearted," and felt that "he understood the problems of people in trouble." There is a further conclusion, drawn by some fabricators of the legend, that he read widely and studied deeply during his illness and developed a firm social outlook that aligned him forever with the underprivileged. This notion is not sustained by Roosevelt's history during the prosperity of the 1920's. His human capacity, enlarged though it probably was, was not crystallized in either a new philosophy or a heightened interest in reforms.

For anyone of Roosevelt's background and character to have turned to serious social study or unorthodox political views would have been most unusual. From boyhood to the time of his illness he had led an outdoor athletic life, spending his indoor leisure on such diversions as stamp collections, ship models, naval history, and the like, not on sociological literature. His way of thinking was empirical, impressionistic, and pragmatic. At the beginning of his career he took to the patrician reform thought of the Progressive era and accepted a social outlook that can best be summed up in the phrase *noblesse oblige*.[2] He had a penchant for public service, personal philanthropy, and harmless manifestoes against dishonesty in government; he displayed a broad, easygoing tolerance, a genuine liking

---

2. "Frankness, and largeness, and simplicity, and a fine fervor for the right are virtues that some must preserve, and where can we look for them if not from the Roosevelts and the Delanos?" wrote Franklin K. Lane to Roosevelt, August 1920.

for all sorts of people; he loved to exercise his charm in political and social situations. His mind, as exhibited in writings and speeches of the twenties, was generous and sensible, but also superficial and complacent.

Roosevelt's education in politics came in a period of progressive optimism when it was commonly assumed that the most glaring ills of society could be cured by laws, once politics fell into the hands of honest men. If women worked endless hours in sweatshops, if workingmen were haunted by fear of unemployment or stricken by accidents, if the aged were beset by insecurity, men of good will would pass laws to help them. As a state senator and as governor this was what Roosevelt tried to do. But the social legislation of the states, however humane and useful, was worked out in provincial theaters of action, dealt more with effects than causes, touched only the surface of great problems like unemployment, housing, taxation, banking, and relief for agriculture. The generation that sponsored these laws got from them a good deal of training in practical politics and welfare work, but no strong challenge to think through the organic ills of society.

Roosevelt's biographers have largely ignored his life in the twenties except his fight for physical recovery, his role as peacemaker in the faction-ridden Democratic Party, and his return to politics as governor of New York. John T. Flynn, however, has pointed with malicious pleasure to his unsuccessful career in business, which certainly deserves attention, not as a reflection on his ethics or personal capacities, but on his social views during the years of prosperity. The ventures with which Roosevelt was associated—chiefly, one suspects, for the promotional value of his name— were highly speculative, and with one exception they failed. Perhaps the most illuminating of these was the

Consolidated Automatic Merchandising Corporation, of which he was a founder and director along with Henry Morgenthau, Jr. This was a holding company, whose promoters were stirred by the typically American idea of a chain of clerkless stores to sell standard goods by means of automatic vending machines. In 1928 the chairman of its board announced that a large store staffed with such machines would soon be opened in New York City. Although it promised fabulous returns to investors, the firm lost over two million dollars within three years and closed its affairs in a bankruptcy court. Since Roosevelt promptly resigned his interest when he became governor, his connection with it was brief and, in a business way, unimportant; but the social implications of the clerkless store and the jobless clerk, not to mention the loose and speculative way in which the enterprise was launched, do not seem to have troubled his mind.

In 1922 Roosevelt became president of the American Construction Council, a trade organization of the building industry. The council had been conceived in the light of Secretary of Commerce Hoover's philosophy of self-regulation by business, and Hoover presided over the meeting at which Roosevelt was chosen. In his address to the council Roosevelt endorsed the Hoover doctrine:

> The tendency lately has been toward regulation of industry. Something goes wrong somewhere in a given branch of work, immediately the public is aroused, the press, the pulpit and public call for an investigation. That is fine, that is healthy . . . but government regulation is not feasible. It is unwieldy, expensive. It means employment of men to carry on this phase of the work; it means higher taxes. The public doesn't want it; the industry doesn't want it.

Seven years later in a Fourth of July speech at Tammany Hall, Governor Roosevelt warned of dangers inherent in "great combinations of capital." But he explained that "industrial combination is not wrong in
itself. The danger lies in taking the government into
partnership." The chief theme of his address was
summed up in the sentence: "I want to preach a new
doctrine—complete separation of business and government"—which was an ironic message for the future
architect of the New Deal.

Even Mr. Flynn concedes that as governor Roosevelt was "a fair executive." On social justice and humane reform his record was strong; in matters of long-
range economic understanding and responsibility it
was weak. He worked earnestly and effectively with a
hostile Republican legislature to extend reforms that
had been started by Al Smith. He secured a program
of old-age pensions, unemployment insurance, and labor legislation, developed a forthright liberal program
on the power question,[3] and took the initiative in calling a conference of governors of Eastern industrial
states to discuss unemployment and relief. His state

3. Roosevelt believed that the vast potential of the St. Lawrence should be developed to shake down the unreasonable rates
of the power companies. He wanted great power sites like the
St. Lawrence, Muscle Shoals, and Boulder Dam to be developed
by federal or state authority so that they would "remain forever
as a yardstick with which to measure the cost of producing and
transmitting electricity." This yardstick could be used to test the
fairness of private utility rates. He proposed that New York
build power structures and market the power they generated
through contracts with private companies. If the state failed to
get satisfactory contracts it would go into the business of selling
power directly to consumers. In 1931 the legislature created the
New York Power Authority, embodying his proposals, but the
necessary treaty with Canada was first blocked by the Hoover administration and later defeated by the Senate in 1934 when it
failed to get the necessary two-thirds majority.

was in the vanguard of those taking practical steps to relieve distress.

Along with most other Americans, however, Roosevelt had failed to foresee the depression that began when he was governor. Six months before the crash he found New York industry "in a very healthy and prosperous condition." In his addresses and messages he ignored the significance of the depression until its effects became overwhelming. His signal failure was in the realm of financial policy.

On December 11, 1930 the Bank of United States in New York City was closed by the State Superintendent of Banks, in substantial default to 400,000 depositors, mostly people with small savings. It had long been a practice of some New York commercial banks to create special "thrift accounts," which, although much the same as ordinary savings accounts, stood outside the control of state laws regulating savings-bank investments and gave bankers a wide latitude with other people's money. Another device was to create bank affiliates which were manipulated in sundry complicated ways to milk depositors and stockholders for the benefit of insiders.

A few months before the collapse of the Bank of United States, the failure of the City Trust Company had led to an investigation of the State Banking Department, and in Roosevelt's absence Acting Governor Herbert Lehman appointed Robert Moses as investigator. Moses's report roundly condemned many bank practices, especially "thrift accounts" and bank affiliates, and referred to the Bank of United States as an especially flagrant case.

Roosevelt ignored the Moses report and created another commission to study the same subject, appointing as one of its members Henry Pollak—a director and counsel of the Bank of United States! Not surprisingly, the new commission rejected Moses's recommendations. Shortly afterward, when the Bank of United States failed, Roosevelt was self-assured, unabashed, impenitent. To the state legislature he boldly wrote: "The responsibility for strengthening the banking laws rests with you." Insisting that the protection of the laws be extended to depositors in thrift accounts, he waxed righteously impatient: "The people of the State not only expect it, but they have a right to demand it. The time to act is now. Any further delay is inexcusable. . . ."

This incident, particularly Roosevelt's sudden espousal of a reform he had opposed, foreshadows a great part of the history of the New Deal. There is an irresistible footnote to it. When Roosevelt came to power the banks of the nation were in paralysis. In his first press conference he was asked if he favored federal insurance of bank deposits. He said that he did not. His reason was that bad banks as well as good ones would have to be insured and that the federal government would have to take the losses. Nevertheless the Federal Deposit Insurance Corporation was soon created as a concession to a bloc of insistent Western Senators. The FDIC thus took its place among a company of New Deal reforms that add to the lustre of Roosevelt's name and will presumably be cited by historians as instances of his wise planning.

When the task of conducting a presidential campaign fell upon him, Roosevelt's background of economic innocence was dappled by only occasional traces of knowledge. "I don't find that he has read much about economic subjects," wrote Raymond Moley in a family letter, April 12, 1932. "The frightening aspect of his methods is FDR's great receptivity. So far as I know he makes no efforts to check up on anything that I or anyone else has told him." On occasion his advisers were astounded by his glib treatment of complicated subjects. Once when his campaign speeches on the tariff were being prepared, and two utterly incompatible proposals were placed before him, Roosevelt left Moley speechless by airily suggesting that he should "weave the two together." That "great receptivity" which frightened Moley, however, was the secret of Roosevelt's political genius. He became an individual sounding-board for the grievances and remedies of the nation, which he tried to weave into a program that would be politically, if not economically, coherent.

Roosevelt's 1932 campaign utterances indicate that the New Deal had not yet taken form in his mind. He was clear on two premises: he rejected Hoover's thesis that the depression began abroad, insisting that it was a home-made product, and he denounced Hoover for spending too much money. He called the Hoover administration "the greatest spending Administration in peace time in all our history." The current deficit, he charged, was enough to "make us catch our breath." "Let us have the courage," he urged, "to stop borrowing to meet continuing deficits." And yet he was "unwilling that economy should be practiced at the expense of starving people." Still, he did not indicate how he proposed to relieve starving people. Public works? They could be no more than a "stopgap," even if billions of dollars were spent on them. He was firm in ascribing the depression to low domestic purchasing power, and declared that the government must "use wise measures of regulation which will bring the purchasing power back to normal." On the other hand, he surrendered to Hoover's idea that America's productive capacity demanded a large outlet in the export market. "If our factories run even 80 percent of capacity," he said (quite inaccurately),[4] "they will turn out more products than we as a nation can possibly use ourselves. The answer is that . . . we must sell some goods abroad."

Roosevelt made several specific promises to the farmers. There was one aspect of Hoover's farm policies that made him especially bitter—the attempt of the Farm Board to organize retrenchment in production, which Roosevelt called "the cruel joke of advising farmers to allow twenty percent of their wheat lands to lie idle, to plow up every third row of cotton and shoot every tenth dairy cow." His own program involved "planned use of the land," reforestation, and aid to farmers by reducing tariffs through bilateral negotiations. Later he backtracked on the tariff, however, promising "continued protection for American agriculture *as well as* American industry."

All Roosevelt's promises—to restore purchasing power and mass employment and relieve the needy and aid the farmer and raise agricultural prices and balance the budget and lower the tariff and continue protection—added up to a very discouraging performance to those who hoped for a coherent liberal program. The *New Republic* called the campaign "an obscene spectacle" on both sides.

Roosevelt delivered one speech at the Commonwealth Club in San Francisco, however, which did generally foreshadow the new tack that was to be taken under the New Deal. In this address Roosevelt

---

4. "The United States," concluded the authors of *America's Capacity to Consume*, "has not reached a stage of economic development in which it is possible to produce more than the American people as a whole would like to consume."

clearly set down the thesis that the nation had arrived at a great watershed in its development. Popular government and a wide continent to exploit had given the United States an unusually favored early history, he asserted. Then the Industrial Revolution had brought a promise of abundance for all. But its productive capacity had been controlled by ruthless and wasteful men. Possessing free land and a growing population, and needing industrial plant, the country had been willing to pay the price of the accomplishments of the "ambitious man" and had offered him "unlimited reward provided only that he produced the economic plant so much desired." "The turn of the tide came with the turn of the century." As America reached its last frontiers, the demand of the people for more positive controls of economic life gave rise to the Square Deal of Theodore Roosevelt and the New Freedom of Woodrow Wilson. In 1932 the nation was still faced with the problem of industrial control.

A glance at the situation today only too clearly indicates that equality of opportunity as we have known it no longer exists. Our industrial plant is built; the problem just now is whether under existing conditions it is not overbuilt. Our last frontier has long since been reached, and there is practically no more free land. More than half of our people do not live on the farms or on lands and cannot derive a living by cultivating their own property. There is no safety valve in the form of a Western prairie to which those thrown out of work by the Eastern economic machines can go for a new start. We are not able to invite the immigration from Europe to share our endless plenty. We are now providing a drab living for our own people. . . .

Just as freedom to farm has ceased, so also the opportunity in business has narrowed. . . . The unfeeling statistics of the past three decades show that the independent business man is running a losing race. . . . Recently a careful study was made of the concentration of business in the United States. It showed that our economic life was dominated by some six hundred odd corporations who [sic] controlled two-thirds of American industry. Ten million small business men divided the other third. More striking still, it appeared that if the process goes on at the same rate, at the end of another century we shall have all American industry controlled by a dozen corporations, and run by perhaps a hundred men. Put plainly, we are steering a steady course toward economic oligarchy, if we are not there already.

Clearly, all this calls for a re-appraisal of values. A mere builder of more industrial plants, a creator of more railroad systems, an organizer of more corporations, is as likely to be a danger as a help. The day of the great promoter or the financial Titan, to whom we granted anything if only he would build, or develop, is over. Our task now is not discovery or exploitation of natural resources, or necessarily producing more goods. It is the soberer, less dramatic business of administering resources and plants already in hand, of seeking to reestablish foreign markets for our surplus production, of meeting the problem of underconsumption, of adjusting production to consumption, or distributing wealth and products more equitably, of adapting existing economic organizations to the service of the people. The day of enlightened administration has come. . . .

As I see it, the task of government in its relation to business is to assist the development of an economic declaration of rights, an economic constitutional order. . . .

Happily, the times indicate that to create such an order not only is the proper policy of Government, but it is the only line of safety for our economic structures as well. We know, now, that these economic units cannot exist unless prosperity is uniform, that is, unless purchasing power is well distributed throughout every group in the nation.

In cold terms, American capitalism had come of age, the great era of individualism, expansion, and opportunity was dead. Further, the drying up of "natural" economic forces required that the government step in and guide the creation of a new economic order. Thus far Roosevelt had left behind the philosophy of his 1929 Tammany Hall speech. But in the Commonwealth Club speech two different and potentially inconsistent lines of government action are implied. One is suggested by the observation that the industrial plant is "overbuilt," that more plants will be "a danger," that production must be "adjusted" to consumption; the other by phrases like "meeting the problem of underconsumption," making prosperity "uniform," distributing purchasing power, and "an economic declaration of rights." The first involves a retrogressive economy of trade restriction and state-guided monopoly; the second emphasizes social justice and the conquest of poverty. In 1931 the United States Chamber of Commerce's Committee on Continuity of Business and Employment had declared in terms similar to Roosevelt's: "A freedom of action which might have been justified in the relatively simple life of the last century cannot be tolerated today. . . . We have left the period of extreme individualism." The committee then proposed a program very closely resembling the NRA as it was adopted in 1933. It is evident that Roosevelt's premises, far from being intrinsically progressive, were capable of being adapted to very conservative purposes. His version of the "matured economy" theory, although clothed in the rhetoric of liberalism and "social planning," could easily be put to the purposes of the trade asso-

ciations and scarcity-mongers. The polar opposition
between such a policy and the promise of making prosperity uniform and distributing purchasing power anticipated a basic ambiguity in the New Deal.

IV

At one of his earliest press conferences Roosevelt
compared himself to the quarterback in a football
game. The quarterback knows what the next play will
be, but beyond that he cannot predict or plan too rig-
idly because "future plays will depend on how the next
one works." It was a token of his cast of mind that he
used the metaphor of a game, and one in which chance
plays a very large part. The New Deal will never be
understood by anyone who looks for a single thread of
policy, a far-reaching, far-seeing plan. It was a series
of improvisations, many adopted very suddenly, many
contradictory. Such unity as it had was in political
strategy, not economics.

Roosevelt had little regard for the wisdom of economists as a professional caste. "I happen to know," he
declared in his third fireside chat, "that professional
economists have changed their definition of economic
laws every five or ten years for a long time." Within
the broad limits of what he deemed "sound policy"—
and they were extremely broad limits—he understood
that his administration would not be politically durable
unless it could "weave together" many diverse, conflicting interests. He had built a brilliantly successful
career in the Democratic Party on his flair for reconcil-
ing or straddling antagonistic elements, and he was too
practical to abandon a solid bedrock of political har-

mony in favor of some flighty economic dogma that might be abandoned in "five or ten years." Frances Perkins tells how Lord Keynes, whose spending theories were influential with some New Deal economists, paid a brief visit to the President in 1934 and talked about economic theory. Roosevelt, bewildered at Keynes's "rigamarole of figures," told his Secretary of Labor: "He must be a mathematician rather than a political economist." Keynes for his part was somewhat disappointed, remarking that he had "supposed the President was more literate, economically speaking." The Britisher's mistake is likely to become a model for Roosevelt legend-makers.

Raymond Moley, in his *After Seven Years*, has compiled a fairly long but not exhaustive enumeration of the sharp swerves and tacks in Rooseveltian policy. It will be more simple and profitable to speak only of the two New Deals that were foreshadowed in the Commonwealth Club speech. In a sense both of them ran concurrently; but it is roughly accurate to say that the first was dominant from Roosevelt's inauguration to the spring and summer of 1935 and that the second emerged during that period and lasted until the reform energies of the nation petered out.

The first New Deal, the New Deal of 1933-4, was conceived mainly for recovery. Reform elements and humane measures of immediate relief were subsidiary to the organized and subsidized scarcity advocated by the Chamber of Commerce, the Farm Bureau Federation, and the National Grange, and incarnated in the NRA and AAA. These great agencies, the core of the first New Deal, representing its basic plans for industry and agriculture, embodied the retrogressive idea of recovery through scarcity.

The AAA was the most striking illustration of organized scarcity in action. Although successful in raising farm prices and restoring farm income, it did just what Roosevelt had found so shocking in Hoover's Farm Board. To the common-sense mind the policy seemed to have solved the paradox of hunger in the midst of plenty only by doing away with plenty. In an address at Atlanta, in November 1935, Roosevelt implicitly conceded that the whole policy was geared to the failure of the American economy. He pointed out that the average American lived "on what the doctors would call a third-class diet." If the nation lived on a first-class diet, "we would have to put more acres than we have ever cultivated into the production of an additional supply of things for Americans to eat." The people lived on a third-class diet, he said candidly, because they could not afford to buy a first-class diet.[5]

The mainspring of the first New Deal was the NRA, which Roosevelt called "the most important and far-reaching legislation ever enacted by the American Congress . . . a supreme effort to stabilize for all time the many factors which make for the prosperity of the nation." Under it business received government sanction for sweeping price agreements and production quotas and in return accepted wage stipulations improving the condition of many of the poorest-paid workers.[6] It is not unfair to say that in essence the NRA

5. The Ever Normal Granary Plan, enacted in 1938, was widely hailed as a more satisfactory policy. Although it promised greater price stability and other benefits, it still involved familiar plans for marketing quotas and the shadow of abundance still hung over it. Its sponsor, Henry Wallace, admitted that "several years of good weather" and good crops would "embarrass" the government.

6. It may be necessary to say that NRA was not a universal business policy. A poll taken in 1935 showed that Chamber of Commerce members were almost three to one for continuing NRA, while NAM members opposed it three to one.

embodied the conception of many businessmen that recovery was to be sought through systematic monopolization, high prices, and low production.[7] In spite of the enthusiasm with which its "planned" features were greeted, it retarded recovery, as the Brookings economists concluded, and a strong, sustained advance in business conditions began only after the Supreme Court killed it in May 1935.[8] Roosevelt was nevertheless slow to give up the NRA idea. In February 1935, asking for a two-year extension, he said that to abandon its "fundamental purposes and principles . . . would spell the return of industrial and labor chaos."

The initial New Deal was based upon a strategy that Roosevelt had called during the campaign "a true concert of interests," and that meant in practice something for everybody. Farmers got the AAA. Business got the NRA codes. Labor got wage-and-hour provisions and the collective-bargaining promise of Section 7 (a). The unemployed got a variety of relief measures. The middle classes got the Home Owners' Loan Corporation, securities regulation, and other reforms. Some debtors were aided by inflation. As new discontents developed they were met with new expedients.

Despite all Roosevelt's efforts, however, the nation insistently divided into right and left, and his equivocal position became more difficult to maintain. Pressure

7. NRA Administrator Hugh Johnson declared in an early press conference: "We are going to ask something in the nature of an armistice on increased producing capacity, until we see if we can get upward spiral started. . . . We are going to plead very earnestly . . . not to use any further labor-saving devices or anything further to increase production for the present."

8. The end of NRA was certainly not the only factor in the recovery that began in the summer of 1935, but it is beyond argument that the most sustained period of economic advance under the New Deal took place in the two years after the Blue Eagle was laid to rest.

from the organized and enheartened left became stronger; but Roosevelt was also baited into a leftward turn by die-hard conservatives. He was surprised and wounded at the way the upper classes turned on him. It has often been said that he betrayed his class; but if by his class one means the whole policy-making, power-wielding stratum, it would be just as true to say that his class betrayed him. Consider the situation in which he came to office. The economic machinery of the nation had broken down and its political structure was beginning to disintegrate. People who had anything to lose were frightened; they were willing to accept any way out that would leave them still in possession. During the emergency Roosevelt had had practically dictatorial powers. He had righted the keel of economic life and had turned politics safely back to its normal course. Although he had adopted many novel, perhaps risky expedients, he had avoided vital disturbances to the interests. For example, he had passed by an easy chance to solve the bank crisis by nationalization and instead followed a policy orthodox enough to win Hoover's approval. His basic policies for industry and agriculture had been designed after models supplied by great vested-interest groups. Of course, he had adopted several measures of relief and reform, but mainly of the sort that any wise and humane conservative would admit to be necessary. True, he had stirred the masses with a few hot words about "money changers" and chiselers, but he had been careful to identify these as a minority among businessmen. It was, after all, not Roosevelt but the terrible suffering of the depression that had caused mass discontent, and every sophisticate might be expected to know that in such times a few words against the evil rich are necessary to a politician's effectiveness.

Nothing that Roosevelt had done warranted the vituperation he soon got in the conservative press or the obscenities that the hate-Roosevelt maniacs were bruiting about in their clubs and dining-rooms. Quite understandably he began to feel that the people who were castigating him were muddle-headed ingrates. During the campaign of 1936 he compared them with the old man saved from drowning who berated his rescuer for not salvaging his hat—and again with a patient newly discharged from the hospital who had nothing but imprecations for his physician. Before 1935 Roosevelt had engaged in much political controversy, but he had generally managed to remain on friendly terms with his opponents. Surrounded from childhood with friendship, encouragement, and indulgence, he might have been able to accept criticism offered in the spirit of good-natured banter or the proposal of constructive alternatives (which he would simply have appropriated), but the malice and deliberate stupidity of his critics made him angry, and his political struggle with the "economic royalists" soon became intensely personal. Professor Moley, who in 1932 had admired his lack of "a bloated sense of personal destiny," was saddened to hear him say in 1936: "There's one issue in this campaign. It's myself, and people must be either for me or against me." In public he grew aggressive. He would like to have it said of his second administration, he stated, that in it "the forces of selfishness and of lust for power . . . met their master."

The development of Roosevelt's relation to the left is of critical importance to the Roosevelt legend. Perhaps no aspect of his public relations has been so quickly forgotten as his early labor policy. At the beginning of his administration Roosevelt was an acquaintance, not a friend, of organized labor. Although he was eager to do something about the poorest-paid workers through the NRA codes, his attitude toward unions themselves was not overcordial. The NRA itself had been rushed into shape partly to head off the strong pro-labor provisions of the Black-Connery bill. Section 7(a) of NRA, which guaranteed the right of collective bargaining, did not ban individual bargaining, company unions, or the open shop. Workers at first rallied to the NRA with enthusiasm and entered the more aggressive unions by the thousands in response to the plausible but false appeal: "The President wants you to join." But when disputes arose under Section 7(a), General Hugh Johnson and Donald Richberg handed down interpretations that, in the language of the Brookings Institution economists, "had the practical effect of placing the NRA on the side of anti-union employers in their struggle against the trade unions. . . . The NRA thus threw its weight against labor in the balance of bargaining power." Roosevelt stood firmly behind his administrators. Further, his last appointee as NRA administrator was a notorious foe of labor, S. Clay Williams. By early 1935, when there were few in the ranks of organized labor who had any expectation of help from the White House, workers were calling the NRA the "National Run Around." On February 2 William Green threatened that the entire labor movement would oppose Roosevelt.[9]

In the meanwhile another political threat was rising. Huey Long, who had achieved the position of a major

---

9. An article in the *New York Times*, February 3, 1935, under the heading "LABOR UNIONS BREAK WITH THE NEW DEAL," reported that labor leaders were "almost in despair of making headway toward union recognition in the face of powerful industrial interests and an unsympathetic administration."

leader of mass opinion in the hinterland through his demagogic "share-the-wealth" movement, was talking about a third party. In his *Behind the Ballots* James A. Farley recalls that the Democratic National Committee, worried about the 1936 election, conducted a secret national poll to sound Long's strength. They were dismayed at what they learned. "It was easy to conceive a situation," reports Farley, "whereby Long . . . might have the balance of power in the 1936 election." Democrats also had private reports that he would be well financed if he ran. By mid-spring Professor Moley was horrified to hear Roosevelt speak of the need of doing something "to steal Long's thunder." [10]

It was at this point that the Supreme Court broke the mainspring of the original New Deal by declaring the NRA unconstitutional. Roosevelt, looking forward to 1936, now found himself in a difficult position. The Court had torn up his entire program for labor and industry. Labor seemed on the verge of withdrawing political support. Huey Long's popularity showed the dissatisfaction of a large part of the electorate. And no sign of a really decisive turn toward business recovery had yet come. The result was a sharp and sudden turn toward the left, the beginning of the second New Deal.

In June 1935 two striking measures were added to the President's list of "must" legislation: the Wagner labor-disputes bill and a drastic new "wealth tax" to steal Long's thunder. By the end of the 1935 legislative session the original New Deal, except for the AAA, was scarcely recognizable. In place of the NRA codes and the masquerade of Section 7(a) there was now a Labor Relations Board with a firm commitment to collective

---

10. The Townsend old-age pension movement was a menace of comparable importance, although it had not taken political form.

bargaining. A strong holding-company act and a stringent wealth tax stood on the books. None of these measures as they were finally enacted had been contemplated by Roosevelt at the beginning of the year. In the WPA a new relief program had been organized, with larger expenditures and a better wage scale. A Social Security Act had been passed. And at the close of the year the chief executive told Moley he was planning a "fighting speech" for his next annual message to Congress because "he was concerned about keeping his left-wing supporters satisfied."

Roosevelt's alliance with the left had not been planned; it had not even grown; it had erupted. The story of the Wagner Act, the keystone of his rapprochement with labor, and in a sense the heart of the second New Deal, is illustrative. The Wagner Act had never been an administration measure. It had been buffeted about the legislative chambers for more than a year without winning Roosevelt's interest. His Secretary of Labor recalls that he took no part in developing it, "was hardly consulted about it," and that "it did not particularly appeal to him when it was described to him." Nor did he altogether approve of the vigorous way in which it was later administered by the NLRB. Miss Perkins recalls that he was "startled" when he heard that the Board had ruled that no employer was to be able to file a petition for an election or ask the Board to settle a jurisdictional dispute. Yet under the stimulus of recovery and the protection of the NLRB, unions grew and flourished and provided the pressure in politics that gave the second New Deal its dynamic force. "A good democratic antidote for the power of big business," said Roosevelt.

Since Roosevelt was baited and frustrated by the right and adopted by the left, his ego was enlisted along with his sympathies in behalf of the popular point of view. During the formative period of the second New Deal he seems to have begun to feel that his social objectives demanded a crusade against the "autocracy." Early in 1936 at a Jackson Day dinner he made an elaborate and obvious comparison between Jackson and himself in which he observed of Jackson's hold on the common people: "They loved him for the enemies he had made." It is doubtful whether, even in Jackson's day, there had ever been such a close feeling of communion between a President and the great masses of the people as in the 1936 campaign. One incident that Roosevelt recalled for reporters touched him especially. He was driving through New Bedford, Massachusetts, when a young girl broke through the secret-service guards and passed him a pathetic note. She was a textile worker. Under the NRA she had received the minimum of eleven dollars a week, but had recently suffered a fifty per cent wage cut. "You are the only man that can do anything about it," her note ended. "Please send somebody from Washington up here to restore our minimum wages because we cannot live on $4 or $5 or $6 a week." [11] Here was common ground: the "resplendent economic autocracy" that imposed such a pitiful wage scale was the same interest that was flaying the President. Without design by either, and yet not altogether by accident, Roosevelt and the New Bedford girl had been thrown together in a league of mutual defense.

Roosevelt's second inaugural address was a lofty and benign document in which he remarked with satisfaction on the improvement of "the moral climate of

11. See Roosevelt's *Public Papers*, V, 624.

America," declared that the proper test of progress is "whether we provide enough for those who have too little," and called attention to "one-third of a nation, ill-housed, ill-clad, ill-nourished." In the first two years of his second administration he sponsored, in addition to the controversial Supreme Court reform bill, four new reform measures of broad economic importance: the Housing Act of 1937, the Fair Labor Standards Act, the Farm Security Act, and an unsuccessful proposal to set up a national string of seven TVA's. But the New Deal was designed for a capitalistic economy that, as Miss Perkins says, Roosevelt took as much for granted as he did his family. For success in attaining his stated goals of prosperity and distributive justice he was fundamentally dependent upon restoring the health of capitalism. The final part of the New Deal story can be told not only in political battles and reform legislation but in jagged movements on the business-cycle graphs.

Early in 1937, administration circles, watching the rapid rise of the business index almost to 1929 levels, became fearful of a runaway boom. Federal Reserve officials put a brake upon credit, Roosevelt called upon Congress for economies, and WPA rolls were sliced in half. Roosevelt had never publicly accepted spending as a permanent governmental policy; although he had operated upon yearly deficits, he had always promised that when the national income reached a satisfactory level he would return to balanced budgets. But events proved that he had become a prisoner of the spending expedient. As Alvin Hansen has characterized it, the 1935-7 upswing was a "consumption recovery," financed and spurred by huge government outlays. When government expenditures were cut, a sharp downward trend began, which reached alarming dimensions early in 1938. Just at this time the National

Resources Committee, an executive fact-finding agency, placed upon the President's desk a careful survey of consumer incomes for 1935–6. The committee estimated that 59 per cent of the families in the land had annual cash incomes of less than $1,250, 81 per cent less than $2,000. When this report reached him, Roosevelt knew that business conditions had again declined. There were still about 7,500,000 workers unemployed. Plainly something fundamental, something elusive, was wrong.

The New Deal had accomplished a heart-warming relief of distress, it had achieved a certain measure of recovery, it had released great forces of mass protest and had revived American liberalism, it had left upon the statute books several measures of permanent value, it had established the principle that the entire community through the agency of the federal government has some responsibility for mass welfare, and it had impressed its values so deeply upon the national mind that the Republicans were compelled to endorse its major accomplishments in election platforms. But, as Roosevelt was aware, it had failed to realize his objectives of distributive justice and sound, stable prosperity.[12]

In April 1938 Roosevelt adopted two expedients that signalized the severity of the crisis in the New Deal: one was a return to spending on a large scale, the other a crusade against monopoly. The first expedient solved the immediate crisis: Congress readily appropriated new funds, business conditions responded quickly, and

---

12. Cf. the comment of Professor Tugwell in *The Stricken Land*: "It was in economics that our troubles lay. For their solution his progressivism, his new deal, was pathetically insufficient. . . . I think . . . that he will be put down as having failed in this realm of [domestic] affairs."

the "Roosevelt recession" was soon liquidated. Henceforth Roosevelt took it for granted that the economy could not operate without the stimulus of government funds. In his memorable budget message of 1940 he finally accepted in theory what he had long been doing in fact, admitted the responsibility of government retrenchment for the recession, credited the revival of spending for the revival in business, and in general discussed the problem of the federal budget in Keynesian terms.[13]

The second expedient, the call for an attack upon monopoly, was a complete reversal of Roosevelt's philosophy of 1933 and the NRA policy. The message to Congress in which the crusade was announced—and which led to the fruitful TNEC investigations—was one of the most remarkable economic documents that has ever come from the White House. Roosevelt viewed the structure of economic and political power in broad social perspective. "Private power," he declared, was reaching a point at which it became "stronger than the democratic state itself." In the United States "a concentration of private power without equal in history is growing," which is "seriously impairing the effectiveness of private enterprise." "Private enterprise is ceasing to be free enterprise and is becoming a cluster of private collectivisms." A democratic people would no longer accept the meager standards of living caused by the failure of monopolistic industry to produce. "Big business collectivism in industry compels an ultimate collectivism in government." "The power of the few to manage the economic life of the Nation must be diffused among the many or be

13. The Hoover administration, which Roosevelt had accused of extravagance in 1932, was now criticized for having failed to spend enough to fight the depression.

transferred to the public and its democratically responsible government."

Like Wilson, Roosevelt saw the development of big business and monopoly as a menace to democratic institutions, but like Wilson and all other politicians who touched upon the so-called trust problem, he was equivocal about how this menace was to be controlled. Although his argument carried to the brink of socialism, it was not socialism that he was proposing. Nor did he propose to reverse the whole modern trend of economic integration by trying to dissolve big business, a course of action the futility of which had been demonstrated by almost fifty years of experience. The economists whose guidance he was following believed that the rigid price structure of the semi-monopolized heavy industries was throwing the whole economy out of gear. Presumably anti-trust measures were not to be used to break up big corporations but to discipline their pricing policies. How the reformist state was to police the corporations without either destroying private enterprise or itself succumbing to the massed strength of corporate opposition was not made clear. Roosevelt did not tackle such problems in theory, and events spared him the necessity of facing them in practice.

Roosevelt's sudden and desperate appeal to the ancient trust-busting device, together with his failure in the fall elections of 1938 to purge the conservative elements in his party, augured the political bankruptcy of the New Deal. The reform wave had spent itself, and the Democratic Party, divided by the Supreme Court fight and the purge and hamstrung by its large conservative bloc, was exhausted as an agency of reform. Always the realist, Roosevelt rang the death knell of the New Deal in his annual message to Congress on January 4, 1939. "We have now passed the period of internal conflict in the launching of our program of social reform," he declared. "Our full energies may now be released to invigorate the processes of recovery in order to preserve our reforms." Almost three years before Pearl Harbor his experimentation had run its course. "The processes of recovery" came only with war. "Our full energies" were never successfully released for peacetime production. What would have happened to the political fortunes of Franklin D. Roosevelt if the war had not created a new theater for his leadership?

V

When the Second World War elevated Roosevelt to a position of world importance, he had no consistent history of either isolationism or internationalism. Having begun his career in national politics as a strong navalist, an admirer of Mahan, who believed that every nation like every schoolboy was bound to come to blows with its fellows, he had turned about in the 1920 campaign to defend the League of Nations; but even then the Haiti incident revealed that he was thinking more in the lines of *Machtpolitik* than highflown internationalism. As the tide of isolationism rolled higher in the 1920's and his party dropped the League, Roosevelt went along with the trend, refusing to expose himself by defending an unpopular cause in which he had no vital interest. In 1932 he became the first Democratic candidate who explicitly repudiated the League: when William Randolph Hearst demanded a disavowal from Roosevelt in an open letter threatening to use his powerful newspaper chain against any internationalist, Roosevelt quickly capitulated. He had no regrets, he said, for his work in behalf of the League in 1920. But now the League was no longer the instrument Wilson had designed. Instead of working for world peace, it had become a mere agency for the discussion of European affairs. Had the United States entered at the beginning, the League might have become what Wilson wanted, but since it had not, "I do not favor American participation." The statement was an intense disappointment to internationalists. "Roosevelt," wrote Henry F. Pringle in the *Nation*, "hauls down banners under which he has marched in the past and unfurls no new ones to the skies."

In spite of Cordell Hull's reciprocal-trade program, New Deal economics was based essentially upon playing a lone hand. It was Roosevelt's campaign thesis that recovery must be based upon independent domestic action rather than world arrangements, and it was he who killed the London Economic Conference of 1933 with a message minimizing the importance of international monetary agreements and affirming the intention of the United States to go its own way. Busy with domestic affairs, he showed no interest in international action up to the fall of 1937, except for an unsuccessful attempt to get Congress to affiliate with the World Court. His overt policy may not have reflected his private convictions. (In 1933 he had implicitly endorsed the "Stimson doctrine" of non-recognition of Japanese penetration of China,[14] and his intimates heard him expressing a desire in the spring of 1935 "to do something" about Hitler.) But he was in no mood to try to remold the dominant isolationist and pacifist feeling

14. When Moley and Tugwell objected, the President referred to the fact that his ancestors had been active in the China trade. "I have always had the deepest sympathy with the Chinese. How could you expect me not to go along with Stimson on Japan?"

of the country. Although he was opposed to its mandatory embargo provision, he signed the isolationist Neutrality Act of 1935. The Spanish war showed how unwilling he was to lose domestic support or take the slightest risk of foreign conflict to embark upon a crusade against fascist aggression. Since the Spanish war was a civil war, the mandatory embargo on war supplies did not apply to it, but the administration tried to maintain an informal embargo against both sides. When two American exporters insisted on their legal right to sell to the Spanish Republican government, Roosevelt asked Congress to amend the Neutrality Act to cover civil wars, and the Spanish government was definitively cut off from American markets.[15] This move not only violated American diplomatic precedent and what is known as international law, but also breached the 1902 Treaty of Madrid between the United States and Spain. After Franco's victory the Roosevelt administration quickly gave official recognition to his government.

Roosevelt's first sign of a swing toward collective security came on October 5, 1937, when he proposed to "quarantine" aggressor nations and asserted that "there

15. Editing his public papers in 1941, Roosevelt insisted that it was "useless to argue" that Spain was the proper place for the European democracies to have stopped the aggressor nations. As for the United States, its people were unwilling to risk "the slightest chance of becoming involved in a quarrel in Europe which had all the possibilities of developing into a general European conflict." Further, he said, the fascists had more shipping than the Republican government, and if American goods had been available to both sides the fascists would probably have bought more. This was a shifty argument. The United States was not limited to the alternative of selling to both sides or neither. It would have been more consistent with American precedent, "international law," and American treaty obligations to continue normal economic relations with a government recognized *de jure* and to embargo shipments to a revolutionary faction.

is no escape" for the United States from international anarchy and instability "through isolation or neutrality." It remains a matter of conjecture what caused this turnabout. Hitler's power had already become imposing and, not long before, Japan had resumed its invasion of China. Hostile critics also charged, without more than circumstantial evidence, that Roosevelt was trying to distract attention from the developing business recession. What is certain is that the "quarantine speech" produced no sharp turn in public sentiment; almost a year later, in September 1938, the Gallup poll showed that only 34 per cent of American voters favored selling arms and ammunition to England and France in case of a war with the Axis. Within seven months Hitler violated the Munich agreement and took Prague and Memel, and the figure went from 34 to 68 per cent.

During this period a deep fissure appeared in the American public mind. The typical American was afraid that if Germany overwhelmed the western democratic powers, the United States would ultimately have to face the military might of fascism alone. But he was also desperately anxious to stay out of war. When war began he wanted to aid the Allies, to become a silent partner against the Axis, and yet to avoid hostilities. Roosevelt's foreign policy had always been shaped with due regard to the state of domestic opinion, and now his public statements closely reflected this ambiguity in American intentions. "We know," he said to Congress in January 1939, "what might happen to us of the United States if the new philosophies of force were to encompass the other continents and invade our own." When the war began, however, he said: "I hope the United States will keep out. . . . Every effort of your government will be directed toward that end." On January 3, 1940 he noted that "there is a vast difference between keeping out of war and pretending that this war is none of our business." The fall of France, which broke down all pretense of American "neutrality," did not end the general hope that actual involvement could be avoided. In 1940 Roosevelt and Willkie and their party platforms promised aid to countries fighting the Axis; both promised again and again that they would not take the country into war. Shortly after the campaign was over, Roosevelt said: "Our national policy is not directed toward war. Its sole purpose is to keep war away from our country and our people." In the same speech, however, he described the United States as "the great arsenal of democracy," and stated that "no dictator, no combination of dictators," could weaken American determination to aid Britain. During 1940 and 1941 he sponsored many measures that flouted neutrality, including the trade of destroyers for naval bases, the Lend-Lease Act, occupation of Greenland and Iceland, patrolling the waters between the United States and Iceland, and constructing a naval base in Northern Ireland. In September 1941 hostilities took place between a German submarine and an American destroyer. The following month the President announced in a Navy Day speech that "America has been attacked," and "the shooting has started." The nation was already engaged in undeclared naval hostilities, but the final public reluctance to wage open warfare made decisive use of national resources impossible. Roosevelt was in a difficult position, but the Japanese attack at Pearl Harbor did for him what the Confederate attack on Sumter had done for Lincoln.

Roosevelt died before the practical direction of his postwar policies became clear. He left a good deal in words, promises, and statements of general objectives, but not much to tell how they were to be translated into action. Since 1935 he had become accustomed to appeal to a liberal audience at home, and presumably to think in the popular humanistic language of the progressive tradition. During the 1944 campaign he talked of guaranteeing broad security and welfare to the people through an "economic bill of rights," of which the most vital was "the right of a useful and remunerative job." But lest anyone imagine that this involved a drastic reconstruction of economic life going far beyond the New Deal, he also spoke of "full production and full employment under our democratic system of private enterprise, with Government encouragement and aid whenever and wherever that is necessary." "I believe in free enterprise and always have," he reiterated. "I believe that private enterprise can give full employment to our people." Abandoning the "matured economy" theory of his Commonwealth Club speech, he spoke hopefully of "an expansion of our peacetime productive capacity that will require new facilities, new plants, new equipment —capable of hiring millions of men." With the economy operating at full speed under wartime conditions it was easy for him to forget the incompleteness of recovery under the New Deal and to refer proudly to the manner in which "we . . . fought our way out of the economic crisis."

He showed a like optimism about foreign relations. In January 1945 he told Congress that the misuse of power could no longer be a controlling factor in international life. "Power must be linked with responsibility and obliged to defend and justify itself within the framework of the general good." He spoke of "a people's peace" based upon independence and self-determination, and expressed his intention that the United Nations should have "the power to act quickly and

decisively to keep the peace by force, if necessary."
Returning from Yalta shortly before his death, he said
cheerfully of his relations with Churchill and Stalin:
"We achieved a unity of thought and a way of getting
along together." The Crimean conference spelled "the
end of the system of unilateral action and exclusive
alliances and spheres of influence and balance of power
and all the other expedients that have been tried for
centuries and have always failed."

That Roosevelt ever had deep faith in the United
Nations as an agency of world peace is doubtful. His
original and spontaneous reaction was to seek for peace
and stability not through a general concert of all the
nations but rather through a four-power establishment
of the United States, Great Britain, Russia, and China,
which was to police the world. Cordell Hull reports
that in the spring of 1943 Roosevelt wanted all other
nations, including France, to be disarmed. "He believed," says Hull, "in the efficacy of direct personal
contact between Churchill, Stalin, Chiang Kai-shek,
and himself, and he thought that this direct relationship among the chiefs of the four nations would result
in efficient future management of the world." Rather
than an overall world organization he favored regional
organizations, which were to leave all questions of
peace and security to the four great powers. Once
when Secretary Hull and some internationalist visitors
who wanted a world organization asked him: "Aren't
you at least in favor of a world secretariat?" he laugh-
ingly replied: "I'll give you the Pentagon or the Empire
State Building. You can put the world secretariat there."
By the summer of 1943, however, he had accepted the
idea of world organization and in the fall he approved
the draft of the four-nation declaration adopted at the
Moscow Conference of that year, which called for "a

general international organization . . . for the maintenance of international peace and security."

Roosevelt has often been criticized for a tendency to think that a clash of interests or principles can be resolved by bringing together two representatives of opposing forces and persuading them to shake hands and be convivial. It was natural to his mode of thought to rest his hopes for future peace upon personal amenability and personal understandings among the leaders of the great powers. In this sense his philosophy of international relations, however democratic as to ends, was far from democratic as to means. In the case of Russia he seems at one time to have had the curious idea that dealing with a dictatorship might be easier than dealing with a parliamentary democracy. "What helps a lot," Vice Admiral Ross T. McIntire remembers him saying, "is that Stalin is the only man I have to convince. Joe doesn't worry about a Congress or a Parliament. He's the whole works." [16] His position between Churchill and Stalin was that of a compromiser and mediator, in the spirit of "weave the two together," and he evidently felt that it would continue to be necessary to "referee" between Britain and Russia. As he had once stood between the Al Smith men and the rural Protestant Democrats, later between the NAM and William Green, and still later between Jesse Jones and Henry Wallace, he now felt that he stood between Soviet and British imperialisms.

How did he propose to deal with these imperialisms? The answer is clearer in the case of England and the

---

16. Arthur Bliss Lane, in *I Saw Poland Betrayed*, comments on Roosevelt's "exaggerated confidence in the power of his charm to persuade diplomatic and political adversaries of his point of view. He seemed to feel that this charm was particularly effective on Stalin."

other western European imperial powers. Roosevelt was moved by the plight of the colonial peoples,[17] he hoped to better their condition, and felt that it would be necessary to loosen the bonds of the British, French, and Dutch empires; he believed that the British and French were informally leagued together to sustain each other's colonial possessions. Further, the United States was handicapped in its conduct of the war in the East by the keen resentment of British imperialism among Oriental peoples. During the war American influence was thrown on the side of the colonial peoples, and ultimate independence for India, Burma, Syria, and Lebanon was proposed. At one time Roosevelt said to his son Elliott that postwar discussions should take up the status of India, Burma, Java, Indo-China, Indonesia, the African colonies, Egypt, and Palestine. Secretary Hull records, however, that Britain, France, and the Netherlands were not pressed at any time for an immediate grant of self-government to their colonies. This, it was expected, "would come in time."

Roosevelt's opposition to the colonial empires was not simply altruistic; American commercial interests—for instance, the vast oil concessions that had been made to American companies in Saudi Arabia—were much in his mind. Although he believed that "imperialists"—he

---

17. In a memorandum to Cordell Hull, January 12, 1944, he wrote concerning the plight of Iran that ninety-nine per cent of its people were in bondage to the other one per cent and "do not own their own land and cannot keep their own production or convert it into money or property." "I was rather thrilled," he added, "with the idea of using Iran as an example of what we could do by an unselfish American policy. . . ." Not long afterward he wrote to Hull of his conviction that Indo-China should become independent, rather than revert to France. "France has had the country—thirty million inhabitants—for nearly one hundred years, and the people are worse off than they were at the beginning."

used the word as an epithet—had been short-sighted in taking a purely exploitative view of the colonies and that much greater potentialities lay in them if the welfare of the colonial peoples was taken into account, he was also aware of the possibilities for American trade in an economic revivification of the colonial areas under American encouragement. Elliott Roosevelt pictures him talking with the Sultan in Churchill's presence about concessions for American firms in Morocco, and promising Chiang Kai-shek that if Chiang came to terms with the Chinese Communists and democratized his government he would support him in trying to terminate the special rights of the Western empires in Hong Kong, Shanghai, and Canton.

Roosevelt appears to have believed that the ruthless imperialism of the older colonial powers might be replaced by a liberal and benevolent American penetration that would be of advantage both to the natives and to American commerce.[18] He believed that British and German bankers had had world trade "pretty well sewn up in their pockets for a long time," to the disadvantage of the United States. Arguing that "equality of peoples involves the utmost freedom of competitive trade," he appealed to Churchill to open markets "for healthy competition" and to dissolve the British Empire trade agreements.[19]

---

18. During the nineteenth century Britain had played some such role in Latin America and southern and eastern Europe, supporting nationalism and independence for oppressed peoples and reaping trade advantages from the disintegration of other empires.

19. Roosevelt was by no means indifferent to the coming post-war problems of Great Britain's economy. He was much concerned with maintaining Britain's export market, which he felt should be done at Germany's expense. His dominating conception was that Britain's economic fortunes were inverse to Germany's. Although he privately repudiated the idea expressed in the Que-

All this seems characteristic—the quick sympathy with oppressed colonials, the ideal of liberation and welfare, and yet the calculating interest in American advantage. Just as the Chamber of Commerce's NRA idea had been clothed in the language of the liberal social planners and had brought gains to the most hard-ridden sections of the working class, so a new American conquest of world markets might well go forth under the banner of international welfare work.

It was not as evident during Roosevelt's life how critical American-Russian relations would be, and in this sphere his conceptions were not so sharply defined. In February 1940, at the time of the Russo-Finnish war, he had said that Russia, "as everybody who has the courage to face the facts knows, is run by a dictatorship as absolute as any other dictatorship in the world." But when he met the absolute dictator at Teheran he found him "altogether impressive." "I'm sure we'll hit it off," he said to Elliott, and later remarked that he liked working wtih Stalin because there was "nothing devious" about his talk. He seemed to think that he had impressed upon Stalin that the United States and Britain were not allied in a bloc against the Soviet Union. "If I can convince him," he said to Vice Admiral McIntire, "that our offer of cooperation is on the square and that we want to be comrades rather than enemies, I'm betting that he'll come in." If Roosevelt ever outlined a specific strategy to cope with an aggressive Soviet imperialism, it has not yet been pub-

bec Conference of making Germany an "agricultural and pastoral nation," he did feel that postwar control of the German economy should be so managed as to work to Britain's advantage. The British Empire must not be permitted to collapse while Germany built up her exports and a new armaments capacity. "The real nub of the situation," he wrote to Hull, "is to keep Britain from going into complete bankruptcy at the end of the war."

lished. At the time of his death the pattern of the "cold war" was only beginning to emerge. Certainly he had no magic formula for getting along with the Russians. James F. Byrnes has taken pains to blast "the legend that our relations with the Soviet Union began to deteriorate only after his death," by revealing that Stalin charged the Anglo-American allies with making separate and secret peace arrangements with Germany in the spring of 1945 and that he angered Roosevelt by questioning the truthfulness of Roosevelt's denials. On the day of his death Roosevelt sent a message to Churchill advising that in a forthcoming speech to the House of Commons "the general Soviet problem" should be minimized. He added: "We must be firm, however, and our course thus far is correct."

It was an ambitious plan of action that Roosevelt outlined in the last year of his life—to lead the nation toward full production and full employment, to realize a sweeping bill of economic rights under private enterprise, enlarge American trade abroad, serve as a diplomatic buffer between Britain and Russia and between China and all the powers that harassed her, dissect the great colonial empires, and bring sanitation, justice, and freedom to the colonial underdogs. This combination, as motley as the various undertakings of the early New Deal, has come to seem even less feasible in the years since Roosevelt's death than it did during his lifetime; but the world of 1942-5 has been transformed, and it is idle to project too far into the future the plans of such a changeable statesman. To take his statements literally, to look upon them as anything more than a rhetorical formulation of his preferences, would be a mistake; there seems no more reason to take his words as a literal guide to his projected action than there would have been to expect him to fulfill both his 1932 pledges to balance the budget and give adequate relief to the unemployed.

Roosevelt seems a more flexible and a cleverer politician than Wilson, much his superior in the craft of maneuver, but less serious, less deliberate, and less responsible. What we know of his conduct at the international conferences with Stalin and Churchill compares unfavorably in moral tone if not in practical effect with Wilson's at Versailles. It is hard to imagine Wilson trying to smooth over a conflict between Stalin and Churchill over the prospective treatment of captured Nazis with a joke about the precise number that would have to be killed. It is almost as hard to imagine Roosevelt expressing any such poignant understanding of the human consequences of the war on the home front as Wilson expressed to Frank Cobb, or straining as desperately at Yalta or Teheran as Wilson did at Paris for detailed factual understanding, for intellectual consistency and moral responsibility.

Roosevelt's reputation, however, will remain greater than Wilson's, and in good part because the circumstances of his martyrdom were more auspicious. Wilson died only after his defeat was a matter of historical record; Roosevelt died in the midst of things, and it is still possible for those under his spell to believe that everything would have been different if only he had survived to set the world on the right path in the postwar period. Further, the very lack of confidence in the American future and of a positive program of ideas increases popular faith in the wonder-working powers of the great man. Roosevelt is bound to be the dominant figure in the mythology of any resurgent American liberalism. There are ample texts in his writings for men of good will to feed upon; but it would be fatal to rest content with his belief in personal benevolence, personal arrangements, the sufficiency of good intentions and month-to-month improvisation, without trying to achieve a more inclusive and systematic conception of what is happening in the world.

ACKNOWLEDGMENTS

Oₙₑ who attempts a work of this sort is singularly dependent upon the counsel and criticism of friends. I have received a great deal of patient and invaluable criticism at several stages in the preparation of the manuscript, and my moments of complaisance here admitted many improvements; my bursts of obstinacy, however, should spare others all responsibility for the eccentricities and errors of my interpretations. The manuscript was read in whole or in large part by Frank Freidel, Alfred Kazin, William Miller, C. Wright Mills, Irving Sanes, Roger Shugg, Kenneth M. Stampp, Harold Strauss, and Harvey Swados. Chapters I and II were read by John A. Krout and Dumas Malone, III by Walton Bean, V by Reinhard Luthin, IX by Howard Beale, XI and XII by Virginia Buckner Miller. I am especially indebted to my wife, Beatrice Kevitt Hofstadter, for several perceptive readings and for her fine editorial talent.

BIBLIOGRAPHICAL ESSAY

❦

These bibliographical comments are intended to exhaust neither the available literature on the subjects nor the materials I have consulted. They do include, however, my chief sources of factual matter and the writings that have directly influenced my interpretations.

I. THE FOUNDING FATHERS

THE literature on the making of the Constitution is voluminous. Max Farrand, ed.: *The Records of the Federal Convention* (4 volumes, New Haven, 1911–37) is indispensable. The records of convention proceedings have also been rearranged in topical order by Arthur T. Prescott in *The Framing of the Constitution* (Baton Rouge, 1941), an extremely useful work. Jonathan Elliot: *Debates* (5 volumes, Washington, 1836–45) is the standard collection of debates over ratification. A fund of primary material, chiefly in the form of letters, may be found in the valuable pages of Charles Warren's *The Making of the Constitution* (Boston, 1928), which suffers at points from its apologetic tone. There are innumerable editions of *The Federalist*, by Hamilton, Madison, and Jay. John Adams's *Defence of the Constitutions of Government of the United States of America* and *Discourses on Davila* are in his *Works*, ed. by Charles F. Adams (Boston, 1851), Vols. IV and VI, and the quoted letters to John Taylor of Caroline as well as other letters with illuminating matter on his social ideas are in Vol. VI. Adrienne Koch and William Peden: *The Selected Writings of John and John Quincy Adams* (New York, 1946) is a volume of well-chosen documents.

Among secondary works on the Constitution-makers first place belongs to Charles A. Beard's great study: *An Economic Interpretation of the Constitution of the United States* (New York, 1913). I have used the more recent 1935 edition with the new introductory essay by Professor Beard. His observations on the same subject in *The Republic* (New York, 1943) have a somewhat different emphasis. J. Allen Smith's *The Spirit of American Government* (New York, 1907) still stands out for its perceptive treatment of the intentions and political ideas of the Constitution-makers. Robert L. Schuyler in *The Constitution of the United States* (New York, 1923) sets forth convincingly the thesis that the points of agreement among the Convention delegates were far more important than the differences that had to be compromised.

V. L. Parrington's brief account of the ideas behind the debate over the Constitution in Vol. I of *Main Currents in American Thought* (New York, 1927) is deft and informative. Merle Curti: *The Growth of American Thought* (New York, 1943) is extremely valuable in placing the intellectual issues in their social context. The conservative spirit of the Enlightenment thinkers is stressed in Charles A. and Mary R. Beard: *The American Spirit* (New York, 1943). I have been greatly stimulated by the treatment of seventeenth- and eighteenth-century political thinking in George H. Sabine's masterful *A History of Political Theory* (New York, 1937), and I have also used William S. Carpenter's *Development of American Political Thought* (Princeton, 1930). Two delightful books by Carl Becker: *The Declaration of Independence* (New York, 1922, 1942) and *The Heavenly City of the Eighteenth Century Philosophers* (New Haven, 1932) are superb guides to the eighteenth-century mind.

There are valuable essays on the intellectual background of the Constitution in Conyers Read, ed.: *The Constitution*

Reconsidered (New York, 1938), among which I found especially helpful the contributions of Stanley Pargellis, R. M. MacIver, Gaetano Salvemini, and Roland Bainton. Walton Hamilton and Douglass Adair stress the mercantilist economic ideas of the Fathers in *The Power to Govern* (New York, 1937). Information on foreign influences on the Fathers' political ideas may be found in Paul Spurlin: *Montesquieu in America, 1760–1801* (Baton Rouge, 1940), and Archibald Cary Coolidge's suggestive essay: *Theoretical and Foreign Elements in the Formation of the American Constitution* (Freiburg, 1892). I have profited much from several chapters in the first volume of Joseph Dorfman's *The Economic Mind in American Civilization* (2 volumes, New York, 1946). H. F. Russell Smith: *Harrington and His Oceana* (Cambridge, 1914) is valuable. Correa M. Walsh: *The Political Science of John Adams* (New York, 1915) is a thorough study. A perceptive short account of Adams's ideas may be found in chapter xi of Charles A. Beard's *Economic Origins of Jeffersonian Democracy* (New York, 1915). Rexford Guy Tugwell and Joseph Dorfman in two articles, "Alexander Hamilton, Nation Maker," *Columbia University Quarterly*, December 1937 and March 1938, have said much in little. Harold W. Bradley: "The Political Thinking of George Washington," *Journal of Southern History*, Vol. XI (November 1945), pp. 469–86, is a good brief analysis.

Among general histories of the Confederation period, Allan Nevins: *The American States during and after the Revolution 1775–1789* (New York, 1924) stands out for fullness of information on affairs within the states. E. B. Greene: *The Revolutionary Generation* (New York, 1943) has some background material. Merrill Jensen: *The Articles of Confederation* (Madison, 1940) is a distinguished study. My conception of the larger historical background of this period owes much to the perceptive interpretations of Curtis Nettels's outstanding history of colonial America: *The Roots of American Civilization* (New York, 1938). Louise B. Dunbar: *A Study of "Monarchical" Tendencies in the United States from 1776 to 1801* (Urbana, 1922) proved valuable.

The standard biography of Madison is Gaillard Hunt's *Life of James Madison* (New York, 1902), but Irving Brant has brought out the first two volumes of a more recent study. Gilbert Chinard's *Honest John Adams* (Boston, 1933) is useful, but the definitive biography has yet to be written. See also James Truslow Adams: *The Adams Family* (Boston, 1930). Frank Monaghan's *John Jay* (New York and Indianapolis, 1935) is the source of the maxim by Jay.

I have found the following classic writings of special help in understanding the intellectual background of the Constitution: Aristotle's *Politics*, especially Book III, chapter viii, and Book IV, chapters xi–xii; Montesquieu: *Spirit of Laws*, especially Book XI; Harrington: *Oceana;* Locke: *Of Civil Government;* and Hobbes: *Leviathan.*

II. THOMAS JEFFERSON

NONE of the editions of Jefferson's writings is entirely adequate. I have used the edition of Paul L. Ford (10 volumes, New York, 1892–9). Saul Padover: *The Complete Jefferson* (New York, 1943) has all of Jefferson's systematic writings in one convenient volume, but only a handful of his letters. There is a good selection of important letters in Adrienne Koch and William Peden: *The Life and Selected Writings of Thomas Jefferson* (New York, 1944). Bernard Mayo in *Jefferson Himself* (Boston, 1942) has arranged in chronological order from varied writings a full Jefferson autobiography that is of exceptional value. See also Paul Wilstach, ed.: *Correspondence of John Adams and Thomas Jefferson* (Indianapolis, 1925), and Dumas Malone, ed.: *Correspondence between Thomas Jefferson and Du Pont de Nemours* (Boston and New York, 1930).

The classic biography upon which other biographers have always relied is Henry S. Randall's *The Life of Thomas Jefferson* (3 volumes, New York, 1858). A full, well-rounded modern biography is yet to appear. Gilbert Chinard: *Thomas*

Jefferson, the Apostle of Americanism (Boston, 1929), the product of years of careful and original investigation into Jefferson's intellectual life, is outstanding among modern studies. Albert Jay Nock's *Jefferson* (New York, 1926) is a superb biographical essay, beautifully written and penetrating in analysis; Mr. Nock understands Jefferson so well that one despairs of going at all beyond him, especially in a brief essay. Marie Kimball: *Jefferson, the Road to Glory* (New York, 1943), which covers Jefferson's early career, contains some remarkably loose thinking about the significance of his Virginia reforms. By far the best work on Jefferson's life to 1784 is Dumas Malone's *Jefferson the Virginian* (Boston, 1948).

The work which above all others sheds light on the Jeffersonian period in American politics is Charles A. Beard's *Economic Origins of Jeffersonian Democracy* (New York, 1915), and like everyone else who touches on the period I am under especial obligation to it. Claude Bowers: *Jefferson and Hamilton* (Boston and New York, 1933) and *Jefferson in Power* (Boston, 1936) are partisan but useful. C. M. Wiltse: *The Jeffersonian Tradition in American Democracy* (Chapel Hill, 1935) is a stimulating discussion of intellectual currents. A competent study of Jefferson's abstract interests can be found in Adrienne Koch: *The Philosophy of Thomas Jefferson* (New York, 1943). On Jefferson and classical antiquity see Karl Lehmann: *Thomas Jefferson, American Humanist* (New York, 1947). Two institutional aspects of Jefferson's democracy are studied in Roy Honeywell: *The Educational Work of Thomas Jefferson* (Cambridge, 1931), and Frank L. Mott: *Jefferson and the Press* (Baton Rouge, 1943). Henry Steele Commager: *Majority Rule and Minority Rights* (New York, 1943) deals with Jefferson's attitude toward the judiciary and his belief in periodic constitutional revision.

On the world-historic context of Jefferson's liberalism I have benefited by reading Harold J. Laski's *Rise of European Liberalism* (London, 1936), and of course Carl Becker's *The Declaration of Independence* (New York, 1922, 1942). On Jefferson's economic views the essay by Joseph Dorfman in *The Economic Mind in American Civilization* is valuable. On Jefferson and the physiocrats see the excellent introduction by Gilbert Chinard in his edition of *The Correspondence of Jefferson and Du Pont de Nemours* (Baltimore, 1931), and Richard Hofstadter: "Parrington and the Jeffersonian Tradition," *Journal of the History of Ideas,* Vol. II (October 1941), pp. 391–400. There is a perceptive account of Jefferson in France in Charles D. Hazen: *Contemporary American Opinion of the French Revolution* (Baltimore, 1897). On John Taylor of Caroline, whose work sheds so much light on Jeffersonian democracy, see Eugene T. Mudge: *The Social Philosophy of John Taylor of Caroline* (New York, 1939), and Taylor's own writings, especially *Arator* (Georgetown, 1814) and *Inquiry into the Principles and Policy of the Government of the United States* (Fredericksburg, 1814). See also H. H. Simms: *Life of John Taylor* (Richmond, 1932). Manning J. Dauer and Hans Hammond in "John Taylor: Democrat or Aristocrat?" *Journal of Politics,* Vol. VI (November 1944), pp. 381–403, take a view of the subject that is congenial to the thesis of this chapter. A. Whitney Griswold: "The Agrarian Democracy of Thomas Jefferson," *American Political Science Review,* Vol. XL (August 1946), pp. 657–81, is successful in putting Jefferson in his historical context.

On Jefferson's local environment Charles H. Ambler: *Sectionalism in Virginia from 1776 to 1861* (Chicago, 1910) is helpful, as is H. J. Eckenrode: *The Revolution in Virginia* (Boston and New York, 1916). Clarence R. Keim: *The Influence of Primogeniture and Entail in the Development of Virginia,* unpublished doctoral dissertation, University of Chicago, 1926, helps to set the Virginia reforms in proper perspective. Henry Adams: *History of the United States of America* (9 volumes, New York, 1889–98) has many insights. There is a mass of material in Albert J. Beveridge: *Life of John Marshall* (4 volumes, Boston and New York, 1916–19), but on the interpretative side the work is a Federalist tract. Louis M. Sears: *Jefferson and the Embargo* (Durham, 1927) takes as favorable a view as possible of that ill-fated experiment. Julius W. Pratt: *Expansionists of 1812* (New York, 1925) is the classic account of the aims of Republican Party War Hawks. On the circumstances under which the Republicans chartered a second national bank, see Ralph H. C. Catterall: *The Second Bank of the United States* (Chicago, 1903), chapter i.

III. ANDREW JACKSON

THE most important sources for Jackson are John Spencer Bassett, ed.: *Correspondence of Andrew Jackson* (6 volumes, Washington, 1926–33), and J. D. Richardson, ed.: *Message and Papers of the Presidents* (Washington, 1896), Vols. II and III. The old study by James Parton: *A Life of Andrew Jackson* (3 volumes, New York, 1859–60) is based on letters and interviews with contemporaries. For biographical matter I have generally followed the more recent critical study by John Spencer Bassett: *Life of Andrew Jackson* (2 volumes, New York, 1928). See also Marquis James: *The Life of Andrew Jackson* (2 volumes, Indianapolis, 1938). The old study by William Graham Sumner: *Andrew Jackson* (Boston, 1882) is especially good on financial matters. Thomas Perkins Abernethy, in *From Frontier to Plantation in Tennessee* (Chapel Hill, 1932) and his sketch of Jackson in the *Dictionary of American Biography*, is indispensable on Jackson in Tennessee, but takes an unduly hostile view of his subject. Professor Abernethy is bitterly critical of Jackson's pretensions to democracy. A contrary view is argued by Arda Walker in "Andrew Jackson: Frontier Democrat," *East Tennessee Historical Society Publications* No. 18 (1946), pp. 59–86; although her conclusion is questionable, her review of the evidence is of considerable value.

On the frontier, frontiersmen, and the Jackson period in general, I with all students of American history have benefited from the great work of Frederick Jackson Turner, especially *The Frontier in American History* (New York,

1921), *The Rise of the New West* (New York, 1906), and *The United States, 1830–1850* (New York, 1935). W. J. Cash's brilliant impressionistic work, *The Mind of the South* (New York, 1941), has been highly suggestive. On the early background of the Jacksonian period I have profited by reading Carl Russell Fish: *The Rise of the Common Man* (New York, 1927), John Krout and Dixon Ryan Fox: *The Completion of Independence* (New York, 1944), Wilfred E. Binkley: *American Political Parties* (New York, 1943), Kirk Porter: *A History of Suffrage in the United States* (Chicago, 1918), W. E. Stanwood: *A History of Presidential Elections* (Boston, 1884), Dixon Ryan Fox's study *The Decline of Aristocracy in the Politics of New York* (New York, 1919), and Samuel Rezneck: "The Depression of 1819–22, A Social History," *American Historical Review*, Vol. XXXIX (October 1933), pp. 28–47. Herman Hailperin: "Pro-Jackson Sentiment in Pennsylvania," *Pennsylvania Magazine of History and Biography*, Vol. L (July 1926), pp. 193–238, is a case study in the rise of Jackson support in a Jackson stronghold. M. Ostrogorski, in his classic work *Democracy and the Organization of Political Parties* (New York, 1902), Vol. II, chapters i–ii, traces with brilliant insight the revolution in political techniques and political personnel that I believe to be the essence of the origins of Jacksonian democracy. See also Carl Russell Fish: *The Civil Service and the Patronage* (New York, 1905). However, the late E. M. Eriksson's important paper "The Federal Civil Service under President Jackson," *Mississippi Valley Historical Review*, Vol. XIII (March 1927), pp. 517–40, is a definitive refutation of the charge that Jackson was in some special sense the founder of the national spoils system; his findings lead to the contrary suggestion that, especially considering the circumstances that brought him to office, Jackson exercised commendable restraint in the removal of public officials. On the decline of the caucus in this relation see, in addition to Ostrogorski, Frederick Dallinger: *Nominations for Elective Office in the United States* (New York, 1897), and C. S. Thompson's brief essay: *The Rise and Fall of the Congressional Caucus*

(New Haven, 1902). The important campaign that brought Jackson to power is treated with illumination in Florence Weston: *The Presidential Election of 1828* (Washington, 1938), and in Culver H. Smith: "Propaganda Technique in the Jackson Campaign of 1828," *East Tennessee Historical Society Publications* No. 6 (1934), pp. 44–66. For a bitter account of some of Jackson's political methods, see Richard R. Stenberg, "Jackson, Buchanan, and the 'Corrupt Bargain' Calumny," *Pennsylvania Magazine of History and Biography*, Vol. LVIII (January 1934), pp. 61–85.

Arthur M. Schlesinger, Jr.: *The Age of Jackson* (Boston, 1945), is a major work which, among its other merits, serves as a valuable corrective of the Turner emphasis on the West. See, however, the judicious criticism of Schlesinger in Bray Hammond's review, *Journal of Economic History*, Vol. VI (May 1946), pp. 79–84, which expresses a view of the significance of the period more akin to my own. William E. Dodd presents a shrewd analysis in parts of his *Expansion and Conflict* (Boston, 1915). *The Autobiography of Martin Van Buren* (Washington, 1920), edited by John C. Fitzpatrick, and Thomas Hart Benton's *Thirty Years' View* (2 volumes, New York, 1854–6) are important sources.

Ralph C. H. Catterall: *The Second Bank of the United States* (Chicago, 1903) remains the indispensable source on the bank and the bank war. Bray Hammond: "Jackson, Biddle, and the Bank of the United States," *Journal of Economic History*, Vol. VII (May 1947), pp. 1–23, is a defense of Biddle that does not ignore the banker's failings; but more important, it has, to my knowledge, the wisest and best-balanced estimate of the bank controversy, and it does justice to some of the complexities of the problem that I have had to pass by. Perhaps the best account of the controversy from the Jacksonian standpoint is in Carl Brent Swisher's excellent *Roger B. Taney* (New York, 1935). All the quotations I have taken from Nicholas Biddle are in Reginald C. McGrane's useful collection: *The Correspondence of Nicholas Biddle* (Boston, 1919). See also McGrane's *The Panic of 1837* (Chicago, 1924). For the bank issue in the campaign see

S. R. Gammon, Jr.: *The Presidential Campaign of 1832* (Baltimore, 1922), and Glyndon G. Van Deusen: *The Life of Henry Clay* (Boston, 1937). The limitations of the Jacksonian position on bank notes and the source of the distinction between the function of note issue and the functions of discount and deposit are explained in Harry E. Miller's scholarly study: *Banking Theories in the United States before 1860* (Cambridge, 1927). Sister M. Grace Madeleine's *Monetary and Banking Theories of Jacksonian Democracy* (Philadelphia, 1943) views wildcat banking as a phase of the history of laissez-faire in America. On some sources of anti-bank views see also William E. Smith: *The Francis Preston Blair Family in Politics*, Vol. I (New York, 1933). St. George L. Sioussat: "Some Phases of Tennessee Politics in the Jackson Period," *American Historical Review*, Vol. XIV (October 1908), concludes that Jackson's ideas about banks were deep-seated prejudices and not the results of local experience.

Two invaluable sources on the views of hard-money Jacksonians are Theodore Sedgwick, Jr., ed.: *A Collection of the Political Writings of William Leggett* (2 volumes, New York, 1840), and William M. Gouge: *A Short History of Paper Money and Banking in the United States* (Philadelphia, 1833). See also F. Byrdsall: *The History of the Loco-Foco or Equal Rights Party* (New York, 1842). An important article on the split in the Democratic Party is William Trimble: "Diverging Tendencies in New York Democracy in the Period of the Locofocos," *American Historical Review*, Vol. XXIX (April 1919), pp. 398–421. The same author in "The Social Philosophy of the Locofoco Democracy," *American Journal of Sociology*, Vol. XXVI (May 1921), pp. 705–15, views this left wing of the Jacksonian movement, mistakenly I believe, as "nascent proletarianism." For a corrective of this viewpoint see the treatment of Jacksonian democracy in Joseph Dorfman's *Economic Mind in American Civilization*, Vol. II, and in the same author's interesting essay: "The Jackson Wage-earner Thesis." There is a concurrent view in Richard Hofstadter: "William Leggett,

Spokesman of Jacksonian Democracy," *Political Science Quarterly*, Vol. XLVIII (December 1943), pp. 581–94, and much substantiating evidence in Walter Hugins: "Ely Moore, the Career of a Jacksonian Labor Leader," unpublished master's essay, Columbia University, 1947. On the continuity between Jeffersonian and Jacksonian laissez-faire ideology, see Hofstadter: "Parrington and the Jeffersonian Tradition."

The literature on economic development and social structure in the Jackson period is very inadequate. Bray Hammond's article: "Free Banks and Corporations: The New York Free Banking Act of 1838," *Journal of Political Economy*, Vol. XLIV (April 1936), is very valuable. General corporation history has been too little explored, but William Miller: "A Note on the History of Business Corporations in Pennsylvania," *Quarterly Journal of Economics*, Vol. LV (November 1940), pp. 150–60, is valuable bibliographically and otherwise. Charles Haar: "Legislative Regulation of New York Industrial Corporations, 1800–1850," *New York History*, Vol. XXII (April 1941), pp. 191–207, emphasizes the growing control of the industrial type of corporation by the legislature. Guy S. Callender: "Early Transportation and Banking Enterprises of the States in Relation to the Growth of Corporations," *Quarterly Journal of Economics*, Vol. XVII (November 1902), pp. 111–62, covers a great deal of territory. John R. Commons et al.: *History of Labour*, Vol. I, is helpful but not definitive on the state of labor development. On Taney's Court in relation to property rights and corporations, see Benjamin F. Wright: *The Contract Clause of the Constitution* (Cambridge, 1938), chapter iii, and the discriminating discussion in chapter xii.

IV. JOHN C. CALHOUN

CALHOUN's *Works* (New York, 1854) were edited in six volumes by his friend Richard K. Crallé, with brief and sometimes inaccurate commentary. His formal political writings, *A Disquisition on Government* and *A Discourse on the Constitution and Government of the United States,* both posthumously published, are in Vol. I. The indispensable *Correspondence of John C. Calhoun* (Washington, 1900), edited by J. Franklin Jameson, contains most of the Carolinian's letters and many written to him. There are more of the latter in *Correspondence Addressed to John C. Calhoun, 1837–1849* (Washington, 1930), edited by Chauncey S. Boucher and R. P. Brooks.

William M. Meigs: *The Life of John Caldwell Calhoun* (2 volumes, New York, 1917) is the most substantial biography despite its intellectual superficiality. Gaillard Hunt: *John C. Calhoun* (Philadelphia, 1907) is an interesting biographical essay. Hermann von Holst's hostile study: *John C. Calhoun* (Boston, 1900) is outmoded at several points by modern scholarship. Charles M. Wiltse in his *John C. Calhoun: Nationalist, 1782–1828* (Indianapolis, 1944) has made the only recent biographical study of scholarly worth. I have followed Professor Wiltse on several points, including the still arguable question whether the authorized campaign biography of Calhoun published in 1843 was written by the Carolinian himself; Meigs and Hunt say yes, Wiltse no. Richard Current in his brilliant essay: "John C. Calhoun, Philosopher of Reaction," *Antioch Review* (Summer 1943), pp. 223–34, has done more than anyone else in the past generation or so to say something new about Calhoun's ideas; he emphasizes very strongly the aspects of Calhoun's thinking that I have chosen to dwell upon, and I am most intensely indebted to him. Gamaliel Bradford's sensitive essay on the Carolinian in *As God Made Them* (Boston, 1929) is one of his best psychographs. William E. Dodd's treatment in *Statesmen of the Old South* (New York, 1911) is suggestive, although not always precise.

The Carolina background is treated illuminatingly in William A. Schaper: *Sectionalism and Representation in South Carolina* (Washington, 1901); C. S. Boucher: "Sectionalism, Representation, and the Electoral Question in Ante-Bellum South Carolina," *Washington University Studies,*

Vol. IV (1916), which shows Calhoun as a powerful opponent of any attempt to agitate local questions and thus weaken the state in its relation to the federal government; Boucher's "The Secession and Cooperation Movements in South Carolina, 1848 to 1852," ibid., Vol. V (1918); John H. Wolfe: *Jeffersonian Democracy in South Carolina* (Chapel Hill, 1940); and Philip M. Hamer: *The Secession Movement in South Carolina, 1847–1852* (Allentown, 1918). The nullification movement has been studied almost to death. Most pertinent for my purposes was Frederic Bancroft's tart little study: *Calhoun and the South Carolina Nullification Movement* (Baltimore, 1928). See also David F. Houston: *A Critical Study of Nullification in South Carolina* (Cambridge, 1896), and C. S. Boucher: *The Nullification Controversy in South Carolina* (Chicago, 1916). The economic difficulties of the state and the South are recorded soberly in John G. Van Deusen: *Economic Bases of Disunion in South Carolina* (New York, 1928) and Robert R. Russel: *Economic Aspects of Southern Sectionalism* (Urbana, 1924). See also Van Deusen's *The Ante-Bellum Southern Commercial Conventions* (Durham, 1926). Herman V. Ames: "John C. Calhoun and the Secession Movement of 1850," American Antiquarian Society *Proceedings*, N.S., Vol. XXVIII (April 1918), pp. 19–50, is an excellent study of Calhoun's return to extreme militancy in the late forties.

Biographies of other Carolinians are very helpful in setting Calhoun in perspective. Laura A. White: *Robert Barnwell Rhett* (New York, 1931) is a scholarly study of a militant who often wanted to go farther than Calhoun. Lillian A. Kibler: *Benjamin F. Perry* (Durham, 1946) is a thorough study of a Unionist who opposed Calhoun bitterly. A Charleston intellectual who stood at the opposite pole from Calhoun and finally snubbed him roundly is portrayed in Linda Rhea's *Hugh Swinton Legaré* (Chapel Hill, 1934). Theodore D. Jervey: *Robert Y. Hayne and His Times* (New York, 1909) is a full study of one of the Carolinians who on occasion took up arms with Calhoun but were often annoyed with him; it sheds special light on the transportation problems of the state and their relation to politics. Elizabeth Merritt's *James H. Hammond* (Baltimore, 1923) is a disappointing work on an interesting figure. Dumas Malone's excellent biography: *The Public Life of Thomas Cooper* (New Haven, 1926) traces the work of a militant Southern thinker who had some influence on Calhoun.

William S. Jenkins's sober and unimaginative *Pro-Slavery Thought in the Old South* (Chapel Hill, 1935) is the best study of its subject. Jesse T. Carpenter: *The South as a Conscious Minority* (New York, 1930) traces the effect of the South's minority position upon its political theory; it is full of the most suggestive material. Clement Eaton's *Freedom of Thought in the Old South* (Durham, 1940) has an interesting chapter on Calhoun's influence. Charles E. Merriam contributed a good essay on "The Political Philosophy of John C. Calhoun" to *Studies in Southern History and Politics* (New York, 1914). C. M. Wiltse in "Calhoun and the Modern State," *Virginia Quarterly Review*, Vol. XIII (Summer 1937), pp. 396–408, argues that representation by economic interest groups exercising mutual checks, as proposed by Calhoun, is necessary to modern democracy. William E. Dodd's "The Social Philosophy of the Old South," *American Journal of Sociology*, Vol. XXIII (May 1918), pp. 735–46, is incisive. Wilfred Carsel's "The Slaveholder's Indictment of Northern Wage Slavery," *Journal of Southern History*, Vol. VI (November 1940), pp. 504–20, shows that Calhoun's critique of Northern industrialism became common intellectual currency in the South.

Arthur M. Schlesinger, Jr.: *The Age of Jackson* has good material on the attitude of radical Northern Democrats toward Calhoun. James H. Hammond: *Speeches and Letters* (New York, 1866) contains Hammond's famous "mud-sill" speech and an interesting eulogy of Calhoun. C. S. Boucher: *"In re* That Aggressive Slavocracy," *Mississippi Valley Historical Review*, Vol. VIII (June–September 1921), pp. 13–79, argues very plausibly that the South was essentially on the defensive from 1835, especially on the question of Texas and the territories. See E. D. Adams: *British Interests and*

Activities in Texas (Baltimore, 1910) on the source of Calhoun's worries over the Texas question. See also J. D. P. Fuller: *The Movement for the Acquisition of All Mexico* (Baltimore, 1936).

V. ABRAHAM LINCOLN

THE standard collection of Lincoln's writings is the *Complete Works of Abraham Lincoln* (2 volumes, New York, 1894), edited by John G. Nicolay and John Hay; I have used the early edition. The two volumes must be supplemented by four others: Paul Angle: *New Letters and Papers of Lincoln* (Boston and New York, 1930); Ida M. Tarbell: *The Life of Abraham Lincoln* (New York, 1900), Vol. II, Appendix; and Gilbert A. Tracy: *Uncollected Letters of Abraham Lincoln* (Boston and New York, 1917)—all three of which contain material of significance upon which I have drawn—and *Lincoln Letters Hitherto Unpublished in the Library of Brown University and Other Providence Libraries* (Providence, 1927), which consists mostly of routine communications. There are countless selections from Lincoln's works; I have used with profit T. Harry Williams's *Selected Writings and Speeches of Abraham Lincoln* (Chicago, 1943), which has a good introductory essay and a useful enumeration of the chief sources.

Among the biographies, I have consulted Nicolay and Hay's monumental *Abraham Lincoln: a History* (10 volumes, New York, 1890), which is firmly in the hero-worshipping tradition. I am heavily indebted to the classic two-volume study by Albert J. Beveridge: *Abraham Lincoln* (Boston and New York, 1928), which carries Lincoln's life to 1858 and places him in his historical setting as does no other work. There are passages in Claude Bowers: *Beveridge and the Progressive Era* (Cambridge, 1932) relating Beveridge's struggles in interpreting Lincoln's early career which should be read by every student of Lincoln. James G. Randall's

Lincoln the President: Springfield to Gettysburg (2 volumes, New York, 1945) is a work of outstanding scholarship. The same author's *Lincoln and the South* (Baton Rouge, 1946) is excellent, and his *Lincoln the Liberal Statesman* (New York, 1947) has some enlightening essays. I have enjoyed, but not used for this essay, Carl Sandburg's *Abraham Lincoln: the Prairie Years* (2 volumes, New York, 1926), and have used, without similar pleasure, the four fat volumes of *The War Years* (New York, 1939), a monumental bodying-forth of the Lincoln legend. Not knowing what criteria Mr. Sandburg used to separate the authentic stories from the inevitable mass of legend, I have accordingly used his volumes with great care. L. Pierce Clark's study: *Lincoln, a Psychobiography* (New York, 1933), which has a few insights, is sometimes credulous and on the whole disappointing. Lord Charnwood's *Abraham Lincoln* (New York, 1917) is the most readable, and as a character study the most penetrating of the shorter biographies. Nathaniel Wright Stephenson: *Lincoln* (Indianapolis, 1922) has a far more adequate coverage of the war years than other short biographies. Edgar Lee Masters: *Lincoln the Man* (New York, 1931) is one of the most fascinating of all Lincoln books; a fierce and malicious diatribe, without friendship or pity, it combines some remarkable insights with atrocious judgment.

Primary material indispensable for any estimation of Lincoln is presented in William H. Herndon and Jesse Weik: *Herndon's Lincoln*, which should be read in the one-volume edition by Paul M. Angle (New York, 1930). The biography is supplemented by the even more revealing Herndon letters edited by Emanuel Hertz in *The Hidden Lincoln* (New York, 1938), a work of great fascination. Herndon's facts are not always reliable. He is responsible, among other things, for a sentimental exaggeration of the story of Ann Rutledge and a not-so-sentimental exaggeration of some of the circumstances surrounding Lincoln's marriage; his judgments of Lincoln during the Springfield years are, however, invariably pertinent and honest. Herndon played an important part in providing Lincoln with abolition and proslavery literature, as well as other intellectual fodder. Illuminating in this connection is Joseph Fort Newton: *Lincoln and Herndon* (Cedar Rapids, 1910), which has many of the letters exchanged by Herndon and Theodore Parker; it was from Parker that Lincoln took his great phrase: "of the people, by the people, for the people." For the role of Fitzhugh in Lincoln's ideological strategy, see Harvey Wish: *George Fitzhugh* (New Orleans, 1944). Some of the difficulties facing serious Lincoln biographers are set forth by James G. Randall in his interesting essay: "Has the Lincoln Theme been Exhausted?" *American Historical Review,* Vol. XLI (January 1936), pp. 270–94.

Among special works, William E. Baringer: *Lincoln's Rise to Power* (Boston, 1937) sheds much light on the intra-party maneuverings that brought Lincoln the presidential nomination, but neglects economic and social forces. See also Baringer's *A House Dividing* (Springfield, 1945). Arthur C. Cole's pamphlet: *Lincoln's "House Divided" Speech: Does It Reflect a Doctrine of Class Struggle?* (Chicago, 1923) throws light on Lincoln as a dialectician. Rufus Rockwell Wilson: *What Lincoln Read* (Washington, 1932) is short and useful. Reinhard Luthin: *The First Lincoln Campaign* (Cambridge, 1944) is a first-rate study of the election of 1860. Charles W. Ramsdell set forth his thesis on the Fort Sumter incident in "Lincoln and Fort Sumter," *Journal of Southern History,* Vol. III (August 1937), pp. 259–88. The same general point of view is expressed at much greater length and with much less detachment by John Shipley Tilley in *Lincoln Takes Command* (Chapel Hill, 1941). See also James G. Randall's temperate answer to Ramsdell: "When War Came in 1861," *Abraham Lincoln Quarterly,* Vol. I (March 1940), pp. 3–42. "To say," observes Randall, "that Lincoln meant that the first shot would be fired by the other side *if a first shot was fired,* is by no means the equivalent of saying that he deliberately maneuvred to have the shot fired." The most careful and illuminating review of the Sumter crisis is Kenneth M. Stampp's "Lincoln and the

Strategy of Defense in the Crisis of 1861," *Journal of Southern History*, Vol. XI (August 1945), pp. 297–323. David M. Potter: *Lincoln and His Party in the Secession Crisis* (New Haven, 1942) believes Lincoln was pressing a peace policy, but charges him with ineptitude. On Lincoln's shrewd use of party patronage as a cement for the Union cause, see Harry J. Carman and Reinhard Luthin: *Lincoln and the Patronage* (New York, 1943). James G. Randall: *Constitutional Problems under Lincoln* (New York, 1926) covers more than the title suggests. T. Harry Williams: *Lincoln and the Radicals* (Madison, 1942) is an important study, which, however, suffers from an excessive emphasis on the military aspects at the cost of the political. Harry E. Pratt: *The Personal Finances of Abraham Lincoln* (Springfield, 1943) tends to substantiate Herndon's estimate that Lincoln "had no avarice of the *get* but had the avarice of the *keep*."

Among general works on Lincoln's period I have made much use of James G. Randall's compendious history: *The Civil War and Reconstruction* (New York, 1937), especially of its chapters on Civil War politics and the emancipation question. Carl Russell Fish: *The American Civil War* (London and New York, 1937) is a keen and readable interpretation. Wood Gray: *The Hidden Civil War* (New York, 1942) gives a valuable account of the economic and social roots of the Copperhead opposition and of its activities. George Fort Milton's life of Douglas: *The Eve of Conflict: Stephen A. Douglas and the Needless War* (Boston, 1934) is an important and scholarly contribution that helps to place Lincoln in perspective. A. C. Cole: *The Era of the Civil War 1848–1870* (Chicago, 1922), the third volume of the *Centennial History of Illinois,* is a solid study of Lincoln's state which illuminates politics and social attitudes. Roy Basler: *The Lincoln Legend* (Boston, 1935) is valuable.

VI. WENDELL PHILLIPS

THE only collection of Phillips's writings, *Speeches, Lectures, and Letters* (2 volumes, Boston, 1894), is inadequate for an understanding of his career, particularly for its later phases. I have supplemented this by reading the reports of his speeches in Garrison's paper, the *Liberator*, from 1860 to 1875, and in papers associated with Phillips, the *National Anti-Slavery Standard*, 1865 to 1870, and the *Standard*, 1870 to 1871. Among his more extended writings, see *Can Abolitionists Vote or Take Office under the United States Constitution?* (New York, 1845), *Review of Lysander Spooner's Essay on the Unconstitutionality of Slavery* (Boston, 1847), and *The Constitution: a Pro-Slavery Compact* (New York, 1856). Three important later speeches, *Remarks of Wendell Phillips at the Mass-meeting of Workingmen in Faneuil Hall, November 2, 1865* (Boston, 1865), *The People Coming to Power!* (Boston, 1871), and *Who Shall Rule Us, Money or the People?* (Boston, 1878) are available in pamphlet form.

The standard biography by Carlos Martyn: *Wendell Phillips* (New York, 1890) is a valuable source; Martyn was a friend of the subject, and much of the personal material is unique. The best biography, Oscar Sherwin's *Prophet of Liberty*, is an unpublished doctoral dissertation, New York University, 1940, which is rich with original quotations from Phillips. See also G. L. Austin: *The Life and Times of Wendell Phillips* (Boston, 1893), Lorenzo Sears: *Wendell Phillips* (New York, 1909), and Charles Edward Russell: *The Story of Wendell Phillips* (New York, 1914). All of these take a favorable view of the subject, as does V. L. Parrington in his brief essay in *Main Currents in American Thought*, Vol. III (New York, 1930). For a hostile view of Phillips see almost any standard recent history of the slavery controversy, the Civil War, or Reconstruction.

The work of Gilbert Hobbs Barnes: *The Antislavery Impulse* (New York, 1933) is of especial importance in estimating the place of William Lloyd Garrison and his immediate followers, as it is in tracing the outlines of doctrinal controversies among the abolitionists. For a similar thesis, see William Birney: *James G. Birney and His Times* (New York, 1890). Jesse Macy: *The Abolitionist Crusade* (New Haven, 1919) and Albert Bushnell Hart: *Slavery and Abolition* (New York, 1900) are helpful works. Dwight L. Dumond: *Antislavery Origins of the Civil War in the United States* (Ann Arbor, 1938) is a sympathetic revaluation of the work of the abolitionists, which has given me several important suggestions. The massive four-volume biography by Garrison's sons: *William Lloyd Garrison* (New York, 1885–9) is valuable. Arthur Young Lloyd: *The Slavery Controversy, 1831–1860* (Chapel Hill, 1939) is partisan to the South. *Letters of Theodore Dwight Weld, Angelina Grimke Weld, and Sarah Grimke* (New York, 1934), edited by G. H. Barnes and Dwight L. Dumond, and *Letters of James G. Birney* (New York, 1938), edited by Dwight L. Dumond, are good sources on the spirit of abolitionism. Journals, memoirs, and biographies of such friends and contemporaries of Phillips as Emerson, Thoreau, Theodore Parker, Samuel J. May, and others have interesting sidelights. The quotation from Phillips in the first paragraph of section III is from John R. Commons et al., eds.: *A Documentary History of American Industrial Society*, Vol. VII (Cleveland, 1910–11), pp. 219–21. There is important material on the background of Phillips's career as a labor reformer in Commons, ed.: *History of Labour in the United States*, Vol. II (New York, 1918).

VII. THE SPOILSMEN

I HAVE found the following general accounts useful on the political and industrial developments of the post-Civil War era: Louis M. Hacker and Benjamin B. Kendrick: *The United*

States since 1865 (New York, 1939), Charles A. and Mary R. Beard: *The Rise of American Civilization* (2 volumes, New York, 1933), Samuel Eliot Morison and Henry Steele Commager: *The Growth of the American Republic,* Vol. II (New York, 1942), Harold U. Faulkner: *American Political and Social History* (New York, 1945), and Thomas C. Cochran and William Miller: *The Age of Enterprise* (New York, 1942). There is an evocative portrait of the Gilded Age in V. L. Parrington: *Main Currents in American Thought,* Vol. III. Three volumes in the History of American Life Series are valuable: Ida M. Tarbell: *The Nationalizing of Business, 1878–1898* (New York, 1936), Arthur M. Schlesinger: *The Rise of the City, 1878–1898* (New York, 1938), and Allan Nevins: *The Emergence of Modern America, 1865–1878* (New York, 1927). On conditions among the farmers see Solon J. Buck: *The Granger Movement* (Cambridge, 1913), and *The Agrarian Crusade* (New Haven, 1928), and John D. Hicks: *The Populist Revolt* (Minneapolis, 1931). The first chapter of Henry David: *The Haymarket Affair* (New York, 1936) is excellent on the condition of the workers; see also Norman J. Ware: *The Labor Movement in the United States, 1860–1895* (New York and London, 1929), and John R. Commons et al.: *History of Labour in the United States* (New York, 1918), Vol. II. For a brief perspective of the men of this generation the *Dictionary of American Biography* (21 volumes, New York, 1928–44) is indispensable.

On the businessmen I have been enlightened by Matthew Josephson: *The Robber Barons* (New York, 1934) and parts of Gustavus Myers: *A History of the Great American Fortunes* (3 volumes, Chicago, 1910). Burton J. Hendrick: *The Life of Andrew Carnegie* (2 volumes, New York, 1932) and Allan Nevins: *John D. Rockefeller* (2 volumes, New York, 1940) are oustanding among biographies of industrialists. C. Wright Mills: "The American Business Elite: a Collective Portrait," Supplement V to the *Journal of Economic History* (December 1945), is an invaluable statistical study. The philosophy of this business civilization is brilliantly outlined in chapter vi of Cochran and Miller: *The Age of Enterprise;* see also the opening chapters of Richard Hofstadter: *Social Darwinism in American Thought, 1860–1915* (Philadelphia, 1944), chapter xxv of Merle Curti: *The Growth of American Thought* (New York, 1943), and chapter xiii of Ralph Gabriel: *The Course of American Democratic Thought* (New York, 1940).

By far the most illuminating book on the politics of the entire period is Matthew Josephson's superb study: *The Politicos* (New York, 1938). Lord Bryce's *American Commonwealth* (3 volumes, London and New York, 1888) is a great commentary, and there are fine insights in *The Education of Henry Adams* (Boston and New York, 1918) and Henry Adams's novel of Washington, *Democracy* (New York, 1880). On the major parties Wilfred Binkley: *American Political Parties* (New York, 1943) is useful. Howard Beale: *The Critical Year* (New York, 1930) is indispensable on the early strategy of Republican Party leaders, and Earle D. Ross: *The Liberal Republican Movement* (New York, 1919) is a significant study of the bolt of 1872. The best biography of Grant is William B. Hesseltine: *Ulysses S. Grant* (New York, 1935), but Allan Nevins: *Hamilton Fish* (New York, 1936) is invaluable on the Grant administration. Significant personal material can be found in Vol. III of Charles R. Williams, ed.: *Diary and Letters of Rutherford B. Hayes* (Columbus, 1924). Theodore Clarke Smith: *James A. Garfield, Life and Letters* (2 volumes, New Haven, 1925) is rich in detail. Stewart Mitchell: *Horatio Seymour of New York* (Cambridge, 1938) and Alexander C. Flick: *Samuel Jones Tilden* (New York, 1939) are substantial biographies of Democratic leaders.

There is no satisfactory biography of Roscoe Conkling, but Donald Barr Chidsey: *The Gentleman from New York* (New Haven, 1935) is helpful, and the older eulogistic work by Alfred R. Conkling: *The Life and Times of Roscoe Conkling* (New York, 1889) has significant material. David Saville Muzzey's sympathetic *James G. Blaine* (New York, 1934) is the best study of the Plumed Knight; Charles Edward Russell's *Blaine of Maine* (New Lork, 1931) is more critical. Two pamphlets published by the New York *Evening Post* are important: *Mr. Blaine and the Little Rock and Fort Smith Railroad* (New York, 1884) and *Mr. Blaine's Railroad Transactions . . . Including All the Mulligan Letters* (New York, 1884). Blaine's *Political Discussions* (New York, 1887) is a collection of major speeches, and *Twenty Years of Congress* (2 volumes, Norwich, 1886) is a work of substance. See also Harriet S. Blaine Beale, ed.: *Letters of Mrs. James G. Blaine* (2 volumes, New York, 1908).

The complete presidential papers of Grover Cleveland are in Volumes VIII and IX of J. D. Richardson, ed.: *Messages and Papers of the Presidents* (11 volumes, Washington, 1898), but there is an extremely useful compilation of presidential and other papers and speeches up to 1892 in George F. Parker: *The Writings and Speeches of Grover Cleveland* (New York, 1892). Allan Nevins, ed.: *Letters of Grover Cleveland* (Boston and New York, 1933) is an invaluable personal source; the introduction is the source of the characterization of Cleveland by Professor Nevins near the close of the chapter. Cleveland's *Presidential Problems* (New York, 1904) has important essays evaluating phases of his presidential acts. Cleveland's essay *The Self-Made Man in American Life* (New York, 1897) is a major source on his social values. The best biography is Allan Nevins's sympathetic portrait: *Grover Cleveland, a Study in Courage* (New York, 1932); see also Robert McElroy: *Grover Cleveland* (2 volumes, New York, 1923).

VIII. WILLIAM JENNINGS BRYAN

DEPENDENT for a large part of his income on his publications, Bryan wrote a good deal. His *Memoirs* (Philadephia, 1925), finished after his death by his wife, is a revealing source, but must be used with care. *The First Battle* (Chicago, 1896) is essentially a handbook of the campaign, valuable because it contains all Bryan's major speeches. *The Second Battle* (Chicago, 1900) does the same for the campaign of 1900. Bryan's *Speeches* (2 volumes, New York and London, 1909) has the most significant addresses from the beginning of his public career to the campaign of 1908. *A Tale of Two Conventions* (New York, 1912) is a compilation of Bryan's syndicated newspaper reports of the 1912 conventions. *Heart to Heart Appeals* (New York, 1917) is a collection of religious and political speeches. *The Old World and Its Ways* (St. Louis, 1907) is an account of Bryan's 1905–6 trip around the world; it has a brief sequence on his interview with Tolstoy which is of special interest. American (Christian) and Chinese (Confucian) civilizations are contrasted, to no surprising end, in *Letters to a Chinese Official* (New York, 1906). Such of Bryan's religious opera as *Famous Figures of the Old Testament* (New York, 1923), *Seven Questions in Dispute* (New York, 1924), and *Christ and His Companions* (New York, 1925) are dismal reading, but cannot be ignored by those who want to see Bryan's mind in action. In the most important of these, *In His Image* (New York, 1922), Bryan goes to bat against all forms of infidelity, including Darwinism. The files of Bryan's periodical, the *Commoner* (1901–23), which contain many speeches and addresses not found elsewhere, are the best source for Bryan's occasional political views.

Paxton Hibben: *The Peerless Leader* (New York, 1929), which was finished by C. Hartley Grattan after Mr. Hibben's untimely death, is by far the best of the Bryan biographies; I have followed its interpretations again and again. M. R. Werner's *Bryan* (New York, 1929) is less thorough, but valuable. Wayne C. Williams: *William Jennings Bryan* (New York, 1936) is apologetic throughout, but contains information not to be found elsewhere. See also Merle Curti: *Bryan and World Peace* (Northampton, 1931).

Biographies and autobiographies of such contemporaries as Hanna, Altgeld, Cleveland, Champ Clark, David Houston, Wilson, Taft, Theodore Roosevelt, Robert M. La Follette, McAdoo, and others have gleanings on Bryan's career, but offer little specifically on Bryan that has not been culled by his biographers. There are interesting discussions with good personal material in Charles Willis Thompson: *Presidents I Have Known and Two Near Presidents* (Indianapolis, 1929), Oswald Garrison Villard: *Prophets, True and False* (New York, 1928), and Dixon Wecter: *The Hero in America* (New York, 1941). *Bryan and Darrow at Dayton* (New York, 1925), edited and compiled by Leslie H. Allen, presents the most significant parts of the Scopes proceedings bearing on Bryan's homespun metaphysics.

Among articles on particular phases of Bryan's career, George R. Poage: "The College Career of William Jennings Bryan," *Mississippi Valley Historical Review,* Vol. XV (September 1928), pp. 165–82, is especially helpful. Thomas A. Bailey asks: "Was the Presidential Election of 1900 a Mandate on Imperialism?" ibid., Vol. XXIV (June 1937), pp. 43–52, and emerges with a negative answer; Professor Bailey is critical of Bryan for including the free-silver plank in the platform of 1900. Estal E. Sparlin: "Bryan and the 1912 Democratic Convention," ibid., Vol. XXII (March 1936), pp. 537–46, sheds light on Bryan's relations with Champ Clark. Selig Adler: "Bryan and Wilsonian Caribbean Penetration," *Hispanic American Historical Review,* Vol. XX (May 1940), pp. 198–226, is an excellent reinterpretation. Malcolm M. Willey and Stuart A. Rice in "William Jennings Bryan as a Social Force," *Social Forces,* Vol. II (March 1924), pp. 338–44, measure the influence of Bryan's anti-evolutionist broadsides on Dartmouth undergraduates and conclude that they had some effect. A. Vandenbosch summarizes "Bryan's Political Theories" in *American Review,* Vol. IV (May 1926), pp. 297–305.

For the campaign of 1896 see Harvey Wish: "John P. Altgeld and the Background of the Campaign of 1896," *Mississippi Valley Historical Review,* Vol. XXIV (March 1938), pp. 503–18; Irving Bernstein: "Samuel Gompers and Free Silver, 1896," ibid., Vol. XXIX (December 1942), pp. 394–400; and William Diamond: "Urban and Rural Voting in 1896," *American Historical Review,* Vol. XLVI (January

1941), pp. 281–305. James A. Barnes: "Myths of the Bryan Campaign," *Mississippi Valley Historical Review*, Vol. XXXIV (December 1947), pp. 367–404, is a significant article. For the situation of farmers see Fred A. Shannon: *The Farmer's Last Frontier* (New York, 1945).

For the background of Bryan's political activities, John D. Hicks: *The Populist Revolt* (Minneapolis, 1931) is invaluable. I have also drawn upon Matthew Josephson: *The Politicos* (New York, 1938), and *The President Makers* (New York, 1940), Allan Nevins: *Grover Cleveland* (New York, 1932), and Harry Barnard: *Eagle Forgotten: A Life of John P. Altgeld* (Indianapolis, 1938). Samuel Flagg Bemis in his *Latin American Policy of the United States* (New York, 1943) concurs with Selig Adler's intepretation of Bryan's imperialism. On World War neutrality I have used Charles Callan Tansill: *America Goes to War* (Boston, 1938), and the unsigned sketch of Bryan by Joseph V. Fuller in S. F. Bemis, ed.: *American Secretaries of State and Their Diplomacy* (New York, 1929).

IX. THEODORE ROOSEVELT

I HAVE used the National Edition of Roosevelt's *Works*, published under the auspices of the Roosevelt Memorial Association in twenty volumes (New York, 1926), edited by Hermann Hagedorn. *Selections from the Correspondence of Theodore Roosevelt and Henry Cabot Lodge, 1884–1918*, edited by Henry Cabot Lodge (2 volumes, New York, 1925), is extremely valuable. There are a few important items in *Letters from Theodore Roosevelt to Anna Roosevelt Cowles, 1870–1918* (New York, 1924). Roosevelt's opinions on a great variety of subjects can be found in the useful *Roosevelt Cyclopedia* (New York, 1941).

The authorized biography by Joseph Bucklin Bishop: *Theodore Roosevelt and His Time* (2 volumes, New York, 1920) has been dubbed "The Concealment of Theodore

Roosevelt" by the late Professor N. W. Stephenson: however, it contains many selections from correspondence. The best biography, Henry F. Pringle's *Theodore Roosevelt* (New York, 1931), is a critical and objective work of unusual discernment. W. F. McCaleb: *Theodore Roosevelt* (New York, 1931) is less satisfactory but of some value. *My Brother, Theodore Roosevelt* (New York, 1921), by Corinne Roosevelt Robinson, is very revealing at points. An extremely penetrating interpretation, to which I am heavily indebted, is that of Matthew Josephson in *The President Makers* (New York, 1940). See also Lewis Einstein: *Roosevelt, His Mind in Action* (Boston, 1930).

Among the many specialized studies I have been much influenced by Howard Hurwitz's first-rate survey of *Theodore Roosevelt and Labor in New York State* (New York, 1943). Charles W. Stein: *The Third Term Tradition* (New York, 1943) is good on the campaign of 1912 and in general on Roosevelt and the question of the third term. Harold F. Gosnell: *Boss Platt and His New York Machine* (Chicago, 1924) is informative on Roosevelt in New York State politics. Howard C. Hill: *Roosevelt and the Caribbean* (Chicago, 1927) for the most part looks indulgently on Roosevelt's policies. Dwight C. Miner: *The Fight for the Panama Route* (New York, 1940) is a thorough, scholarly, and devastating review of the Panama question. See also Tyler Dennett: *Theodore Roosevelt and the Russo-Japanese War* (New York, 1925). Stuart Sherman has a penetrating essay on the Rough Rider in *Americans* (New York, 1922). J. C. Malin: "Theodore Roosevelt and the Elections of 1884 and 1888," *Mississippi Valley Historical Review*, Vol. XIV (June 1927), pp. 23–38, surveys Roosevelt's first lessons in political opportunism and concludes sadly that he cared less at this early date for high standards of public morality than for "narrow and exaggerated nationalism which he felt could not be realized except under a Republican administration." George Mowry: "Theodore Roosevelt and the Election of 1910," *Mississippi Valley Historical Review*, Vol. XXV (March 1939), pp. 523–34, argues with a good show of evidence the La Follette thesis that Roosevelt in that year had no ambitions for 1912 but was looking forward to 1916, a position that is sustained by Roosevelt's friend Charles G. Washburn in "Roosevelt and the 1912 Campaign," *Proceedings* of the Massachusetts Historical Society, Vol. LIX (May 1926), who believes that Roosevelt did not plan his candidacy long in advance, but made a sudden *volte-face*. The best review of Roosevelt's political course from 1910 to his death, which has the most plausible conjectures on his motives and impulses, George Mowry's *Theodore Roosevelt and the Progessive Movement* (Madison, 1946), which abounds in suggestive material. The political strategist is treated with shrewd realism by N. W. Stephenson in "Roosevelt and the Stratification of Society," *Scripps College Papers*, no. 3 (1930). Earle D. Ross offers a few sidelights on Roosevelt's more general views in "Theodore Roosevelt and Agriculture," *Mississippi Valley Historical Review*, Vol. XIV (December 1927), pp. 287–310. Roosevelt's attitude toward the World War is carefully surveyed in Russell Buchanan: "Theodore Roosevelt and American Neutrality," *American Historical Review*, Vol. XXII (April 1923), pp. 97–114. There are two rather critical evaluations of Roosevelt's historical work, one by John H. Thornton in *The Marcus W. Jernegan Essays in American Historiography* (Chicago, 1937), and the other by Raymond C. Miller in *Medieval and Historiographical Essays in Honor of James Westfall Thompson* (Chicago, 1938). The background of the "new" Roosevelt of 1910–12 is illuminated by two books that influenced his thinking at that time: Herbert Croly's *The Promise of American Life* (New York, 1909), and Charles R. Van Hise's *Concentration and Control* (New York, 1912). The convergence of Roosevelt's and Perkins's views of the trust question become crystal-clear in George W. Perkins's pamphlet: *The Sherman Law*. Harold L. Ickes: "Who Killed the Progressive Party?" *American Historical Review*, Vol. XLVI (January 1941), pp. 306–37, throws the blame on Perkins and glides innocently over Roosevelt's part, but concedes that Perkins's undue private influence in the Progressive Party can be traced to the fact that the party "was the personal political vehicle of Theodore Roosevelt."

Biographies of contemporaries throw much light on Roosevelt. N. W. Stephenson: *Nelson W. Aldrich* (New York, 1930) is excellent on Roosevelt's close relations with the conservatives in the Senate. Thomas Beer's *Hanna* (New York, 1929) is the source of some priceless anecdotes. See also Herbert Croly: *Marcus A. Hanna* (New York, 1912). Claude Bowers: *Beveridge and the Progressive Era* (Cambridge, 1932) is especially good on the fate of the Progressive Party. Roosevelt is seen critically in Henry F. Pringle: *The Life and Times of William Howard Taft* (2 volumes, New York, 1939), Tyler Dennett: *John Hay* (New York, 1933), and Henry Adams: *Education of Henry Adams*, and with bitterness in Robert M. La Follette: *La Follette's Autobiography* (Madison, 1913). For the muckrakers' retrospect see the pertinent comments by Ray Stannard Baker: *American Chronicle* (New York, 1945), Lincoln Steffens: *Autobiography* (2 volumes, New York, 1931) and *The Correspondence of Lincoln Steffens* (2 volumes, New York, 1938), edited by Ella Winter and Granville Hicks. See also Phillip C. Jessup: *Elihu Root* (2 volumes, New York, 1938) for the view of a conservative friend who understood Roosevelt well. There are sidelights in Karl Schriftgiesser: *The Gentleman from Massachusetts* (New York, 1945), a biography of Lodge.

On Roosevelt's times I have consulted with special advantage Walter Millis: *The Martial Spirit* (Boston, 1931), John Chamberlain: *Farewell to Reform* (New York, 1932), Louis Filler: *Crusaders for American Liberalism* (New York, 1940), and Harold Underwood Faulkner: *The Quest for Social Justice* (New York, 1931).

X. WOODROW WILSON

WOODROW WILSON's public writings are collected in *The Public Papers of Woodrow Wilson* (6 volumes, New York, 1925-7), edited by Ray Stannard Baker and William E. Dodd. *The New Freedom* (New York, 1913), culled from 1912 campaign speeches, is readable and important. Among Wilson's other writings, *Congressional Government* (Boston, 1885) is of considerable importance; *The State* (Boston, 1889) is a rather dull survey. *Constitutional Government in the United States* (New York, 1908) represents his matured opinions on American politics. See also *Division and Reunion* (New York, 1893), *An Old Master* (New York, 1893), *Mere Literature and Other Essays* (New York, 1896), and *A History of the American People* (6 volumes, New York, 1902).

The most inclusive biography, Ray Stannard Baker's *Woodrow Wilson, Life and Letters* (8 volumes, New York, 1927-39), which has a liberal selection from Wilson's letters, is far more critical and detached than most authorized biographies. See also Baker's *American Chronicle* (New York, 1945). Arthur S. Link: *Wilson, the Road to the White House* (Princeton, 1947), the first volume of a new scholarly biography, is a shrewd and discriminating work that contains a balanced estimate of Wilson's public career to 1912. H. C. F. Bell's *Woodrow Wilson and the People* (New York, 1945) is a brief and sympathetic personal study. *Woodrow Wilson as I Know Him* (New York, 1921), by Joseph Patrick Tumulty, Wilson's secretary, is an illuminating source, but not always reliable. A perceptive study by a New Jersey acquaintance, James Kerney's *The Political Education of Woodrow Wilson* (New York, 1926), remains one of the best books on the man; it is the source of the letter from George Record quoted in section V. For the New Jersey Progressives, see Ransom E. Noble's excellent study: *New*

Jersey Progressivism before Wilson (Princeton, 1946). There is priceless material in *The Intimate Papers of Colonel House* (4 volumes, Boston and New York, 1926), edited by Charles Seymour. The photographs in *Woodrow Wilson as the Camera Saw Him* (New York, 1944), edited by Gerald W. Johnson, are evocative.

Among special studies of Wilson, William Diamond: *The Economic Thought of Woodrow Wilson* (Baltimore, 1943) stands out for thoroughness of research and excellence of interpretation; I am much indebted to it. Walter Lippmann's *Drift and Mastery* (New York, 1914) is a sharp critique of the New Freedom from the standpoint of a liberal socialist. On the philosopher of the New Freedom see Alpheus T. Mason: *Brandeis* (New York, 1946). There is interesting material on the period in Oswald Garrison Villard's autobiography: *Fighting Years* (New York, 1939). Harley Notter: *The Origins of the Foreign Policy of Woodrow Wilson* (Baltimore, 1937) contains a fund of valuable material, badly organized. For the neutrality period and its problems I have relied most heavily on Charles Callan Tansill's *America Goes to War* (Boston, 1938), which is critical of the Wilson policies. Charles A. Beard: *The Devil Theory of War* (New York, 1936) is stimulating. Charles Seymour: *American Diplomacy during the World War* (Baltimore, 1934) is of unusual value for its use of material from the House Collection at Yale and for its sympathetic understanding of Wilson's problems, intentions, and plans. Paul Birdsall: "Neutrality and Economic Pressures, 1914–1917," *Science and Society*, Vol. III (Spring 1939), pp. 217–28, argues an important thesis about the economic background of America's entrance into the war. J. L. Heaton: *Cobb of "The World"* (New York, 1924) is the source of Wilson's agonized words to Frank Cobb. For the Peace Conference I have drawn heavily upon Paul Birdsall: *Versailles Twenty Years After* (New York, 1941), and Thomas A. Bailey: *Woodrow Wilson and the Lost Peace* (New York, 1944). Ray Stannard Baker's *Woodrow Wilson and World Settlement* (3 volumes, New York, 1922), although outmoded on many points of interpretation, remains valuable. A classic but harsh view of Wilson is to be found in John Maynard Keynes: *The Economic Consequences of the Peace* (New York, 1920). On the basic conceptions underlying the peace I have been much influenced by Edward H. Carr's brilliant work: *Conditions of Peace* (New York, 1942). James T. Shotwell's thoughtful little book: *What Germany Forgot* (New York, 1940), excellent on the economic consequences of the war, serves as an antidote to the classic liberal view of Versailles. Thomas A. Bailey's *Woodrow Wilson and the Great Betrayal* (New York, 1945) is a masterly survey of the fight over the League in the United States, which, despite its sympathy with Wilsonian internationalism, leaves no doubt of the ineptness of Wilson's political strategy.

XI. HERBERT HOOVER

THE standard source on Hoover's presidential writings and speeches is *The State Papers and Other Public Writings of Herbert Hoover* (2 volumes, New York, 1934), edited by William Starr Myers. I found far more useful, however, *The Hoover Policies* (New York, 1937), edited by Ray Lyman Wilbur and Arthur M. Hyde, which, in addition to providing an excellent selection of Hoover's speeches and writings in topical arrangement, draws upon his entire public career from 1920 to 1934; it contains an apologetic commentary. Among Hoover's writings, *Principles of Mining* (New York and London, 1909) is significant to this study chiefly for brief passages on labor relations. *American Individualism* (New York, 1922) outlines the major premises of his social philosophy. *The New Day* (Stanford, 1928) is a collection of 1928 campaign speeches. *The Challenge to Liberty* (New York, 1934) and *The Problems of Lasting Peace* (New York, 1942) are discussed in the text. *America's First Crusade* (New York, 1942) has revealing matter on Hoover's international ideas and his role at Paris. *Addresses upon the*

American Road, 1933–1938 (New York, 1938) and *Further Addresses upon the American Road* (New York, 1940) are collections of speeches on the New Deal and foreign policy. A pamphlet by Hoover, *Since the Armistice* (n.p., 1919), reprinted from *The Nation's Business*, illustrates excellently his reaction to State economic policy as a result of his wartime experiences; another, *Why the Public Interest Requires State Rather than Federal Regulation of Electric Public Utilities* (Washington, 1925), is a clear statement of his philosophy of regulatory legislation. The *Annual Reports* of the Secretary of Commerce from 1921 to 1927 have material on Hoover's career as a bureaucrat. Hoover's article: "Economics of a Boom," *Mining Magazine*, May 1912, pp. 370–2, is the source of the quotation in the second paragraph of section III.

There is no biography of Hoover at all comparable to William Allen White's superb study of Coolidge. The biographical literature consists of a spate of superficial books turned out during the presidential campaign years from 1920 to 1932, which are either eulogies or bitter and often irrelevant tirades. Herbert Corey: *The Truth about Hoover* (Boston and New York, 1932) is a tiresome refutation of the latter. The most substantial of the hostile works, Walter W. Liggett's *The Rise of Herbert Hoover* (New York, 1932), is based upon some research and investigation. Vernon Kellogg: *Herbert Hoover, the Man and His Work* (New York, 1920) has some first-hand reporting on Hoover's career in European relief and reflects accurately the public view of him in 1920. Probably the best biography is the work of a personal friend, Will Irwin's *Herbert Hoover, a Reminiscent Biography* (New York, 1928). I found William Hard: *Who's Hoover* (New York, 1928) suggestive at several points. Edwin Emerson: *Hoover and His Times* (Garden City, 1932), an inchoate compilation, has some useful material. The brief sketch of Hoover in *Current Biography* for 1943 was helpful as a guide to Hoover's more recent career. Many gaps were filled by consulting the files of the New York *Times*, 1920–44; Hoover's statements on foreign policy summarized in the early paragraphs of section V are from addresses and press statements reported in the *Times* on these dates: April 1, October 27, 1938; October 11, 1939; June 26, 1940; September 17, 1941.

Hoover's relief work is surveyed in Part I of *American Food in the World War and Reconstruction Period* (Stanford, 1931), edited by Frank M. Surface and Raymond L. Bland, a mine of information. Other original material, including some important letters from Hoover to Wilson, is in *Organization of American Relief in Europe* (Stanford, 1943), edited by Suda Lorena Bane and Ralph H. Lutz. For the relation between relief and anti-Bolshevik politics see Louis Fischer: *The Soviets in World Affairs* (2 volumes, London, 1930), and a series of frank articles by T. T. C. Gregory, one of Hoover's subordinates in the ARA: "Stemming the Red Tide," *World's Work*, Vol. XLI (1921), pp. 608–13; Vol. XLII, pp. 95–100, 153–64. See also William Starr Myers: *The Foreign Policies of Herbert Hoover* (New York, 1940).

A few biographies of contemporaries were of value. William Allen White's study of Coolidge: *A Puritan in Babylon* (New York, 1938) is a remarkable book. Samuel Hopkins Adams: *Incredible Era: the Life and Times of Warren Gamaliel Harding* (Boston, 1939) has a few sidelights on Hoover; and Alfred Lief; *Democracy's Norris* (New York, 1939) sees him through the hostile eyes of the Progressive Senator. Harvey O'Connor: *Mellon's Millions* (New York, 1933) is an excellent study. Hoover's courtship of the utilities is the subject of two excellent, well-documented articles by Amos Pinchot: "Hoover and Power," the *Nation*, Vol. CXXXIII (August 5, August 12, 1931), pp. 125–8, 141–53. For Hoover's relations with his successor see Raymond Moley: *After Seven Years* (New York, 1939).

For the depression and its background I have drawn on many volumes, but am particularly indebted to the brilliant survey of the period in Louis Hacker's *American Problems of Today* (New York, 1938). Also suggestive are Gilbert Seldes: *The Years of the Locust* (Boston, 1933), Henry

Bamford Parkes: *Recent America* (New York, 1941), Charles and Mary Beard: *America in Midpassage* (New York, 1939), and Frederick Lewis Allen: *The Lords of Creation* (New York, 1935).

The general style of social thinking represented by Hoover is analyzed in Thurman Arnold's clever book: *The Folklore of Capitalism* (New Haven, 1937), which does not deal specifically with Hoover himself. William Starr Myers and Walter H. Newton: *The Hoover Administration: a Documented Narrative* (New York, 1936) is an informative chronological survey of Hoover's words and deeds as President and also presents a stubborn defense of his record. There is a brief critique of Hoover's economic policy in George Soule: *The Coming American Revolution* (New York, 1934). On economic conditions see the hearings of the Temporary National Economic Committee, *Investigation of Concentration of Economic Power,* Part 9, "Savings and Investment." See also Alvin Hansen: *Business Cycles and Fiscal Policy* (New York, 1941); *America's Capacity to Consume* (Washington, 1934), by Maurice Leven, Harold G. Moulton, and Clark Warburton. Joseph M. Jones, Jr.: *Tariff Retaliation* (Philadelphia, 1934) is a good study of repercussions of the Smoot-Hawley tariff.

XII. FRANKLIN D. ROOSEVELT

THE standard source of Franklin D. Roosevelt's presidential writings and of selected gubernatorial writings is *The Public Papers of Franklin D. Roosevelt* (9 volumes, New York, 1938 and 1941), edited by Samuel Rosenman. In addition to his speeches and messages there are useful commentaries by Mr. Roosevelt and extended selections from press conferences. Roosevelt's statements on foreign affairs can be more easily traced in the useful compilation: *Roosevelt's Foreign Policy, 1933–1941* (New York, 1942). The material in *Looking Forward* (New York, 1933) and *On Our Way*

(New York, 1934) consists chiefly of speeches and writings that can be better consulted in the *Public Papers*. *The Happy Warrior, Alfred E. Smith* (Boston and New York, 1928) contains Roosevelt's 1928 nominating speech and a brief tribute. *F. D. R., Columnist* (Chicago, 1947), edited by Donald Scott Carmichael, is a collection of brief newspaper columns written by Roosevelt in 1925 and 1928; although of little intrinsic interest, the columns illustrate the qualities of Roosevelt's mind for the period in which they were written. *Government—Not Politics* (New York, 1932) is a collection of magazine article from 1931 and 1932, most of them as empty as the title. Roosevelt's early navalism is expressed in four articles: "The Problem of Our Navy," *Scientific American*, Vol. CX (February 28, 1914), pp. 177–8; "The Naval Plattsburg," *Outlook*, Vol. CXIII (June 28, 1916), pp. 495–501; "On Your Own Heads," *Scribner's*, Vol. LXI (April 1917), pp. 413–16; "What the Navy Can Do for Your Boy," *Ladies' Home Journal*, Vol. XXXIV (June 1917), p. 25. A more pacific viewpoint is expressed in Roosevelt's article: "Our Foreign Policy," *Foreign Affairs*, Vol. VI (July 1928), pp. 573–87, and also in "Shall We Trust Japan?" *Asia*, Vol. XXIII (July 1923), pp. 476–8. Roosevelt's attitude on power was set forth in "The Real Meaning of the Power Problem," *Forum*, Vol. LXXXII (December 1929), pp. 327–32.

Primary material on Roosevelt's early days is contained in Sara Delano Roosevelt's *My Boy Franklin* (New York, 1933), an extremely revealing work, and in *F. D. R.: His Personal Letters, Early Years* (New York, 1947), edited by Elliott Roosevelt. See also Rita Halle Kleeman's *Gracious Lady* (New York, 1935), a biography of Sara Delano Roosevelt. Frank D. Ashburn: *Peabody of Groton* (New York, 1944) is amply informative about Roosevelt's prep school and has a good chapter on Roosevelt's relations with Peabody. Eleanor Roosevelt: *This Is My Story* (New York, 1937), although candid about its author, says little about her husband; but it has interesting sidelights on early domestic life and is the source of the priceless story about Henry Adams. Elliott

Roosevelt: *As He Saw It* (New York, 1946) is an account of several conversations between the author and his father at the time of some of the great international conferences. On the quality of Roosevelt's relationship with Churchill, see Louis Adamic's *Dinner at the White House* (New York, 1946).

Among the "inside" books on Roosevelt and the New Deal thus far published, I am much impressed with Frances Perkins's *The Roosevelt I Knew* (New York, 1946), which, although friendly and sympathetic, is also detached, critical, intelligent, and rich in important factual detail. Of like value, although unfriendly, is Raymond Moley's *After Seven Years* (New York, 1939), to which I am very heavily indebted; it is an absolutely indispensable book on the development of the New Deal, and one with which the late President's ardent admirers must reckon. Although my outlook does not coincide with Professor Moley's, I have relied upon him again and again for factual matter. James A. Farley: *Behind the Ballots* (New York, 1938) is useful only at a few points, and hardly comparable in frankness, much less in insight. Charles Michelson: *The Ghost Talks* (New York, 1944), the report of a Democratic publicity agent, is interesting, and so is Merriman Smith's *Thank You, Mr. President* (New York, 1946), the record of the United Press White House correspondent. Rexford Guy Tugwell: *The Stricken Land* (New York, 1947), which is mostly about Puerto Rico, contains some interesting reflections on Roosevelt. James M. Cox: *Journey through My Years* (New York, 1946) is pertinent on the campaign of 1920 and other aspects of Roosevelt's career. See also the affectionate record in the volumes of Josephus Daniels's autobiography. There is much of value in Hugh Johnson's *The Blue Eagle from Egg to Earth* (New York, 1935). Useful for its account of the 1937–8 spending crisis is Joseph Alsop and Robert Kintner: *Men around the President* (New York, 1939), although I have not relied upon it for specific detail. See also Vice Admiral Ross T. McIntire: *White House Physician* (New York, 1946).

There are already a good many journalistic biographies

of Roosevelt, which I find valuable as media through which to study the emergence of a Roosevelt hero-image. Among them I might mention works by Alden Hatch, Gerald W. Johnson, Compton Mackenzie, and Emil Ludwig. The biography that I found most useful and most respectable is, curiously enough, the first, Ernest K. Lindley's *Franklin D. Roosevelt, a Career in Progressive Democracy* (Indianapolis, 1931), which has the decisive advantage of being written at an early period and *not* seeing the subject from the presidential perspective; Lindley was a personal witness of many events of Roosevelt's governorship. Mauritz Hallgren: *The Gay Reformer* (New York, 1935), although good on the early New Deal, was written too early for a fair appraisal of Roosevelt as President. John T. Flynn in his *Country Squire in the White House* (New York, 1940) is one of the few people who have shown any interest in Roosevelt's extra-political career during the 1920's; although his little book contains many suggestive criticisms, it is vitiated by its bitterness and by the extravagant thesis that everything that happened in the Roosevelt era was the result of Roosevelt's personal peculiarities and deficiencies. Noel Busch: *What Manner of Man?* (New York, 1944), a superficial attempt at psychoanalysis, has a few insights that suggest the hidden hand of a professional psychoanalyst. A more serious effort to classify Roosevelt psychologically is Sebastian de Grazia's "The Character of Franklin Delano Roosevelt: A Typological Analysis," an unpublished article the proofs of which the author was kind enough to show me. Dan Wharton, ed.: *The Roosevelt Omnibus* (New York, 1934) has excellent material, including an informative article on the Roosevelt family income from *Fortune*, October 1932. For biographical and historical detail I have turned again and again to the files of the *New York Times*.

On the Bank of United States affair, which deserves a book of its own, see Norman Thomas: "The Banks of New York," the *Nation*, Vol. CXXXII (February 11, 1931), pp. 147–9; Thomas was a representative of an organization of Bank of United States depositors. On power see Samuel I. Rosenman:

"Governor Roosevelt's Power Program," the *Nation,* Vol. CXXIX (September 18, 1929), pp. 302–3.

Basil Rauch in his *History of the New Deal, 1933–1938* (New York, 1944) has undertaken a difficult task and performed it extremely well. On the New Deal see also Louis Hacker's excellent *American Problems of Today* (New York, 1938), Charles and Mary Beard: *America in Midpassage* (New York, 1939), and Charles Beard and George E. Smith: *The Old Deal and the New* (New York, 1940). In evaluating the NRA I have relied on the study by the Brookings Institution economists, Leverett Lyon et al.: *The National Recovery Administration* (Washington, 1935). *Labor and the Government* (New York and London, 1935), prepared under the auspices of the Twentieth Century Fund, and Edward Levinson: *Labor on the March* (New York, 1938) have been useful. Wesley C. Clark: *Economic Aspects of a President's Popularity* (Philadelphia, 1943) correlates Roosevelt's popularity, as measured in public-opinion polls, with trends in the business cycle. The economics of government spending and of the 1937 recession in particular is discussed in Alvin Hansen's *Industrial Stagnation or Full Recovery* (New York, 1938). The theory behind the anti-monopoly phase of the New Deal is exponded in Thurman Arnold's *The Bottlenecks of Business* (New York, 1940). On fluctuations in foreign policy to 1940 see Charles A. Beard: *American Foreign Policy in the Making* (New Haven, 1946).

Among the most recent writings, the Morgenthau diaries confirm the view of Roosevelt as a facile improviser. See also the interesting material in Edward J. Flynn: *You're the Boss* (New York, 1947), James F. Byrnes: *Speaking Frankly* (New York, 1947), James A. Farley: *Jim Farley's Story* (New York, 1948), and *The Memoirs of Cordell Hull* (2 volumes, New York, 1948); I am indebted to the Macmillan Company for granting me access to the text of the last-named work prior to its publication.

INDEX

A NOTE ABOUT THE AUTHOR

Richard Hofstadter, who died in October 1970, was DeWitt Clinton Professor of American History at Columbia University. He received his B.A. from the University of Buffalo and his M.A. and Ph.D. from Columbia University. He taught at the University of Maryland from 1942 until 1946, when he joined the History Department at Columbia. He also served as Pitt Professor of American History and Institutions at Cambridge University in 1958–9. The first of his books on American History was *Social Darwinism in American Thought*, published in 1944, followed by *The American Political Tradition*, in 1948. *The Age of Reform* (1955) won the Pulitzer Prize in history, and *Anti-intellectualism in American Life* (1963) received the Pulitzer Prize in general nonfiction, the Emerson Award of Phi Beta Kappa, and the Sidney Hillman Prize Award. Mr. Hofstadter's other books include *The Paranoid Style in American Politics* (1965), *The Progressive Historians* (1968), *The Idea of a Party System* (1969), and *America at 1750* (1971). He also edited, with Michael Wallace, *American Violence: A Documentary History* (1970).